Intonation and Meaning

OXFORD SURVEYS IN SEMANTICS AND PRAGMATICS

GENERAL EDITORS: Chris Barker, New York University, and Chris Kennedy, University of Chicago

ADVISORY EDITORS: Kent Bach, *San Francisco State University*; Jack Hoeksema, *University of Groningen*; Laurence R. Horn, *Yale University*; William Ladusaw, *University of Southern California*; Beth Levin, *Stanford University*; Richard Larson, *Stony Brook University*; Anna Szabolcsi, *New York University*; Mark Steedman, *University of Edinburgh*; Gregory Ward, *Northwestern University*

PUBLISHED

1 *Modality*
Paul Portner

2 *Reference*
Barbara Abbott

3 *Intonation and Meaning*
Daniel Büring

IN PREPARATION

Questions
Veneeta Dayal

Aspect
Hana Filip

Lexical Pragmatics
Laurence R. Horn

Mood
Paul Portner

Intonation and Meaning

DANIEL BÜRING

OXFORD
UNIVERSITY PRESS

Great Clarendon Street, Oxford, OX2 6DP,
United Kingdom

Oxford University Press is a department of the University of Oxford.
It furthers the University's objective of excellence in research, scholarship,
and education by publishing worldwide. Oxford is a registered trade mark of
Oxford University Press in the UK and in certain other countries

First Edition published in 2016
Impression: 1

Published in the United States of America by Oxford University Press
198 Madison Avenue, New York, NY 10016, United States of America

British Library Cataloguing in Publication Data
Data available

Library of Congress Control Number: 2015956590

ISBN 978–0–19–922626–9 (Hbk)
ISBN 978–0–19–922627–6 (Pbk)

Printed in Great Britain by
Clays Ltd, St Ives plc

Contents

Supplementary material for this book is available on a companion website at www.oup.co.uk/companion/Buring

General Preface

Oxford Surveys in Semantics and Pragmatics aims to convey to the reader the life and spirit of the study of meaning in natural language. Its volumes provide distillations of the central empirical questions driving research in contemporary semantics and pragmatics, and distinguish the most important lines of inquiry into these questions. Each volume offers the reader an overview of the topic at hand, a critical survey of the major approaches to it, and an assessment of what consensus (if any) exists. By putting empirical puzzles and theoretical debates into a comprehensible perspective, each author seeks to provide orientation and direction to the topic, thereby providing the context for a deeper understanding of both the complexity of the phenomena and the crucial features of the semantic and pragmatic theories designed to explain them. The books in the series offer researchers in linguistics and related areas—including syntax, cognitive science, computer science, and philosophy—both a valuable resource for instruction and reference and a state-of-the-art perspective on contemporary semantic and pragmatic theory from the experts shaping the field.

The study of intonational meaning, or information structure, is concerned with those conventionalized aspects of meaning that are embodied in the way that a sentence is pronounced, and which interact in key ways with the way that the sentence is structured. Research in this domain cuts across multiple subfields of linguistics, including phonetics, phonology, syntax, semantics, pragmatics, and typology, making it a challenging topic for novices and experts alike. In this book, Daniel Büring has drawn on his extensive research experience in this area to develop a comprehensive guide to this difficult terrain, exhaustively documenting the empirical phenomena that have driven work on intonational meaning over the past 40 years, and providing a clear and accessible overview of contemporary lines of analysis, some of which are rooted in quite distinct scholarly traditions. We are pleased to present Professor Büring's contribution to *Oxford Surveys in Semantics and Pragmatics*, which we anticipate will be the starting point for the next generation of scholarship on intonational meaning.

Chris Barker
New York University
Christopher Kennedy
University of Chicago

Preface

When, as a beginning graduate student, I stumbled into issues of intonational meaning (I wanted to become a syntactician when I grew up), that area was definitely a niche market, as far as grammatical theory was concerned. Twenty-five years, hundreds of workshops, thousands of papers, and various major national and international research groups later, it is fair to say intonational meaning, or information structure, as it is now usually referred to, has taken a permanent and rather central place in theoretical linguistics (it was even a bit of a fashion *du jour* at some point, I think).

Combining, as it does, aspects of (in alphabetical order) phonetics, phonology, pragmatics, semantics, syntax, and typology, information structure research provides a perfect example of what Linguistics, with a capital L, is all about. At the same time, due to that very fact, any researcher in that area, no matter how experienced, will be a bit of a dilettante regarding some aspects of it, and for non-specialists, who—like I did back in the day—suddenly realize that their research topic cannot be fully understood without considering aspects of information structure, the complexity of the area can be intimidating, creating an obstacle for engaging the issues.

My intention in writing this book was to provide a reliable travel guide for first time visitors, but also for people familiar with the terrain, who are ready to explore a little further, perhaps to go off the beaten path now and then. How not to get lost, and how to avoid the tourist traps. The first three chapters provide a rather closely guided tour to the core phenomena, focussing and givenness deaccenting, concentrating on the natural history of the phenomena, their formal representation and their semantic/pragmatic interpretation. After that, readers are more or less free to choose their own destinations, though the tour loosely continues in Chapters 6 and 7, which elaborate more on prosodic structure and its role in realizing focus and givenness.

With this book, I hope to offer as much of a common ground—terminologically, formally, and as far as known generalizations are concerned—as is possible in a rapidly progressing field, a knowledge base from which I hope readers can develop their own research in a maximally accessible way, modifying and expanding where necessary, but—and here I confess to having an agenda—without reinventing the wheel (which, more often than not, will not come out quite as round as the ones on offer already; but one tends to realize that only when it's too late).

Other than that, however, this book does not advocate one particular approach to the exclusion of others, but aims to present a plurality of perspectives and analytical options, hopefully made commensurable and, where possible, compatible. As I regularly tell my students at the beginning of a class: The question is not which theory is the right one. The question is which parts of each we should retain for the next, slightly less wrong one.

Naturally, the field has not had the good grace of suspending development while I was working on this book, and while I tried to incorporate much of the work up to 2015, there is no attempt at comprehensiveness, especially when it comes to cross-linguistic and experimental-phonetic work. Also, while I tried to cover all aspects of the phenomena, the perspective is, probably undeniably, that of a formal semanticist (or pragmaticist) with ties to syntax and prosodic phonology. In some ways I see this book as a companion piece to Ladd's (2008) *Introduction to Intonational Phonology* (though I cannot hope to match the clarity of that book), to which I refer any readers who want to explore the 'P-side' of things further.

Many colleagues and friends generously helped me during the writing of this book, and I want to thank them all, particularly Stefan Baumann, Ivano Caponigro, Silvio Cruschina, Katharina Hartmann, Daniel Hole, Manfred Krifka, Martin Prinzhorn, Arndt Riester, Vieri Samek-Lodovici, Roger Schwarzschild, Arnim von Stechow, Kriszta Szendrői, Michael Wagner, and Malte Zimmermann. Special thanks go to Manuel Križ for double-checking the complicated stuff, and preparing the index, Max Prüller for proofreading, and all those who patiently provided data. Wholehearted thanks to my Herzallerliebste Summer and all of my family, for their support and patience. It took me about seven years longer to write this book than my original contract with OUP anticipated, which I will blame on the many excellent distractions that came along during that period: internet music sites, Hulu, the Nord Electro, a professorship in Vienna. And last, but certainly not least, Lillian and Edwin; this book is dedicated to them, and to my parents Christel and Jürgen, who taught me all the essentials.

List of Abbreviations

1/2/3O	1st/2nd/3rd person object
1/2/3TS	1st/2nd/3rd person transitive subject
ACC	accusative case
AP	adjective phrase
AS	accessibility status
ASS	assertive case
AwF	association with focus
BON	background overrides newness
CSM	contextually salient meaning
CT	contrastive topic
DAT	dative case
DEC	declarative marker
DEM	demonstrative
DET	determiner
DP	determiner phrase
EMPH	emphatic
FAL	flexible accent language
FOC	FOC(us) (in Selkirk, 1995)
FRP	Focus Realization Position
FSE	focus sensitive element
FUT	future tense
GEN	genitive case
INSTR	instrumental case
INT	interrogative
IP	intonational phrase
iP	intermediate phrase
IRL	irrealis
MDL	middle
NEG	negation marker
NOM	nominalizer
NP	noun phrase
NPA	nuclear pitch accent

NSR	Nuclear Stress Rule
OBL	oblique case
OCE	open class element
OCP	Obligatory Contour Principle
OOTB	out of the blue
PA	pitch accent
PAM	pitch accent meaning
PAST	past tense
PBTM	phrase and boundary tone meanings
PERF	perfect tense/aspect
PH	Pierrehumbert and Hirschberg (1990)
PL	plural
POW	power set
PP	prepositional phrase
pP	phonological phrase
PREV	preverb
PRT	particle
PS	possessive marker
pWd	prosodic word
QAC	question–answer congruence
QED	quod erat demonstrandum (what was to be shown; end of proof)
REL	relative form of the verb (Hausa)
RFR	rise–fall–rise
SAAR	sentence accent assignment rule (Gussenhoven, 1983)
SG	singular
TP	tense phrase
TR	control transitivizer in Nɬʔkepmxcin
XP	asyntactic phrase of any category

1

Prominence, accent, focus

1.1 Prominence, accent (and stress)

1.1.1 Perceived prominence and pitch accenting

Speakers of English will pronounce sentence (1) very differently in response to different contexts. Three cases are exemplified in (1a–c), with some significant changes in intonation indicated by capitalization:

(1)   Margaritas are a good source of vitamins.
    a. What are Margaritas a good source of?—Margaritas are a good source of VITamins.
    b. What's a good source of vitamins?—MargaRITas are a good source of vitamins.
    c. Are margaritas a poor source of vitamins?—No, margaritas are a GOOD source of vitamins.

Asked about the difference in intonation, speakers will variously answer that the words ⟨vitamins⟩, ⟨margaritas⟩, and ⟨good⟩, respectively (or perhaps the syllables ⟨vi, ri⟩, and ⟨good⟩) are the 'strongest,' 'loudest,' or 'most prominent' in the sentence. Asked about the difference in meaning, they may say (answers here differ more in my experience) that 'vitamins,' 'margaritas,' and 'good' are the most important, informative, or new pieces in the sentence.

This is the essence of focussing: A difference in the prosodic realization of an utterance corresponds in an—ostensibly—systematic way with a difference in interpretation. More generally, it is the essence of the connection between intonation and meaning, the subject matter of this book. Much of it (the book, that is) will be devoted to explicating such concepts as 'strength', 'prominence', 'informative,' or 'new', and most of all, their systematic connection. And focussing as in (1a–c), being by far the best studied among all intonation-and-meaning phenomena, will occupy the better part of it.

It will be useful to introduce some technical terms right here at the beginning. We already mentioned PROMINENCE, a speaker's intuitive sensation of strength in an utterance he or she hears. These intuitions regard relative prominence, either that one syllable is more prominent than the other, or that one syllable is the most prominent one in a given utterance (or part thereof). Prominence judgments are part of our raw material, as it were. But what is it that we hear when we hear prominence? It turns out that the main correlate of perceived prominence in English is what intonational phonologists call PITCH ACCENTS. Figure 1.1 shows

Intonation and Meaning. First edition. Daniel Büring.
© Daniel Büring 2016. First published 2016 by Oxford University Press.

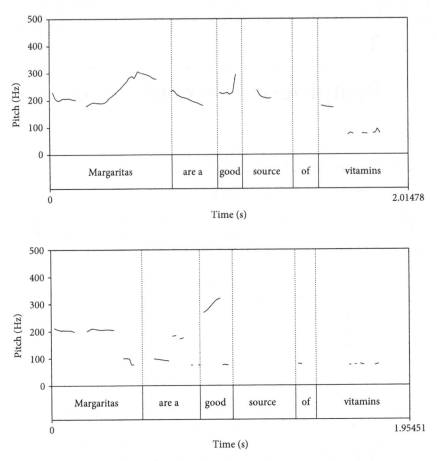

FIGURE 1.1   Annotated pitch track for the neutral rendering of ‹Margaritas are a good source of vitamins› (top), and the version with focus on ‹good› (bottom).

a pitch track for a neutral rendering of (1), as well as the focussed version (1c). The pitch tracks show the fundamental frequency of the first harmonic, or, put differently, the frequency of the vibration of the vocal chords of the speaker, as it changes over time (it will thus be a solid line during those segments only which involve periodic vibrations of the vocal chords, that is, sonorants) in Hertz.

In the top diagram (the neutral rendering), pitch maxima on ‹margaritas›, ‹good›, ‹source›, and ‹vitamins› are clearly visible, with the latter two discernibly lower than the first two. Still, ‹vitamins› is perceived as the most prominent element here, a phenomenon we will say more about in Section 1.1.2 and Chapter 6.

In the second pitch track, the location of the main perceived prominence, ‹good›, corresponds to a discernible local maximum in the pitch contour. On closer inspection, we see another local maximum on the syllable ‹ri› in ‹margaritas›. Perceived prominence almost always correlates with such pitch accents, though the "shape" of those accents, i.e. whether they are "bumps" or "dips" (more technically:

high or low), steep or gradual, where within the syllable they reach their peak (or "valley") etc. may vary.

It is worth stressing that pitch accents are not purely acoustic (or phonetic) phenomena. It takes a person's intuitive judgment about prominence, combined with skilled investigation of the pitch track to locate and classify pitch accents with a satisfactory degree of intersubjective agreement. No computer program can, to this day anyway, reliably detect those and only those pitch movements that correspond to speakers' intuitions of prominence.

Often, prominent syllables are acoustically distinguished in other ways, too: they are louder (more intense) and longer than they would be otherwise, or show changes in their formant structure. We will return to these cues at various points, but it turns out that none of them are as important for the perception of prominence as pitch movements. For example, artificially enhancing a pitch movement reliably leads to perceived prominence, and compression reliably makes prominence disappear. Manipulations of length and loudness are far less effective in that way.[1]

A term often used in the discussion of intonation is STRESS. In fact, many authors appear to use it synonymously with (pitch) accent or prominence, but in this book we will be careful not to do so. Stress and accent are intimately related, as we will see, but are not the same. Crucially, stress is a more abstract concept than pitch accent, and its definition may vary from author to author. I will postpone discussion of stress until Chapter 6.

1.1.2 The nuclear pitch accent

Within a short sentence, we usually perceive one syllable as the strongest. The pitch accent on that syllable is referred to as the NUCLEAR PITCH ACCENT (NPA). In English, and in the Germanic languages in general, the NPA is not, in fact, the accent with the biggest pitch excursion (or the highest loudness or some such thing). Rather, it is last pitch accent in the sentence. Looking at the pitch track, the NPA in fact often corresponds to the *lowest* pitch peak. Yet we inevitably hear it as the strongest.[2]

In the previous section we talked about 'short sentences'; the situation is more complicated for complex sentences such as (2):

(2)   If you send the data to my office, I can immediately start working on them.

Each of the two clauses—the ‹if›-clause and the main clause—will correspond to an intonational unit in many renderings of (2). Within each, one syllable is strongest, presumably ‹o(ffice)› and ‹wor(king)› (I include the rest of the word to make identification of the syllable easier). We say that ‹office› bears the nuclear

---

[1] See Fry (1955, 1958); Terken and Hermes (2000) and the references in the latter. Pitch might be less of a central cue for the automatic recognition of prominence, see the results in Howell (2011).

[2] Currie (1980, 1981), Liberman and Pierrehumbert (1984: pp.182ff), Ladd (1996: esp. chap. 6). Katz and Selkirk (2011) argue that there are instances in which a non-final pitch accent is in a grammatical sense stronger than the final one. If so, the picture is more complicated than outlined here.

pitch accent in ‹if you send the data to my office›, and ‹working› bears the NPA in ‹I can immediately start working on them›.

Of course, we should say more about why the two clauses in (2) are counted as separate intonational units, each with its own NPA. Characteristically, the two are separated by a drop in pitch at the end of ‹office›, and, optionally, by a pause between ‹office› and ‹I›; additionally, the final syllable(s) of the first domain will be slightly lengthened. The orthography, obviously, reflects this by a comma (though this is not always the case). We speak of a BOUNDARY between the two intonational units. The units thus delimited we will also call (PROSODIC) DOMAINS or PROSODIC PHRASES. The most prominent element within a given prosodic domain is called the HEAD of that domain. So in clausal and similar prosodic domains, the prosodic head of the domain bears the final, nuclear pitch accent within that domain.

Contraposing this last point, we hypothesize that whenever speakers hear two (or more) maximally (and equally) prominent syllables in a given utterance, that utterance consists of two (or more) prosodic phrases, each containing exactly one NPA; accordingly, closer inspection should also reveal the presence of one (or more) boundaries, realized by a characteristic turn of the pitch contour, lengthening of syllables, and/or a pause.

In intonational phonology, the term NPA is often used more narrowly for heads of INTERMEDIATE PHRASES only (presumably because intermediate phrases are typically the smallest prosodic domains to contain more than one PA). Here, we will use the term more generally whenever we have a prosodic phrase that contains more than one pitch accent, one of which is perceived as the most prominent. Since most cases discussed in the literature involve sentences which are standardly realized by a single intermediate phrase, the difference will be of little consequence, however.

As said above, what we hear as the most prominent pitch accent is the last one in a domain. Put differently, there are, by definition, no post-nuclear pitch accents (again, we will return to the finer points about this in Chapter 6). There can be, on the other hand, any number of pre-nuclear pitch accents.

1.2 Default intonation

So far, we have described intonation, and hinted at its phonological representation. But where does it come from? Can we predict the location of pitch accents, the NPA, domain boundaries, etc.? And if so, what are the predictors? Is prosody just a deterministic realization of syntactic structure? Or would you indeed have to be—as Bolinger (1972) puts it—a mind-reader to predict it? Rather than trying to answer these questions in the abstract, let us approach them hands-on. Let us try to predict, and then see how well it works!

1.2.1 Default accenting

For the moment, I will narrow the question down to just one aspect of intonation: Can we predict where pitch accents will go? To answer this question, it is best to start at the bottom. Speakers are certainly very consistent in where, within a given word, when uttered in isolation, they will put main, and, where applicable, secondary prominence(s). It has to be ‹PArrot› and ‹giRAFFE›, rather than *‹parROT› and *‹GIraffe›. The Golden State is called ‹CAliFORnia›, where ‹cal› is more prominent than ‹li› and ‹nia›, and ‹for› is more prominent than all of them.

Presumably, such facts about prominence (or whatever its grammatical counterpart is) have to be learned when we learn the pronunciation of individual morphemes (though English shows a number of regularities in this regard, too[3]).

Likewise, for complex words, we know that it is ‹UNderEStimate›, ‹LAWNmower› and ‹STATECApitol›. We describe our knowledge of this as part of our morphological rules, or the lexical entries of certain affixes.

Unlike in the case of simplex words like ‹giraffe›, changing prominence relations in a complex word might not automatically lead to judgments of ill-formedness. ‹UNderestimate› is not an unacceptable pronunciation; it would be appropriate, for example, in a sentence like ‹I thought they had overestimated the danger, but if anything, they UNderestimated it›. Yet, most speakers and researchers alike find the claim that the *normal* ('neutral', 'natural') pronunciation is ‹UNderEStimate› as unobjectionable as the parallel one about ‹giRAffe›.

As we turn from words to phrases, assessments become more varied. As mentioned above, Dwight Bolinger, talking about sentence accent, famously claimed that "accent is predictable (if you're a mind-reader)" (Bolinger, 1972), suggesting that "the distribution of sentence accents is not determined by syntactic structure but by semantic and emotional highlighting", and contended that syntax might at most be useful to deliver a classification of structures which differ in which accent pattern is statistically most likely to be found on them (see Bolinger, 1972: 644). To be clear: Bolinger's contention wasn't just that no existing theory successfully predicted accent patterns, but that indeed in many examples, two or more accent patterns are equally acceptable, but not, as he put it, "informationally" equivalent (i.e. not in free variation, once one considers meaning).

It seems to me that the standard position nowadays takes Bolinger's objections seriously in that it acknowledges that virtually any phrasal accent pattern can be found acceptable under certain conversational circumstances—or the speaker's communicative intentions formed in them. In fact, as the title of this book indicates, I believe that a sufficiently fine-grained theory of meaning ought to be able to capture the very "semantic and emotional" factors Bolinger was talking about, and how they influence intonation. By the end of the day, we should be able to predict, if not *the* accent pattern of a sentence, then at least the class of (semantically and pragmatically equivalent) accent patterns acceptable for a sentence, *given a sufficient characterization of the relevant "semantic and emotional" (i.e. non-morpho-syntactic) factors*. Much of this book is about those among the semantic and emotional factors that we presently understand reasonably well.

Most researchers also seem to hold, on the other hand, that actual intonation patterns are determined by the interaction of Bolingerian "semantic and emotional" factors (such as focus) on the one hand, with certain structural defaults, even above the word level, on the other (see e.g. the excellent discussion in Ladd,

---

[3] See Hayes (1982); Liberman and Prince (1977); Pater (2000); Selkirk (1980) among many others.

1996: chs 6 & 7). Structural defaults in this sense may be rules that assign accents in relation to syntactic configurations or labels (e.g. linear order in Chomsky and Halle, 1968, argument structure in Gussenhoven, 1983a; Selkirk, 1984).

This is not *per se* incompatible with Bolinger's position. Even if there is a structural component to accent placement (and I am not sure Bolinger meant to debate that), it may be that no single uttered accent pattern, naturally occurring or elicited, is ever free of all semantic and emotional factors, and thus accent is, indeed, only predictable if you know what these factors happened to be.

On the other hand, it is possible that, at least for those sentences for which speakers do have clear and intersubjectively consistent judgments about what the "citation form" accent patterns are, these correspond to what the structural factors alone determine, *without any specific semantic and emotional factors*.[4]

Höhle (1982) provides an insightful discussion of this topic. He takes speakers' intuitions about what he calls *Normalbetonung*, 'normal intonation,' as part of the primary data to be captured by a grammatical theory (to be sure, Höhle does not claim that there is such an intuitively normal intonation for *every* given sentence, only that grammar should predict it in those cases where there is).

The general perspective I take in this book follows Höhle's view. Accordingly the theory (or family of theories) to be explored does, among other things, generate an accent pattern even where all non-structural factors are unspecified, which is meant to correspond to the intuitive out-of-the-blue intonation. I will refer to that accent pattern as DEFAULT ACCENTING (and, starting in chapter 6, DEFAULT PROSODY or DEFAULT INTONATION).

A note on terminology: Default accenting/intonation in the sense intended here goes by various names in the literature, most often NEUTRAL, NORMAL, UNMARKED, or OUT-OF-THE-BLUE (OOTB) intonation (or, in the case of single words, the CITATION FORM). Analogously for accenting in particular, and prosody in general. For the remainder of this book I will stick to "default" or "out-of-the-blue," since, as we will see momentarily, the other terms may potentially lead to confusion.

1.2.2 Predicting default accenting: a sketch

To illustrate the issue in the previous section, consider the following set of Toy Rules for assigning default accents.

(3^{DEF})   DEFAULT ACCENT ASSIGNMENT FOR ENGLISH (DUTCH, GERMAN), TOY VERSION

---

[4] By "sentence" we mean here "sentence under a syntactic analysis." That is, we are not interested in different renderings of ambiguous sentences, e.g. the fact that (i) will have the main prominence on ‹leave› when construed as "my instructions are that I must leave," but on ‹(in)struc(tions)› when analyzed as meaning "I have instructions which I must leave" (cf. Bresnan, 1971):

(i) I have instructions to leave.

In this case, we wouldn't speak of one sentence, but of two.

Step 1: Put pitch accents on open class elements; put the minimal number to guarantee that each syntactic phrase contains at least one PA.

Step 2: a. *Delete* pitch accents if they are followed by at least one other
(optional)   PA,
             or alternatively

         b. *add* pitch accents on open class elements (OCEs), if they are followed by at least one other PA.

Step 1—a rather direct adaptation of Truckenbrodt's (1995) constraint Stress-xp—does the main work of accent assignment. First, it will ensure that OPEN CLASS ELEMENTS (OCEs)—nouns, adjectives, and main verbs—may bear accents, but pronouns, prepositions, determiners, and auxiliaries will not. Second, rather than assigning a pitch accent to *every* OCE, Step 1 assigns pitch accents by syntactic phrase. If a phrase XP contains exactly one OCE, that is, if it does not contain a complement, specifier or adjunct—(4a),(4b)—that OCE gets a PA. The same holds if the complement does not contain an OCE—structures (4c) and (4d). If, on the other hand, a phrase contains a complement, YP, with an OCE in it, *that* YP will get the PA—structures (4e) and (4f). (We will return to the case of specifiers and adjuncts in Chapter 6; suffice it to say at this point that, being phrasal, these will, by Step 1, have to bear a PA if open class, regardless of the presence of any other pitch accents in XP.)

$$
\begin{array}{ll}
& \text{PA} \qquad\qquad\qquad\qquad\qquad \text{PA} \\
& | \qquad\qquad\qquad\qquad\qquad\quad | \\
(4)\quad a.\ [_{AP}\text{blue}] \qquad\qquad\quad b.\ [_{VP}\text{dance }]
\end{array}
$$

(4)   a. [_{AP}blue]   PA   b. [_{VP}dance]   PA

         PA   PA
          | |
     c. [_{DP}[_{NP}pictures [_{PP}of himself]]]   d. [_{VP}see [_{DP}someone]]

                       PA   PA
                        | |
     e. [_{DP}[_{NP}pictures [_{PP} of Mary]]]   f. [_{VP}see [_{DP}the sunset]]

Note that in structures (4e) and (4f), *every* syntactic phrase contains a PA: the NPs ‹Mary› and ‹sunset› contain a pitch accent by virtue of having a pitch accented head. All other XPs contain a pitch accent by virtue of containing that NP; there is no need, by Step 1, to put additional pitch accents on the embedding heads, even though these are OCEs.

   The effect of this will be particularly noticeable in head-final structures, such as the German VP in (5).

                    PA
                     |
(5)   a. [_{VP}[_{DP} die [_{NP} SOnne]] sehen]   'to see the sun'   (German)
               the   sun   see

                 PA   PA   PA
                  | | |
     b. #die Sonne SEhen.   c. # die SONne SEhen.

By the same logic as before, the NPA on the NP ‹Sonne› within the complement DP is the only one licensed by Step 1: given its presence, NP, DP, and VP all contain a PA. The well-documented consequence of this is that the NPA, rather than falling on the last content word—the verb—falls on the complement, an effect called INTEGRATION (to which we will return in detail in Chapters 4, 6, and 8).[5] In fact, accenting the final head leads to a decidedly marked accent pattern, signaled by # in examples (5b) and (5c) above.

Step 2 in definition (3) introduces a certain amount of optionality into the picture. It allows deletion of any but the final accent in a sentence, or addition of pitch accents *before* the final PA. Thus, (6a), the result of Step 1, could be transformed into (6b) or (6c) by Step 2 (of course, Step 2 being optional, (6a) could also remain as it is):

$$
\begin{array}{lll}
& \text{PA} & \text{PA} \\
& | & | \\
(6) \quad \text{a.} \ [_s[_{DP}[_{NP}\text{Kim}]][_{VP}\text{saw }[_{DP}[_{NP}\text{Sam}]]]]. & \text{b. Kim saw Sam.}
\end{array}
$$

$$
\begin{array}{c}
\text{PA} \quad \text{PA} \quad \text{PA} \\
| \quad\ | \quad\ | \\
\text{c. Kim saw Sam.}
\end{array}
$$

In keeping with our earlier observation that NPAs need not, in fact, be any different from pre-nuclear pitch accents since they are identifiable solely as the final ones, Step 1 in definition (3) above does not award any special status to the NPA. Step 2, however, crucially alludes to the final PA: it effectively exempts that accent from optional deletion, and it ensures that no "new NPA" can be created by adding a pitch accent *after* the final pitch accent as determined by Step 1. Thus, (6a) cannot be turned into (7a), nor (5a) into (7b):

$$
\begin{array}{ll}
\text{PA} & \text{PA} \quad \text{PA} \\
| & | \quad\ | \\
(7) \quad \text{a. Kim saw Sam.} & \text{b. die Sonne sehen}
\end{array}
$$

What Step 2 effectively predicts, then, is that there is a certain optionality regarding pre-nuclear accents, but not regarding the nuclear accent. This corresponds reasonably well to the empirical picture: Speakers easily agree on where in a given utterance they hear the NPA, or where they would put it if asked to read a sentence out-of-the-blue, much more so than when it comes to pre-nuclear accents.

Let us call the accent patterns created by the Toy Rules in (3) DEFAULT ACCENTING, which at present is our stand-in for default prosody.

To be sure, the rules in definition (3) above are not meant as a complete theory of default accenting in English, nor even as an accurate description thereof.[6] Still,

---

[5] See a.m.o. Bresnan (1971); Fuchs (1976); Schmerling (1976) for early discussion.

[6] A laundry list of what I think their major shortcomings are is given in (i):

(i) a. The integration effect is both more general and more restricted than entailed by Step 1.
   b. There are probably additional restrictions on pre-nuclear pitch accent deletion (and possibly addition) as allowed by Step 2.

they do a reasonably good job of generating the intuitively natural out-of-the-blue accent pattern(s) for a great deal of English examples (as well as other, similar Germanic languages such as German and Dutch). What is more, while these rules will be replaced by more precise and refined ones in Chapters 6 and 7, the Toy Rules in (3) (and their imminent refinement in the next section) are very much in the same "spirit," in terms of what the operative concepts and generalizations are, as the final formal system.

What these rules completely ignore (rather than simply get wrong or under-determine) is any influence of Bolinger's "semantic and emotional factors." It is to these that we now turn.

1.3 Focus

1.3.1 When default accenting is not normal accenting

In the foregoing discussion we talked about default intonation and citation forms. I floated the idea that, given a lexicon that specifies stresses for all morphemes, a sufficiently sophisticated system of rules should be able to predict accent loca-tions within complex words, phrases, and sentences, and that those predictions correspond, at least in many cases, to speakers' judgments about out-of-the-blue intonation.

For example, the NPA in (8), read out of the blue, will be on ‹shell(fish)›, as predicted by Step 1 (with pre-nuclear accents possible on ‹Jerome› and ‹hav(ing)›):

(8)   Jerome is having shellfish.

But if used to answer the inquiry in (9), the NPA would unequivocally be found on ‹Jerome› (and accordingly, no other pitch accents may occur in the sentence):

(9)   (Who is having shellfish? —) JeROME is having shellfish.

A word on the representations here: I will indicate the syllable bearing the NPA by capitalization. This represents that it bears a pitch accent, no pitch accents follow it, and pitch accents preceding it are distributed in keeping with the Toy Rules in (3). Linguistic contexts are given in parentheses, where a dash indicates a change of speaker, as in a question–answer sequence like (9). No claims are made about the *prosody* of these context sentences, and hence no capitals or other markings are found in them. When I refer to, for example, 'sentence (9)', I thereby refer to the non-bracketed part of (9), unless otherwise noted.

Sentence (9) does not show default accenting, but its accenting is perfectly natural, perhaps even the only one possible in the context of the question in (9).

---

c. These rules always treat the entire sentence as a domain; realistically, especially complex sentences should be broken up into several domains, in each of which Step 2 should operate; the formation of these domains itself should be part of the default rules.

Why is that? The obvious hypothesis is that it is caused by the preceding question, or more carefully: by contextual factors (a.k.a. Bolinger's "semantic and emotional factors") reflecting the presence of that question. A more specific, yet widespread version of this hypothesis is that these contextual factors cause ⟨Jerome⟩ in (9) to be FOCUSSED, and that focus in turn causes non-default accenting.

In example (10), too, the NPA in the final ⟨if⟩-clause will very likely be on ⟨Jerome⟩, again, ostensibly, due to context.

(10)   (I don't much care for seafood, but I will have shellfish if) JeROME is having shellfish.

Here, too, we can say that ⟨Jerome⟩ is focussed, namely as a CONTRASTIVE FOCUS. Alternatively, we may say here (and perhaps in example (9) above, as well) that ⟨is having shellfish⟩ has been DEACCENTED (note that ⟨Jerome⟩ will bear a pitch accent by Step 1 in definition (3) above, which would be nuclear after deaccenting of ⟨is having shellfish⟩). We will say more about the relation between focussing and deaccenting later, but stick to the former term for the time being.

So to a first approximation, we talk of focussing in at least those cases in which the contextually appropriate intonation, in particular the accent placement, is *different* from the default one, due to contextual, non-structural reasons. Note that, considering such cases of focussing, it may be misleading to call the default accent pattern "neutral" (if it were, should it not be felicitous in any context?) or "normal" (at least if "normal" means "what would normally be produced" *in a given context*), which is why I decided to use "default" or "out-of-the-blue" instead.[7] Likewise, if we call the accent pattern in examples (9) and (10) MARKED, we must understand "marked" to mean "non-default" in the technical sense, rather than "intuitively marked/less acceptable in the context given" (which examples (9) and (10) clearly are not); put differently, "marked" here means "intuitively inappropriate in an out-of-the-blue utterance."

It will be useful to clarify a number of points right here. First, we will say that in (9), the *word* ⟨Jerome⟩ has been focussed (or is in focus, or is a focus), as opposed to the syllable ⟨rome⟩, or the meaning of the word (though that certainly will figure in the interpretation of the focussing). The latter choice—foci are words, rather than meanings—is made in most formal works on the topic, though some sources, explicitly or implicitly, may assume otherwise.

Second, we are not claiming that there is anything special about the PA on ⟨Jerome⟩ in (9), as opposed, say, to that on ⟨shellfish⟩ in (8) (e.g. that it is in some sense quantitatively more extreme, or qualitatively different). Though naive speakers may characterize focussing as involving "added stress" or "extra loud" words, we restrict our attention here to the syntagmatic effects of focussing:

---

[7] To be entirely precise: "default" is a theory-dependent notion—"as predicted by the focus/context-independent rules of accent assignment/prosodic realization"—while "out-of-the-blue" is an empirical notion—"as produced by speakers when no context is given." By using these near-synonymously we already presuppose that the structural default rules establishing prosodic structure do indeed succeed in producing the intuitively felicitous out-of-the-blue intonation.

pitch accents that are obligatory in an out-of-the-blue utterance (and predicted as default accenting by our Toy Rules in (3) above) are omitted.

Whether, in addition to the *distribution* of pitch accents in sentences like (9), there is anything about the NPA itself that is indicative of focussing is far less clear. It is often claimed, especially in studies based mostly on introspection, that the NPA in (9) is itself qualitatively different from that in, say, (8) in that it shows a higher pitch excursion, a different alignment of the pitch peak with the syllable, longer duration, higher intensity, or a different shape of pitch movement (e.g. a steeper slope towards the peak). Others claim that either there are no such differences, or where there are, that these can be reduced to other properties of the utterance, such as the rather early occurrence of the NPA in the string, the lower total number of pitch accents in the sentence, or effects of the pragmatic type of utterance.

To test these claims experimentally while controlling for all these factors turns out to be extremely difficult, and many results, it seems to me, are open to different interpretations. In addition, inter-speaker variation on these points seems to be considerable.[8]

Eady and Cooper (1986), for example find that in English,

sentence-initial focus does not result in an increased F_0 value on the focused item [as compared to the same word in the same position in a neutral sentence; DB]. Instead, the presence of emphatic stress at this position is realized by an increase in word duration . . . and by a very sharp post-focus F_0 drop. (Eady and Cooper, 1986: 408)

While Cooper et al. (1985) reach essentially the same conclusion, Eady et al. (1986) find no increased duration effect in longer words, whereas in shorter words, early focus resulted in increased duration *and* higher pitch excursion. Eady and Cooper (1986) and Eady et al. (1986) find that the pitch accent on a subject occurs earlier within the syllable in a subject-focus environment than in a neutral sentence, whereas Shue et al. (2007) find that subject focus is realized by a *later* pitch accent. In contradistinction, post-focal deaccenting (or extreme compression of pitch accents) is universally found in all studies that I am aware of.

In sum, then, the term CONTRASTIVE ACCENT should be used with caution, or rather: be either explicated further, or avoided. That said, we can use the term CONTRASTIVE ACCENT PATTERN to refer to patterns that do not accord to the default, out-of-the-blue intonation, and, derivatively, to the NPA in such structures as a contrastive accent. To forestall misunderstandings, though, we will use the term NON-DEFAULT ACCENT PATTERN instead.

1.3.2 Focus realization and focus projection

In the previous section, we apprehended the notion of "marked accent pattern" by suggesting that these involve focussing. More precisely, we said that in such

---

[8] A proper investigation would have to compare two pitch accents in identical phonotactic environments (i.e. surrounded by the same number of syllables, preceded by the same number of pitch accents at the same distance, etc.), of which one is intuitively neutral, while the other one is not.

sentences, one element (or perhaps several) has been focussed, and that that focussing influences NPA placement—ostensibly overwriting default rules of accent placement.

Let us now take a first closer look at the relation between focus and NPA: what are the regularities in FOCUS REALIZATION? In the examples in the previous section, the focussed element ‹Jerome› bore the NPA. This will turn out to be the case in all standard cases of focussing.

Of course only the most prominent syllable of the focus, ‹ROME› is pitch accented. So the focus is bigger than the accent bearing syllable; yet, if the relation between focus and accent is always as straightforward as this ("the focus is the word that bears the NPA"), it would seem like overkill to introduce a separate term "focus" for this, rather than generalizing the term "accented" to words. But *is* the focus always the word (or morpheme) that bears the NPA, or can it be bigger (or smaller) than that?

The answer is that it can be both smaller, and bigger. But to show that, obviously, we first have to have a way of diagnosing focus independent of accent. The strategy we apply is the following: First, identify pragmatic factors that steer the NPA onto a particular word in simple examples of non-default accenting. Second, elicit this very pragmatic effect on some larger constituent. Third, examine the structural relation between that larger constituent and the accenting found in the elicited sentence.

To illustrate, we suggested above that putting the NPA on the subject ‹Jerome› is necessary in the context of a question like ‹Who ordered shellfish?› We now hypothesize the following general pragmatic rule (much more on this in chapters 2 and 3):

(11^{DEF})   QUESTION–ANSWER CONGRUENCE (QAC)
           In an answer to a constituent question, the element corresponding to the
           ‹wh›-phrase in the question must be a focus.

Casual inspection of various question–answer pairs confirms this generalization for cases in which the element corresponding to the ‹wh›-phrase in the question is a single word: the predicted focus word always bears the NPA, including in example (9) above, repeated in (12a). Now what happens if that element is a complex phrase?

(12)   (Who ordered shellfish?)
        a. JeROME ordered shellfish.
        b. My next door NEIGHbor ordered shellfish.
        c. The guy at the table over by the WINdow ordered shellfish.

All of the answers in (12a–c), with the NPA as indicated, are felicitous. Assuming (11), the entire subject *phrases* in (12b–c), ‹my next door neighbor› and ‹the guy at the table over by the window›, respectively, are foci.

At this point it will be useful to introduce a notational device. Following Jackendoff (1972: ch.6), we will mark the focussed constituents by []_F-brackets (where the focus is a single word, as in (13a), I may sometimes write the F-MARKER on the word itself, e.g. ‹JeROME$_F$›):

(13) Q: Who ordered shellfish?
     a. [JeROME]$_F$ ordered shellfish.
     b. [My next door NEIGHbor]$_F$ ordered shellfish.
     c. [The guy at the table over by the WINdow]$_F$ ordered shellfish.

This allows us to omit repeating the context when discussing the prosodic effects of focus, while still having an unambiguous way of indicating the intended focussing. Terminologically, (13b) and (13c) illustrate FOCUS PROJECTION (see Sections 2.4, 2.5, 4.4, and 8.4). The focus, as identified by pragmatic rules, is bigger than the NPA-bearing word.

Before going on, I should make it clear that the foregoing discussion was not intended to *prove* that one needs to distinguish a category f(ocus) in the grammar, much less that it needs to be represented in the syntax in the way done in (13). The purpose was rather to illustrate the concept and introduce a notational device. The question of whether our grammatical representations need to contain F-markers, and whether our theory needs to make reference to the notion of focus is a rather abstract and difficult one, and will be addressed in Chapter 5, after we have seriously introduced our various pragmatic conditions related to pitch accent placement in Chapters 2, 3, and 5.

Returning to the issue of focus projection, one rather obvious constraint appears to be that the focus contains the NPA. Put differently, any accent on ‹ordered› or ‹shellfish› in (13a–c) would clearly render these infelicitous as answers to the question given. But note that the following variants of (13) are unacceptable, too:

(14) (Q: Who ordered shellfish?)
     a. #[MY next door neighbor]$_F$ ordered shellfish.
     b. #[The guy at the TAble over by the window]$_F$ ordered shellfish.
     c. #[The GUY at the table over by the window]$_F$ ordered shellfish.

I use # here to mean that the sentences are unacceptable given the context provided (i.e. the question in (14)), as opposed to ungrammatical (which would warrant an*). Echoing our earlier discussion of default intonation, I should add that perhaps even these renderings of (14a–c) *are* acceptable under special circumstances as answers to that question, for example if one imagines the entire question–answer sequence embedded in a larger discourse, but that they are certainly not judged as the normal pronunciations given the question, and nothing else; the reader should mentally add this caveat to every #-marked example that follows.

All of the answers in (14) should meet (11) if we simply assume that focus has to contain the NPA. The fact that they are infelicitous here indicates that the focus–pitch accent relation is more complex than just containment.

Jackendoff (1972: sec. 6.2) already offers a generalization on this, which, transposed into our current setting, can be rendered as in (15).

(15^{GEN}) FOCUS–PITCH ACCENT RELATION, FOLLOWING JACKENDOFF (1972)
The last default pitch accent within the focus is the last pitch accent in the sentence.

According to (15), there are no special rules of pitch accenting within a larger focus. Focus "narrows down" the space within which the NPA is to be found, and as such "overwrites" default accenting. But within a larger focus, default accenting takes over again.

We can capture the effect of definition (15) in our Toy Rules (3) above by inserting two new steps.

(16^{DEF}) Step 1:   Put pitch accents on open class elements; put the minimal number to guarantee that each syntactic phrase contains at least one PA.

Step F+:   If the focus does not contain a PA, assign one to the last word within the focus.

Step F−:   Delete all pitch accents after the focus.

Step 2:   a. Delete pitch accents if they are followed by at least one
(optional)   other PA,
                 or alternatively
            b. *add* pitch accents on open class elements (OCEs), if they are followed by at least one other PA.

Step F+ is only there for cases in which the focus consists of function words only, for example ‹HE$_F$ *ordered shellfish*›. The crucial work is done by Step F−, which achieves POST-FOCAL DEACCENTING. (Note that in a different setting the effect of both Step F+ and Step F− could be achieved by simply demanding that the focus must contain the NPA, as will be done in Chapter 7.)

The effect of Step F− is illustrated in (17); (17a) is the outcome of Step 1, which gets transformed into (17b) by Step F− (Step F+ has no effect here):

```
         PA        PA              PA       PA        PA
          |         |               |        |         |
(17)  a. [some guy at the table over by the window]_F ordered shellfish.
         PA        PA              PA
          |         |               |
      b. [some guy at the table over by the window]_F ordered shellfish.
```

Structure (17b) (or rather, the various results of applying Step 2 to it) corresponds to example (13c) above, as desired. It should be easy to see that (13b), as well as, almost trivially, (13a) are derived by the procedure given here as well.

1.3.3 Introducing information structure

In Sections 1.3.1 and 1.3.2 I introduced the notion of focus—particularly: answer focus and contrastive focus—mainly to demonstrate how, in principle, it interacts with default accenting. I did not give a serious account of when and on which constituent(s) focus will be marked in an utterance, or conversely, how (the prosodic effect of) focussing will be interpreted in general (that I will turn to in the subsequent chapters). What is crucial at this point is that focus, whatever its eventual explication may be, is a *meaning-related* influence on prosody, in contradistinction to the rules and principles of default accenting (which relate accent placement to aspects of syntactic structure).

In all likelihood, focus is not the only meaning-related factor of this sort. Semantic or pragmatic properties like topicality, contrast, and givenness, to name just a few, have been claimed to likewise influence prosody, and, accordingly, been modeled by features like T, C, or G, analogous to F(ocus). The sum total of such non-structural factors is usually referred to by the term INFORMATION STRUCTURE, or sometimes INFORMATION PACKAGING. In this book I, too, will use the term information structure in this sense: as a cover term for the list of whatever non-structural factors like focus, topic, etc. we identify and model as influences on prosody, or grammar more in general.

In a more narrow sense the term information structure may refer to just the *representation* of these categories; currently, that would be the distribution of F-markers in a syntactic tree. One way or the other, information structure as understood here (and most places in the literature) is not a (level of) representation in its own right, like, say, s(urface)-structure, Logical Form and its offsprings in Principles and Parameters Approaches, F(unctional)-structure in Lexical Functional Grammar, or Prosodic Structure in Prosodic Phonology; it is merely the *marking* of syntactic nodes or constituents as focus, topic, etc. in a regular syntactic representation.

1.4 Summary and outlook

In this chapter we have introduced in very broad strokes a theory of default prosody (here: accenting), and how it interacts with focussing (as representative of other non-structural factors influencing prosody), in the form of the Toy Rules in (16). Although these rules will be subsequently refined and reformulated, their essential properties will remain unchanged throughout this book, and it is worth highlighting some of these here.

First, these rules for default prosody make rather minimal reference to hierarchical syntactic structure, namely in Step 1 (and only there), in which the head-vs-phrase distinction plays a crucial role. All other rules, including the focus-related Step F+ and Step F− are purely linear. Second, it is crucial that Step 1 produces entire accent patterns, rather than just placing the NPA. This not only results in a more realistic (or more complete) description of sentence intonation, it also captures systematic similarities among accent patterns across various focus placements and sizes (e.g. aspects of default accenting may be preserved even in subject focus). Third, the rules entail a fundamental asymmetry between accenting of focal and pre-focal material on the one hand, and post-focus material on the other. The former is almost exclusively determined by default prosody, and subject to considerable optionality in accenting (Step 2); the latter is strictly accentless as a matter of grammar (Step F—). Lastly, the Toy Rules allow for various accent patterns to be "functionally equivalent" (i.e. to realize the same focussing), with Step 2 as a stand-in for a more fine-grained account of accent addition and deletion; however, this optionality never regards the placement of the NPA.

What of the question which started Section 1.2: Is accenting predictable? The answer that emerges from the foregoing discussion, and will (hopefully) take shape further throughout the rest of this book, is that we presumably can predict if not *the* accent pattern, then the *set* of acceptable accent patterns (and maybe ultimately: of acceptable prosodic realizations) for a sentence, based on its syntactic structure on the one hand, and a sufficiently detailed model of its discourse context on the other. Neither one by itself determines the distribution of accents, but both *influence* it.

When illustrating this basic idea, we used the rule of Question–Answer Congruence in definition (11), which directly relates focussing to the discourse context, as a proxy for Bolinger's (1972) "semantic and emotional highlighting." Evidently, other, and more precise, rules will have to be devised. If these, like Question–Answer Congruence, merely include reference to the discourse context, they clearly do not require mind-reading. But even if we were to include rules or principles that make reference to certain attitudes of the speaker, this would not jeopardize the project in general, as long as the attitudes in question are in principle accessible and sufficiently intersubjective. For example, if instead of requiring an overt question as in Question–Answer Congruence, we said that the speaker needs to be *interested* in learning the answer to certain question, this still makes for a testable generalization. And while it would take mind-reading to predict which question a speaker may, on a given occasion, be interested in, we still get mileage out of such a rule: We can predict, how a speaker *with a certain question on their mind* would (and would not) accent a sentence; and we can predict what conclusions a competent addressee would draw on the basis of that accentuation.

2

Focus and givenness in flexible accent languages

Marked tonicity occurs, in general, under either (or both) of two conditions. Either some element other than the one just specified is "contrastive"; or the element just specified . . . is "given"—has been mentioned before or is present in the situation.

(Halliday, 1967a: 23)

The Germanic and Slavic languages, among others, instantiate what I will call FLEXIBLE ACCENT LANGUAGES (FALs); languages in which the placement of pitch accents varies due to focussing and other information structural factors. Since these are by far the most well-studied languages in the field of information structure, and virtually the only ones that have informed the development of semantic theories of information structure, we will exclusively focus on these in the next few chapters.

As discussed informally in Chapter 1, the perspective adopted in this book is that the most noticeable prosodic effect of focus on intonation in such languages consists in changes to the default prosody, first and foremost the *omission* of pitch accents after the focus, and, in some cases, the addition of pitch accents where the focus contains no default accents. What we will concentrate on in this chapter is the concomitant pragmatic question: Under what pragmatic (or semantic) circumstances can or must a constituent be designated for the omission or addition of pitch accents?

After introducing the core concepts, givenness and focussing (Sections 2.1 and 2.2), the central Section 2.3 develops a complete, if in parts informal, system for representing, interpreting, and realizing these. Finally, central concepts and the terminology related to them are laid out in Sections 2.4 and 2.5, so as to provide the foundations for the discussions in the rest of this book.

Any account of information structure-related accent placement in FALs involves one or both of the concepts of (contrastive) FOCUS and GIVENNESS. It is important to get a pre-theoretic, yet clear understanding of these concepts in order to appreciate the differences and convergences between the various formal accounts to be discussed.

Intonation and Meaning. First edition. Daniel Büring.

2.1 Givenness

Givenness, as we use the term here, is a property of expressions in utterance contexts. An expression counts as given in a context if its meaning, or some related meaning, is salient in that context. The prototypical case of givenness is coreference between two expressions, as in example (1); more precisely, we will say that ‹the singer› is GIVEN, because its referent, Frank Sinatra, is SALIENT in the context.

(1) (Sinatra's reputation among industry musicians grew swiftly, and) James always supPORted the singer.
                                                    ⏜
                                                  given

Where contextual saliency is due to a previous utterance, such as that of the name ‹Sinatra› in example (1), we can speak of that constituent, which *makes* the meaning salient, as the GIVENNESS ANTECEDENT. In other cases, such as (2) and (3), linguistic or non-linguistic context may make a concept salient without there being a particular expression which would count as a givenness antecedent.

(2) (A: The opposition wants to impeach the president.)
     B: I HATE politics.
                  ⏜
                given

(3) [seeing someone's new pack of cigarettes] I thought you QUIT smoking.
                                                                    ⏜
                                                                  given

As these examples show, too, givenness is not limited to referring expressions; meanings of any semantic category can be salient and thereby make any kind of syntactic category given (see also Section 5.1.1).

What is the exact relation that has to hold between a salient meaning and the denotation of an expression for that expression to count as given? Apart from coreference and synonymy, various other semantic relations between givenness antecedents and given expressions have been discussed in the literature, the most important of which may be hyponymy as in example (4) from van Deemter (1999: 7): mentioning ‹viola› makes violas salient, and since viola is a hyponym of string instruments, ‹string instruments› is given.

(4) (Bach wrote many pieces for viola.)
                                    He must have LOVED string instruments.
                                                          ⏜
                                                        given

In such cases, too, we will call the hyponym, ‹viola› in (4), the givenness antecedent for ‹string instruments›.

The *prosodic effect* of givenness in all the examples in this section is omission of any accenting on the given expressions. A more precise characterization, as we will see in Section 2.3 (and Section 7.2 of Chapter 7), is that given expressions must not bear the *nuclear* pitch accent. As the reader can verify, the given expressions in examples (1)–(4) would all bear the NPA in out-of-the-blue utterances of the clauses they are in.

2.2 Focus and background

Focussing is a relation between three things: a FOCUS, a FOCUS DOMAIN (F-domain), and a CONTEXT. For example, in (5), ‹Sam› is focussed in the F-domain ‹the boss gave Sam a raise›. This is appropriate (according to virtually any account of focussing) because the context makes salient the proposition that the boss gave *Kim* a raise, which is identical to the meaning of the F-domain, except for the meaning of the focus itself.

(5)   (The boss gave Kim a raise.—) No, the boss gave SAM a raise.

Analogous to the case of givenness, we may speak of the contextual expression ‹the boss gave Kim a raise› as the FOCUS ANTECEDENT for the focussing of ‹Sam› in its F-domain. Those expressions within the F-domain that are not focussed (‹the boss›, ‹gave›, and ‹a raise› in (5)) are said to be in the BACKGROUND of the F-domain.

The semantic relation between the focus antecedent, the F-domain, and the focus in example (5) can, to a first approximation, be characterized as in condition (6).

(6^{CON})   CONTRASTIVE FOCUS CONDITION
         Replacing the focus within the F-domain by some alternative, one can
         obtain an expression whose meaning is the same as, or closely related to,
         that of the F-antecedent.

Replacing ‹Sam› with ‹Kim› in example (5), we obtain ‹the boss gave Kim a raise›, the meaning of which is the same as that of the preceding utterance, its F-antecedent, in accordance with condition (6).

In virtually every proposal in the literature, focus conditions like (6) (or Question–Answer Congruence in definition (11) of Chapter 1) are formalized semantically. That is, rather than replacing one part of an expression with another, one calculates the set of *meanings* which would be obtained by such a replacement. I will use pseudo-logical expressions such as formula (7) to characterize these meanings (here: those of example (5) above).

(7)   the boss gave x a raise

If we call the meaning of a declarative sentence—that the boss gave Sam a raise for ‹the boss gave Sam a raise›—a PROPOSITION, then formula (7) symbolizes a *set of propositions*, namely all those propositions obtained by assigning an individual to x. It bears pointing out again that formulae like (7) are merely shorthand notations for sets of semantic objects (such as propositions); those sets, but not the formulae used to characterize them, are part of the 'official' theories to be discussed.

2.2.1 F-alternatives

It will be helpful to introduce the bulk of terminology and notation at this point, even before we make them precise and formalize them. As is standard in much of the semantic literature, we will write $[\![\, E\,]\!]_O$ for the denotation ('meaning') of an expression E. We will then—following the convention introduced in Rooth (1992b: 76)—write $[\![\, E\,]\!]_F$ for the set of F-ALTERNATIVES to E, which is a set of meanings.

To exemplify, $[\![$ the boss gave SAM_F a raise $]\!]_F$—crucially with focus/F-marking on *Sam*—is the set containing the propositions that the boss gave Lee a raise, that the boss gave Kim a raise, that the boss gave Sandy a raise, and so forth for any individual. $[\![$ the boss gave SAM_F a raise $]\!]_O$ is just the proposition that the boss gave Sam a raise; focussing has no effect on $[\![\ ]\!]_O$. Formula (7) above, then, is a shorthand notation to characterize the set $[\![$ the boss gave SAM_F a raise $]\!]_F$.

The elements in $[\![\, E\,]\!]_F$ are called the F-ALTERNATIVES of E, the entire set $[\![\, E\,]\!]_F$ is variously referred to as the FOCUS SET, ALTERNATIVE SET, FOCUS SEMANTIC VALUE, or FOCUS ALTERNATIVE VALUE. Analogously, $[\![\, E\,]\!]_O$ is called the ORDINARY MEANING or ORDINARY SEMANTIC VALUE of E.

It is important to keep the technical notion of "alternative" separate from the question of which alternatives are in fact salient in the context. Thus one may say, at least informally, that the relevant alternative to ‹KIM_F› in (8) is just Jo (and hence 'Sam called Jo' at the sentence level):

(8)   (Did Sam call Kim, or Jo?—) Sam called [KIM]_F.

But technically, the set of F-alternatives in the answer in (8) is still the set of *all* individuals. The Contrastive Focus Condition in (6) is formulated in such a way that only one of those needs to be salient in the context (generally, focus conditions never make statements about the entire class of F-alternatives, it seems); but calculating the F-alternatives of the answer is a "blind" process: it only restricts F-alternatives by semantic class. This is in part why we call the proposition 'Sam called Jo' in a context like that in (8) a salient proposition, rather than a "salient alternative": Focus Conditions like (6) match a context, with its specific salient elements, against a pragmatically unrestricted, "raw" set of F-alternatives.

2.2.2 Focus and accenting

The effect of focussing on accenting is virtually the inverse of the givenness effect: the focussed constituent must contain the main accent within its F-domain. As in the Toy Rules in Chapter 1, this requirement will lead to amendments to the DEFAULT PROSODY, in particular:

- within the F-domain, no accents may occur *after* the focus;
- if the focus does not contain an accent by default prosody (e.g. focus on a function word or integrated predicate), it will be assigned an additional accent.

This characterization will be sufficient for the discussion to follow.

2.2.3 Focus semantics, first inspection

As sketched above, the conditions on felicitous focussing in an expression E are usually stated in terms of relations between the alternative value of E and E's context. The prototypical case, illustrated in formula (7) above, is that of CONTRASTIVE FOCUS: there is a contextually salient meaning—call it T, the TARGET of the contrastive focussing—and focus in E is placed in such a way that T is among the F-alternatives, $[\![\,E\,]\!]_{\mathcal{F}}$, of E.

Though this is not usually done in the literature, I will now introduce a preliminary taxonomy of focus uses, which will hopefully prove useful in the following discussion. For that, consider sentence (10) as (part of) a response to any of the sentences in (9).

(9)   a. They bought a blue table.
   b. They bought some kind of table.
   c. What kind of table did they buy?
   d. They bought a round table.

(10)   They bought a RED table.

As a response to (9a), (10) is clearly—intuitively and formally—an instance of contrastive focus: replace the focussed ‹red› in (10) by ‹blue› to get the meaning of (9a). (I will continue to speak about focus semantics in this way, although, as mentioned before, replacing of expressions is not meant to be taken literally as part of the theory.)

Next consider (9b) as a context to (10). Intuitively, (10) does not so much contrast with (9b) as it *elaborates* on it. On a more formal level, whether or not this qualifies as a contrastive focus depends on whether an expression like ‹some kind of›, or indeed some trivial property (i.e. one that holds of any object at all) counts as a licit F-alternative to ‹red› (in which case we could replace ‹red› in (10) by ‹some sort of›—or nothing at all—to obtain the meaning of (9b)).

I will henceforth refer to examples of this kind as ELABORATION FOCUS, informally characterized as follows:

(11^{DEF})   ELABORATION FOCUS
          The EXISTENTIAL F-CLOSURE, of the F-alternatives is contextually salient.

The notion of existential F-closure is illustrated in formula (12), the ∃F-Clo of example (10) (see Section 3.5 in Chapter 3 for a formal definition).

(12)   ∃P [they bought a P table]

Informally speaking, the ∃F-Clo of a F-domain is symbolized by the same formula as the focus value of that domain, but with all free variables existentially bound.[1]

---

[1] This will only work for propositional expressions. The necessary generalizations will be discussed in Section 3.5.2. For the case of propositional expressions E, ∃F-Clo(E) is in fact the same as the disjunctive closure of $[\![\,E\,]\!]_{\mathcal{F}}$, $\bigcup[\![\,E\,]\!]_{\mathcal{F}}$, provided E does not contain quantifying elements that outscope the focus.

In the case of formula (12), it turns out that the ∃F-Clo is simply the proposition that they bought a table, which we will assume to be the denotation of (9b) above as well. In cases like (13b), the ∃F-Clo is not quite that trivial.

(13)   a. (They saw someone.)
       b. They saw NELson.
       c. ∃x [they saw x]

The ∃F-Clo of example (13b) is formula (13c), the proposition that they saw something or someone, which is (virtually) the meaning of example (13a). Unlike in the case of a focussed adjunct as in example (10), ∃F-Clo here binds a variable that is necessary to retrieve a proposition from the F-alternatives.

Turning now to context (9c) above, here the putative F-alternative is a question. What is the pertinent relation that needs to hold between a question meaning and the F-value of the answer? In answering this question, we can rely on the vast body of literature that concerns itself with ANSWER FOCUS, characterized informally as in (14), which simply describes the configurations meeting QUESTION–ANSWER CONGRUENCE (QAC), as discussed in Section 1.3.2 of Chapter 1.

(14^{DEF})   ANSWER FOCUS
            There is a salient (non-polar) question in the discourse, and every (literal) answer to that question is among the F-alternatives of E.

Note that in the case of answer focus, the focus antecedent is the entire question, its denotation a *set* of propositions, rather than a single proposition.

Cases like (15) appear to straddle the boundary between answer focus and contrastive focus; it clearly is an answer focus, but it also seems to relate to exactly one alternative, Elwood's brother Jake, and the question, arguably, makes both brothers salient.

(15)   (Which one of the Blues Brothers plays the harmonica?—) ELwood plays the harmonica.

In what follows, I will restrict the term contrastive focus to instances where exactly one alternative is contextually salient before the utterance, not a multiplicity of alternatives, however small, disqualifying (15) as a contrastive focus.[2]

To complete the introduction of characters that play significant roles in the discussion to follow, compare context (9a) to context (9d). To the extent that things

___

[2] The opposite position seems to be taken e.g. in Chafe (1976: 34) according to which 'the only consistent factor [in contrastive focus sentences; DB] seems to be that the speaker assumes that a *limited number* of candidates is available in the addressee's mind (whether or not the addressee could in fact list all of them). Often the number is one, often it is larger, but when it is unlimited the sentence fails to be contrastive' (my emphasis).

But since this idea requires access to (a speaker's assumption about) the addressee's mind, rather than just inspection of the context, it is problemantic to adopt it for taxonomic purposes (see also Section 5.2.2).

have been made precise at this point, both of these are clear instances of contrastive focus: ‹blue› and ‹round› are both intersective adjectives, and as such both are *bona fide* alternatives to focussed ‹red› in (10).

But intuitively, there is a clear difference between these cases, and that intuitive difference is reflected in the acceptability difference between (16) and (17).

(16)   (They bought a blue table.—) $\left\{ \begin{array}{c} \text{No,} \\ \text{I thought} \end{array} \right\}$ they bought a RED table.

(17)   (They bought a round table.—) # $\left\{ \begin{array}{c} \text{No,} \\ \text{I thought} \end{array} \right\}$ they bought a RED table.

While (16) seems entirely natural, (17) feels like a *non-sequitur*; there simply is no obvious contrast between the first utterance and the second.

We will refer to this contrast as the distinction between EXCLUSIVE CON-TRASTIVE FOCI ('red' vs 'blue') and UNRELATED CONTRASTIVE FOCI ('red' vs 'round'), trusting that the concepts are sufficiently clear intuitively.

In introducing this taxonomy of foci, I do not intend to claim that there are different ways in which these are realized or even grammatically represented (at least in FALs). To the contrary, my impression is that these foci behave identically in all respects. Rather, the taxonomy will be useful in comparing various theories of focussing, which routinely lump several, but not all of them.

Before turning to such theories, I will briefly elaborate on the semantic strength of the respective focus types in relation to one another. A context which makes salient an exclusive contrastive focus thereby also makes salient a contrastive focus *simpliciter*, but not *vice versa*. More interestingly, if a context provides a salient antecedent for a contrastive focus (exclusive or unrelated), it presumably also provides an antecedent for an elaboration focus. For example, if a context makes the proposition that they saw Nelson salient, it presumably thereby makes the proposition that they saw *someone* salient, too.

So it appears that any case which meets the condition on exclusive contrastive focus automatically also meets the condition on independent contrastive focus, and both in turn meet the condition on elaboration focus. The inverse is not the case.

Finally, what about answer focus? It seems at least plausible to claim that raising a certain question makes salient the proposition that the question has a true answer. In other words, the question ‹Who did they see?›, while not *implying* that they saw someone (after all, one can answer ‹no one›), would be said to nevertheless *make salient* the proposition that they saw someone. If so, answer focus would be the same as elaboration focus, and any context that licenses the former should also license the latter.

2.3 A grammar of focus and givenness

2.3.1 Representation

Jackendoff (1972) proposed to use a grammatical marker ("feature") F to label a constituent as focussed. Analogously, a privative feature G is often assumed to mark, in the syntactic representation, a constituent which is given. Since it will be useful to have an easy way of representing focus and givenness in the discussion to follow, we will now define a first model of focus/givenness representation, its realization, and its interpretation, based on such markers.

2.3.2 Interpretation

We have already seen that both focus and givenness conditions relate an expression to a CONTEXTUALLY SALIENT MEANING, henceforth CSM. Summing up the discussion so far, here is what we have:

(18^{CON}) GIVENNESS CONDITION

A G-mark on constituent E is licensed in a context Cx if Cx provides a CSM, and that CSM stands in a G-RELATION to the ordinary denotation of E.

(19^{DEF}) G-RELATIONS

a. CSM is the referent of E in Cx, or
b. CSM and E are synonymous, at least contextually
c. CSM is a hypernym of E, at least contextually

(20^{CON}) FOCUS CONDITION

An F-domain D is licensed in a context Cx if Cx provides a CSM which stands in an F-RELATION to the F-alternatives of D.

(21^{DEF}) F-RELATIONS

a. CSM is one of D's F-alternatives   (contrastive F)
b. CSM is or entails the existential focus closure of D's F-alternatives
(elaboration F)
c. CSM is a question, and each direct answer to CSM is an F-alternative of D (answer F)

Both conditions start with the CSM, but while givenness relates to the ordinary meaning, focus relates to the F-alternatives. The particular relation that has to hold between the CSM and the ordinary meaning and F-alternatives, respectively, I called G- and F-relations. For the moment, these are just the ones discussed informally so far. But we can plug in, as it were, different, more accurate and precise conditions later, without having to redefine the entire system. Also keep in mind that (21a) is really just a sub-case of (21b), and (21c) might be, too, under certain assumptions, as discussed in Section 2.2.3. I just keep them all for greater transparency, or in case we want to apply them to different types of focus later on.

The formulation of condition (20) might seem to disavow my earlier insistence that focus is at its core relational; like condition (18) it only relates *one* thing, the F-alternatives, to a CSM. Still, since it is a condition on the entire *F-domain*, rather than just the focus, it has access to everything it needs to know about the focus *and* its background via the F-alternatives.

2.3.3 Realization

The G- and F-conditions (18) and (20) regulate when G-marking and F-domain formation are permitted in a given structure in a given context. The following INFORMATION STRUCTURE REALIZATION CONDITIONS regulate how G- and F-marking influence accenting.

(22^{CON}) a. F-REALIZATION CONDITION
          For any F-domain D, the final accent in D lies in a focus of D.
      b. G-REALIZATION CONDITION
          A G-marked constituent does not contain the nuclear accent, unless forced by the F-Realization Condition.
      c. PROSODIC INERTIA
          Default Intonation is preserved as much as possible, while meeting the F-Realization Condition and the G-Realization Condition.

The following examples illustrate the interplay of these conditions.

(23) (They bought a red table.) No, they bought a [BLUE]$_F$ table.
          $\underline{\hspace{6cm}}$
                                    F-domain
      a. CSM for F-condition: that they bought a red table
      b. F-alternatives of F-domain: they bought an x table
      c. CSM is an element of the F-alternatives (and entails their ∃F-Clo, 'they bought a table'); (20) is met.
      d. final pitch accent in F-domain is on the only element of the focus; (22a) is met.

(24) (Bach wrote many pieces for viola.)
                          He must have LOVED [string instruments]$_G$.
      a. CSM for Givenness-Condition: viola
      b. ‹viola› is a hyponym of ‹string instrument›; (18) is met.
      c. ‹string instruments› is 'deaccented'; (22b) is met.

It is worthwhile to review why the accent in (24) will be on ‹loved› by Prosodic Inertia. Recall our toy rules for producing default prosody from Chapter 1.[3]

(25^{DEF}) DEFAULT PROSODY
      Step 1:   Put pitch accents on open class elements; put the minimal number to guarantee that each syntactic phrase contains at least one PA.
      Step 2:   a. *Delete* pitch accents if they are followed by at least one other
      (optional)   PA,
                or alternatively
                b. *add* pitch accents on open class elements (OCEs), if they are followed by at least one other PA.

---

[3] Since conditions (18) and (20) now take care of the information structure-related aspects of prosody, we can leave out the F-related Step F+ and Step F− from Section 1.3.2.

As discussed in Chapter 1, transitive verbs like ‹loved› in (24) can get a pitch accent only through Step 2; by Step 1, the complement of V, a syntactic phrase, has to contain a pitch accent, and another pitch accent on V would yield *two* pitch accents within VP, in violation of the minimality requirement in Step 1.

But things are different now: The G-Realization Condition prohibits an accent on ‹string instruments›, and default prosody is only to be realized inasmuch as allowed without violating the G- and F-Conditions. So while Step 1 is prohibited from putting a pitch accent on the DP ‹string instruments›, it *can* still put one within the VP without violating the G-condition, namely on V itself. So instead of leaving DP *and* VP accentless, it can "save" the latter. Finally Step 2 cannot delete that accent, since it is the last in the clause (nor can it add any accents after it). The important thing is that we understand "Default Intonation is preserved as much as possible . . ." in (22c) above to mean "Step 1 is to be carried out as much as possible . . ." (rather than "the output of Step 1 without regard to information structure has to be preserved as much as possible . . .").

Finally in example (26) we see the reason why the F-condition "outranks" the G-Condition. If an F-marker is present in addition to a G-marker, the latter has no effect on accenting.

(26)   (Who will Kim's boss send to the meeting?—)

$$\text{Kim's boss will send } \underline{[\text{KIM}]_{\text{G,F}}.}$$
$$\text{F-domain}$$

2.3.4 Enforcement

The G- and F-Conditions outlined in Sections 2.3.2 and 2.3.3 provide sufficient conditions for F- and G-marking, but not necessary ones. They never *force* G-marking, or the construction of a F-domain. But that seems wrong, since it would predict that default prosody is always an option if the speaker chose not to G- or F-mark.

(27)   (Who nominated Smith?—) # Jones nominated SMITH.

In other words, while the rules correctly predict (28a) and (28b) to be fine in this context, they do not enforce that a speaker will answer the question in (27) with either of (28), rather than the answer in (27).

(28)   a. JONES [nominated Smith]$_G$
       b. JONES$_F$ nominated Smith
       $$\text{F-domain}$$

In anticipation of later discussions, we stipulate, for the time being, the following guidelines.

(29^{CON})   MAXIMIZE INFORMATION STRUCTURE MARKING
       a. If G-Marking of a constituent is licensed by (18), it is obligatory ("G-mark as much as possible").

    b. If a constituent can be in the background of an F-domain by (20), it
       has to be ("background as much as possible").

Note that condition (29b) indirectly encourages focussing: For a constituent to be
in the background, there needs to be an F-domain; and an F-domain needs to
contain a focus to meet the Focus Condition (20) above.[4] Finally, given the choice
between more or less focussing within an F-domain, condition (29b) will opt for
the structure with more background, that is, less focussing.

    Inasmuch as backgrounding can be understood as a device to link the
backgrounded elements to the context—and we will see that it is plausible to view
things that way—the two clauses of (29) have a common denominator: they force
the speaker to maximize relations to the context. In fact, various authors, following
the lead of Williams (1997), Truckenbrodt (1995) and Sauerland (2005) assume
precisely that: that one or both of (29) are just theorems of a general principle
like "Maximize Background," "Maximize Anaphoric Relations," or "Maximize
Presuppositions" (we will return to this in Chapters 4 and 5).

2.4 Arguments for keeping focussing and givenness separate

In many instances, focussing and givenness yield the same prosodic result. For
example, (30) could be analyzed as a contrastive focus on ‹Sam›, with ‹won the
race› backgrounded and the previous sentence as its focus antecedent; or it could
be analyzed as givenness deaccenting of the VP ‹won the race›, with the VP of the
previous sentence as givenness antecedent.

(30)   (Kim won the race.—No,) SAM won the race.

In fact, if we follow the letter of (29), the representation for the correction in (30)
has to be as in (31).

(31) $[SAM]_F$ [won the race]$_G$
               F-domain

This seems highly redundant. There are configurations, however, in which this
complementarity breaks down, namely when focus and given elements overlap,
partially or completely. These then provide *prima facie* reasons to have both
givenness and focussing as parts of the theory (and have been presented as such
in the literature[5]). It is therefore worthwhile to discuss them in turn.

---

[4] Unless the F-domain happens to be entirely given, a fact exploited in Schwarzschild's (1999)
GIVENness Theory, to be discussed in Chapter 3.

[5] See in particular Ladd (1980: pp.81ff), Selkirk (1984: sec. 5.2.1, esp. pp. 214–25), as well as
(Schwarzschild, 1999: pp.145ff).

2.4.1 Partially given foci: given elements within a broader focus

Where a focus contains more than one word, the accent assignment within the focus is usually determined by default prosody. If however, one of these elements is given, we can observe givenness deaccenting within a focus, as in (32) and (33).[6]

(32)   (What did John's mother do?—) She PRAISED him.

(33)   (After what Kim did, her mother should probably leave the country.—No!)
       a. She should [TALK to Kim]$_F$
       b. She should [TALK to the poLICE]$_F$.

Both the contrastive context in (33) and the question context in (32) should lead to a VP-focus in the next utterance. This in turn should yield the NPA on the direct object, which seems the correct prediction in light of answer (33b). However, in answer (33a) the direct object is given, and the NPA 'shifts' leftwards onto the verb. This suggests a more elaborate representation along the lines of (34), in which a G-marker occurs *within* a focus.

(34)   she should [TALK to Kim$_G$]$_F$
       ⎯⎯⎯⎯⎯⎯⎯⎯⎯⎯⎯⎯⎯
            F-domain

One might be tempted to try, alternatively, to argue that (32) and (33a) involve narrow focus on V, which would immediately explain the accent pattern. But note that none of the F-relations discussed so far would license such narrow V-focus: the question that antecedes the focussing is not "What did John's mother do to John?"; nor does example (32) contrast with a proposition of the form "Kim's mother should Q Kim" (witness also the answer in (33b) again, which is clearly *not* compatible with these).

   Therefore we cannot, given our assumptions, say that examples like (32) and (33) involve narrow focus; givenness within the focus not only seems intuitively correct, it also fits the overall theory without any problem.

2.4.2 Completely given foci

Where a focus is completely given, accenting takes place as usual (as we already saw in (26)):

(35)   (A: Kim's mother nominated Sam./ Who did Kim's mother nominate?)
       B: She nominated KIM$_F$.

(36)   (A: The young king's mother nominated Sam for a promotion./ Who did the
           young king's mother nominate for a promotion?)
       B: She nominated [the YOUNG KING]$_F$ for a promotion.

---

[6] (32) is Schwarzschild (1999: ex. (9)).

Like partially given foci, completely given foci challenge the idea of a reduction of focus to givenness: both ‹She nominated...for the job› and ‹Kim/the young king› are entirely given. Yet, the latter bears the NPA, and this seems due to focussing (the default NPA would be on ‹promotion› in this structure). This is readily explained if ‹Kim/the young king› were focussed in addition to being given, assuming, as we did in (22b), that focussing "overrides" givenness when in direct conflict. The representation for this case would look as in example (37).

(37)   She$_G$ nominated$_G$ KIM$_{F,G}$ for a promotion$_G$
       _____
                                        F-domain

As mentioned at the outset of this section, (partially) given foci play an important role in the history of focus theory, as they militate against any simple reduction of focus to non-givenness, or *vice versa*. We will come back to examples illustrating them at various points to see if and how the proposals we discuss meet this challenge.

We now have in place a full system of focus and givenness interpretation, representation, and realization, which will provide the reference point for the rest of this book. Before going on to more theoretical matters, I will discuss a few more aspects of the natural history of focussing.

2.5 Larger foci and focus ambiguities

2.5.1 Focus ambiguity

In this chapter we have concentrated so far on cases in which the focus was a single word or non-complex constituent, that is where the focus pretty much coincides with the smallest constituent containing the NPA. When I introduced the concept of focussing in Chapter 1, I mentioned the existence of cases in which focus 'projects' to complex constituents, and how to investigate them. We are now in a position to do this more systematically.

Having established the basic licensing conditions for focussing using one-word-focus cases, we now reverse our investigative strategy, and *use* those licensing conditions, for example the F-condition in (20) above, to construct contexts in which the focus is predicted to be on larger constituents (the analogous maneuver was illustrated cursorily for answer focus in Section 1.3.2), in order to see how such foci will be realized. Consider the sentence ‹No, the boss gave Kim a raise› in three different contexts.

		PREDICTS...
(38)	a. Did the boss keep the wins for herself?	VP-focus
	b. Why the turmoil. Did someone die?	S-focus
	c. Did the boss give Kim the pink slip?	DP-focus
		...FOR
	No, the boss gave Kim a RAISE	↵

As indicated, in any of these contexts, the reply will be naturally produced with the NPA on ‹raise›, and indeed may be pronounced with the same overall accent *pattern* (accent on all content words). That is to say, the sentence ‹the boss gave Kim a RAISE›, with the NPA as indicated, can be said to be Focus-Ambiguous.[7]

We (like virtually all of the literature) use the term focus *ambiguous*, rather than "focus underspecified" or "focus vague" because, by assumption, focus is a grammatical category, and therefore ‹the boss gave Kim a RAISE› is a different grammatical object in each of the contexts in (38). Using F-markers, we can represent these objects, unambiguously, as in (39).

(39)   a. No, the boss [gave Kim a RAISE]$_F$.
       b. No, [the boss gave Kim a RAISE]$_F$
       c. No, the boss gave Kim [a RAISE]$_F$

Technically, we can characterize a Focus Ambiguity as: different F-markings on otherwise identical syntactic structures converge on the same accent pattern. If we assume F-markers to be a *bona fide* part of the syntactic representation, focus ambiguities turn out to be a regular case of syntactic ambiguity.

That different F-markings may converge on the same NPA placement (and indeed the same accent pattern) is in fact compatible with Jackendoff's rule, alluded to in Chapter 1 already, which we paraphrased as generalization (40).

(40^{GEN})   The last default pitch accent within the focus is the last pitch accent in the sentence.

In Chapter 1 we implemented this generalization by an extra step in the Toy Rules that assign accents, Step F−, which deletes all pitch accents after the focus. In condition (22a) above we simply stated it as a condition on the final representation instead, which requires the last/nuclear pitch accent to be within the focus.

Either way, the result, in keeping with generalization (40), is that the focus contains the NPA (the last pitch accent in the sentence). More precisely, the following holds:

(41)   Corollary on the Relation between NPA Placement and Focus:
       NPA on a terminal X is compatible with focus on any constituent Y which
       a. contains X, and
       b. within which X would get the final/nuclear PA by default accenting.

As mentioned in Chapter 1, cases like (39a) and (39b) are usually said to involve Focus Projection—descriptively: a non-terminal (and usually branching) node being interpreted as focus. The term "projection" presumably goes back to implementations of focus theory in which the terminal bearing the NPA is necessarily itself syntactically F-marked, and that F-marker is literally copied onto higher

---

[7] A fact perhaps first noted in Worth (1964: 701) and discussed in Halliday (1967b: 207f) (as "domain of focus").

nodes, including the eventual pragmatic focus, possibly constrained by syntactic "projection rules" (e.g. Selkirk, 1984, 1995b: see Chapter 4 for detailed discussion).

The representations in (39) do not have that property; only the pragmatic answer focus is F-marked, hence our more neutral characterization of focus projection in this chapter.

Focus projection is most commonly illustrated with sentence-final focus, as in example (38). But as we saw in Section 1.3.2 of Chapter 1, focus projection can, for example, also occur in subject position. Example (42) repeats the example given there in a yes/no question context.

(42)   Did Jacques order shellfish?—No,
       a. [JANE]$_F$ ordered shellfish.
       b. [My next door NEIGHbor]$_F$ ordered shellfish.
       c. [The guy at the table over by the WINdow]$_F$ ordered shellfish.

By the same token, the accent pattern in, say, example (42c) gives rise to focus ambiguities, in keeping with corollary (41):[8]

(43)   a. (Did the guy at the bar order shellfish?—) No, the guy [at the table over by the WINdow]$_F$ ordered shellfish.
       b. (Did the guy at the table over by the exit order shellfish?—) No, the guy at the table [over by the WINdow]$_F$ ordered shellfish.

2.5.2 Focus sizes: broad, wide, narrow

In the previous section we saw foci of different sizes, from single-word to sentence-wide. The former are often called NARROW FOCI; the antonymous term BROAD FOCUS is sometimes used to mean sentential (i.e. maximum-size) focus, sometimes any focus bigger than a single word or main-clause constituent (e.g. VP-focus, focus on embedded clauses, or on complex DPs).

Occasionally the terms narrow focus and contrastive focus are used for the focus in any sentences in which the NPA is not where default prosody would put it. Indeed, such examples very often display narrow focus, but the correlation is far from perfect. "Early" NPAs may still project sizeable foci, as in example (42c), and we already saw in example (33) in Section 2.4.1 that givenness deaccenting may make a VP focus sound like a narrow verb focus. In fact, such cases can even project S-focus, if everything following the NPA is properly given, as in (44).

(44)   Q: (What happened after Kim absconded to Iceland?)
       a. [The company's stock hit rock BOTTom]$_F$.
       b. [The company SUED [Kim]$_G$]$_F$
       c. [LEE [went to Iceland]$_G$]$_F$ (too).

---

[8] By corollary (41), the foci in examples (43a) and (43b) could be even narrower, namely on the NPs ‹table over by the window› and ‹window›, respectively. I know of no tests to decide between these options.

Recall at this point that we treat the question–answer configuration as an authoritative diagnostic for focus size; but also, answer (44a) is used as a Focus Size Control, showing that the question clearly does not limit possible answers any more narrowly than the question "What happened?" would suggest. Note also that (44b) and (44) (c) would require *different* questions to be the meaning of (44Q)— 'What happened to Kim?' and 'Who went to Iceland?', respectively.

Let me add a plea once more for carefully distinguishing the *size* of a focus from the *domain* of a focus (and using these terms accordingly): in a broad focus example like (42c), ‹the guy at the table over by the window› itself *is* the focus. The F-domain in that example is the entire clause, that is to say, that constituent containing the focus that is related to the question in (42) by one of the F-relations (here (21c) above; a precise representation of F-domains will be introduced in Section 3.1). Especially in older writings, the term F-domain is sometimes used for broad/projected foci (e.g. Halliday, 1967b)—presumably because the term "focus" is reserved for the accented word alone (what we will call the Focus Exponent in Section 4.4); given pragmatic definitions of focus such as the one used here, however, there is no reason to call a broadly focussed constituent anything other than "the focus," and using any other term will only lead to confusion (worst of all if, as in the case of "F-domain", there is another meaning attached to it).

It is sometimes said that the smaller or narrower a focus is, the more contrastive it is.[9] This is not correct, though. What we may say is that a narrower focus needs a more specific context. For illustration, (45a) needs a context that makes salient a proposition of the form "Sam called x," whereas (45b) merely needs a salient proposition of the form "Sam Q" (which basically just means that Sam must be salient in the context—instantiate Q with "exists"), and finally, (45c) imposes no requirements on the context at all.

(45) a. Sam called [KIM]$_F$.   Sam called x
      b. Sam [called KIM]$_F$ Sam Q
      c. [Sam called KIM]$_F$ p

Still, as we have seen, any size of focus can be used in a correction, and any size of focus can be used in plain juxtapositions or as an elaboration. It is therefore advisable to keep the issue of focus size distinct from the issue of whether or not a focus is corrective, contrastive, or what have you.

2.5.3 Focus and ellipsis

As discussed in connection with examples (33) and (44), givenness deaccenting may obscure the actual size of a broader focus. Apart from controlling the context (by questions or the like), we can apply one other diagnostic to determine focus size, based on the following generalization.

---

[9] E.g. Guéron (1980).

(46^{GEN})   FOCUS–ELLIPSIS GENERALIZATION
> A term answer cannot be smaller than the focus. (Focal elements cannot
> be elided.)

Some observations motivating this generalization are presented in examples (47)
through (49): Even though ‹Alex› can be a term answer, as in (47), this is illicit when
the question requires a VP-focus answer, (48).

(47) (Who was Kim going to kiss?)
      —ALEX./ Kim was going to kiss ALEX.

(48) (What was Kim going to do?)
      a. Kim was going to kiss ALEX.
      b. Kiss ALEX.
      c. #ALEX.

While this might seem unsurprising in (48), note that even if the verb ‹kiss› is
actually given, as in (49), a DP term answer remains impossible.

(49) (What was Kim going to do, after kissing Sam?)
      a. Kim was going to kiss ALEX.
      b. Kiss ALEX.
      c. #ALEX.

Finally, even if partial givenness of a broad focus demonstrably licenses deaccenting, as in (50) (note that the normal pattern is ‹Kim reSIGNED›, not ‹KIM
resigned›), it is still impossible to omit the given item, even though the resulting
term answer is possible as a narrow focus, (51).

(50) (What will happen if Sam resigns?)
      a. (Then) KIM will resign.
      b. #KIM.

(51) (Who will oversee the project if Sam resigns?)
      a. (Then) KIM will oversee the project.
      b. KIM.

All of this shows the validity of (46), and, consequently, of ellipsis as a test for
teasing apart narrow focus from broader focus plus givenness deaccenting.
   Curiously, the test actually works the other way around, too (though this is not
expressed in generalization (46)): ‹kiss ALEX› is unacceptable as an answer to the
question in (47); a term answer *bigger* than the focus (but still smaller than the

entire clause) is impossible, too, meaning we can in principle use term answers to explore not just the minimum size, but also the maximum size of a focus.[10]

The limit of this test is that the putative narrow focus must in principle be a possible term answer. Thus from the unacceptability of (52b) one cannot conclude that we are dealing with a broader focus than V in (52), since a term answer consisting of a transitive verb alone seems to be impossible in English in general (whence the *, rather than #).

(52)   (What are they going to do to Kim's family if they find out?)
    a.   TICKLE 'em.
    b.   *TICKLE.

Keeping this limitation in mind, though, term answers, and likely ellipsis more generally, can be a good probe to test whether an apparently narrow focus is in fact broader.

2.5.4 Sentential contrastive focus?

In example (38) above, we introduced sentential focus in a corrective focus setting, repeated in (53).

(53)   (Why the turmoil. Did someone die?—) No, [the boss gave Kim a RAISE]$_F$

Any proposition (sentence meaning) is a F-alternative of the correction in example (53); since there is no unfocussed material in the sentence, the set of F-alternatives is not further restricted at all. Evidently, then, the proposition "someone died," made salient by the previous utterance, is among the F-alternatives to the answer, so sentential focus is predicted by condition (6) above, or clause (21a) of definition (21), to be acceptable in example (53).

Now recall that contrastive focus (clause (21a)) is not limited to corrections. Rather, clause (21a) predicts that any salient proposition, and hence derivatively *any sentence*, could figure as the target of focussing in example (53). This may seem surprising and counter-intuitive. It licenses, for example, sentential focus on the second utterance in (54).

(54)   (It was a beautiful day.) [Children were playing in the park]$_F$

One could avoid this consequence by requiring that any focus needs to have *some* background, or semantically speaking, the sentential F-alternatives must exclude *some* propositions. On the face of it, this would rule out not just (54) (as a sentential focus, that is), but also example (53). But it is arguable that in example (53), the full answer is really ‹*The turmoil is because [the boss gave Kim a raise]$_F$*›, with only the embedded clause being a focus, and the main clause its domain, accounting

---

[10] Discussion of this phenomenon is found in connection with the so-called MAXELIDE constraint; see Merchant (2008); Takahashi and Fox (2005) a.o.

for at least a weak sense of exclusion and alternatives here (other reasons for the turmoil). None of that is the case in (54), which also does not have any obvious "hidden embedding."

On the other hand, sentence-wide focus always results in the same accent pattern as default prosody alone. This is so because within the focus, default prosody applies, so if the entire sentence is focussed, the resulting prosody will be the same as that of a focus-less sentence (in which default prosody applies, by definition). There is thus no reason *not* to assume that (54) is a sentence-wide focus.

In fact, any context that makes *some* proposition(s) salient licenses sentence-wide focus on any declarative sentence. It is arguable that this is the case even for discourse initial contexts, with salient propositions including "you (the addressee) and me (the speaker) are having a conversation," "we are currently at..." (place of the conversation), etc. If so, all-new sentences would also be analyzable as involving sentential focus; there might be no focus-less sentences.

What is important is that at this point, there is no empirical difference between these choices, as they both predict the same, default accent pattern in non-specific contexts. By the same token, the choice to analyze example (53) above as an instance of sentential focus, rather than a focus-less sentence, is guided by a desire to classify it together with the other instances of (narrow) focus, rather than the need to predict a marked, focus-specific accent pattern. Accordingly, researchers and proposals differ on whether and under which circumstances they assume sentential focus.

2.6 Chapter summary

This concludes our initial presentation of focus and givenness representation, interpretation, and realization, which will serve as the general background for the rest of this book. In the following chapters, I will discuss several, sometimes competing, elaborations and modifications of this general system.

In particular, I will continue to use the descriptive labels contrastive focus, elaboration focus, and answer focus, as well as the distinction between privative givenness and relational focussing, the latter crucially involving F-domains, which in turn consist of one or several foci plus a background.

Likewise, F- and, where applicable, G-conditions of the general form in (18) and (20) in this chapter ("there is a contextually salient meaning which bears a F-/G-relation to...") are assumed throughout the remainder of this book. What will change, as far as *interpretation* of information structure is concerned, is the specification of the F-/G-relations (19) and (21) (Chapters 3 and 5). Details of the representation and realization of focus and givenness are the subject of Chapters 4 and 8.

3

Focus and givenness theories

In this chapter I introduce some of the most influential theories of focus/ givenness interpretation. Despite first appearances, the differences between some of the theories are minimal, and often one is simply an improved or more complete version of another.

Any one of the theories discussed in this chapter includes, if to varying degrees, aspects of focus representation in addition to focus interpretation. I will try to separate out these aspects as much as possible, concentrating on F-/G-interpretation in this chapter, and on F-/G-representation in Chapter 4.

3.1 Alternative Semantics: Rooth (1985, 1992b)

3.1.1 Composing alternatives

Rooth (1985) develops a compositional way of deriving the F-alternatives informally introduced in Chapter 2, that is it defines what amounts to the function $[\![\ ]\!]_{\mathcal{F}}$ introduced earlier. The technical details are given in the appendix to this chapter; at this point, an informal characterization will suffice.

If, and only if, a constituent ‹C› is itself F-marked, it is *eligible to introduce* F-alternatives. What kind of F-alternatives it introduces depends on its *semantic type*: if ‹C› is a name and denotes an individual, its F-alternatives, $[\![\,C\,]\!]_{\mathcal{F}}$, will be the set of all individuals; if ‹C› is a transitive verb and denotes a two-place relation, its F-alternatives will be the set of all two-place relations; if ‹C› is a clause and denotes a proposition, $[\![\,C\,]\!]_{\mathcal{F}}$ will be the set of all propositions, and so forth. If a terminal node is not F-marked, it is not eligible to introduce alternatives. However, technically, it still has a set of F-alternatives: the singleton set of its ordinary denotation. So ‹Kim›, unfocussed, has the F-alternative set {Kim} (we could also write ‘{$[\![\,Kim\,]\!]_{o}$}’). If we write **laughed** for the property denoted by ‹laughed›, $[\![\,\mathbf{laughed}\,]\!]_{\mathcal{F}}$—again unfocussed—is {**laughed**} (or {$[\![\,\mathbf{laughed}\,]\!]_{o}$}), etc.

What is the reason to let unfocussed terminals introduce such TRIVIAL ALTERNATIVES (i.e. singleton sets containing their ordinary meaning)? It allows Rooth to give a uniform rule for PROPAGATING F-alternatives for branching nodes: take each F-alternative of the one daughter, combine it with each F-alternative of the other daughter, and collect the results in a set; that set will be the set of F-alternatives of the mother.

Figure 3.1 schematizes this process, continuing to write formulae with variable symbols as shorthand for sets of meanings (and singleton sets as ‘{Kim}’ etc.). Alternative Propagation, as in Figure 3.1 is the standard mode to get $[\![\ ]\!]_{\mathcal{F}}$, the F-alternatives, for a non-terminal node that is not itself F-marked.

Intonation and Meaning. First edition. Daniel Büring.
© Daniel Büring 2016. First published 2016 by Oxford University Press.

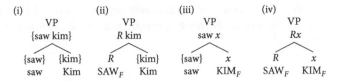

FIGURE 3.1 F-alternatives for a transitive VP for all combinations of F-marked and not F-marked; any formula containing a variable symbol abbreviates a set of meanings, i.e. every node has a set of ordinary meanings as its $\llbracket \ \rrbracket_{\mathcal{F}}$.

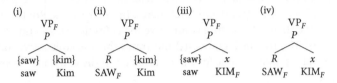

FIGURE 3.2 F-marking on a non-terminal introduces the full set of F-alternatives, P, the set of all VP-denotations (properties); any F-marking "below" is ignored.

F-marked non-terminals simply get to introduce a new set of alternatives, regardless of the F-alternatives of their daughter(s), as shown in Figure 3.2.

Note at this point that the focus semantic value of constituent α which is not itself F-marked is not necessarily equal to $\{\llbracket \alpha \rrbracket_{o}\}$. If α *contains* any F-marked sub-constituents, the F-alternatives of those constituents will propagate (in the sense just introduced), and so $\llbracket \alpha \rrbracket_{\mathcal{F}}$ will also be a multi-membered (non-trivial) set. This is the case for the VP node in the trees in Figure 3.1(ii)–3.1(iv).

3.1.2 The Squiggle Theory

Rooth (1992b) integrates the compositional derivation of F-alternatives just discussed (essentially that from Rooth, 1985) with a comprehensive approach to the representation and pragmatic interpretation of focus. Rooth proposes a single operator $\sim$, the SQUIGGLE, which retrieves focus semantic values and makes them accessible to compositional semantics.

In Rooth's formulation, $\sim$ combines with an unpronounced pronoun, which I will call the F-DOMAIN VARIABLE, conventionally written as C_i, and then with a syntactic constituent ⟨δ⟩ of arbitrary syntactic category. This is felicitous only if the value of the unpronounced pronoun stands in one of two specific relations to the focus semantic value of ⟨δ⟩ (Rooth 1992b: 93).

(1^{CON})   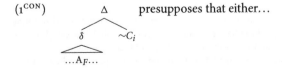   presupposes that either...

a. INDIVIDUAL CASE: The contextually supplied value of C_i is identical to an element of the focus semantic value of δ (formally: $[\![\, C_i \,]\!]_O \in [\![\, \delta \,]\!]_F$).[1]

or

b. SET CASE The contextually supplied value of C_i is identical to, or a subset of, the focus semantic value of δ (formally: $[\![\, C_i \,]\!]_O \subseteq [\![\, \delta \,]\!]_F$). The ordinary meaning of Δ is that of δ (formally: $[\![\, \Delta \,]\!]_o = [\![\, \delta \,]\!]_o$).[2]

The alert reader will have noticed that Rooth's Individual Case and Set Case correspond to the F-relations contrastive focus and answer focus, respectively, as discussed in Section 2.3 ((21a) and (21c) there). In other words, Rooth's definition of $\sim$ allows the theory to capture contrastive focus (exclusive and unrelated) and answer focus. The tree in Figure 3.3(i) illustrates this for contrastive focus, with the contextually supplied value for the F-variable C indicated on C for expository convenience.

For answer focus it is crucial to adopt a theory of question meanings on which the denotation of a constituent question is a set of literal answers to it (here I assume Hamblin's (1973) semantics, which has questions denoting the set of all literal answers, true or false). In that case, if each literal answer is an element of the answer's focus semantic value, it holds that $[\![\, \text{question} \,]\!]_o \subseteq [\![\, \text{answer} \,]\!]_F$ whenever the Set Case (1b) is met. This is illustrated in the tree in Figure 3.3.

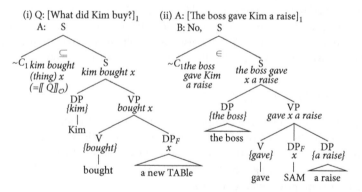

FIGURE 3.3   Answer focus and contrastive focus in a Squiggle Theory. For ease of reading, the structure is annotated with the F-alternatives at every node, the value of the F-variable C, and an indication of which case (set/$\subseteq$ or individual/$\in$) applies in the example (between $\sim C$ and its sister).

---

[1] "Individual Case" here does not mean that this case involves focus on individual denoting expressions only; in fact, it has nothing to do with the semantic class of individuals. It is so called because the value of C in this case is a single ("individual") meaning, not a *set* of such meanings.

[2] I will postpone discussion of the question what $[\![\, \delta \sim C \,]\!]_F$ is until Section 10.5.4 in Chapter 10.

3.1.3 Notable properties

I will now highlight some of the noteworthy aspects of Rooth's proposal.

Focus conditions as presuppositions: The conditions on $\sim$ in (1) above are formulated as presuppositions. This is a formal implementation of our earlier observation that sentences with "wrong" accent placements are judged as inappropriate or infelicitous (in the given context), rather than as false or ungrammatical, and one that is shared by most accounts of focus semantics: what we pretheoretically describe as appropriateness conditions are implemented as presupposition.

F-domains: The formalism in Rooth (1992b) appears to be the first to include an explicit representation of F-domains, by including $\sim$ in the syntactic representation (at Logical Form); any sister to a $\sim C_i$ is an F-domain. This allows the theory to capture cases like the, by now legendary, beginning of a farmer joke in (2).

(2)   An AMERICAN farmer met a CANADIAN farmer.

The tree in Figure 3.4 is Rooth's (1992b) representation of this example: both NPs are F-domains, and each domain bears a (different) F-domain variable. The coindexing of the C variables with the (remote!) NPs indicates that C_1 is to be assigned the value 'Canadian farmer', and C_2 the value 'American farmer'. In this case, both $\sim C_1$ and $\sim C_2$ qualify as Individual Cases in the sense of condition (1) above.

Relation to context, givenness, and saliency: A surprising feature of the proposal is the apparent absence of any reference to context, antecedents, or saliency. Yet, given certain assumptions about how the F-domain variable, C, has to relate to context, Rooth's proposal is at its very heart an anaphoric theory of focus. An F-domain involves an empty pronoun C_i, introduced as argument to the squiggle. While Rooth (1992b) does not discuss this aspect of the proposal in detail, it is

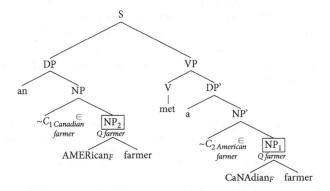

FIGURE 3.4   A Logical Form representation of a sentence with two subsentential F-domains (boxed nodes).

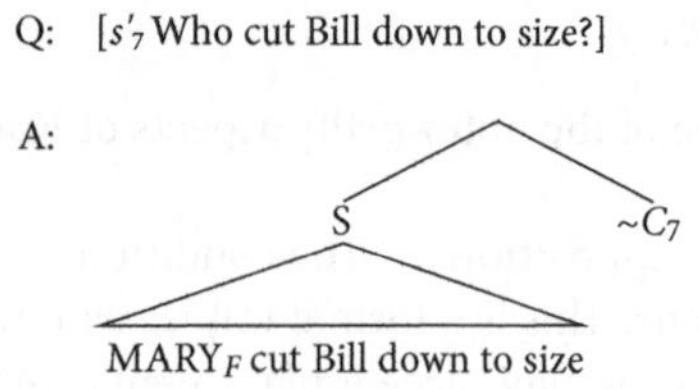

Q: [s'_7 Who cut Bill down to size?]

A:

MARY$_F$ cut Bill down to size

FIGURE 3.5   Rooth's (1992b) representation of an answer focus example.

clear from his examples that C_i may be assigned the ordinary semantic value of previously uttered sentences (or parts thereof), as in the tree in Figure 3.5 (ex. (41a) in Rooth, 1992b), where the coindexing between the contextual question and the F-domain variable again indicates that the variable gets assigned the same meaning as the ordinary meaning of the preceding question.

Rooth (1996a) explicitly states the logic behind this.

The advantage of casting [Question–Answer Congruence] in terms of the $\sim$ operator is that we do not need to state a rule or constraint specific to the question–answer configuration. Rather, focus interpretation introduces a variable which, like other free variables, needs to find an antecedent or be given a pragmatically constructed value. Identifying the variable with the semantic value of the question is simply a matter of anaphora resolution. (Rooth, 1996a:279)

If we assume that the values available for assignment to the F-domain variables are all and only contextually salient meanings, Rooth's Focus Conditions do, indirectly, make reference to contextually salient meanings (in the form of available meanings for the F-domain variables), and correspond in fact exactly to our earlier formulations of the contrastive focus and answer focus conditions (albeit it in a more formal and explicit fashion, and in the more general context of anaphora resolution).[3]

Contrast: Although Rooth's theory is commonly referred to as a theory of contrastive focus, it is contrastive only in the weak sense of what I called UNRELATED contrastive focus earlier (Section 2.2.3). That is, even in the individual case the choice of antecedent is not constrained by any stronger condition than identity of semantic class (see e.g. example (14) in Rooth, 1992b: 81). In fact, Rooth argues this to be a virtue of his account:

---

[3] Rooth (1992b: 8of) explicitly juxtaposes the "analysis based on contrast" given there with "an account based on anaphoricity," which is argued to fail for the ⟨farmer⟩ example (2). The objection there seems to be, however, that, in our terms, there can be no "mutual givenness antecedence" (i.e. the first ⟨farmer⟩ G-antecedes the second, and the second the first). On the analysis in the tree in Figure 3.4, NP$_2$ is the F-antecedent to C_2/NP$_1$ and NP$_1$ is the F-antecedent to C_1/NP$_2$.

Whether this is really a less "odd position from the standpoint of our understanding of anaphora in general" (1992b: 80) is not a question I will go into here. In any event Rooth (2009: 15ff) explicitly calls the proposal in Rooth (1992b) "anaphoric," so we will, too.

Possibly there is a lot to say about [exactly what it is to construe two phrases as contrasting]. ... my strategy in this paper will be a different ... one which will eventually strip away any reference to contrast. (Rooth, 1992b: 81f)

It is important to keep this in mind, especially when comparing Rooth's approach to others later on. Anything can be F-marked as a "contrastive focus" with anything salient in the context, as long as their semantic types are the same.

3.1.4 Rooth (1992a): bridging by entailment

Rooth (1992a) discusses some cases of BRIDGING BY ENTAILMENT, such as (3) (Rooth, 1992a: ex. (14a)).

(3) (First, John told Mary about the budget cuts, and then) SUE$_F$ heard about them.

Intuitively, the proposition "that John told Mary about the budget cuts," made salient by the first clause, can license the focussing in ⟨Sue$_F$ heard about them⟩ because that John told Mary about the budget cuts entails, or at least implies via inference, that Mary heard about the budget cuts, which is an F-alternative of ⟨SUE$_F$ heard about them⟩.

(Rooth, 1992a: sec. 4) proposes, as an "expository device", a squiggle representation akin to that proposed in Rooth (1992b). Using our informal notation, example (3) would be represented as in Figure 3.6.

As indicated in Figure 3.6, this variant of the Individual Case is not well-formed according to clause (1a) of the squiggle definition. Clause (1a), needs to be reformulated so as to incorporate entailment: the contextually supplied value of C need not be an element of its sister's F-alternatives, but merely entail one (using an assumed axiom, e.g. that if someone is told about something, they hear about it). Note that this still subsumes the original individual case, since if C's value is an element of the focus semantic value, it a fortiori entails one.

(4^{CON}) REPLACEMENT OF INDIVIDUAL CASE (1A) (preliminary)
        the contextually supplied value of C_i entails one of the F-alternatives of δ
        (formally: $\exists \alpha \in [\![\delta]\!]_F [[\![C]\!]_O \Rightarrow \alpha]$)

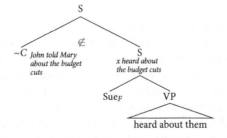

FIGURE 3.6 An example of bridging by entailment from Rooth (1992a: (14b)).

However, unlike the original individual case, the amended definition (4) will only work for propositional constituents, since it relies on entailment. Consider the ⟨farmer⟩ case in example (2) and Figure 3.4, for example, where the F-domains were NPs. "Canadian farmer" is an *element* of $[\![$ AMERican$_F$ farmer $]\!]_F$, but does not *entail* any element of it, simply because it is not a proposition in the first place.

Although Rooth (1992a) only discusses examples with clausal F-domains, one can construct examples in which the NP-focus appears to be bridged in the same way, such as in (5), the beginning of yet another joke.

(5)   You know the difference between BerLIN, and an [AMERican city]$\sim C_1$...?

The bridging here goes from "Berlin" to "German city," which is an element of $[\![$ AMERican$_F$ city $]\!]_F$. This seems entirely parallel to example (3) above, but it requires a generalization of the notion of entailment to something like hyponymy. This can be achieved by applying EXISTENTIAL CLOSURE, ∃Clo, to the contextually salient meaning as well as to the F-alternatives.

(6^{CON}) REPLACEMENT OF INDIVIDUAL CASE (1A)
the ∃Clo of the contextually supplied value of C_i entails the ∃Clo of one of the F-alternatives of δ (formally: $\exists \alpha \in [\![\delta]\!]_F[\exists\text{Clo}([\![C]\!]_O) \Rightarrow \exists\text{Clo}(\alpha)]$)

∃Clo is similar to ∃F-Clo, introduced in Section 2.2.3 (see Section 3.5.2 below for a formal definition), in that it existentially binds ("closes") free variables, except that in the case of ∃Clo these variables are not focus-related, but are the variables necessary to turn a non-propositional meaning into a proposition. For example, the ∃Clo of ⟨Berlin⟩ is something like "Berlin exists" or "Berlin has some properties," whereas that of "German city" (an F-alternative of ⟨AMERican$_F$ city⟩) is that a German city exists. The former entails the latter (assuming as an axiom that Berlin is a German city), meeting the entailment-based Individual Case.

It is worth noting here that ∃Closures alluded to in (6)—say of ⟨Berlin⟩—is not claimed to be *asserted*, or otherwise implied or presupposed, by the sentence containing a given element—such as example (5) (though this would not hurt in this particular case); the ∃Clos are merely used "internally," for checking the F-condition.

3.1.5 Desiderata

Rooth's theory is very successful in modeling what happens where focussing takes place, or more precisely, what has to be the case if $\sim C$ is present in a tree. It does not, however, contribute anything to the question of *when* focussing should take place. At the same time, it contains no theory of givenness deaccenting, so that in the end it can *rule out* many possible F-marking and F-domain assignments, but never *force* any focussing or the concomitant deaccenting.

In a little more detail: First, nothing ever forces the adjunction of $\sim$, that is, the construction of an F-domain; a sentence without any $\sim$ does not invoke the

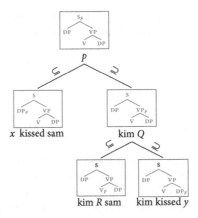

FIGURE 3.7   Upsize permissiveness, demonstrated for the sentence ‹Kim kissed Sam›. Each node shows what the F-alternatives of the entire sentence would be if that node were the F-marked one.

Squiggle Condition (1) above at all, and hence it is not clear what would rule it out, that is, what could possibly *require* focussing and accent shift.

Second, while an F-domain needs to contain *some* F-marking,[4] condition (1) above hardly determines the correct *size* of the focus, owing to the following fact: If an F-domain D, containing an F-marked constituent E meets condition (1) above (in a given context), the same domain with F-marking on E', where E' dominates E, is guaranteed to meet condition (1) as well. In plain words, making a focus *bigger* will never be excluded by the $\sim$/F-condition as given by Rooth (nor in fact by those discussed in the previous chapter).

This general property of Alternative Semantics, which I will call UPSIZE PER-MISSIVENESS, is illustrated informally in Figure 3.7, where dominance in the tree stands for the (improper) superset relation.

So the $\sim$/F-Condition (1) as given by Rooth is upsize permissive: since the well-formedness of ‹$\delta \sim C_i$› solely depends on whether the value of C_i is a *subset*, or element, of $[\![\delta]\!]_{\mathcal{F}}$, any *super*set of $[\![\delta]\!]_{\mathcal{F}}$ will meet condition (1) if $[\![\delta]\!]_{\mathcal{F}}$ does.[5] The

---

[4] Rooth's official algorithm rules out F-domains without F in them categorically by requiring that the focus semantic value of an F-domain must contain at least one other element, apart from the ordinary meaning of that constituent (Rooth, 1992b: 90). But even if this requirement were removed, note that an F-less F-domain D could only meet (the individual case) condition (1) if the context provides an antecedent with the *exact same* meaning as D, i.e. if D is given entirely.

[5] For a focus condition to not be upsize permissive, it would have to put a requirement on *all* F-alternatives, for example $C = [\![\delta]\!]_{\mathcal{F}}$ or $[\![\delta]\!]_{\mathcal{F}} \subseteq C$. But such conditions will not work in general, since that would mean that a contrastive focus has to generate its specific contextual target as its *only* F-alternative. Likewise, the answer ‹I visited JORDAN_F›, with its F-alternatives 'I visited x' would have to have 'x an individual' in the context of the question 'Who did you visit', 'x a place' on the context of 'Where did you visit?', and '$x = $ one of the speaker's siblings' in the context of 'Which of your siblings did you visit?'

Since we cannot contextually restrict a sentence's F-alternatives through context, on pain of circular-ity ("S meets the Focus Condition if those of its F-alternatives that are contextually salient are equal to a contextually salient antecedent"), this route seems in general untenable.

concomitant problem of allowing foci that are intuitively too big is usually called the PROBLEM OF OVERFOCUSSING.[6] It is illustrated in (7).

(7) (What is Kim doing in Paris?—)
    a.   She [WORKS]$_F$ in Paris.
    b. #She [works in PARis]$_F$.
    c. $[\![\,(7a)\,]\!]_{\mathcal{F}}$ = kim Q in Paris
    d. $[\![\,(7b)\,]\!]_{\mathcal{F}}$ = kim Q

$[\![\,(7a)\,]\!]_{\mathcal{F}}$ is clearly a proper subset of $[\![\,(7b)\,]\!]_{\mathcal{F}}$, so if every answer to the question is in the former, it is also in the latter. But as indicated in (7b), VP-focus would be realized with an accent on the final adverb, rather than the verb; Rooth's system thus wrongly predicts the accenting in (7b) to also be acceptable in this context.

It bears mentioning that this problem should be more accurately called the PROBLEM OF OVERACCENTING, since it is not the larger focus, but the lack of prosodic backgrounding that poses the problem here. Still, for conformity with the literature, I will stick to the term "overfocussing" in what follows.

It is worthwhile to note that the problem of overfocussing has been mentioned before, when we informally discussed our system of F- and G-marking and -interpretation in Section 2.3. I remarked there that an adequate account should force F-domains to be as big as possible, and foci to be as small as possible, in other words: to maximize the background. The same is true for Rooth's account, as we will discuss in more detail later.

3.2 F/FOC-Theory: Selkirk (1984, 1995b)

Selkirk (1984 1995b) and Rochemont (1986) develop theories of the accent-to-interpretation relation. We discuss here the theory given in Selkirk (1995b), which can be seen as the cumulation of those developments.

Selkirk's theory, like Rooth's, employs only one grammatical marker, F. However, an F-marked constituent that is not dominated by another F-marker, called a FOCus of the sentence in Selkirk (1995b), has a different status from all other F-markers. It corresponds quite closely to answer focus or contrastive focus in our previous discussion, as well as the F-marked constituent(s) in Rooth (1992b). Selkirk does not go into the details of what the F-relations look like, so for now we will take them to be the same as Rooth's, with the F-domain being the entire sentence.

What I want to concentrate on here is the interpretation of the other (non-FOC) F-marks in Selkirk's (1995b) proposal, which serve a very different purpose, much more closely related to the phenomena we discussed under the rubric of *givenness* in Chapter 2. For these it holds that a node is F-marked if and only if it is not given. This is summarized in clauses (8a) and (8b).[7]

---

   [6] The term "overfocussed" appears to originate in Schwarzschild (1993: 4).

   [7] The corresponding notion in Rochemont (1986) is C-CONSTRUABLE, which, like givenness in Section 2.3 is defined by a number of potential G-relations such as coreference/antecedence etc. (cf. Rochemont, 1986: 62f).

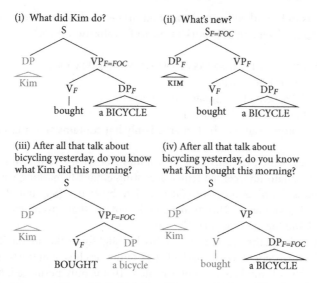

FIGURE 3.8   Representations à la Selkirk (1995b); accents indicated by capitals for the NPA and small caps for pre-nuclear pitch accents. Nodes that need to be given (because they are F-less) are in gray.

(8^CON)   F(OC)-INTERPRETATION ACCORDING TO SELKIRK (1995B)
  a. FOCus
      A constituent that is FOC marked (=_def F-marked but not dominated by any F-markers) is interpreted as focus in some larger domain
  b. NON-GIVEN ⇆ F-MARKERS
      Any other constituent is F-marked if and only if it is not given.

Typical representations as required under this approach are sketched in Figure 3.8.

As can be seen in Figure 3.8(i), a regular VP-focus now contains numerous STACKED F-MARKERS. In fact, if everything within the focus is new (non-given), as in Figure 3.8(i), every node within the focus must itself be F-marked. So in an all-new case like Figure 3.8(ii), the subject needs to be F-marked, too, as it is not given.

The tree in Figure 3.8(iii) involves givenness deaccenting: ‹Kim› and ‹a bicycle› are given, hence not F-marked. The verb, being the only non-given terminal in the sentence, bears an F-marker and the nuclear pitch accent, projecting, as it were, FOCus on the VP. Finally, Figure 3.8(iv) shows a case of narrow object focus. Note that ‹a bicycle› is given in Figure 3.8(iv); yet, since it is the FOCus of the sentence, this does not matter (clause (8b) only applies to non-FOCi).

The use of subordinate (or "stacked") F-markers in this type of approach serves to address some of the shortcomings we noted in Rooth's (1992b) account. In particular, deaccenting of given constituents can be enforced by banning pitch accents on non-F-marked constituents. In Selkirk (1995b) this is done by restricting pitch accents to F-marked heads. Definition (9) below illustrates how this is done, using a simplified version of Selkirk's (1995b) F-realization rules.[8]

(9^{CON})   ACCENTS $\leftrightarrows$ F-MARKERS (simplified Selkirk (1995b) version)
   a. BASIC FOCUS RULE
      All accented terminals are F-marked.
   b. PROJECTED FOCUS RULE
      A non-head may be F-marked only if it contains an F-marker.

By clause (9a), which is equivalent to Selkirk's rule of the same name, all given heads must remain unaccented (since accenting entails F-marking which entails non-givenness)—unless they are FOCi (which, by clause (8a), may be accented regardless of givenness). This transparently entails that given *phrases* will be unaccented, too (again, unless FOCussed).

Clause (9b) is not the exact inverse of this, but slightly weaker in that it allows for a head to be unaccented, yet F-marked. This option is chosen in the tree in Figure 3.8(i): ‹bought› is F-marked, but not accented. This is only permitted, however, if the *projection* of that head (which will not be given, since it contains a non-given head) still manages to contain an accent, that is if, as in Figure 3.8(i), the head has a complement which is not given and hence accented. Otherwise, as in Figure 3.8(iii), the head *has* to be accented, not for its own sake, but so that its projection can meet clause (9b).

Note that accenting an F-marked head with an accented complement is still *allowed* by clause (9a) (just not required). Alongside the tree in Figure 3.8(i), then, the rules predict a pragmatically equivalent option with a pre-nuclear accent on ‹bought› (and the NPA on ‹bicycle›), which, for English at least, seems generally adequate (though see Section 4.4.2 for more discussion).

The net effect of all this is that within a FOCus, all and only non-given constituents will be F-marked and accented; givenness—within a FOCus as well as outside of it—entails lack of accent.

3.2.1 Notable properties

Selkirk's (1995b) system effectively takes a theory of focus like Rooth's (1992b) and adds to it a givenness check at every node, except the FOCus: Given phrases cannot be accented, and non-given phrases *must* be accented. In a way, the F-marker is used as a "newness" marker.

By forcing given phrases to be unaccented (by way of forcing them to be F-less), this system forces deaccenting. More precisely, it assumes that what we call default accenting here is really the result of F-marking (recall that, as noted in

---

[8] Selkirk (1995b), and many leading up to it, proposes rather complex restrictions on the relation between F-marks and accents, which I will come back to in Chapter 4, when discussing the details of F-representation. For the discussion here, the simplified and less restricted version in definition (9), essentially that given in Schwarzschild's (1999) adaption of the Selkirk (1995b) approach, suffices.

Section 2.5.4, all-focus sentences are predicted to have default accenting), whereas the absence of F-markers corresponds to deaccenting.

This does not rule out overfocussing, but it neutralizes its prosodic (ill-)effects. Take example (10), repeated from (7b).

(10)   (What is Kim doing in Paris?—)# She works in PARis.

      she [$_{VP}$ works$_F$ [$_{PP}$in Paris]$_{\neq F}$]$_{FOC}$

Even if VP is 'wrongly' chosen as the FOCus, ⟨in Paris⟩ would still not be entitled to an accent, since it is given and hence F-less, leaving ⟨works⟩ to project the VP focus. The resulting accenting is the same as if there were narrow focus on V. So while it may be counter-intuitive to FOC-mark VP, rather than V, no harm is done, since the accenting comes out right anyway (and recall that semantically there is no problem: every answer to the question is an element of ⟦ she [works in Paris]$_{F(OC)}$ ⟧$_F$; this is what ruled in overfocussing in the first place).

In fact, the only effect FOCus—as opposed to F/non-givenness-marking—will have on accenting in this model is that it will force a pitch accent on a narrow focus, even if given.[9]

3.2.2 Problems

The Selkirk/Rochemont approach is rightly seen as a milestone in the theory of focus, and one that any other theory has to measure up to. Yet, there are some clear shortcomings of the theory, which it is good to be aware of.

First, the theory requires that any constituent that is not given be F-marked. Regardless of the finer points of the givenness definition one assumes, it seems clear that a constituent that contains an F-marked constituent will, in virtually all cases, not itself be given. Take again example (11) below, the structure of which was given in the tree in Figure 3.8(iv).

(11)   (After all that talk about bicycling yesterday, guess what Kim bought this
      morning?—) [$_S$Kim [$_{VP}$bought [a BIcycle]$_{FOC}$]

According to clause (8b) above, S and VP must be given, since they are not F-marked. But evidently ⟨(Kim) bought a bicycle⟩ is *not* given. If we were to faithfully F-mark *all* non-given constituents, we would have to F-mark VP and S in example (11) too; in fact, we would have to F-mark every node dominating the focus in virtually all cases. But if we do so, S, not DP in example (11) is the FOCus (since a FOCus is defined as an F-marker *not* dominated by other F-markers); again, this will hold quite generally. In a case like (11), this will not only be unintuitive, it will also make it impossible to accent ⟨a bicycle⟩, which, after all, is given. In fact, since only FOCi are exempted from the 'NON-GIVEN ⇆ F-MARKER' requirement in

[9] See Selkirk (1984: 214–25) for an insightful and thorough explication of the points summarized in this subsection.

clause (8b), none of the major constituents in example (11) qualifies for accenting if the highest F(OC) is on the S-node; the sentence should effectively be ineffable.

The correct diagnosis for this problem is, I think, this: Exceptions to Non-GIVEN ⇆ F go both ways: FOCi may be F-marked despite being given (as said in clause (8b)), and nodes that *dominate* the FOCus may be non-given despite being F-less. This can be accommodated by changing clause (8b) to say that any node that is *or dominates* FOC may or may not be given, whereas Non-GIVEN ⇆ F holds for all other nodes. Still, one would hope to find some deeper reason for this state of affairs (and we will, I think, in Section 3.3).

The second problem I want to point out is arguably related, but pertains even under the assumption that, somehow, nodes above the FOCus can generally be F-less. As discussed in Section 2.4, a given constituent may still bear the (nuclear) accent provided it is itself the focus. At first glance, exempting FOCi from Non-GIVEN ⇆ F achieves this very same effect, as in example (11) and Figure 3.8 (iv).

However, this will fail in cases in which an all-given focus is syntactically complex, as in (12).

(12)   (Has anyone seen the young king's murderer?—Well, I suppose) [the young KING]$_F$ has seen his murderer

While ‹the young king› itself can legitimately be F-marked *and* given (it is the FOCus), none of its parts can: all of ‹the›, ‹young›, and ‹king› are given, yet none of them is a FOCus (by definition—a FOCus cannot be dominated by another FOCus—as well as prosodically—at least ‹the› clearly does not contain a pitch accent). But by definition (9) above, a phrase cannot be F-marked unless it contains an accented and F-marked head, too. Therefore the answer in (12), too, should in fact be ineffable: The DP ‹the young king› must be F-marked, but then so must be a head within it, yet neither of those is allowed to be, because they are given and not FOCus.

The problem here, it seems, lies with the assumption that within a larger focus there *have to be* further F-markers, at least one on some terminal. On the other hand, allowing accents *without* corresponding F-markers in this setting would be fatal, as it would effectively allow all sorts of overaccenting.

A final problem, though not for F-*interpretation* but for F-*realization* is that the Basic Focus Rule (9a) combined with Non-GIVEN ⇆ F predicts that given XPs in general must be accent-less. This, however, is certainly too strong a claim. Given XPs cannot bear the NPA (unless in narrow focus), but they are happily accented in pre-nuclear position. The system we sketched in Chapter 2 accommodates this observation, since neither focus nor givenness ever prohibit the realization of pre-focal accents.

3.3 GIVENness Theory: Schwarzschild (1999)

Schwarzschild (1999) arguably presents the most comprehensive approach to focus and givenness in English to date. It takes as its starting point Selkirk's theory (see

Section 3.2), on which any non-given constituent has to be F-marked, but aims to eliminate the disjunctive interpretation of F-marking, which was: non-maximal F-marker means non-given, maximal F-mark (FOCus) means (contrastive) focus.

This involves three essential steps: First, a new semantic notion, called GIVEN, is introduced, which unifies givenness and focussing (effectively subsuming the former under the latter). Second, while maintaining that all non-given constituents need to be F-marked, the inverse condition—that *only* non-given constituents may be F-marked—is dropped. Third, in order to prevent unwanted proliferation of F-marks (which is in principle possible given the second step), a syntactic principle AVOIDF is introduced, which requires the number of F-markers in a structure to be as small as possible, while still F-marking all non-GIVEN constituents.

3.3.1 The GIVEN relation

Schwarzschild's (1999) notion of GIVEN makes essential use of EXISTENTIAL-F-CLOSURE, $\exists$F-Clo, which we informally introduced in Section 2.2.3 in connection with our characterization of ELABORATION FOCUS. Continuing to speak informally, $\exists$F-Clo replaces all focussed elements in a constituent by variables, and existentially binds these, so as to obtain a proposition. This is exemplified in (13).

(13) a. KIM$_F$ won.

      $[\![\ ]\!]_{\mathcal{F}}$: x won (where x is a variable over individuals)

      $\exists$F-Clo : $\exists x[x$ won$]$ = the proposition that somebody won

    b. Kim WON$_F$.

      $[\![\ ]\!]_{\mathcal{F}}$: Kim Q (where Q is a variable over properties)

      $\exists$F-Clo : $\exists Q[$Kim $Q]$ = the proposition that Kim did something or

                                     has some property

Where the constituent to be $\exists$F-Closed is not a complete clause, $\exists$F-Clo—like plain $\exists$Clo in Section 3.1.4—provides additional variables to make it a complete clause and existentially binds these, too.

(14) a. won [the RACE]$_F$

      $[\![\ ]\!]_{\mathcal{F}}$: won x (replace focus by individual variable)

      $\exists$Clo: $\exists y[y$ won $x]$ (supply additional individual variable to get a

                                   complete clause and $\exists$-bind them)

      $\exists$F-Clo : $\exists x\exists y[y$ won $x] \approx$ the proposition that someone (or something)

                               won something (or someone)

    b. red APPLE$_F$

      $[\![\ ]\!]_{\mathcal{F}}$: $\lambda x.P(x)$ & $red(x)$ ($\equiv$ red P)

      $\exists$F-Clo : $\exists P\exists x[P(x)$ & $red(x)] \approx$ the proposition that something red

                               exists

Thus the $\exists$F-Clo of any constituent will be a proposition, required for the definition of GIVEN in (15).

TABLE 3.1 The relation between F-antecedents and foci, as defined by '∃Clo(antecedent) → ∃F-Clo(S)' in Schwarzschild (1999).

ANTECEDENT (UNDERLINED)	∃Clo(ANT.)		∃F-Clo($‹KIM_F$ won›)
Someone won.	$\exists x[\text{person } x \ \& \ x \text{ won}]$	$\rightarrow$	$\exists x[x \text{ won}]$
Jack won.	jack won	$\rightarrow$	$\exists x[x \text{ won}]$
Having won is wonderful.	$\exists x[x \text{ won}]$	$\leftrightarrow$	$\exists x[x \text{ won}]$
Who won?	$\exists x[\text{person } x \ \& \ x \text{ won}]$	$\rightarrow$	$\exists x[x \text{ won}]$
Which player won?	$\exists x[\text{player } x \ \& \ x \text{ won}]$	$\rightarrow$	$\exists x[x \text{ won}]$

(15^{DEF})   Definition: GIVEN
    A constituent E is GIVEN in a context Cx iff Cx provides a salient meaning which is in $[\![E]\!]_{\mathcal{F}}$ (if E denotes an individual), or which (after existential closure, if necessary) entails the ∃F-Clo of E.

Setting aside the case of individual-denoting expressions, being GIVEN as per (15) amounts to a slightly weakened version of being an expression containing an elaboration focus, as discussed in Section 2.2.3. But where an elaboration focus requires that the F-domain's ∃F-Clo itself be salient, (15) is content already if it is merely *entailed* by something salient. Due to this weakening, GIVENness can be met for, say, (16) not only if the proposition that someone won is salient (i.e. elaboration focus), but also if any particular proposition, like that Sam won, is salient (i.e. (unrelated) contrastive focus).

(16) KIM_F won.

In fact, sentence (16) will be GIVEN even if merely the property of winning (or having won) is salient; this is so because the ∃Clo of the property of winning is that someone wins, which (tense aside) entails—in fact is the same as—the ∃F-Clo of (16). This is illustrated in the third case from the top in Table 3.1.
    I should emphasize that in all the contexts in Table 3.1, not just the verb or VP ‹won› is GIVEN, but the entire sentence is. GIVENness is thus a very different notion from (lower case) givenness discussed up to now. In fact, to be GIVEN is much closer in empirical scope to being a legitimate F-domain in Rooth's terms, cf. fact (17).[10]

---

[10] In order to emphasize the difference between GIVENness and givenness, I have referred to the former as CONTEXT-CONNECTEDNESS in Büring (2012b). Here I will stick with the original term, distinguished from the more common sense term "givenness" only by capitalization. The reader may be well advised, though, to read "GIVENness" as "GIVENness in the technical sense as defined in Schwarzschild (1999)" and "givenness" as "givenness *simpliciter* in the traditional and intuitive sense" throughout.

(17^{FACT})   If ⟨[$_E$...F...]⟩ is a legitimate F-domain (in the sense of Rooth, 1992a, 1992b) in a context Cx, E will be GIVEN (in the sense of Schwarzschild, 1999) in Cx.

Table 3.1 should help us to see why fact (17) holds regarding Rooth's individual case. Assume E denotes a proposition. Then ∃F-Clo(E) is the same proposition as the disjunction of all F-alternatives in ⟦ E ⟧$_{\mathcal{F}}$. Therefore, if the value of C is (or entails) *one* of the F-alternatives in ⟦ E ⟧$_{\mathcal{F}}$, it necessarily entails ∃F-Clo(E).[11]

For questions—taken care of by the set case in Rooth (1992b)—suffice it to say at this point that the ∃Clo of a question meaning will turn out to be the proposition that the question has a true answer, or put informally: the result of replacing the ⟨wh⟩-word with an indefinite pronoun (e.g. 'someone won' for the question ⟨Which person won?⟩ etc.), so that answer focus turns out to be a special case of elaboration focus.

Despite the major differences between GIVENness and givenness, the choice of terminology (though potentially confusing) is not arbitrary; in addition to fact (17), it also holds that

(18^{FACT})   If a constituent E is given in a context Cx, it is also GIVEN in Cx.

This fact is rather easy to appreciate: If a hyponym or synonym A of E is salient (as required to make it given), the ∃Clo of A will necessarily entail the ∃F-Clo of E: if violins are salient, both ⟨violin⟩ and ⟨string instrument⟩ are given, and likewise the proposition that there is a violin entails the propositions that there is a violin and that there is a string instrument. In fact, we can strengthen the above fact to the following:

(19^{FACT})   Fact (18), strengthened:
             If a constituent E is given in a context Cx, it is also GIVEN in Cx, *without the necessity to F-mark anything within E.*

So descriptively speaking, a constituent E is GIVEN, according to definition (15) above if any of the following are met.

- C is given (including by hyponymy);
- C is a legitimate F-domain according to the individual case in Rooth (1992b) (contrastive focus);
- C would qualify as an elaboration focus in the sense of definition (11) in Chapter 2 (includes answer focus).

In short, GIVENness unifies givenness and "being a legitimate sister to ∼" (i.e. being a F-domain).

---

[11] If E denotes something non-propositional, the same reasoning applies *mutatis mutandis*: ∃F-Clo(E) equals the disjunction of the ∃Clo of all F-alternatives in ⟦ E ⟧$_{\mathcal{F}}$ (formally: ∃F-Clo(E) = ⋃{∃Clo(α) | α ∈ ⟦ E ⟧$_{\mathcal{F}}$}). Therefore, if the ∃Clo of the value of C entails the ∃Clo of one F-alternative in ⟦ E ⟧$_{\mathcal{F}}$, it will entail the disjunction of the ∃Clos of all of them. QED.

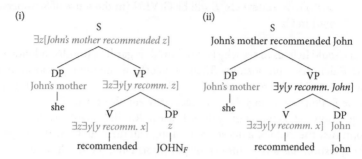

FIGURE 3.9   F-marking on a given element—‹John›—saves the GIVENness day for a higher node—VP. The ∃F-Clo is given on each constituent, grayed out where it is entailed by the F-antecedent.

Since it is so comprehensive a notion, Schwarzschild (1999) can now define contextual appropriateness of F-marking simply as in condition (20).[12]

(20^{CON})   GIVENness Requirement
          Every constituent must be GIVEN.

The use of the term GIVENness might lead one to expect that, like previous givenness conditions, condition (20) would run into problems with all-given foci (cf. Section 2.4.2), such as in example (11) above, or (21).[13]

(21)   (Who did John's mother recommend?—) She recommended [JOHN]$_\text{F}$.

There, is, however, no problem.

---

[12] See Schwarzschild (1999: 155), definition (32), given in (i). (i) restricts the applicability of GIVENness to non-F-marked constituents (see also his footnote 3):

(i^{CON})   GIVENness Requirement
          If a constituent is not F-marked, it must be GIVEN.

As best as I can tell, this makes no difference for the discussion here. Note in particular that the ∃F-Clo of an F-marked constituent E is the proposition corresponding to ∃e[∃P[P(e)]], where e is a variable of the same semantic type as E, and P a variable over functions mapping elements of that category to propositions. In other words, the ∃F-Clo of an F-marked constituent is the set of all worlds, and hence entailed by the ∃Clo of *anything* salient. Similarly, the focus semantic value of a focussed individual denoting expression is the set of all individuals, so as long as *any* individual at all is salient (e.g. the speaker), such an expression counts as GIVEN by definition (15).

Presumably the reason Schwarzschild (1999) uses (i) is that his final *informal* definition of GIVEN (p.151)—unlike our definition (15)—has no special proviso for F-marked individual denoting expressions, so that those can only be GIVEN by coreference, focussed or not. The final *formal* version, his (28), however does include such a proviso and is thus much closer to the version discussed in the main text here, according to which all F-marked expressions are basically trivially GIVEN. See also Section 3.5.3 below.

[13] Based on (3) in Schwarzschild (1999: 142).

Figure 3.9(i) shows that with F-marking on the given DP ‹John›, every node's ∃F-Clo is entailed by the F-antecedent, as required by the GIVENness Requirement (20). Moreover, Figure 3.9(ii) shows that without F-markers, neither VP nor S would qualify as GIVEN: the combination of two given elements does not necessarily yield another given element. And if that is the case, only an F-marker on one of its given daughters will save VP from violating condition (20).

3.3.2 AVOIDF

The above only works because there is nothing in the system so far that *prohibits* F-marking, that is, no equivalent of Selkirk's (1995b) requirement that given elements remain F-less. This brings us to the third and final piece in the GIVENness system, the principle AVOIDF.[14]

(22[CON])   AVOIDF
            F-mark as little as possible, without violating the GIVENness Requirement (20).

AVOIDF will ensure that GIVENness is met using the *minimum* number of F-markers. Like the other proposals discussed so far, the GIVENness Requirement by itself is upward permissive, meaning that adding F-markers to an already legitimate (by GIVENness) structure necessarily preserves legitimacy. At an extreme, F-marking *every* constituent in a sentence would guarantee that sentence's compliance with the GIVENness condition in any context whatsoever. But it would in virtually all cases violate AVOIDF.

As the reader has probably sensed already, AVOIDF is a rather direct implementation of Maximize Information Structure Marking (condition (29) at the end of Section 2.3), or similar strategies to avoid overfocussing. Very transparently, adding a superfluous F-marker, as in (23b) violates AVOIDF.

(23)   (Who informed Smith?)
        a.   [KING]$_F$ informed Smith.
        b.   #[KING]$_F$ informed [SMITH]$_F$.

Likewise, accenting a given (and hence GIVEN) element *within* a focus involves unneeded F-markers, see (24):

(24)   (What did you do when you realized what Kim was up to?—)
        a.   I [tried$_F$ to STOP$_F$ Kim]$_F$.
        b.   #I [tried$_F$ to STOP$_F$ KIM$_F$]$_F$

And finally, spuriously "expanding" a focus, even where no new accents are added, will be blocked, too.

---

[14] See Schwarzschild's (1999: 156, ex. (34)).

(25) (What did you do to Cooper?—)
    a. I [igNORED]$_F$ Cooper.
    b. #I [[igNORED]$_F$ Cooper]$_F$

Crucially, however, AvoidF is not violated by F-marking a given focus, as in example (21) above (‹(*Who did John's mother vote for?—) She voted for [JOHN]$_F$*›). As discussed there, ‹*she voted for John*›, without any F-marking, would violate the GIVENness Requirement (20); F-marking ‹*John*› is in fact the minimal way of F-marking to make the sentence comply with condition (20).

3.3.3 Notable properties

Despite what the name may suggest, GIVENness Theory is in effect a focus theory. But it manages to unify focussing à la Rooth and regular givenness deaccenting, essentially by recognizing that an F-marked constituent as well as an "F-free" constituent are limiting cases of F-domains, with the latter corresponding to traditional givenness, and the former to a trivial GIVENness requirement (the ∃F-Clo of an F-marked constituent is the necessary proposition, which is entailed by anything at all).

Where a constituent contains F-markers, Rooth's and Schwarzschild's treatments of focussing are extremely similar conceptually and empirically, though not completely equivalent, since the GIVENness system is slightly more permissive (i.e. the inverse of fact (17) above is not true).

Another notable feature of GIVENness Theory is the absence of any marking of F-domains, that is, an equivalent of the squiggle. This, however, is not a very substantial difference: On reflection, by having the GIVENness requirement (20) apply to *every* constituent, every constituent α is subjected to requirements (nearly) equivalent to an F-domain: find a contextually salient meaning whose ∃Clo entails α's ∃F-Clo. A minor difference is that GIVENness Theory invokes the F-less F-domain as well as the trivial F-domain, shown in Figure 3.10.[15]

In the end, all we seem to lose here is the ability to explicitly represent the relation between an F-domain and its F-antecedent in the grammatical representation (i.e. coindexing the F-domain variable with its antecedent).

The main point of departure for GIVENness Theory, compared to the Squiggle Theory is that it explicitly forces focussing, just like Selkirk's proposal: A non-given constituent, terminal or nor, must contain (or bear) a F-marker. Not having any F-marking is just not an option in any context.[16]

Like Selkirk (1995b) it does so by way of tying accents to F-marking, forcing F-markers as newness markers. Unlike Selkirk (1995b) it does not need to exempt

---

[15] An F-less F-domain could, in principle, be made compatible with Rooth's proposal. Its sole FA would be its literal meaning, which therefore would have to be (entailed by something) salient in the context, i.e. given. Therefore, one might even say that Schwarzschild's theory simply makes every node a Roothean F-domain, with a slightly weakened notion of what may be an antecedent for such a domain, due to its appeal to entailment, rather than synonymy.

[16] Except in repetitions or contextually uninformative statements, which I will not be concerned with here.

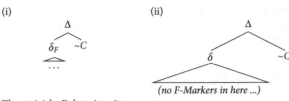

(i)

(ii)

The trivial F-domain: its ∃F-Clo is the trivial proposition, so it has no requirements at all.

The F-less F-domain; its GIVEN-ness requirement is tantamount to traditional givenness.

FIGURE 3.10   Two unusual kinds of F-domain implicit in GIVENness Theory.

FOCi from the usual interpretation rules by stipulation, since there is nothing that says that only non-given things may be F-marked (only the other way around). The desired effects of such a requirement in Selkirk's approach is achieved by AVOIDF in GIVENness Theory.

GIVENness Theory also has no problem with nodes dominating a focus (recall Section 3.2.2). Even though such nodes will not be given, they are GIVEN. Put differently, as in Rooth (1992b), F-alternatives are "propagated" upwards, and GIVENness, unlike givenness, is based on F-alternatives. In many respects, a focus contained in a constituent functions as a "wild card" in the search for a F-antecedent.

3.3.4 Open ends

GIVENness Theory as presented so far shares with the proposal in Selkirk (1995b) the two problems mentioned last in Section 3.2.2: It prohibits all-given complex foci (since a given node within a given constituent does not need to be F-marked and hence, by AVOIDF, must not be; cf. Section 3.2.2); and it prohibits non-focal, pre-nuclear pitch accents. While the latter is not taken up in Schwarzschild (1999), that paper does discuss example (26) (ex. (67), Schwarzschild, 1999: 172), which is parallel to our example (12) above (‹Has anyone seen the young king's murderer?— Well, I suppose) [the young king]$_F$ has seen his murderer›).

(26)   (The rising of the TIDES depends upon the MOON being full, and) [the BOAT$_F$ being empty$_F$]$_F$ depends upon [the rising of the TIDES]$_F$

The problem with this kind of example, recall, is that no terminal may be accented unless it is F-marked, a feature Schwarzschild's (1999) proposal inherits from Selkirk's (1995b) rules relating F-markers to pitch accents (see definition (9) above). But ‹the›, ‹rising›, ‹of›, and ‹tides› are each given and thus should not be F-marked, on pain of violating AVOIDF (crucially, the GIVENness Requirement is already met by F-marking the entire object DP).

Schwarzschild proposes that the noun ‹tides› in example (27) will in fact bear an F-marker, even though that marker is not forced by the GIVENness Requirement (20). This is of course a violation of AVOIDF. In order to allow for that, one has to assume that the rules that require accents within foci, and F-markers on accented heads—definition (9) above—may also license violations of AvoidF (just like (20)). So AvoidF should read as in (27).

(27^{CON}) AvoidF (Exegesis)
          F-mark as little as possible without violating the GIVENness Require-
          ment (20) and the Accents $\leftrightarrows$ F-markers rules in (9) above.[17]

For some further discussion of potentially problematic aspects of GIVENness Theory and the definitions underlying it, see Chapter 5.

On a last note, just like Selkirk (1995b) explicitly unifies the *representation* and *realization* of focus and (non-)givenness, GIVENness Theory does the same for their *interpretation*. This is of course its central aim, but it also presupposes a deep, intrinsic relation, likely even identity, of the two phenomena, focussing and givenness.

But, as we will see in Chapter 8, there may be reasons to prefer a theory that actually keeps those two separate at the core: while in virtually any language discussed in the literature, focussing has some effect on grammar, and very often on prosody in particular, not all languages show givenness effects such as anaphoric deaccenting. It is not obvious how to deal with such languages in GIVENness Theory, where the effects of focussing follow from the very same principles as those of givenness.

3.4 Chapter summary

Following the line of exposition in Chapter 2, esp. Section 2.3, it may be useful to tease apart each of the three approaches' F-condition from the F-relation which that condition refers to. Figure 3.11 attempts to visualize this.

3.4.1 Comparing F-conditions

The F/FOC-Theory imposes a simple condition on all given (that is: F-less) constituents: that they have a givenness antecedent (in addition it also involves a FOC condition, which we took to be the same as in the Squiggle Theory). The squiggle theory imposes a condition on all F-domains: they have to be answer foci or (unrelated) contrastive foci (this ignores the bridging by entailment cases for the moment, but see Section 3.4.2). GIVENness Theory, finally, imposes a condition on *every* constituent α: That it be GIVEN (i.e. $\exists\text{Clo(antecedent)}\Rightarrow\exists\text{F-Clo}(\alpha)$).

From this point of view it is evident how GIVENness Theory, on the level of F-conditions, subsumes the other two. The next step in our comparison, then, are the F-relations.

---

[17] Schwarzschild (1999) integrates AvoidF with all other constraints in an Optimality Theoretic account, so violability is actually to be expected.

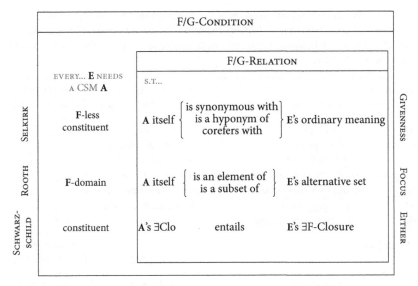

FIGURE 3.11   Comparison of the three conditions and the relation(s) they involve. Each line represents one of the three approaches, with corresponding parts aligned in columns.

3.4.2 Comparing F-/G-relations

I already pointed out in Section 3.3 that the GIVEN relation is, technically, an F-relation (there are no G-markers in GIVENness Theory), and that it is strictly weaker than the F-relations required of F-domains by the presupposition of the squiggle.

The exact relation between the two can perhaps be understood best by looking at Table 3.2.

The $\in$-/$\subseteq$-based presupposition of the squiggle in Rooth (1992b) captures the basic contrastive focus and answer focus cases, but neither elaboration focus nor bridging by entailment. Once entailment is built into the F-relation (Rooth, 1992a), we get bridging for propositions, or, assuming ∃Clo in the case of non-propositional constituents, for all types of constituents. This means that, except for elaboration focus, Rooth's (1992a) squiggle presupposition (with ∃Clo for non-propositions) and Schwarzschild's (1999) GIVENness Requirement are equivalent.

The final step from Rooth's Squiggle Condition to GIVENness is to use ∃F-Clo(E) rather than $[\![E]\!]_{\mathcal{F}}$ for formulating the F-condition. As said before, anything that entails *one* F-alternative of E entails ∃F-Clo(E), but in addition something denoting ∃F-Clo(E) *itself* may also function as a GIVENness/focus antecedent (since it, naturally, entails ∃F-Clo(E)). This gives us elaboration focus (where the F-antecedent denotes ∃F-Clo(E)). But it also gives us answer focus: the ∃Clo of a question Q is the proposition that Q has a true answer, which will entail the ∃F-Clo of a well-focussed answer.[18]

---

[18] It holds that if $[\![\text{question}]\!]_{\mathcal{O}} \subseteq [\![\text{answer}]\!]_{\mathcal{F}}$ (Rooth's set case, clause (1b) above), ∃Clo($[\![\text{questions}]\!]_{\mathcal{O}}$) ⇒ ∃F-Clo(*answer*).

TABLE 3.2   Successively weaker versions of the F-relation lead to coverage of successively more cases: (i) contrastive focus, (ii)/(iii) answer focus (unrestricted and restricted), (iv) contrastive focus with bridging, (v) answer focus with bridging, (vi) elaboration focus, (vii) anaphoric deaccenting.

Rooth (1992b) ANTECEDENT (UNDERLINED)	C(ONTEXTUALLY) S(ALIENT) M(EANING)	RELATION TO $[\![\text{KIM}_F \text{ SAW IT}]\!]_F$	
(i) Jack saw it.	jack saw it	$\in$	
(ii) Who saw it?	person x & saw it x	$\subseteq$	*x saw it*
(iii) Which player saw it?	player x & saw it x	$\subseteq$	
(iv) Jones showed it to Sam, and then ...	jones showed it to sam	$\not\subset, \not\subseteq$	
(v) Who did they show it to?	person x & they showed it to x	$\not\subset, \not\subseteq$	
(vi) Someone saw it.	$\exists x[\text{person } x \,\&\, \text{saw it } x]$	$\not\subset, \not\subseteq$	
(vii) Having seen it is disturbing.	saw it	$\not\subset, \not\subseteq$	

Rooth (1992a)	$\exists\text{Clo(CSM)}$	RELATION TO $[\![\text{KIM}_F \text{ SAW IT}]\!]_F$	
(i) Jack saw it.	jack saw it	$\Rightarrow \in$ see caption	
(ii) Who saw it?	person x & saw it x	$\Rightarrow \subseteq$ see caption	*x saw it*
(iii) Which player saw it?	player x & saw it x	$\Rightarrow \subseteq$	
(iv) Jones showed it to Sam, and then ...	jones showed it to sam	$\Rightarrow \in$	
(v) Who did they show it to?	person x & they showed it to x	$\Rightarrow \subseteq$	
(vi) Someone saw it.	$\exists x[\text{person } x \,\&\, \text{saw it } x]$	$\not\Rightarrow \in$	
(vii) Having seen it is disturbing.	$\exists x[x \text{ saw it}]$	$\not\Rightarrow \in$	

Schwarzschild (1999)	$\exists\text{Clo(CSM)}$	RELATION TO $\exists$F-CLO$(\text{KIM}_F \text{ SAW IT})$	
(i) Jack saw it.	jack saw it	$\Rightarrow$	
(ii) Who saw it?	$\exists x[\text{person } x \,\&\, \text{saw it } x]$	$\Rightarrow$	$\exists x[x \text{ saw it}]$
(iii) Which player saw it?	$\exists x[\text{player } x \,\&\, \text{saw it } x]$	$\Rightarrow$	
(iv) Jones showed it to Sam, and then ...	jones showed it to sam	$\Rightarrow$	
(v) Who did they show it to?	$\exists x[\text{person } x \,\&\, \text{they showed it to } x]$	$\Rightarrow$	
(vi) Someone saw it	$\exists x[\text{person } x \,\&\, \text{saw it } x]$	$\Rightarrow$	
(vii) Having seen it is disturbing.	$\exists x[x \text{ saw it}]$	$\Rightarrow$	

The symbols $\Rightarrow\in$ and $\Rightarrow\subseteq$ stand for "entails one of" and "each entail one of," respectively. I assume for the question case à la Rooth (1992a) that $\exists$Clo vacuously applies to each answer in $[\![$ Who... $]\!]_O$, not to the question denotation as a whole (which would give us the existential statement again, as in (ii)/(iii)/(v) in the bottom center column (under Schwarzschild, 1999)); whence the lack of $\exists$ in (ii)/(iii)/(v) in the center column in the middle.

As hinted at in case (v) in Table 3.2, GIVEN also covers what we may call answer focus with bridging, as in (28).

(28)   (Whom did they tell about the budget cuts?—) SUE$_F$ knows about them.

To that we may add elaboration focus with bridging, which would be a case like (29).

(29) (John told someone about the budget cuts.—Yeah,) SUE$_F$ heard about them.

Given that these cases appear as natural as those discussed in Rooth (1992a), it seems fair to conclude that GIVEN is in fact the empirically most successful F-relation. Put differently, even if we choose to have an F-condition, for example associated with the squiggle, we should use GIVEN as the pertinent F-relation.

3.4.3 Comparison of the theories

The main remaining difference between Squiggle Theory and GIVENness Theory is the choice and number of F-domains. Schwarzschild's (1999) GIVENness Requirement condition (20) above, requires every constituent to be GIVEN, while Rooth (1992b) imposes the parallel requirements only on nodes that are F-domains.[19] We can, accordingly, discuss the question which algorithm for domain formation is more adequate independently of the question what the correct F-relation should be.

The main argument in favor of GIVENness Theory is that it enforces F-marking on (or within) all non-given constituents—its legacy from F/FOC Theory. This becomes possible because GIVENness Theory unifies givenness and focussing; the key to that is the realization that G-relations and F-relations are virtually identical, once one utilizes ∃Clo; and that givenness's reference to the ordinary meaning of a constituent E (right column in Figure 3.11) is tantamount to reference to E's F-alternatives in case there is no focus in/on E (in which case the F-alternatives are just the singleton of the ordinary meaning).

The final innovation with GIVENness Theory is that it explicitly adds a cure for overfocussing, in the form of the constraint AVOIDF. This in turn allows GIVENness Theory to do away with the restriction that only non-given elements can be F-marked (which was part of F/FOC Theory's recipe against overfocussing), and in turn eliminate the semantic distinction between F and FOC.

These two aspects of GIVENness Theory directly rely on the use of stacked F-markers, and thus indirectly on a version of ACCENTS ⇆ F-MARKERS ((9) above). As I pointed out in Sections 3.2.2 and 3.3.4, these assumptions face some empirical challenges in the realm of F-realization, first and foremost that they exclude any pre-focal accenting. We will therefore revisit the question of which constituents (all, F-less, F-domains only) should be targeted by the F-condition in Chapters 4 and 5.

3.5 Appendix: definitions and technical details

It should be possible to read the rest of this book with just the informal understanding of F-alternatives, $[\![\ ]\!]_F$, focus semantic values, ∃Clo and ∃F-Clo alluded to up

---

[19] Another difference is of course that only the Squiggle Theory includes an explicit representation of F-domains, but that is arguably not a substantial difference if we assume, as we do here, that all and only contextually salient meanings are possible values for Roothean F-variables.

to now, and readers who are in hurry are invited to jump to the next chapter now. For all others, this appendix provides the 'formal underbelly' to these notions.

3.5.1 Focus Semantic Values

In this section I discuss the inner workings of $[\![\ ]\!]_{\mathcal{F}}$, that is, how to derive focus semantic values compositionally. The earliest system to compositionally derive something like F-alternatives can be found in von Stechow (1981), which uses STRUCTURED MEANINGS to represent the meaning of sentences with focussing in them. Rooth (1985) provides the first system to directly derive F-alternatives of the sort we use here; this system has the following general shape:

1. Each expression is assigned two meanings, its ordinary value and its focus alternatives.
2. The focus alternatives are a set of meanings, where each of these meanings belongs to the same domain as the ordinary meaning; sloppily speaking, the alternatives are a set of ordinary meaning.
3. The focus alternatives to an expression that does not contain F-marking is the singleton set containing its ordinary meaning.
4. The focus alternatives to an expression that is F-marked is the entire domain of meanings for expression of that semantic type, i.e. the set of all meanings of the same type as the ordinary meaning of that expression.
5. The focus alternatives to an expression E that contains F-marks but is not itself F-marked is the set of meanings that correspond to expressions that are like E with the F-marked subexpressions in E replaced by type-identical other expressions.

Clauses 3, 4, and 5 above are differentiated for perspicuity, even though the former two are just special cases of clause 5.

Since Rooth (1985) the standard way of defining Alternative Semantics has been as in (30):[20]

(30^{DEF}) a. If A is an F-marked terminal or non-terminal node of semantic type τ, then $[\![\ A\ ]\!]_{\mathcal{F}}$ is the set of possible denotations in the domain of τ.

    b. otherwise (if A is not F-marked)
     (i) If A is a terminal node, $[\![\ A\ ]\!]_{\mathcal{F}} = \{[\![\ A\ ]\!]_{\mathcal{O}}\}$
     (ii) If A is a non-branching node that dominates B, $[\![\ A\ ]\!]_{\mathcal{F}} = [\![\ B\ ]\!]_{\mathcal{F}}$
     (iii) for any branching node $[_{\mathrm{A}}\ B\ C]$, if $\oplus$ is the combination operation such that by the ordinary semantic rules $[\![\ A\ ]\!]_{\mathcal{O}} = [\![\ B\ ]\!]_{\mathcal{O}} \oplus [\![\ C\ ]\!]_{\mathcal{O}}$, $[\![\ A\ ]\!]_{\mathcal{F}} = \{b \oplus c \mid b \in [\![\ B\ ]\!]_{\mathcal{F}} \wedge c \in [\![\ C\ ]\!]_{\mathcal{F}}\}$

It is straightforward to generalize this system to n-ary branching nodes (e.g. Rooth, 1996a: (29c)).

---

[20] See e.g. Rooth (1996a: sec. 4.1).

3.5.2 Existential closure

∃Clo takes a meaning of any type 'ending in t', that is any function whose ultimate range is propositions, and delivers a proposition (note that I take t to be the type of propositions, not truth values; so the domain of t, D_t is the set of all proposisitions, specifically $POW(W)$, the power set of the set W of possible worlds). To formalize this, we follow Schwarzschild (1999) and first define formally what a type 'ending in t', also called a CONJOINABLE TYPE is, and then define ∃Clo for meanings corresponding to those types (generally, for any type τ, D_τ denotes the set of possible denotations for expressions of that type, or the DENOTATION DOMAIN of τ).[21]

(31[DEF])   CONJOINABLE TYPE ('type that ends in t')
        a. t, the type of propositions, is a conjoinable type
        b. if σ is a conjoinable type, then so is $\langle\tau,\sigma\rangle$ for any type τ

(32[DEF])   EXISTENTIAL CLOSURE
        for any conjoinable type τ and meaning $\mu \in D_\tau$
        a. if μ is a proposition, ∃Clo$(\mu)= \mu$
        b. otherwise, where $\mu \in D_{\langle\alpha,\beta\rangle}$, ∃Clo$(\mu) = \lambda w \in W.\exists x \in D_\alpha[$∃Clo $(\mu(x))(w)]$

This definition assumes that, for example, a transitive verb denotes a function from individuals to function from individuals to propositions, for example (33a), and delivers a proposition as the result of ∃Clo, for example (33b).

(33)   a. formula corresponding to the meaning of ‹kiss›:
        $\lambda x \in D_e.\lambda y \in D_e.\lambda w \in W.y$ kisses x in w
      b. formula corresponding to the meaning of ∃Clo(‹kiss›):
        $\lambda w \in W.\exists y \in D_e[\exists x \in D_e[y$ kisses x in $w]]$

3.5.3 Existential focus closure

We characterized the ∃F-Clo informally as "replace all F-marked elements by variables, saturate all open argument positions by variables, and then existentially bind them all" (cf. Section 2.2.3). A formal definition is given in (34).

(34[DEF])   ∃F-Clo (formal definition)
        for any conjoinable type τ and focus semantic value $\phi \in \mathcal{P}(D_\tau)$,
        ∃F-Clo$(\phi) = \bigcup\{$∃Clo$(p) \mid p \in \phi\}$

In other words, the ∃F-Clo for a propositional expression E is simply $\bigcup [\![E]\!]_{\mathcal{F}}$, which is equivalent to a formula with existentially quantified variables.[22]

---

[21] These definitions are direct adaptions from Schwarzschild (1999: 152), with an obvious typo in his (26b) corrected.

[22] Another way of rendering this for a propositional expression α is given in (i) ...

(i) $\lambda w \in W.\exists p[p \in [\![E]\!]_{\mathcal{F}} \& p(w) = 1]$

Schwarzschild's (1999) definitions for ∃Clo and ∃F-Clo exclude expressions of non-conjoinable type, in particular individual denoting expression, that is those of type e. Instead, the theory stipulates that such an expression is GIVEN if it, in present terms, refers to a salient individual. An alternative may be to postulate that the ∃Clo of an expression denoting an individual i is the proposition that i has some property (*modulo* some fix to the more general problem of restricting functor alternatives, see Section 5.4.1), or that i exists.

... and for α of arbitrary conjoinable types ...

(ii) $\lambda w \in W.\exists p[p \in [\![E]\!]_{\mathcal{F}} \, \& \, \exists\mathrm{Clo}(p)(w) = 1]$

These formulations make it perhaps clearer why this is tantamount to existential quantification of the F-variable.

Schwarzschild (1999) does not give a formal definition of ∃F-Clo *per se*, but wraps it into the formal definition of GIVEN (p. 152). We choose a different presentation here to facilitate comparison to other approaches, and to avoid the need to introduce Schwarzschild's particular focus semantics. The result should be equivalent, though, ignoring assignment functions. See Schwarzschild (1999: sec. 2.2) for the original definition of ∃F-Clo without the intermediate step of calculating F-alternatives.

4

More on focus/givenness representation

In Chapter 3 we saw that the GIVEN relation from Schwarzschild (1999) subsumes all F(ocus)-relations and G(ivenness)-relations discussed so far (because it is the weakest notion of them all). Section 3.3 in the previous chapter demonstrated this in the context of a stacked-F-markers approach such as that in Selkirk (1984, 1995b) and Schwarzschild (1999). One essential feature of these approaches is that every pitch accent corresponds to an F-marker on the word bearing it.

This is quite different from the perspective taken in Chapters 1 and 2 where pitch accents—within a focus and outside of it—are virtually always assigned by default prosody, and information structure marking within a focus—G-marking in Chapter 2—is only necessary where a focus includes both given and new material.

Is the wide applicability of GIVENness à la Schwarzschild (1999), then, a reason to abandon that earlier perspective? Does it constitute an argument in favor of stacked F-markers and a close pitch accent–F-mark relation like ACCENTS⇆ F-MARKERS in Section 3.2? The answer is "no," and this chapter will serve to show how GIVENness as an F-relation can also be combined with other ways of representing focus and givenness, that is, that the choice of focus/givenness representation, as well as focus/givenness realization, is by and large independent of the choice of F-relation. This is the topic of Sections 4.1 and 4.2.

But why explore such alternatives to Schwarzschild's (1999) proposal in the first place?

I would argue that stacked F-markers and the concomitant tight relation between F-markers and pitch accents make it much more difficult to formulate an adequate theory of F-realization (see Chapters 6 and 7). It also obscures, in my view, the role of prosody internal principles in the realization of focus, as well as the essential parallelism in the fact that F-interpretation as well as F-realization are fundamentally *relational* in nature (something which is hard to appreciate when they are reduced to F-marking and pitch accenting, which are both privative by nature; see esp. Chapter 7).

A second, more mundane reason is that the majority of the literature on information structure does not use stacked F-markers, but rather a single F-marker to mark 'the focus' (Selkirk's FOC), and occasional G-Markers to mark plain givenness. I think it is important to establish compatibility between the works using either kind of representation, without having to reinvent the semantic/pragmatic wheel, as it were.

Intonation and Meaning. First edition. Daniel Büring.
© Daniel Büring 2016. First published 2016 by Oxford University Press.

The alternatives to be developed in Sections 4.1–4.3 are based on the premise—advocated throughout this book—that within a focus, default prosody and givenness are the sole factors determining accent placement—essentially Jackendoff's (1972) position, as introduced and refined in Chapters 1 and 2 (esp. Sections 1.3.2 and 2.3).

Eschewing stacked F-markers here also implies that "focus projection"—the relation between the focus and the accents realizing it—cannot refer to stacked F-patterns. This, too, is in marked opposition to Selkirk's (1984, 1995b) approach, as well as many others (such as Jacobs, 1991/2c, von Stechow and Uhmann, 1986; and Uhmann, 1991), which argue for additional FOCUS PROJECTION RULES. Section 4.4 presents reasons to be skeptical about such rules and thereby serves to justify their omission.

The remaining Sections 4.5 discusses selected issues about F-representation that do not usually figure prominently in the literature. These are mostly meant for reference, and may be skipped by readers eager to see the "big picture" developed.

4.1 Back to F-marking plus G-Marking

In Chapter 2 (Section 2.3) we started out with a system that marked foci (by F) *and* givenness (by G). In contradistinction, the systems discussed in Chapter 3 only utilize F-marks; even in an approach like Selkirk's (1995b), in which F-markers are interpreted in two different ways, givenness is "marked" by the *absence* of F-markers, whereas F-markers mark "newness."

There is, however, no principled obstacle to integrating any of the F-Conditions discussed—plus squiggle, if desired—with a system that marks givenness by G. To illustrate, the tree in Figure 4.1(i) repeats the "F plus G" notation from Chapter 2 (example (33) there), juxtaposed with the "F(OC) only" representations of the same example in the tree in Figure 4.1(ii).

Straightforward information structure interpretation rules to set up such an F+G system are given in (1).

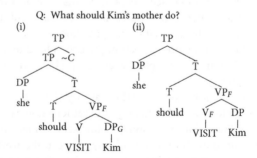

FIGURE 4.1   The same IS pattern represented using F and G, 13(i), and, à la Selkirk/Schwarzschild, using F-markers only, 13(ii).

(1^{CON}) a. 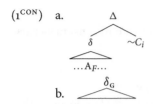 presupposes that the contextually supplied value of C_i makes δ GIVEN.[1]

b. presupposes that δ is given.[2]

Note that—as anticipated in Section 3.4.1 at the end of Chapter 3—condition (1a) (re-)defines, and thereby generalizes, the Roothean squiggle using Schwarzschild's (1999) GIVEN relation instead of Rooth's original Set Case and Individual Case.

Condition (1b) adds to that a simple givenness (not GIVENness!) condition along the lines discussed in Section 2.1 and assumed by, for example Selkirk (1984, 1995b) and Rochemont (1986). Turning to focus realization, we simply assume the Information Structure-Realization Conditions from Chapter 2, repeated in (2).

(2^{CON}) a. F-REALIZATION CONDITION
For any F-domain D, the final accent in D lies in a focus of D.
b. G-REALIZATION CONDITION
A G-marked constituent does not contain the nuclear accent, unless forced by the F-Realization Condition.
c. PROSODIC INERTIA
Default Intonation is preserved as much as possible, while meeting the F-Realization Condition and the G-Realization Condition.

Like its predecessor in Chapter 2, this system needs to be augmented by principles that force F-domain-formation (which in turn will necessitate F-marking) as well as G-marking, leading to anaphoric deaccenting. Clearly, AVOIDF (Section 3.3.2) will not do the job. For one thing, it has no say in the matter of G-marking. For another, it could no longer keep a lid on the "oversized focus" kind of overfocussing, due to the lack of stacked F-markers; for example V, VP, and S focus each involve exactly one F-marker, so AVOIDF could not force, for example, (3a) instead of (3b) or (3c) (repeated from example (7), Section 3.1.5; recall that $[\![(3a)]\!]_{\mathcal{F}} \subset [\![(3b)]\!]_{\mathcal{F}} \subset [\![(3c)]\!]_{\mathcal{F}}$, and hence condition (1a) above is met in all of them).

(3) (What does Kim do in Paris? —)
a. Kim [WORKS]$_F$ in Paris.
b. #Kim [works in PARis]$_F$.
c. #[Kim works in PARis]$_F$.

As in Chapter 2, we therefore add to the system a version of "Maximize Information Structure Marking," which, in anticipation of later discussions, is renamed "Maximize Background" here.

---

[1] Explicitly: ∃Clo(C) entails ∃F-Clo(δ).
[2] That is: there is a contextually salient meaning CSM s.t. ∃Clo(CSM) entails ∃Clo($[\![C]\!]_O$).

(4^{CON})   MAXIMIZE BACKGROUND
In any tree, maximize the number of (non-synonymous) constituents that
are in the background.

(5^{DEF})   BACKGROUND in a F+G-marking system
A constituent E is IN THE BACKGROUND in a tree T iff
a. E is c-commanded by a $\sim C$ in T, and not (part of) a focus of that
$\sim C$,   *or*
b. if E bears, or is dominated by, a G-Marker in T.

(6^{DEF})   FOCUS OF A F-DOMAIN
An F-marked constituent E is a FOCUS of a $\sim C$ in tree T if $\sim C$ minimally
c-commands E in T.
(i.e. $\sim C$ c-commands E in T and there is no closer $\sim C'$ in T, i.e. no $\sim C'$
c-commanding E and c-commanded by $\sim C$)

Apart from quite directly encouraging G-marking due to clause (b) of definition (5), MAXIMIZE BACKGROUND pushes for large F-domains with small foci in
them, since every element within an F-domain but outside of the focus of that
domain is thereby backgrounded. For example, MAXIMIZE BACKGROUND picks the
tree in Figure 4.2(i) over the alternative structures 4.2(ii)–4.2(v), all of which meet
conditions (1a) and (1b) above.

In principle, the effect of MAXIMIZE BACKGROUND in (4) could also be achieved
by strengthening condition (1b) above to a biconditional, that is, by adding: "A node
δ *without* G-Marking presupposes that δ is *not* given"; an all-given focus would
then be F- *and* G-marked, with the G-REALIZATION CONDITION in (2b) above

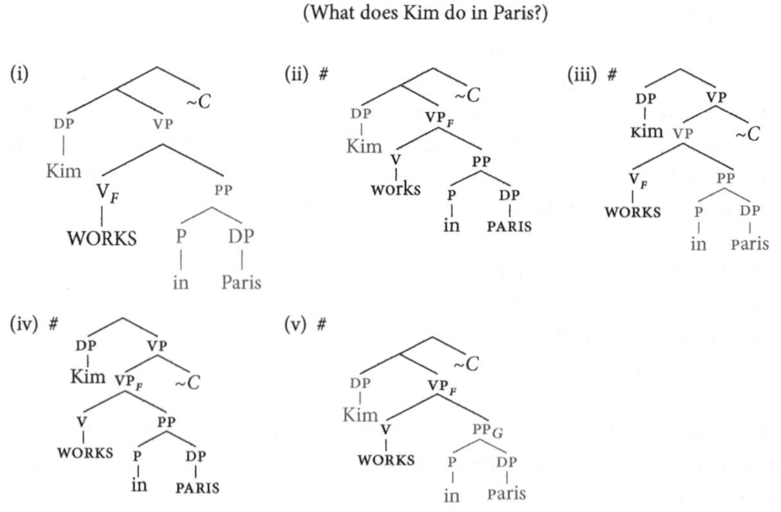

(What does Kim do in Paris?)

FIGURE 4.2   Maximize Background, (4)/(5), at work: structure (i) beats (ii)–(v), which all
have fewer backgrounded constituents (marked in gray). Note that Maximize Background
also entails a preference for narrow focus, (i), over broader focus plus deaccenting, (v), since
VP is backgrounded in the former, but not the latter.

Q: What should Kim's mother do?

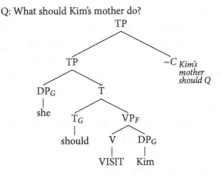

FIGURE 4.3   The information structure pattern from the tree in Figure 4.1(i) once more, this time with all given constituents G-marked (an option we will not adopt).

resolving the conflict.[3] This would still allow for oversized foci, but neutralize the prosodic effect of overfocussing by simultaneous G-marking, as in (7).

(7)   (What does Kim do in Paris? —)
    a. Kim [WORKS]$_F$ in Paris.
    b. Kim [WORKS in Paris$_G$]$_F$.
    c. [Kim$_G$ WORKs in Paris$_G$]$_F$.

Another consequence of having "G-marked↔given" instead of "G-marked→given" would be that we would get representations as in the tree in Figure 4.3 instead of that in Figure 4.3(i), in which all elements in the background of a F-domain are, redundantly, G-marked. Why redundantly? Because these additional G-markers have no effect on prosody: a constituent in the background of a focus will, by condition (2a) never be "in danger" of receiving the NPA in the first place.

So neither of these consequences—"spurious focus oversizing" and redundant G-markers—compromises the empirical coverage of the resulting system, but they strike me as counter-intuitive, and they certainly do not correspond to most of the informal uses of F- and G-marking in the literature, where F marks "the focus" (Selkirk's FOC) and G marks given elements within foci or in the absence of any F-domains. I will therefore stick to MAXIMIZE BACKGROUND (and, accordingly, condition (1b)), as defined in (4) and (5) above, and, accordingly, structures like the trees in Figures 4.1(i) and 4.2(i).

The accent pattern assigned to Figure 4.2(i) will be as in (8). Crucially, the pitch accent assigned to the subject ‹Kim› by default prosody is unaffected by the focussing.

     PA   PA
     | |
(8)   [KIM WORKS in Paris]~C.

---

[3] Unlike in an 'F only' system, condition (1b) does not require that a given node be F-less, only that it be G-marked. Hence Schwarzschild's (1999) original motivation to weaken Selkirk's (1995b) original biconditional—to allow for F-marking on all-given foci—is no longer relevant here.

The effect of focussing on intonation in this case is just that there is an obligatory pitch accent on ‹works›, and crucially no pitch accent on ‹Paris›. In other words, as in Chapter 2, we allow for pre-nuclear, "ornamental," pitch accents even in the background. This became possible because we gave up the assumption that pitch accenting within a broad focus relies on lower F-markers on terminals (as Selkirk, 1984, 1995b and Schwarzschild, 1999 do) and, conversely, that deaccenting is represented locally by the absence of terminal F-marking.

It also bears emphasizing once more that pre-nuclear content words will also be accented if they are G-marked, as in (9).

(9)   (What did the Jamerson's agent say? —)

$$\begin{array}{ccc} \text{PA} & \text{PA} & \text{PA} \\ | & | & | \end{array}$$

[That JAmerson$_G$ is unavAIlable until FRIday]

Note that ‹Jamerson› would be deaccented if it were clause final (‹that he hasn't TALKED to Jamerson yet›), so we are correct to mark it as given. But by condition (2b), there is no need to change default prosody for realizing this G-marker, since ‹Jamerson› is not in a position to receive the NPA in (9) (nor does condition (2a) affect this accent, obviously). As said before, the contrast between being given or in the background vis-à-vis being a (part of the) focus gets prosodically neutralized in pre-nuclear position (this claim will be slightly qualified in Sections 7.1.5 and 7.2.2 of Chapter 7).

This system is also not committed to the dogma that every sentence needs to contain a focus and an F-domain. Completely F-less sentences (e.g. all-new sentences) are possible within this system, and indeed are predicted in a context where truly nothing is given. Their realization, however, will be indistinguishable from that of an all-focus clause or sentence.

What we have done in this section is define a system which combines the Rooth/Schwarzschild-style focus interpretation with a rather transparent and run-of-the-mill F-/G-representation (eschewing stacked F-markers) and an account of F-/G-realization in line with the general assumption about the focus–accent relation in Chapters 1 and 2. The next step from here could be to refine the F-/G-*realization* side of things, which I will do in Chapters 6 and 7.

However, the F+G-marking system developed in this section is not the only way to reach this state of affairs. In the next section, I will review alternative ideas about information structure representation which have been entertained in the literature and/or will be referenced in later chapters, because they appear advantageous in some respects (but disadvantageous in others).

4.2 Using stacked F-domains to replace G-marking

In this section I will discuss a possible modification of the format of information structure representation just developed. The main tenet of this modification is to generalize the application of focussing so as to eliminate the need for G-marking. In a nutshell, whatever ends up G-marked in the system laid out in Section 4.1 above will instead be the background of a subordinated F-domain.

This project—originally pursued in Büring (2012b)—is transparently related to Schwarzschild's (1999) unification of focus and givenness in terms of F-interpretation, and I will try to make the connection as clear as possible towards the end of the section. Crucially, however, the system developed in this section maintains the general view on information structure-realization expressed in Section 4.1 and earlier chapters, according to which pitch accenting is related to, but not predicated on, F-marking. This excludes, as pointed out before, the use of stacked F-markers to guide pitch accent assignment, and thus is the main motivation for not adopting Schwarzschild's (1999) proposal wholesale (another point in favor of this way of doing things—this time related to interpretation rather than realization—will emerge in Section 5.3).

What would happen if we simply jettisoned G-marking and condition (1b), leaving only F-marking and (1a), repeated as (10), as our sole Information Structure Interpretation Condition?

(10^{CON})

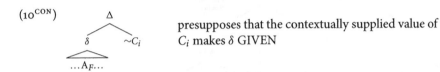

presupposes that the contextually supplied value of C_i makes δ GIVEN

In many cases the result will be the same. Two such cases are illustrated in Figure 4.4: an all-new focus and an all-given focus.

In such a case, focussing will take care of accenting all by itself. In more detail, MAXIMIZE BACKGROUND will favor a maximally big F-domain—ideally the entire sentence—and minimal foci. Since only a focus may bear the NPA within a F-domain, the net effect is that anything outside of the focus will behave as thought it were G-marked and subject to the G-REALIZATION CONDITION (2b).

This much may be unsurprising. But what of partially given foci, which, as already discussed in Section 2.4, are one of the main motivations for having G-marking in addition to F-marking to begin with? On the face of it, focussing alone cannot account for such cases. Consider the structures in Figure 4.5 for the by now all-too-familiar example.

The tree in Figure 4.5(i) correctly F-marks VP, but thereby ends up with the wrong NPA placement, whereas the tree in Figure 4.5(ii), which would have the

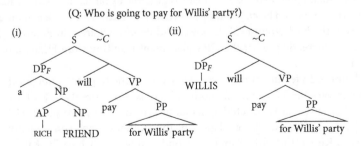

FIGURE 4.4 For sentences with one simple focus, givenness marking does not achieve any additional effect.

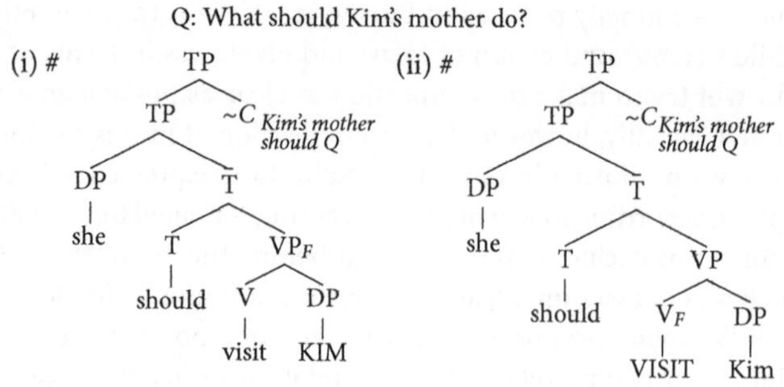

Q: What should Kim's mother do?

(i) #   TP   (ii) #   TP

FIGURE 4.5   Simple F-marking appears to meet its match when it comes to partially given foci.

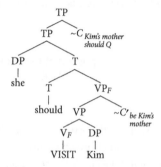

FIGURE 4.6   Could stacked F-domains save the day?

accent in the intuitively right place, does not meet the F-condition, since it is not contextually salient that Kim's mother should do something *to Kim*.

But these two structures do not exhaust the possibilities. We can try to have our cake and eat it too, as it were, if we allow ourselves to stack F-domains, as in the tree in Figure 4.6.

Loosely speaking, the F-Realization Condition (1a) applies twice in the tree in Figure 4.6: For the F-domain TP it requires the NPA to be within VP$_F$, and for the embedded F-domain VP it requires the NPA to be "within" V$_F$, resulting in the sentential NPA on V, as is empirically adequate.

Nothing we have said so far prohibits this kind of F-domain recursion. In fact, whenever such an embedded F-domain is possible as far as the F-condition, (10), is concerned, it would be *enforced* by MAXIMIZE BACKGROUND, since in Figure 4.6, ‹Kim› is in the background (of the lower F-domain), whereas in Figure 4.5(i) it is not. So we correctly predict the NPA placement resulting from Figure 4.6, rather than Figure 4.5(i).

A slightly odd feature of the tree in Figure 4.6 is the required value for the lower F-domain variable, C', 'be Kim's mother'. First, is this property in $[\![\text{VP}]\!]_{\mathcal{F}}$? Given that F-alternatives are restricted by semantic type only, *any* two-place relation will be in $[\![\text{visit}_F]\!]_{\mathcal{F}}$, including the relation 'be the mother of', and consequently 'be the mother of Kim' is in $[\![\text{visit}_F\text{ Kim}]\!]_{\mathcal{F}}$. Second, can we really have 'be Kim's mother' as a focal target for 'visit Kim'? Again, there is nothing in the F-condition (10) that would block this; *some* F-alternative is contextually salient, the F-condition is met.

This is of course a consequence of the fact noted earlier that neither Rooth (1992b) nor Schwarzschild (1999) incorporate any kind of *contrast* requirement worthy of the name in their F-conditions, and neither does our condition (10). As discussed in Section 3.4, any GIVEN constituent is a licit F-domain. Put yet differently, we should be able to systematically replace a focus containing a G-marked constituent, as schematized in (11a), by a focus containing a subordinated F-domain, as in (11b).

(11)   a. $[_{\gamma}...[\,\alpha\,\beta_G\,]...]_F$ b. $[_{\gamma}[_{\gamma}...[\,\alpha_F\,\beta\,]...]{\sim}C\,]_F$

Summarizing, we have defined a system that achieves the same effects as the F+G-marking system in Section 4.1 by utilizing embedded F-domains, and F-marking only. As with Schwarzschild's (1999) proposal, this may be preferable on grounds of parsimony, provided that, first, we can maintain the weak F-semantics used so far, and, second, that we always find givenness and 'background-ness' realized in the same way. Both of these premises will be critically discussed (in Chapters 5 and 8, respectively), but I hesitate to draw firm conclusions on either. So it will comforting to know that, up to this point, either representational option is tenable.

What is the relation of this section's system to the proposal in Schwarzschild (1999)? First and foremost, we maintained here the same assumptions about F-realization as in the previous section, most importantly: default prosody within, as well as to the left of, the focus (*pace* subordinated foci, of course). F-marking, like G-marking before, is only used where there is an *asymmetry* in information structure status between the constituent so marked and its sister; there will never be an F-marked node immediately dominating two F-marked nodes (or a G-marked node immediately dominating two G-marked nodes). Instead, both daughter nodes will remain unmarked, and can be treated alike by the rules and principles of default prosody.

As far as focus interpretation goes, it is instructive to recall that making a constituent α a (subordinate) F-domain (i.e. adjoining a ${\sim}C$ to it) is tantamount to introducing a presupposition that α is GIVEN in the Schwarzschildian sense. This in turn is what requires F-marking within α (to introduce F-alternatives that help to meet that presupposition). So, figuratively speaking, what we are doing is imposing a GIVENness condition on every focus and then assigning F-marks with*in* it so as to meet that condition. Or, for those who prefer anthropomorphic metaphors, within every focus, MAXIMIZE BACKGROUND senses an opportunity to establish a new focus–background structure, just like at the root node, and to thereby maximize overall backgrounding.

But then why do we not have to make *every* node an F-domain, as Schwarzschild (1999) effectively does by requiring that every constituent be GIVEN, in order to be sure that we do not miss any opportunities to further the cause of MAXIMIZE BACKGROUND?

For the sake of concreteness, consider the tree in Figure 4.7.

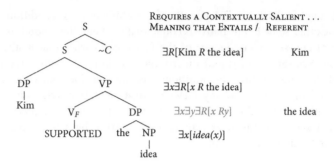

FIGURE 4.7   The referents/∃F-Clos in need of an antecedent/a contextually salient meaning that entails them by a GIVENness Requirement.

Could a squiggle on, say, VP or DP, gain us further backgrounded constituents? Certainly not! Anything without an F-marker is already in the background, and everything *below* an F-marker is by definition *not* in the background (at least not of any F-domain higher than that F). Casually put, the matter of what is backgrounded and what is not is already settled within an existing F-domain all the way "down to" its focus.

Is there, on the other hand, a danger that any constituent in the background of the root F-domain in Figure 4.7 would not itself meet GIVENness? Could we "overlook" non-GIVEN elements by not checking every constituent for GIVENness? In virtually all instances the answer is "no" (see Chapter 5, in particular Section 5.4.2, for why the caveat), due to a fundamental fact about GIVENness: if a constituent α is GIVEN, then so will any sub-constituent β of α, provided β is not (dominated by something) F-marked. Again informally speaking, if α meets GIVENness, we can be sure that everything within α "down to" the next F-marker meets GIVENness as well.

This general fact can perhaps be appreciated by noting that in Figure 4.7 the propositions that need to be entailed by a contextually salient meaning in order for S, VP, and NP to be GIVEN/meet the F-condition (noted to the right of the tree) are ordered by entailment from top to bottom: the GIVENness of S guarantees GIVENness of VP and NP (in addition we have to assume that once such propositions are contextually salient, so are the individuals that "occur in them"; again see Section 5.4.2 for a more careful assessment of this claim).

Therefore there is no need to mark nodes "between" a ~C and its focus as subordinate F-domains, since this will never catch anything in need of F-marking that is not F-marked already.

4.3 Interim summary

In the previous two sections (and the appendix to this section) I have outlined various systems using GIVEN and/or given as their F-/G-conditions, but employing different representations. What they all have in common is that they do not use stacked F-marks as pure newness markers, and thereby fit better with approaches that substantially rely on default prosody to predict the prosody of sentences containing focussing (rather than some version of ACCENTS⇆F-MARKERS, see Section 3.2 above).

What is the key to being able to do this? That the *absence* of F-/G-marking among sister nodes is interpreted as "equality in information structural status," which can be "each is given," but also be "each is new." Only if one, but not all of several sisters is marked is this interpreted as an asymmetry: The sister of an F-marked constituent will be given, and similarly, the mother of a G-marked constituent will be non-given.

A residue of stacked markers will still be necessary to model deaccenting, that is, structural asymmetry, within a focus. This is achieved either by recursively embedding F-domains, as in Section 4.2 and the Appendix to Section 4.3 below, or by embedding G-markers within foci, as in Section 4.1. Are these two ways equivalent? Nearly so, but not completely. A subordinate F-domain may, in principle occur within a focus, but also within the background of another F-domain, or even another *subordinate* F-domain; a G-marker could perhaps occur within the background of an F-domain, but it is unclear what it would mean for one to occur *within* another G-marked constituent. So, clearly, recursive F-domains allow for many more structures than G-markers within F-domains. I have not, however, been able to find an example that would *realize* such recursive F-domain structures differently from "flat" G-within-an-F-domain structures.

In other respects, privative G-marking might, in some instances, at least be easier to conceptualize than embedded F-domains. Take example (12).

(12)   (We got a toy car for Veronica. What else might she like?—)
       She'd probably also like [a gaRAGE for her car]$_F$.

The answer focus in (12) should be on the object DP, as indicated. The deaccenting within that DP would be straightforwardly explained by the givenness of ‹car› (‹garage› being the last non-given content word within the focus). Using subordinate F-domains would lead to the structural representation in Figure 4.8, which leads us to search for a contextually salient meaning (the ∃Clo of) which entails ∃x[x is for her car].[4] Intuitively, that would be "her car" or "the car itself," but it is not obvious that that entailment holds, or if it does, whether this would generalize to other prepositions than ‹for›.

Sloppily put, example (12) feels like a case of, privative, givenness deaccenting, not of, relational, focussing. A technical solution may be forthcoming here, but the analysis in terms of G-marking appears more natural to me in this case. On the other hand, we will see examples of (non-)deaccenting within the focus in Chapter 5 (Section 5.3) which seem to defy any analysis in terms of privative givenness, arguing for the use of subordinate F-domains rather than embedded G-markers.

---

[4] The F-domain in example (12) may also be DP, rather than NP. This would not change the argument much though.

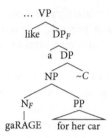

FIGURE 4.8   What is the G-antecedent for ∃F-Clo(‹garage_F for her car›)?

Appendix to Section 4.3: 'G Only' Systems

For the sake of completeness I will mention here the possibility of systems that *only* use G-markings. The simplest version of such a system would interpret G-marking as basic givenness, enforced by some "Maximize G" principle, accompanied by realization principles that steer (nuclear) pitch accents away from G-marked constituents (Sauerland, 2005, proposes a system of this kind). Such a system would, however, exclude all-given foci (because nothing could even indicate the focus as a focus). It is also incapable of distinguishing narrow focus from broader focus plus anaphoric deaccenting; for example, ‹she should VISIT_F Kim› and ‹she should [VISIT_F Kim]_F› would converge on the same representation, the tree in Figure 4.9(i). This may be problematic, inasmuch as this distinction is relevant for interpretation or proper grammatical phenomena such as ellipsis (recall Section 2.5.3 in Chapter 2).

A system more comparable to the ones discussed in this book so far would thus introduce alternatives and retrieve them, for example by the squiggle, but based on a different representation. The key to doing so is to let *all nodes but those marked G* introduce alternatives. That is, the semantics of $[\![\ ]\!]_{\mathcal{F}}$ will be the precise mirror image of what is in Rooth (1985, 1992b), as introduced in Section 3.5.1 above and assumed throughout this book.

(13^{CON})   FOCUS ALTERNATIVES BY G-MARKING (only for this subsection)

      a. If A is G-marked, $[\![\ A_G\ ]\!]_{\mathcal{F}} = \{[\![\ A\ ]\!]_{\mathcal{O}}\}$
         Condition: $[\![\ A\ ]\!]_{\mathcal{O}}$ is given[5]
      b. Otherwise (if A is not G-marked)
         (i)   If A is a terminal node, of semantic type τ, then $[\![\ A\ ]\!]_{\mathcal{F}}$ is the set of possible denotations in the domain of τ.
         (ii) If A is a non-branching node that dominates B, $[\![\ A\ ]\!]_{\mathcal{F}} = [\![\ B\ ]\!]_{\mathcal{F}}$
         (iii) for any branching node $[_A\ B\ C]$, any combination operation $\oplus$ s.t. by the ordinary semantic rules $[\![\ A\ ]\!]_{\mathcal{O}} = [\![\ B\ ]\!]_{\mathcal{O}} \oplus [\![\ C\ ]\!]_{\mathcal{O}}$, $[\![\ A\ ]\!]_{\mathcal{F}} = \{b \oplus c \mid b \in [\![\ B\ ]\!]_{\mathcal{F}} \wedge c \in [\![\ C\ ]\!]_{\mathcal{F}}\}$

---

[5] If G-markers are guaranteed to be c-commanded by a squiggle, the Squiggle Condition might actually subsume this requirement; see again Section 4.2, and Section 5.4.2 in Chapter 5.

According to clause (13b-i) above, every terminal node gets to introduce alternatives as though it were F-marked; alternatives are then propagated, by clauses (13b-ii) and (13b-iii) above. G-marked nodes, on the other hand, block the propagation of alternatives and reset them to the trivial alternative $\{\llbracket\ \rrbracket_o\}$ by clause (13a).

F-alternatives can now be retrieved by adjoining the standard squiggle, presumably as high as possible (approximating the effect of MAXIMIZE BACKGROUND); such a system is presented in Wagner (2006), except that there, F-alternatives are retrieved (to check if there is an antecedent) invariably (and without a $\sim$ in the representation) at the first node dominating the G-marker.

To get all-given foci, establishing F-domains must be more important than marking givenness (in the same way that realizing F(ocus) is more important than realizing G(ivenness) in simple F+G-marking systems). Thus structure (14a)—fewer G-markers but an F-domain—must be preferable to (14b)—maximal possible number of G-markers, but no F-domain.

(14) (Who should Kim's mother call?)
      a. [She_G should_G call_G Kim]$\sim$C
      b. She_G should_G call_G Kim_G.

This could be done by having a principle like "Have F-Domains" outrank "Maximize Givenness"; since the details seem irrelevant at this point, I will not flesh this out further.

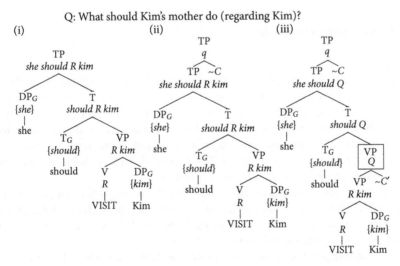

FIGURE 4.9 In a G-only system, F-domains can be made to limit the "scope" of G. This is tantamount to having an F-marker immediately dominating any $\sim$C in a F-marking system. Accordingly, the tree in (ii) represents narrow V-focus, while the tree in (iii) represents VP-focus with a deaccented object DP; note how the VP above $\sim$C' (boxed) introduces, rather than propagates F-alternatives.

Using the standard squiggle from condition (1a) above would essentially treat G as a background marker: the meaning of the G-marked constituent is fixed in all higher focus semantic values. This still would not get us deaccenting within a focus: Figure 4.9(i) could only be interpreted as narrow V-focus, regardless of where $\sim C$ were to attach (see Figure 4.9(ii)).

A more interesting system results if we define the squiggle as in (15):

(15^{CON})   GIVENNESS SQUIGGLE (this subsection only)

a. presupposes that the contextually supplied value of C_i makes δ GIVEN

b. if so $[\![\Delta]\!]_{\mathcal{F}}$ is the set of possible denotations in the domain of $\tau(\Delta)$

Now the squiggle, by clause (15b), acts as if it were itself an F-marker. Put differently: whatever restrictions lower G-markers imposed on $[\![\delta]\!]_{\mathcal{F}}$ (in the tree in (15)) are "lifted" at the next squiggle site. The effect of this is illustrated in Figures 4.9(ii) and 4.9(iii). In the tree in Figure 4.9(ii) a sole squiggle at the root retrieves a narrow V-focus. In the tree in Figure 4.9(iii), on the other hand, the G-marker on ‹Kim› is interpreted locally at the VP-level, whereas the squiggle at the root interprets a "projected" Focus on VP; this corresponds to the trees in Figure 4.1.

If we define a backgrounded constituent as one bearing or dominated by G and c-commanded by a $\sim C$, this system combines with MAXIMIZE BACKGROUND in the usual way and is in fact fully equivalent to that from Section 4.2.

4.4 Focus projection rules

4.4.1 The idea

We introduced the concept of F-projection in Section 2.5.2. F-PROJECTION RULES are meant to determine which element(s) within a larger focus need to be accented, and, inversely, which larger foci an accent on a terminal element might be realizing. The literature sometimes uses the term FOCUS EXPONENT for that terminal that bears the strongest stress or NPA within a focus (and, consequently, the entire F-domain), in which case we may say that F-projection rules should govern what pairings of foci and focus exponents are possible.

Following our earlier assumption that the NPA is simply the last pitch accent (in a given prosodic domain, see Chapter 6), we want F-projection rules to predict what pairings of accent *patterns* and foci are possible. The focus exponent is simply the last pitch accented terminal within a focus.

As a starting point, consider the F-projection rules from Selkirk (1995b).

(16^{CON})   BASIC FOCUS RULE
        An accented word is F-marked. (Selkirk, 1995b: 555)

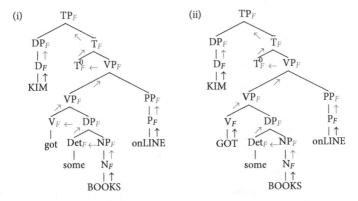

FIGURE 4.10   Some legitimate accent/F-patterns according to Selkirk (1995b). Gray F-markers are optional F-projections, projectable by condition (17a) (vertical: upward/diagonal arrows) or (17b) (horizontal: sidewards arrows) (but every gray F-marker presupposes the presence of an F-marker on the node it gets projected from, i.e. at the tail of the arrow).

(17^{CON})   FOCUS PROJECTION[6]
> a. F-marking of the head of a phrase licenses F-marking of the phrase (henceforth: VERTICAL FOCUS PROJECTION)
> b. F-marking of an internal argument of a head licenses the F-marking of the head (henceforth: HORIZONTAL FOCUS PROJECTION)

These rules between them define the class of grammatical F-marking–accent pattern pairings in English. Using gray F-markers for those assigned by the optionally applying F-Projection Rules in (17) (as opposed to the obligatory Basic Focus Rule (16)), some predicted patterns are shown in Figures 4.10 and 4.11.

Note in particular that broad focus is possible in all these cases, despite the local givenness deaccenting, and that the trees in Figure 4.10(i) and 4.10(ii) only differ in whether or not the verb is accented, but have identical focus potentials.

The patterns in Figure 4.12, on the other hand, are not licensed by rules (16) and (17).

(18) teases apart the various generalizations embodied in these rules, which will be useful for the discussion to follow.

---

[6] In (Selkirk, 1984: 207), this rule read:

(i)   PHRASAL FOCUS RULE
  A constituent may be focus if (ia) or (ib) (or both) is true:
  a. The constituent that is its head is a focus.
  b. A constituent contained within it that is an argument of the head is focus.

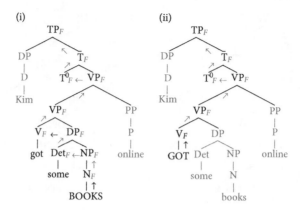

FIGURE 4.11   More legitimate accent/F-patterns according to Selkirk (1995b). Grayed out constituents need to be given.

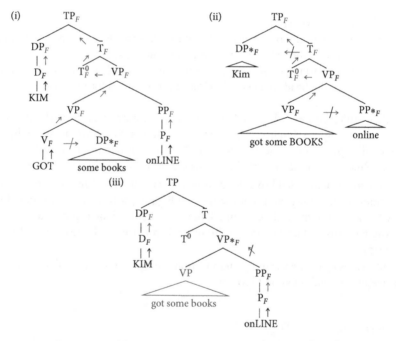

FIGURE 4.12   Some impossible accent/F-patterns according to Selkirk (1995b). No horizontal projection from heads to phrases, (i), or from phrases to sister phrases, (ii), and absolutely no projection from adjuncts, (iii), even if the sister is given.

(18^{GEN})   a. FOCUS CONTAINS ACCENT: Every F-marked projection contains at least one PA.[7]

b. NO PHRASAL FOCUS WITHOUT F-MARKED HEAD: Every F-marked phrase has an F-marked head.[8]

c. NO PROJECTION FROM ADJUNCTS OR EXTERNAL ARGUMENTS: Within an F-marked projection, there must be an accent either on the head or within the internal argument.[9]

d. NO ACCENTS OUTSIDE THE FOCUS: Each accent is dominated by at least one F-mark.[10]

In Büring (2006) I argued that of these, only (18a) is in fact valid, so that—at least in languages like English, Dutch, and German—there is no need for specific rules of F-projection. This position was implicitly adopted already in our use of Jackendoff's rule ("The last default pitch accent within the focus is the last pitch accent in the sentence.") in Chapter 1 and its more formal implementation in the conditions in (2) in this chapter.

I will show how these rules capture the empirical ground, and where the empirical differences to those in (16) and (17) above lie in Section 4.4.3 below. Before that, however, we will take a quick detour to (re)acquaint ourselves with an important aspect of default prosody: integration.

4.4.2 Integration

The term INTEGRATION was coined in Jacobs (1992), but systematic discussion of the phenomena involved goes back at least to Schmerling (1976) for English, and Bierwisch (1966) and Kiparsky (1966) for German. We will use it in a slightly generalized sense here, given in (19).

(19)   INTEGRATION
The grammatically determined non-accenting of a content word within a larger, accent-containing phrase.

The prototypical example of integration is the non-accenting of a final verb in a transitive VP in Dutch or German.

---

[7] By clause (17a), F-marking on the projection is only possible if the head is F-marked. The head, in turn, could be F-marked either (i) because it is accented, clause (16), or (ii) because its internal argument is F-marked, clause (17b). Since an internal argument must be a phrase, the reasoning starts over again; eventually the internal argument (of the internal argument of . . .) will not contain an internal argument itself, so its head must be accented by (i). Since internal arguments are included within the projection of their selecting head, it follows that that projection will necessarily include an accent, either on its head—case (i)—or within it internal argument—case (ii).

[8] A direct consequence of clause (17a) being the only rule that can license F on a phrase. This was not a consequence of the rules in Selkirk (1984); see also note 5 above, as well as Rochemont's (1986) comments on Selkirk (1984).

[9] Follows from the fact that there is no F-projection rule that doesn't start with "F-marking on the head/of an internal argument . . . ."

[10] Direct consequence of rule (16).

(20)   (Was willst du   tun?—) Einen RoMAN schreiben.   (German)
       what want you to do   a-ACC novel   write
       'What are you planning to do?—Write a novel.'

Example (20) illustrates VP focus, yet the verb is, and has to be, unaccented (accenting the verb here would inevitably yield a narrow V-focus interpretation, rendering the exchange in example (20) infelicitous). This meets definition (19) above, since a content word, the verb, is unaccented within a larger phrase that contains an accent, the VP. Importantly, this non-accenting is not due to backgroundedness or givenness since the verb is part of the focus, and not given. Therefore the non-accenting must, by assumption, be grammatically determined (as opposed to information structurally determined).

Transitive verb integration is the default in virtually any object+verb combination, whether it is ‹ein BUCH lesen› ('to read a book') or ‹einen HAIfisch schminken› ('to put make-up on a shark'). Clearly, there is no requirement that the verb be predictable, closely collocational to the object, or "informationally light."

Definition (19) above explicitly excludes function words, which are generally excluded from bearing word or phrasal stress and pitch accents. That verbs, on the other hand, are not generally accentless is evident from examples like (21), an S-focus in which the verb must be accented.

(21)   (Psst! — Was?—) Doris SCHREIBT.
       sssh   what   D.   writes
       'Ssssh!—What?!—Doris is writing.'

It must thus be the particular configuration in examples like (20) that allows for the verb to remain unaccented.

Integration of transitive verbs in English is not obligatory, as it is in German, but it is possible. Example (22) may be felicitously produced without a pitch accent on ‹writing› even in a broad focus context in which writing is not salient.

(22)   (Have you heard the news?—) KIM's writing a NOvel.

In the rare but instructive English cases in which we find predicate-like elements following their argument, English, too, shows obligatory integration, as in (23).

(23)   a. (Did you think of that yourself?—No,) I was advised by a LAWyer I hired.
       b. (What's that noise?—Ooops,) my aLARM went off.

Neither ‹hired› nor ‹went off› are given or in the background in these examples, yet accenting them would render the replies inappropriate, arguably because that would indicate the wrong IS-pattern (focussing of the predicate, or givenness of the argument).

The rules for default prosody given in Chapter 1, repeated in (24) actually capture the basic cases of integration (i.e. within a VP or any other lexical projection).

(24^{DEF})   DEFAULT PROSODY
  Step 1:   Put pitch accents on open class elements; put the minimal
            number to guarantee that each syntactic phrase contains at least
            one PA.
  Step 2:   a. *Delete* pitch accents if they are followed by at least one other
  (optional)   PA,
               or alternatively
            b. *add* pitch accents on open class elements (OCEs), if they are
               followed by at least one other PA.

By Step 1 (the essence of which follows Truckenbrodt, 1995: ch. 6), only one pitch
accent will be assigned in the configurations $[_{XP} X° YP]$ and $[_{XP} YP X°]$. Step 2b, then,
may add an accent on $X°$ in $[_{XP} X° YP]$ (English VP, NP in all three languages), but
cannot in $[_{XP} YP X°]$ (German/Dutch VP) (Step 2a is irrelevant here, since we are
looking at XPs containing the NPA).

   More will be said about integration—where exactly it happens, when it is
blocked, how to include cases like example (23) above—in Sections 6.1 and 8.5 or
below. The cursory discussion here should suffice, though, as background for the
next step, which is to establish an important empirical point, generalization (25).

(25^{GEN})   INTEGRATION–FOCUS INDEPENDENCE
   Integration takes place in the same way within the focus as well as in the
   background.

To establish the validity of generalization (25), we obviously need to look at
cases without focus. Keeping in mind that perhaps even neutral sentences
display (sentence-wide) focus (see Section 2.5.4), the safest environments in
which to do so are transitive VPs in the background of a F-domain, in particular preceding the focus (since there will be no pitch accents after the focus for independent reasons, though see Section 7.3), such as in the examples
in (26).

(26)   a. (You hired a lawyer. What did he recommend?—) The lawyer we hired
          recommended [that we settle]$_F$.
       b. (If I hear an alarm, I stay inside.—Are you nuts?) If an alarm goes off, you
          [run for the door]$_F$!

Example (26a) and example (26b) include an answer focus and a contrastive
focus, respectively, marked by []$_F$ as usual. In the background of these foci are
the integration configurations of interest, ‹lawyer we hired› and ‹an alarm goes off›.
Since these also *precede* the foci, it is still possible (and indeed natural) to find
secondary pitch accents in them, as indicated in structures (27a) and (27b) below.
In both cases, such a secondary PA will go on the argument (‹lawyer› and ‹alarm›),
but not the predicates (secondary accents on ‹recommend› and ‹run› are indicated
for completeness, but do not matter for the argument).

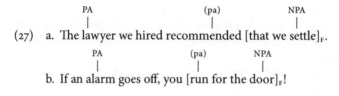

(27)   a. The lawyer we hired recommended [that we settle]_F.

b. If an alarm goes off, you [run for the door]_F!

Choosing a non-integrated pattern as in the structures in (28), on the other hand, is marked here. (28a), even in the context of (26a) above, conveys narrow focus on ‹hired› (in addition to the focus on the object clause): the lawyer we hired, as opposed to some other lawyer. Likewise, (28b) sounds unnatural in the context of (26b), unless the speaker intends a contrast with things to do if an alarm does something else.[11]

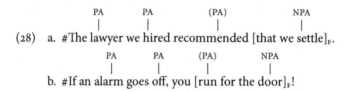

(28)   a. #The lawyer we hired recommended [that we settle]_F.

b. #If an alarm goes off, you [run for the door]_F!

We can contrast examples like these with ones that do not show integration in the first place. ‹Mary resigned› strongly prefers the non-integrated pattern ‹MAry reSIGNED›, even as an all-new sentence, (29). And, put in the background of a narrow focus sentence, the same double accent pattern is found (this time with two secondary accents), see structure (30a).

(29)   (What happened? Why is everybody so pale?—) MAry reSIGNED.

(30)   (If this is a letter of resignation from Mary, what will happen?—) If Mary resigns, we'll have to hire a replacement.

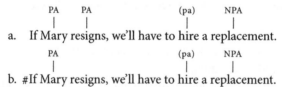

a.   If Mary resigns, we'll have to hire a replacement.

b. #If Mary resigns, we'll have to hire a replacement.

Structure (30b), on the other hand, is marked and evokes an additional contrast between Mary resigning and someone else resigning.[12]

---

[11] Note that this particular characterization of the facts in examples (26)–(30) implies that structures (28) and (30b) (but not those in (27) and (30a)) involve embedded pre-nuclear focus structures. We'll say more about such structures in Chapter 7.

[12] It is even more subtle to make a comparable argument with predicate–argument order, since in general, integration here is optional. For example, it certainly seems natural to put secondary pitch accent on ‹eating› and ‹vegetables› (and the NPA on ‹good›) in (i):

(i)   (Should I avoid vegetables in my diet?—To the contrary:) Eating vegetables is good for you.

Note that all the examples given here are construed in such a way that the integration configuration, although given and backgrounded, is not a *verbatim* repetition of a previous, non-backgrounded version. This was done to exclude the possibility that the purported integration in the background is really just a "copying" of the previous accent pattern.[13]

These examples thus strongly suggest that integration is not a phenomenon of focus realization, but a part of the regular syntax-to-prosody mapping, or as we have usually called it, default prosody. The fact that focussed predicates integrate with their focussed arguments is just a consequence of the fact that within a larger focus, default prosody is assigned.

4.4.3 F-Projection Rules revisited

It was probably evident from the discussion in the previous section that integration, or the rules of default prosody that predict integration, covers the empirical ground of Selkirk's (1995b) Horizontal Focus Projection (clause (17b) above): A head may be F-marked without being accented, provided its internal argument is F-marked (which entails that it is accented).

The FOCUS CONTAINS ACCENT—generalization (18a) above—transparently follows from the Focus Realization Condition, (2a), as does the fact that *after* the (last) focus there will be no more accents (i.e. the juxtaposition of the Basic Focus Rule rule (16) above, but only for the post-focal part of an F-domain).

I have already remarked in chapters 2 and 3 above that generalization (18d) above, No ACCENTS OUTSIDE THE FOCUS, is too strong as it stands: it prohibits any background or "ornamental" accents, wrongly, as pointed out.

But what about No PHRASAL FOCUS WITHOUT F-MARKED HEAD—generalization (18b)—and No PROJECTION FROM ADJUNCTS OR EXTERNAL ARGUMENTS—generalization (18c)? We will now review arguments to the effect that these, too, are overly restrictive.

Starting with No PHRASAL FOCUS WITHOUT F-MARKED HEAD, we should ask if there are cases in which, for example, a VP is focussed, but the V itself is given. Candidates are given in examples (31) and (32) below.[14]

Whether the pitch accent on ⟨eating⟩ can be omitted (i.e. ⟨eating⟩ can integrate) or not is very hard to detect, especially since pre-nuclear PA in general may be omissible here. Yet it seems rather clear to me that it is marked to put a pitch accent on ⟨eating⟩, but none on ⟨vegetables⟩:

(ii) # . . . To the contrary, EAting vegetables is GOOD for you.

Example (ii) invokes an additional contrast ('but smoking them is another matter') which is not there if neither element, both, or just the argument are accented. This pattern wouldn't follow if all pre-nuclear pitch accents were generally optional, but it would if one had to realize either all or none of the pre-nuclear pitch accents, and integration were an option here.

[13] The argument that integration happens in the background was originally presented in (Büring, 2006: sec. 4.1), but the examples used there involved literal repetition, opening up to the possible criticism of "prosodic copying" (whatever that would be). Schwarzschild (1999: sec. 6.2.2) discusses related examples, but still concludes that F-marking is involved, albeit in this case governed by purely structural principles.

[14] Adapted slightly from Büring (2006).

(31)   Q: What did van Dyke do when you teamed up with Stewards?
        A: Van Dyke [teamed up with BROWN]$_F$.
        A': Van Dyke [SUED]$_F$.

(32)   a. What will Messina do if the call doesn't go through?
        A: Messina will [call them AGAIN]$_F$.
        A': Messina will [desPAIR]$_F$.

It should be clear why ⟨team up⟩ and ⟨call⟩ will count as given in these contexts. To make sure that we are nevertheless dealing with VP-focus, both examples include a question that asks for a VP, and can indeed be answered by a VP, including a different, non-given verb, as in the A' answers.

But if the verbs themselves are given, then by Selkirk's (1995b) interpretation rules, they cannot be F-marked (see the discussion in Section 3.2), and examples (31) and (32) are VP foci with F-less heads, in violation of clause (17b) (No PHRASAL FOCUS WITHOUT F-MARKED HEAD) (or they involve given verbs that are nevertheless F-marked, in violation of the F-interpretation rules).[15]

Schwarzschild (1999: 172) provides example (33) to the same effect; it uses contrastive focus, rather than answer focus.

(33)   (The rising of the tides depends upon the moon being full, and) [the MOON being full]$_F$ depends upon [the position$_F$ of the SUN$_F$]$_F$.

The contrast here is of the general form ⟨A depends on B, and B depends on C⟩, which can independently be shown to trigger focus on B and C in the second clause—even though at least B, and everything within it, is given at that point. So no matter where the accent in ⟨the moon being full⟩ falls (Schwarzschild's point was that it falls on the argument, i.e. we see integration here), it either falls on an F-less terminal, or one that is F-marked though given.

The novel examples in (34) conclude this argument with a case involving associated focus (see Chapter 10 above for details on association with focus).

(34)   (He is sure Sue married John after she killed Bill.—I think Sue was framed.)
        I also think Sue married STEVE.

⟨Also⟩ in the final sentence ASSOCIATES with the embedded VP as its focus (the speaker has two beliefs about Sue—she was framed, and she married Steve—not two beliefs about who Sue married). That means that within the focus, there is a given, and presumably deaccented, V, contrary to No PHRASAL FOCUS WITHOUT F-MARKED HEAD.[16]

---

[15] Note that this problem does not reduce to the aforementioned inadequacy of prohibiting ornamental accents. An accent on the verb is neither necessary nor sufficient to license VP-focus by Selkirk's (1995b) F-Projection rules. The issue is that the verb needs to be F-marked for the VP to be a legitimate focus, which would require an exception to the interpretation rules.

[16] Maybe the last clause in example (34) involves S-, rather than VP-, focus as the associate of ⟨also⟩. This would not affect the argument, though, since by the F-Projection Rule, S-focus, too, requires F-marking on the finite verb.

While examples (31) through (34) all arguably show instances of broad foci whose heads cannot be F-marked, they differ in what, if anything, seems to be F-marked, and hence "projecting the focus," instead. In examples (31) and (34), an F-mark is likely on a non-given argument (assuming that the ‹with›-phrase is an argument of ‹team up›), bypassing, as it were, the verbal head. In example (32), the only candidate for a focus exponent within the VP appears to be the non-given adverbial ‹again›, whereas in Schwarzschild's example (33) above, we have an accented argument again, but this time a given one. That is, apart from direct projection from F-marked arguments, the F-Projection rules apparently need to tolerate projection from F-marked adverbials/adjuncts, as well as from F-less elements.

On the other hand, it should be evident that all these cases conform to conditions (2a), (2b), and (2c) at the start of the chapter: Within the focus, the NPA falls on the last non-given element, or, if all elements are given, as in example (33), according to default prosody.

Apart from example (32), many more cases of what would appear to be F-projection from illegitimate F-exponents, that is violations of No PROJECTION FROM ADJUNCTS OR EXTERNAL ARGUMENTS are collected in Büring (2006), among them projection from attributive adjectives, unergative subjects, particles, determiners, and left conjuncts:[17]

(35) a. Ann: What did you buy Ben for Christmas?
          Clara: I got him a blue SHIRT.
          Ann: What did you get for Diane?
          Clara: I got her [a RED shirt]$_F$.

      b. (Jack said the American president drinks. What did Gilles say?)
         He/HE said [the FRENCH president drinks]$_F$.

(36) (Why did Helen buy bananas?—) [Because JOHN bought bananas]$_F$.

(37) (Bill has worn his anti-nuclear power shirt before. Why was he arrested this time?—) [Because he was wearing ONLY his anti-nuclear power shirt]$_F$.

(38) (Your competitor has lowered the prices on every other model. What do you plan to do to answer that?—) We will [lower the prices on ALL models]$_F$.

(39) (What will you do if Bill doesn't want to be hooked up with Mary?—) I'll [hook up JOHN and Mary]$_F$

The combined weight of these examples strongly argues against the kind of specific restrictions on F-patterns embodied in Selkirk's (1995b) and others' F-projection rules. There simply appear to be no structural restrictions on where within a focus an accent needs to be found. Rather, this follows from the interplay of givenness and default prosody alone.

---

[17] Example (35a) is from Delin and Zacharski (1994), (35b) from Schwarzschild (1999); (36)–(39) originally in Büring (2006).

Let me, in closing, speculate on why F-projection rules might have been widely accepted in the pertinent literature, despite the abundance of occasions to show their inadequacy. On the face of it, F-projection rules like the ones in (16) to (17b) provide a straightforward explanation for the infelicity of the responses in (40a) and (40b).

(40) (What did you do?—)
      a. #I imMEDiately called a waiter
      b. #I bought a NEW book.

After all, if focus could project from an adverb or attributive adjective, what is to stop the focus in (40a) and (40b) from projecting to VP, the expected answer focus?

But note that on Selkirk's (1995b) proposal, there are actually *two* things wrong with these answers: First, that VP could not be F-marked, due to the restrictions on F-Projection. And second that ‹called a waiter› and ‹book›, respectively, are not accented, and hence cannot be F-marked, despite the fact that they are not given. That (41) is as odd an answer to the question in (40) as (40a) and (40b) shows that lack of accenting on a non-given phrase *within* a focus is already enough to render a reply inappropriate.

(41)   #I BOUGHT a book.

Note that the accent on V in example (41) could project a VP focus according to clause (17a) (focus projects from V-head to VP), yet is clearly inappropriate *unless*, as Selkirk points out, ‹a book› is at the same time given.

So, what the examples in this section have shown is that the requirement to apply default prosody on non-given elements within a broad focus alone will still successfully block cases like examples (40a) and (40b) above, while at the same time allowing for the various kinds of counter-examples to stricter F-projection rules.

This concludes our main discussion of F-projection rules. The following sub-section attempts to clarify a (minor) conceptual point regularly referenced in the literature regarding F-projection rules. The final subsection, 4.4.5, introduces Reinhart's (1995) competition-based proposal regarding F-projection, but may be skipped without loss of coherence.

4.4.4 Bottom up and top down

Occasionally, reference is made to the "bottom-up" nature of Selkirk's proposal, so called because the algorithm starts from accents on terminal nodes and then regulates—via the licensing clauses (17a) and (17b), which can also be thought of as rules for copying the F-marker onto higher nodes—which non-terminal nodes may be F-marked by virtue of those accents. This contrasts with algorithms such as Krifka (1984), von Stechow and Uhmann (1986), or Jacobs (1988), which start with a focus marked (FOCus in Selkirk's terms) non-terminal and then regulate which terminals must or may receive an accent, and which therefore would be dubbed "top-down." The implication appears to be that a bottom-up algorithm can model what a hearer does upon encountering a certain accent pattern, while a top-down algorithm models what a speaker does when figuring out how to pronounce a given structure in the context they are in, and that neither can do the other.

Like Krifka (1984: 10) I suspect very strongly, though, that this distinction is superficial and in fact without empirical consequences. The following "direction-less" well-formedness rules define the exact same class of possible F-pattern–accent-pattern pairings that Selkirk's algorithm does, without any "directional" implications:

(42^{CON})   a. ANY NODE MAY BE F-MARKED
   b. If there is an F-mark on a projection, there must be an F-mark on its head.
   c. If a head is F-marked, it must be accented, unless it has an F-marked complement.
   d. Only F-marked terminals may bear accents.

It is likewise possible to formulate a "top-down" algorithm that constructs all possible F- and accent patterns for a selected FOCus:

(43^{CON})   a. If the FOCus is a projection, F-mark its head.
   b. If a head is F-marked, accent it and/or F-mark its complement.
   c. Freely F-mark non-complements if dominated by the FOCus.

Like Selkirk's (1995b) original rules, neither of these rule systems is deterministic. For one thing, there is built-in optionality in how to realize an F-pattern whenever it contains an F-marked head with an F-marked internal argument (as most obvious in the formulation in clause (43b)), in which case accenting the head is optional. For another, knowing the focus (FOCus) alone, one cannot predict the entire F-pattern; one also needs to know which elements within the focus are given (recall Figure 4.10; this, of course, holds equally for the top-down approaches in the literature quoted at the start of this subsection).

And of course, the same accent pattern can be associated with various F-patterns, simply because vertical focus projection is, naturally, optional. This is simply the contraposition of the old observation that different foci may be realized by the same accenting.

4.4.5 Competition-based analyses of focus projection

Reinhart (2006, Part III) and, following her, Szendrői (2000, 2001, 2004), propose a system in which the set of possible foci for a given NPA placement is determined via REFERENCE SET COMPUTATION. To illustrate the gist of that proposal, I will try to cast it in present terms as much as possible. Also, at least for starters, I will ignore any effects of givenness and assume focussing only.

First, in keeping with the by now well-known generalization that focus contains the NPA, Reinhart defines the FOCUS SET of a phrase marker with a given NPA as the set of all constituents that dominate the terminal bearing the NPA. Of course, that alone is not sufficient; for example, the root node is in the focus set of *any* NPA placement. To calculate the set of foci that could *actually* be paired with a given NPA placement, one has to remove all those foci that are also in the focus sets of "more neutral" pronunciations. A simple illustration is given in (44):

(44)	Focus Set	Poss. Foci
a. Kim is building a DESK.	$\{DP_{Obj}, VP, S\}$	$\{DP_{Obj}, VP, S\}$
b. Kim is BUILDING a desk	$\{V, VP, S\}$	$\{V\}$
c. KIM is building a desk	$\{DP_{Subj}, S\}$	$\{DP_{Subj}\}$

The set of possible foci for (44b) is the relative complement of (44a)'s focus set with respect to (44b)'s focus set; put differently, all those elements in (44b)'s focus set that are not also in (44a)'s focus set ((44a) being the default, most neutral NPA placement). The set of possible foci for (44c) is the relative complement of (44a)'s focus set with respect to (44c)'s focus set, and so forth.

Note that the set of possible foci for the default NPA placement, (44a), is the same as its focus set. This is necessarily the case: For any NPA placement, those foci in the focus set which could also be achieved by a more default NPA placement are excluded as actual possible foci. Since there is no more default placement than the default placement, the focus set and the set of possible foci for the default NPA placement are one and the same.

Perhaps surprisingly, this method of pairing NPA placements with possible foci turns out to be equivalent to the one we used previously, which entails corollary (45).

(45)　CorOLLARY ON THE RELATION BETWEEN NPA PLACEMENT AND FOCUS:
NPA on a terminal X is compatible with focus on any constituent Y which
a. contains X, and
b. within which X would get the final/nuclear PA by default accenting.

To see why this should be so, note that if X is the default NPA/final PA position in Y, the focus set of Y is the set of all those foci realized by the most neutral NPA placement within Y, which means no other NPA placement within Y could possibly "remove" foci from it. This is the case in (44a), the neutral NPA placement within S, for which the set of possible foci is the same as its focus set. But it is also the case in example (46) (Reinhart 2006: 157ff). ‹Hat› is the last default accent position within the subject DP, therefore example (46) represents the most neutral-like NPA placement possible that has the NPA within the subject; accordingly, the NPA on ‹hat› may signal focus on every node within the subject that dominates ‹hat› (including the DP itself).

(46)　[_DP_The man with the HAT] read the book

Finally, in a case like (47) (Szendrői, 2001; Reinhart, 2006: 160f), ‹man› is the last default accent only within the N ‹man› itself, making it a necessarily narrow focus.

(47)   [$_{DP}$ The MAN with the hat] read the book

In the Reinhart/Szendrői system, we need to subtract from the focus set of example (47), {N_{man}, $NP_{man \backslash what}$, DP_{subj}, S}, the focus set of example (46) above (which is more default-like because it has default accenting within DP, though not within S), {NP_{hat}, DP_{thehat}, PP, $\overline{N}_{man \backslash what}$, DP_{Subj}, S}, as well as that of the default sentential NPA placement ‹the man with the hat read a BOOK›, {NP_{book}, DP_{obj}, VP, S}, leaving us with only {N_{man}} as the set of possible foci for example (47).[18]

Givenness deaccenting in this system is not based on any reference set computation, but works very much as in all other systems discussed so far: A given ("anaphoric" in Reinhart's terms) constituent is automatically labeled "weak" in the default metrical tree. Thus in the classic example (48), ‹books› is unaccented because it is given/anaphoric, so the *default* NPA is on ‹read›, no marked accenting is involved.

(48)   (Has John read *Slaughterhouse Five*?—) John doesn't READ books.

Since example (48) then does not involve marked accenting, the set of its possible foci equals its focus set: {V, VP, S}. Generally, the results will, again, be exactly the same as in the other systems.

There is one crucial difference, though. According to the competition based system, a structure like example (48) could result from two different information structural configurations: Focus on V, VP, or S with ‹books› being given, or narrow focus on ‹read› with ‹books› not being given. All the other systems reviewed so far do not allow the second option;[19] there, the background of an F-domain *has* to be given. We will return to this issue in Section 5.4.3. At this point we merely note that *if* deaccented material is given (anaphoric in the terminology of Reinhart, 2006), the predictions regarding possible foci based on an NPA are the same in the competition-based system as in those discussed before.

Given the convergence in predictions, is the competition based model just a notational variant, or, at any rate, just a (more or less) empirically equivalent competitor to accounts such as Selkirk's (1995b) or Schwarzschild's (1999)? I think it would be, if the computation of reference sets, reduction of focus sets to actually possible foci, etc. were to be conceptualized as parts of the linguistic or grammatical computation proper. But another, perhaps more interesting, way of looking at it, and I am inclined to think the one envisaged by Reinhart, is to see them as communicative strategies *outside* of the linguistic computation proper. Concretely, all that *grammar* delivers is a pairing of accent patterns with focus

---

[18] The actual metric for what is a more default NPA placement in Reinhart (2006) and Szendrői (2001) is based on an operation called (MAIN) STRESS SHIFT on metrical trees, which "swaps" the default weak–strong relation on metrical sisters. The more sister pairs in a metrical tree do not show the default weak–strong relation, the more marked/less default the tree is (more precisely, MT1 is more marked than MT2 if the set of sister pairs with a non-default weak–strong relation in MT1 is a proper super-set of the set of such sister pairs in MT2).

[19] At least as long as we assume that the F-domain variable in Rooth (1992b) is necessarily valued by a contextually salient meaning; see the discussion in Chapter 3, Section 3.1.

sets. So grammatically speaking, even, say, a transitive sentence with the NPA on the subject is ambiguous between subject-focus and S-focus. It is only through considerations of communicative strategies, effort code and similar aspects that conversationalists arrive at further restrictions on what focussings could actually have been intended.

Once this perspective is adopted, the road is clear for further arguments in favor of the underlying theory, of which Reinhart seems to provide at least two kinds. First, if the task of grammar is reduced to focus set computation, this may allow for a simpler and more elegant grammatical formalism than theories that assign the entire task of pairing accent patterns with possible focussings to the core grammatical system. In particular, Reinhart seems to envisage a system that does away with F-marking completely (see especially 2006: 137f).

Second, (Reinhart, 1995: Ch. 5, Sect. 2), points out predictions for focus-related performance measures in children, and compares them tentatively to some re-sults reported in the experimental literature. Note how this move hinges on the idea that the reference set computation is a behaviorally real aspect of language comprehension, which, due to its computational complexity, children below a certain age have difficulty performing. Accordingly, such children are predicted to perform around chance level when trying to identify a pragmatic focus based on a marked NPA placement, a prediction that Reinhart claims to be consistent with the existing findings. Though such behavioral effects *may* be taken to be predictions of theories about grammar (though it is not usually considered fair practice to submit hypothesized operations of "the grammar" to empirical testing in terms of their processing load and time), it seems to me they are more naturally expected on the view that those aspects of comprehension that involve reference set computation are outside of grammar.

Reinhart furthermore argues that the proposal she advances makes such predic-tions for children's comprehension, but not for their production. In production, the speaker must merely check whether their intended focus is in the default intonation's focus set. If not, they will apply stress shift, which they can do following a simple recipe: check all weak–strong assignments on the path from the focus to the root (or the focus domain) and adjust them as necessary to ensure that the focus is dominated by strong nodes only.[20] No comparison of different shifted and unshifted structures is necessary.

The hearer, on the other hand, has to figure out the possible foci (in order to eventually get to *the* intended focus among them by pragmatic reasoning) from the given accent pattern, plus their knowledge of what is contextually given. They have to calculate the focus set of the accent pattern they heard, plus that of the neutral intonation (taking into consideration anaphoric deaccenting at this point already), compare them, and, if they are different, also calculate the focus sets of all accent patterns that are marked, but less so than the one they heard, so as to eventually arrive at the focus set of the actual utterance. And this is where children display difficulties.

---

[20] Reinhart does not, as far as I found, specify this procedure in detail, but it seems to me that this is what is implied by her discussion; see esp. page 250.

This separation of production and comprehension, again, seems a natural line of reasoning on the assumption that we are dealing with pragmatic strategies of disambiguation, rather than aspects of the grammatical system itself.

On the other hand, an argument can presumably be made that these advantages of Reinhart's proposal are indeed independent of virtually all technical aspects of her implementation. Suppose, for concreteness, that violations of Default Prosody (conceived of again as a set of constraints or ideals), in particular STRESS-XP do not, as previously assumed, add to the computation of grammaticality, but merely to an extraneous index of markedness, which then in turn figures in pragmatic reasoning about a speaker's intended focussing (in the same way knowledge about the extent of the grammatically legitimate, but "costly" application of stress shift figures in the computation of actual possible foci in Reinhart's proposal). Such a system could probably be rigged so as to allow for the same kind of conceptual and behavioral arguments we reviewed just above, while maintaining all of the technical aspects of previous proposals.

4.5 Lesser studied focus configuration

In this section I will discuss some cases of focussing which usually do not take center stage in the literature, and point to works that do discuss them.

4.5.1 Discontinuous foci and multiple foci

There are cases in which the expected focus is expressed by a non-constituent:

(49) Where's Kim's homework?/What happened to Kim's homework?
    a. The DOG ate it.
    b. Someone STOLE it.
    c. You're SITTING on it.

In the context of the question 'What happened to Kim's homework?', we would presumably expect property denoting foci, as in (50):

(50) a. it [was eaten by the DOG]$_F$
    b. it [was STOLen]$_F$
    c. it [is right underNEATH you]$_F$

But what to do with cases like those in (49a) to (49c), in which the property in question is not expressed by a syntactic constituent? Such cases are rarely discussed in the literature, so we will only offer a few speculative remarks here.

One way to analyze the cases in (49) is using multiple F-markers:

(51) a. [the dog]$_F$ [ate]$_F$ it
    b. [someone]$_F$ [stole]$_F$ it.
    c. [you]$_F$ [are sitting]$_F$ [on]$_F$ it

The way Alternative Semantics is implemented compositionally (see Chapter 3), this would yield the correct result. Illustrating with structure (51a), the F-alternatives will be (52).

(52) $x \, R$ my homework

Given that R stands for any relation and x for any individual, this is indeed equivalent to (53), where Q ranges over properties in general.

(53)   my homework Q

It is important that on this type of analysis, the two F-markers in structure (51a) above do not signal what we would pre-theoretically call a sentence with multiple foci. This may be disadvantageous, if we want to account for the contrast between (54a) and (54b):

(54)   a. (What happened to your homework?) The DOG ate it.
       b. (First my little brother spilled juice on my homework, and then) the DOG ATE it.

It seems that a pattern with two noticeable accents is quite natural in (54b), but less so in (54a). Example (54b) intuitively is a double focus, ‹dog› contrasting with my little brother, and ‹ate› with 'spill juice on'. But the formal representation of the second sentences in (54a/b) would be the same, structure (51a) above.

   An alternative way of analyzing seemingly discontinuous foci is as sentential foci with givenness deaccenting.[21] This is illustrated in (55), where G marks a constituent as given.

(55)   [the dog ate [it/my homework]$_G$]$_F$

At first glance, such a representation does not qualify as an answer focus; its F-alternatives is the set of all sentence meanings, rather than something like 'my homework Q'. But recall from Section 3.1.5 that focus conditions like Question–Answer Congruence do not themselves prevent overfocussing; in fact we were forced to add a general ban on overfocussing, for example condition (4) from Section 4.1, repeated here.

(56^{CON})   MAXIMIZE BACKGROUND
           In any tree, maximize the number of (non-synonymous) constituents that are in the background.

Is (55) a violation of (56) then? That depends on whether there is a different focussing of ‹the dog ate Kim's homework› that meets the F-condition in the context of the question in (49). We know that there is no structure with a *single* F that

___

[21] This resembles the analysis given in Vallduví (1990) for Catalan.

would (that was our problem to begin with). So if we assumed that condition (56) above only compares structures in which focus is marked by *one* F-marker, (55) is legitimate, despite the appearance of overfocussing. Generally, on such an analysis, any seemingly discontinuous focus would be analyzed as a single focus on the smallest constituent containing all "would-be foci."[22]

Likewise, if we count G-marked constituents as "in the background" in the sense of condition (56), as we did in definition (5) in Section 4.1, example (55) will have as many constituents in the background as structure (50a). (In general $[_\beta \ldots \alpha_G \ldots]_F$ will be equivalent to $[\alpha \, [_\beta \ldots]_F]_{\text{F-domain}}$ in terms of MAXIMIZE BACKGROUND.)

We should also consider the possibility that phrase structure is more flexible than traditional syntactic theories assume. Some syntactic theories, in particular Categorial Grammars (e.g. Steedman, 1994, 2000a, 2000b, 2007, where this property is explicitly related to intonational phrasing and focus) assume that in fact a subject and a transitive verb can form a constituent to the exclusion of the object. If so, ‹The dog ate›, ‹someone stole›, and ‹you're sitting on› may be syntactic constituents and properly F-marked in the same way as simple VP focus examples. From a focus-theoretic perspective, this appears to be the most elegant solution, since it simply makes the initial problem disappear.

It is not clear, however, that the same strategy could be applied to cases in which the putative focus is not even linearly continuous, such as (57).

(57) (What happened to your homework?—) I forgot it on the BUS.

Since ‹I forgot___on the bus› is not a constituent, something else needs to be assumed at least for such cases.

A final possibility may be to ensure continuity of focus at some covert level of syntactic representation like Logical Form. For the cases of discontinuous focus, this would involve GIVEN MOVEMENT, that is, the removal of the non-focal parts from the focus, yielding structures as in (58):

(58) a. $[\text{the dog ate } t_{it}]_F$ it
     b. $[\text{someone stole } t_{it}]_F$ it
     c. $[\text{you're sitting on } t_{it}]_F$ it
     d. $[\text{Kim forgot } t_{it} \text{ on the bus}]_F$ it

Various languages have been argued to have overt given movement, at least for non-pronominal given elements, for example Catalan (López, 2009; Vallduví, 1990), Italian, mostly via right-dislocation, and Czech via leftward scrambling (Kučerová, 2007).

---

[22] By what has been said so far, givenness within a focus does not have any influence on the F-alternatives (nor does it on any formal theory of Alternative Semantics I am aware of). Thus the F-alternatives of (56) are arbitrary propositions, not just propositions like 'my homework Q'. This, like syntactic overfocussing, is not technically a problem since the F-alternatives still include every answer to the question 'what happened to your homework?' But it may be felt to a narrow the appeal of such a solution.

4.5.2 Multiple foci

We already touched upon the issue of multiple foci in Section 4.5.1. Generally, Alternative Semantics "cumulates" foci, that is, each focus locally introduces its F-alternatives, which will ultimately be combined into one set of F-alternatives at the lowest node dominating the foci. Generally, this is what we want. In (59) below for example, the focus semantic value of the answer is "x will talk about y," of which the first utterance's meaning is an element, as required by the usual F-conditions.

(59) (Will Kim talk about snakes tomorrow?—) No, MILLER$_F$ will talk about [POlar bears]$_F$

But Alternative Semantics also has the consequence that structures (60a), (60b) and (60c) all have the same F-alternatives from VP on upwards, and structures (60a) and (60c) even have identical F-alternatives throughout (recall that $Rx \equiv Q$).

(60) a.   b.

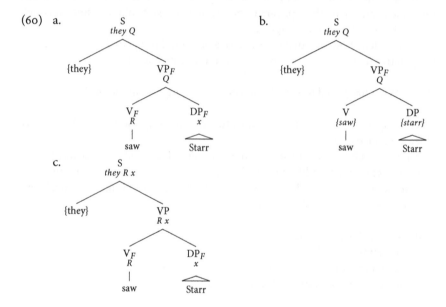

In particular, by any measure of AVOIDF or MAXIMIZE BACKGROUND, structure (60a) should never be allowed, since it is inevitably "undercut" by the other two.[23]

It is tempting to think that the choice between structure (60c), on the one hand, and one of structure (60b) or structure (60a), on the other, corresponds to the distinction between *one broad focus* on VP, and *two narrow foci* on V and DP. As Kehler (2005) observes, these do seem to coexist and have slightly different

---

[23] The differences and choice between (60c) and (60b) will depend on the details of the F-condition, as well as on whether a structure like (60b) is allowed in the first place; (60c), however, is possible even under the most restrictive systems of F-marking, Rochemont (1986) and Selkirk (1995b).

pragmatic meanings, illustrated by the intuitive contrast between (61) (originally from Schwarzschild, 1999) and (62).

(61)   John cited Mary, but ...
       a.   ... he DISSED SUE.
       b. ?... he dissed SUE.

(62)   Fred read the menu and then ...
       a.   ... he ordered a HAMburger.
       b. #... he ORdered a HAMburger.

There is at least a preference to accent both V and the object ‹Sue› in (61a), but comparable double accenting seems distinctly odd in (62b). Let us, for concreteness, represent these choices as in structure (63a) (double focus, parallel to (60c)) and structure (63b) (broad focus, parallel to (60b)).

(63)   a. he [dissed]$_F$ [Sue]$_F$ b. he [ordered a hamburger]$_F$

The problem, as pointed out above, is that the semantics of F-alternatives obliterates the difference between those two structures. Schwarzschild (1997a), discussing similar structures, points out that the F-markers in (63), as well as the top F-marker in structure (60a) (i.e. all FOCi in the sense of Selkirk, 1995b) mark the nodes at which the choice of one particular F-alternative "matters": 'diss' vs 'quote', 'Sue' vs 'Mary', 'read the menu' vs 'order a hamburger.' The subordinate F-markers in structure (60a), on the other hand, are truly just newness markers; even if formally we replace them by a F-alternative, it does not really matter which one (since the chosen alternative will be "overwritten" at the immediately dominating VP node by a VP-type alternative).

This captures the intuitions well enough, but again lacks a counterpart in the formal machinery. For example, why not use the F-alternatives 'read' for ‹ordered› and 'the menu' for ‹a hamburger›, and use a double-F structure as in example (62b)? Both are F-alternatives in the technical sense.

To be sure, this is not to deny the intuition behind the two markings. For example, it seems intuitive to say that 'diss' and 'cite' *contrast* in the context of 'Sue' and 'Mary' (and *vice versa*), whereas 'read' and 'order' do not in the context of 'the menu' or 'a hamburger' (e.g. one may say that he dissed Sue, but not Mary, and that he dissed, rather than cited Sue, but hardly that he ordered the hamburger, rather than the menu, or ordered, rather than read, the hamburger; see Büring, 2012b, for an attempt at a formal analysis along these lines).

But this requires a notion of 'contrast' or 'alternative' that is more restrictive (and context sensitive) than identity of semantic type. Furthermore, it is not obvious how to extend this kind of reasoning to an elaboration focus, including answer focus, where no one particular alternative is contextually salient, or for that matter, obviously identifiable even after the utterance. It seems that for the time being, while we might have a representational device for distinguishing adjacent multiple foci from broad foci, a formal semantic to cash in on that difference is still wanting.

4.5.3 Focus in questions

We have concentrated on focus in declarative sentences so far, but focus ostensibly also occurs in other sentence types, in particular in questions, as in (64).

(64)   a. When did Jones call BARNES?
       b. When did Jones CALL Barnes?
       c. When did JONES call Barnes?
       d. WHEN did Jones call Barnes?

It seems reasonable to think that the givenness requirements in the questions in (64a)–(64d) are the same as in parallel declarative sentences: that Jones called Barnes (at some point), that someone called Barnes, that Jones did something to Barnes, etc. It is important not to conflate these with the EXISTENCE IMPLICATURE found with constituent questions: all of (64) implicate that Jones called Barnes at some point, that is, that there is a true answer among the elements in the question meaning.[24] But only in example (64d) does that also need to be contextually salient for the question to be felicitous.

The givenness requirements, as usual, need not be met by shared beliefs, merely by something salient.

(65)   (We assume Jones didn't meet with Barnes. But) when did Jones CALL Barnes?

Note also that (65) neither presupposes nor evokes another *question* of the form 'When did Jones *R* Barnes?', though of course questions *may*—arguably through their Existential Closure—provide the givenness antecedent.

(66)   (A: When did you call Barnes?—B: I didn't, my secretary did.)
       A: Alright, when did your SECRETARY call Barnes?

In certain cases the two (or more) questions may in fact be parts of a STRATEGY to answer a common SUPER-QUESTION, as in (67).

(67)   (We need to find out who got the information first.) When did JONES get the call? When did BARNES get the call? ...

Still there is no reason to assume that the licensing of the focussings in the two questions in (67) involves anything other than contrasting 'Jones got the call' with 'Barnes got the call'.

It is also instructive that ‹wh›-phrases themselves may be narrowly focussed, as in example (64d). In such cases, too, the antecedent may be another question, or a declarative sentence:

---

[24] I say 'implicate' because, as is well known, this is cancelable: each of (64) can be answered by ‹She didn't›.

(68)   a. (Why did Jones call Barnes? And) WHEN did she call her?
       b. (Jones called Barnes. But) WHY did she call her?

Crucially, though, clause-initial ⟨wh⟩-phrases are not narrowly focussed in general. In fact, ⟨wh⟩-pronouns like ⟨who, what, where…⟩ do not usually bear phrasal stress, just like their non-⟨wh⟩ counterparts ⟨someone, something,…⟩, whereas lexical ⟨wh⟩-phrases like ⟨which singer⟩, etc. appear to display the same prosody (phrasal stress, secondary PA) as full non-⟨wh⟩ phrases in parallel positions.[25] So it seems fair to conclude, as for example Ladd (2008: 244) does, that 'there is nothing…to suggest that the distinction between statements and questions is relevant to sentence stress' (and thus: accent placement).[26]

However, as Ladd also points out, this statement holds for English and most other Germanic languages. We know of an equally sizeable number of languages, though, in which questions have a fixed NPA position, apparently regardless of focus, which is usually on the finite verb for yes-/no-questions, and frequently on the ⟨wh⟩-phrase in constituent questions (Ladd, 2008: 224ff mentions Slavic languages, particularly Russian as well as Romanian and Greek as examples for the former, and Turkish, Bengali, and Romanian for the latter). Though much more empirical work is required here, it appears that this group also includes languages in which, in declarative sentences, accenting is, at least partly, responsive to focussing and/or givenness, such as Russian and other Slavic languages.

In the same vein it is striking to observe that *if* a language has a designated topological position for (narrow) foci, it will also have its ⟨wh⟩-phrases in that position. This holds for the vast majority of African languages, but also for Hungarian (Brody, 1990; É. Kiss, 1987), Armenian (Comrie, 1984), Basque (Saltarelli, 1988), Finnish (Vilkuna, 1989), and Georgian (Harris, 1982). The examples in (69) are from Hausa; note that not only are both ⟨wàà⟩, 'who', in (69b) and ⟨yaarònkà⟩, 'your boy', in (69c) preposed (as opposed to the neutral SVO order), these sentences also usa a special RELATIVE FORM of the verb, which is not found in neutral sentences.[27]

(69)   a. Mun   ga   yaaròn   a   kàasuwaa. (neutral)   (Hausa)
          1PL.PERF see boy   at market
          'We saw the boy at the market.'

       b. Wàà mukà   ganii à   kàasuwaa?
          who 1PL.REL.PERF see   at market
          'Who did you see at the market?'

---

[25] See Jacobs (1991) and Bäuerle (1979) for early investigations of the semantics/pragmatics of focussing in questions.

[26] At least for constituent questions, Ladd seems to find this fact surprising, stating "logic seems to suggest that the ⟨wh⟩-word is the focus of the question, and yet, in English at least, the ⟨wh⟩-word does not normally bear the most prominent accent." My point here is nearly the opposite: pragmatics would suggest that ⟨wh⟩-phrases should *not* be focussed (so English is the expected case); the surprising cases are those in which they appear to be, to be discussed momentarily.

[27] Data from Hartmann (2006: ex.5).

c. Yaarònkà (nee) mukà   ganii à kààsuwaa.
boy.your FM   1PL.REL.PERF see   at market
'We saw your BOY at the market.'

That is to say, syntactically, there is an undeniable cross-linguistic affinity between ⟨wh⟩-phrases and narrow foci.[28] None of the semantic/pragmatic theories we have reviewed here (and none that I am aware of in general) cashes in on that affinity, and, from a pragmatic point of view, for good reasons. ⟨Wh⟩-pronouns in general are semantically "light weight"; contrasting or focussing them makes as little sense as contrasting or focussing an indefinite pronoun. In fact, the ∃Clo of ⟨wh⟩-pronouns, like that of indefinite pronouns (to which, not incidentally, they are identical in many languages) is arguably trivially given in virtually any context ('there exists a thing, there exists a person...'). Also, as we discussed above, the "background" of a ⟨wh⟩-phrase (essentially the existential claim that there is a true literal answer) need not be contextually salient at all, unlike the background of regular foci.

Similarly, to say that focussing resembles questioning because it makes salient a set of alternatives rests, I would argue, on a problematic equivocation: A question *denotes* a set of propositions and maybe makes it salient (though, again, it is not clear what exactly it means for a *set* of propositions to be salient). But focussing does *not* "make alternatives salient" or "evoke them" so much as relate, anaphorically, back to them. So the alleged resemblance is, I would argue, just a consequence of loose talk, mixing up the formal semantics of focus—assign an unrestricted set of alternatives to an expression—with its pragmatic function—anaphorically relating back to one of the alternatives, or their ∃F-Clo.

So to say that, for example, in Hausa, ⟨wh⟩-phrases occur in a focus position *because* they *are* focussed displays, I think, an element of circularity. Neither pragmatically nor semantically does there seem to be anything that the relation between a focus, its background, and its discourse context has in common with the relation between a ⟨wh⟩-phrase, its syntactic scope, and its discourse context. If there is a parallel pragmatic/semantic affinity between foci and ⟨wh⟩-elements (which certainly would make for a good explanation of the syntactic affinity), it has not, to my knowledge, been brought to the fore yet.

---

[28] Apart from Hausa, this seems fairly well established for Tangale, Western Bade, Hindi/Urdu, Turkish, and many other languages.

5

More on the semantics of focus and givenness

This chapter has three main parts. Sections 5.1 and 5.2 compare the discourse-related characterizations of focussing and givenness utilized in the previous chapters to possible alternative characterizations, and provide arguments in favor of the former. Readers who are already sold on the discourse-related meanings for focus and givenness may postpone reading these sections until they need to prepare for a discussion with someone who isn't.

Section 5.3 reviews some recent arguments in favor of strengthening the pragmatic F-relation to include something like True Contrast. It thereby directly extends the discussion in Chapter 3 and points to what I perceive to be genuinely open problems for focus semantics at this time.

Section 5.4 continues by discussing some other, slightly more technical facets of Alternative Semantics and points to a number of open ends, both technically and empirically.

5.1 Givenness

In Section 2.1, I characterized being given as being hyponymous or synonymous with a salient meaning in the context (made salient, for example, by uttering a word with that meaning). Let us now examine this characterization in more detail.

5.1.1 Salient, not familiar

For referring expressions, givenness and FAMILIARITY (in the sense of the familiarity theory of definiteness, e.g. Heim, 1982) boil down to the same effect: If the referent has been introduced by a previous expression, it will be familiar and salient, as in example (1).

(1)   (The Browns introduced me to their neighbors.) I really LIKED
$$\left\{ \begin{array}{c} \text{them} \\ \text{their neighbors} \\ \text{these guys} \end{array} \right\}.$$

However, as already noted in Section 2.1, and illustrated again by examples (2) and (3a), givenness is neither restricted to referring expressions (and thus cannot be

Intonation and Meaning. First edition. Daniel Büring.
© Daniel Büring 2016. First published 2016 by Oxford University Press.

reduced to familiarity), nor does it coincide with it, even for (putatively) referring expressions.

(2)   (Don't jump!)—But I WANT to jump.

(3)   a. (Why do you study Italian?) I'm MARried to an Italian.
       b. (On this house, the roof is missing, whereas on that house), they have already FINished the roof.

5.1.2 Salient, not previously mentioned

By assumption, uttering an expression makes its meaning (at least temporarily) salient. Could we not have defined givenness in terms of (recent) mentioning directly, thereby avoiding the somewhat elusive notion of saliency of meaning? We could, but at the cost of excluding certain other examples. Meanings can become salient in ways other than mentioning. If during my visit to your house a dog walks into the room, I could comment as in (4), where the noun ‹dog› is (and has to be) unaccented:

(4)   a. I thought you HATED dogs.
       b. The building management doesn't ALLOW dogs.

Again, 'dog' counts as salient (and hence ‹dog› is given), although it hasn't been mentioned.[1]

5.1.3 Salient, not presupposed

In many cases a proposition is salient, because it has previously been asserted, as in example (5). Since an assertion of S routinely results in S's content being added to the common beliefs of the discourse participants, givenness of a clause in this case coincides with its content being presupposed (note the factive verb ‹know› in (5)).

(5)   (The Fishers were in town. They were disappointed you hadn't invited them.—) I didn't KNOW they were in town.

However, a clause may be deaccented, even if its content is clearly not presupposed, as in (6).

(6)   (What if the Johnsons show up?—) I DOUBT they'll show up.

---

[1] Many indexical expressions, including all first and second person pronouns, as well as things like ‹here, today, now› etc. strongly tend to be unaccented. If this is an effect of givenness, it suggests that speaker, addressee, speech time and place, etc. are always salient, and hence given, even if they haven't been explicitly mentioned before.

It is possible, however, that these elements are unaccented for other reasons, for example because they are functional, rather than lexical expressions. In that case, no argument against the importance of mentioning is forthcoming from these cases.

And in fact, if we take occurrence under factive verbs as indicative of being presupposed, it is equally easy to find examples where the content of a clause is presupposed, but the clause is accented regularly.

(7)   (Sorry we're late, there was a terrible blizzard on the way here.—) Don't worry, I'm just glad you didn't run out of GAS.

(8)   (The Burtletts don't want to see you.—) Do they know my mother is a SEnator?

It is not difficult to see what is happening in these examples: Something may well be shared knowledge among the participants without therefore being salient: The guests' very presence in example (7) is a very good indidication that they did not run out of gas, yet running out of gas is not salient at that point in the conversation, nor is the meaning of ‹gas›, for that matter. Similarly, beliefs that are shared as a matter of world knowledge (that the speaker's mother is a senator in example (8)), completely unrelated to the discourse situation, do not have to be salient.[2]

   In short, the saliency of a proposition does not entail that that proposition is a shared belief, nor *vice versa*; this is a first, good reason to keep presupposition and givenness apart.

   A second reason is that any lexical category, and all manner of syntactic constituents, may undergo givenness deaccenting, whereas only declarative clauses have the kind of denotation—a proposition—that can be presupposed. Therefore, we couldn't even coherently say that (the meaning of) deaccented ‹jump› or ‹dogs› in examples (2) and (4) is presupposed.

   Of course, we could take the existential closure of those meanings instead, which *is* a proposition. But this will bring back the previously mentioned problems with a vengeance: a proposition may be mutually believed but not salient, as well as salient but not believed. In each case, it is saliency that appears to be crucial for deaccenting and, by assumption, givenness.

---

[2] Kallulli (2006, 2009, 2010) observes that non-factive predicates like English ‹believe› (and its German and Albanian counterparts ‹glauben› and ‹besoj›) when occurring with a pleonastic object ‹it›/‹es›, or a doubling clitic ‹e›, respectively, take on a factive meaning, and typically—and unlike their 'plain' counterparts—occur with deaccented complement clauses:

(i)   a. I beLIEVED, that JOHN LEFT.
       b. I beLIEVE it, that John left.

(ii)   a. Besova   se   Beni SHKOL.   'I believe that Ben left.'
          believe-1SG that   B.   left
       b. E beSOva   se   Beni shkol.
          it believe-1SG that   B.   left

It seems plausible to think that in this case, factivity and givenness do go hand in hand, perhaps due to the anaphoric or topical nature of the pronoun-doubling construction. However, *lexically* factive verbs like ‹know›, or emotive-factives like ‹regret› or ‹be happy›, do not show this behavior, as examples like examples (7) and (8) in the main text clearly show, so Kallulli's (2006: 216) claim that "[i]n order to get a factive reading, the (factive) verb must carry nuclear pitch accent" is likely to only be accurate for the non-factives.

For example, intuitively, it is not a mutual belief in example (2) that someone jumped (someone jumping is salient after the first sentence in (2), but it is not assumed *that* someone jumped—yet). So ⟨jump⟩ should not count as 'presupposed', and hence should not be given. Alternatively, if we insist that its is generally shared knowledge that someone (somewere, at some point) jumped, then that *would* predict that the verb ⟨jump⟩ could be deaccented; but so should (virtually) any other content word, and completely regardless of context, making the presupposition requirement all but vacuous.

Note, finally, that just as a presupposition theory of clausal givenness would wrongly predict any complement clause to factives to be deaccented, an ∃Clo presupposition theory of sub-clausal givenness would wrongly predict every definite DP to be deaccented, a case in point being definites referring to inferable discourse referents (i.e. referents which have not been introduced themselves, but whose existence and uniqueness can be established in relation to another, already established referent), such as ⟨the neck⟩ in example (9):

(9)   Baxter sold this guitar, because he couldn't adjust the NECK properly.

According to standard wisdom, ⟨the neck⟩ in (9) is definite because speaker and addressee know that a guitar has a neck, so that in this context the presupposition of the definite DP—that there is a unique neck—is met.

Yet, ⟨(the) neck⟩ must remain accented in (9), despite its ∃Clo being a mutual public belief; this appears to hold in general for such definites, like ⟨bus—the driver⟩, ⟨story—the beginning⟩, ⟨band—the drummer⟩, etc. Like factivity, definiteness and givenness often go together, for obvious reasons, but they are not completely correlated. The reason, I submit, is because different discourse factors underly them: mutual belief *versus* saliency.

Deaccented elements are also sometimes described as denoting "old information" or being "uninformative." Presumably, this is intended to mean the same as "presupposed," and it seems to me an unfortunate choice of terminology, for the same reasons: To be informative is a property of propositions, but not of words or single phrases; and even where an expression does denote a proposition (or a proposition can be derived from its meaning, for example by ∃Clo), the correlation between that proposition being (non-)informative and the expression being given is, as we have seen, imperfect in both directions: That the Johnsons show up *would* be informative in the context of example (6), but the *proposition* is already salient, whereas that the guest did not run out of gas in example (7) is *not* informative, but new in the sense of not salient. Therefore, apart from the slightly oxymoronic flavor of "old information," "informative," like its pseudo-antonym "presupposed" seems simply inaccurate as a decription of the pragmatics of deaccenting.

In closing, let me point out that the idea that *focussing* has an existential presupposition, while clearly related to the "given=presupposed" idea discussed in this section (and, I believe, equally mistaken, see Section 5.2.1), is also different in crucial respects: Just now, we contemplated the idea that the *ordinary* meaning of a declarative clause or the existential closure of a smaller constituent is presupposed, whereas a focal presupposition theory would assume that the *focus closure* of a clause has to be presupposed. We will return to these issues in Sections 5.4.2 and 5.4.3.

5.2 Focussing

5.2.1 No truth conditions for focussing

It is sometimes suggested that F-domains introduce an existential presupposition, for example ‹KIM took Harry's book› would presuppose that someone took Harry's book.[3] This idea has been refuted in various ways. First, the sentence can answer the questions in (10), neither of which implies (and hence licenses a presupposition to the effect) that someone took Harry's book.

(10)   a. Who, if anyone, took Harry's book?
       b. Did anyone take Harry's book?

Second, as Jackendoff (1972) already observes, a sentence like (11) would be falsely predicted to presuppose that someone took Harry's book (and hence be contradictory).

(11)   NOBody took Harry's book.

Third, there is clear difference between (12a), which—due to the cleft construction—does presuppose that someone took Harry's book, and (12b)—plain free focus—which does not (see Rooth, 1999: for an extended version of this argument).

(12)   a. Was it KIM who took Harry's book?
       b. Did KIM take Harry's book?

Similarly, it is sometimes suggested that free focus entails exhaustiveness of the answer. But again, there is notable difference between plain focus, (13a), and a cleft, (13b), with only the latter truly entailing exhaustivity (and hence creating a contradiction; see again Rooth, 1999).

(13)   a. (Who attended the meeting?) KIM attended the meeting. Maybe Jo did too.
       b. (Who attended the meeting?) It was KIM who attended the meeting. # Maybe Jo did, too.

Data like these show that existence and exhaustivity may be conversational implicatures of focus, but are not parts of truth conditional meaning.

---

[3] E.g. Geurts and van der Sandt (2004); see also the replies in the same issue.

5.2.2 Focus-mentalism

An intuitive characterization of focus meaning would be that focus marks what the speaker intends to highlight, or emphasize, or regards as most important, or most informative (e.g. Miller, 2006). This is an example of what I will call a MENTALIST theory of focus meaning. While such a statement jibes well with our intuitions, and in many case is probably true, too, there is a rather severe problem with using such a mentalist characterization as the meaning of focus: the attitudes it ascribes to speakers are difficult if not impossible to verify independently and systematically. But this is what a theory must allow in order to be testable.

A variant of this problem regards characterizations like "focus presupposes the existence of a closed set of relevant alternatives":[4] if we read this extensionally, then—since we can always find a number of alternatives (i.e. real world entities) for any expression, which exist—this would be trivially met. Understood intensionally, this may mean that discourse participants have to have a number of specific alternatives in mind; but this, again, would be immensely difficult to track down.

More formal-looking characterizations like "focus creates/presupposes an open formula and then provides a unique value for the variable in that formula,"[5] or "focus instructs the hearer to open a new file card and write something on it,"[6] too, are haunted by basically the same problem: They presuppose the reality of a certain kind of representation in the participants' minds (assuming in this case that formulas would not be supposed to be objects in the real world), to which independent access would be needed in order to make the claim falsifiable.

For this reason, Chapter 2 followed most formal work on the interpretation of free focus and took *felicity in a discourse* to be the main data to be accounted for: Which focussing of a given sentence is felicitous as an answer to a particular question, or in response to a particular statement, or as a narrative continuation of a previous text or sentence. The meaning of focus under that view consists of discourse appropriateness conditions. Call these DISCOURSE-RELATED approaches to focus meaning.

(One may argue that on such a view, focus doesn't have *meaning* so much as merely a pragmatic function; this is a valid point, though I will continue to use the term "meaning" in what follows.)

At the same time, many if not most discourse-related approaches will—implicitly or explicitly—assume that, for example, Question–Answer Congruence, does not really constrain the relation between a focussed declarative sentence and a preceding interrogative sentence, but between a focussed declarative sentence and some sort of *context representation construed on the basis of the question* (and maybe additional context as well). This allows the analyst to extend the analysis to cases in which, say, a pertinent question is assumed to be on participants' minds, but never explicitly uttered:

---

[4] Vallduví and Vilkuna (1998: 83).

[5] E.g. López, 2009: 34ff, Vallduví and Vilkuna, 1998: 83ff, a.m.o.

[6] E.g. Erteschik-Shir (1997: 4), Vallduví (1990); see Hendriks (2002) and Dekker and Hendriks (1996) for essentially this criticism.

(14)   [A and B find the door to the classroom locked. Says A:] JONES has keys to
        this room.

Here we can assume that the question of who has keys to the room is on A and
B's minds, even though it hasn't been uttered. A plausible analysis assumes that
focus in A's answer is licensed by Question–Answer Congruence, where "question"
is understood as the QUESTION UNDER DISCUSSION, QUD, in a discourse model
(e.g. Roberts, 1996). Overt question–answer sequences would then be the special
case of a QUD set by an actual question utterance.

So even discourse-related approaches to focus are mentalist in this sense. But
in contradistinction to approaches that talk about "importance," "highlighting," or
open formulae in speakers' minds, discourse-related theories show a direct way
in which to access the pertinent mental discourse representation independently:
when there is an explicit context (e.g. an interrogative utterance), it has a defined
effect on context representation (e.g. setting the QUD); and all relevant aspects of
context representation *can* at least be manipulated by particular utterances such as
explicit questions, statements, etc.

That is, the theory, while (at least in part) ultimately about mental objects, can
be applied and tested purely as a theory about linguistic data.

Most of what I have said in this subsection applies *mutatis mutandis* to the
"inner workings" of focus theories. Characterizing, for example, Rooth's (1985,
1992b) theory as asserting that focus "invokes," "activates," or "raises" alternatives
(in participants' minds) involves what we may call the PSYCHOLOGIZING of focus
semantics.[7]

While it is perfectly possible that mental "activation," etc. of alternative meanings
takes place, at least in some instances, this is not part of any formal theory of
focus I am aware of, nor has it been shown in any psycholinguistic experiments.
Alternative Semantics uses F-alternatives as part of its technical apparatus, but does
not generally claim that F-alternatives become somehow active or salient in the
mind of the person producing or comprehending focus (any more than phonology
claims that the use of [m] "invokes" nasality). In fact, stating things that way not
only does nothing to illuminate the semantics of focus, it also potentially obscures
a discriminating view on cases in which it seems plausible that alternatives *are
made* salient, for example out-of-the-blue uses of contrastive accent patterns, as
opposed to cases in which they *are already salient*, or when used in corrections,
as opposed to cases in which it is not particularly plausible to suppose that anyone
thinks of specific alternatives, such as question–answer pairs or elaboration focus
in general.

5.3 Contrast

We now switch from justifying the basic assumptions we have made so far, to
highlighting some of their limitations. So far we have assumed, with Rooth (1992b)

---

[7] A simple web search will find dozens examples of this.

and Schwarzschild (1999), a rather weak F-condition, which invoked no notion of contrast other than "be/entail an F-alternative of" (Section 3.1.3).

In Section 2.2.3 of Chapter 2 we briefly touched upon the idea of a stronger F-relation, called exclusive contrastive focus there. For concreteness, let us symbolize this condition as in (15).

(15^{CON})   CONTRAST $\notin$:

 is well-formed if the existential closure of the contextually supplied value of C entails the existential focus closure of δ *and the value of C contrasts with the ordinary denotation of δ.*

The crux, as Rooth (1992b) points out, is that the meaning of the word "contrast" in the definition of CONTRAST in (15) is itself in need of explication; existing attempts in the literature have either fallen short of giving an explicit definition, or provided one which is too narrow to capture all the kinds of cases Rooth intended to be subsumed under his proposal. Moreover, Rooth claims, there is no need for such a stronger notion, since the weakest notion—GIVENNess or Rooth's original $\subseteq$ / $\in$ condition—seems to capture all the cases we need to.

This last point, however, has been challenged by Wagner (2006, 2012b), who makes a rather convincing point for using a stronger F-relation, roughly along the lines of definition (15) above. I will now review the arguments to that effect.

5.3.1 Deaccenting requires local contrast

Consider example (16) from Wagner (2006, 2012b):

(16)   (Mary's uncle, who produces high-end convertibles, is coming to her wedding. I wonder what he brought as a present.)
    a. He brought a [CHEAP convertible].
    b. #He brought a [RED convertible]
    c. He brought a red conVERtible.

In the context of (16), (16a), with a deaccented noun, is an acceptable answer, as expected: 'high-end convertible(s)' is an F-alternative to ‹cheap$_F$ convertible›. By the same token, however, (16b) would be expected to be fine, too, since the F-alternatives of ‹RED$_F$ convertible› are the same as those of ‹CHEAP$_F$ convertible›. But deaccenting here seems odd. The natural response in the context provided in (16) in this case is (16c).

Büring (2012b) reports similar judgments for a number of sentences informally surveyed with about a dozen speakers, using a questionnaire. In the following two examples, at least half of the speakers preferred deaccenting the noun and accenting the adjective alone:

(17)   a.   Mary plays many instruments, her favorite being the Spanish guitar. So I asked if she would play on my birthday.—She agreed to play some electric guitar.

b. Steve is a Steinway dealer (the finest pianos in the world). He's also my daughter's godfather. I wonder what she'll get from him for her 5th birthday.—He'll probably get her a cheap piano.

On the other hand, less than a third of the speakers accepted a deaccented noun in the following examples, and nearly everyone preferred a regular accent pattern with accent on both A and N, the latter nuclear:

(18)   a. Sarah is well known for her delicious chocolate cakes. So when we had a potluck dinner, guess what she signed up for bringing?—She signed up to bring a small cake.

   b. Kate has this amazing record collection, which is the apple of her eye. But when she was strapped for cash, guess what she sold?—She sold some classical records.

The contrast between (17) and (18), in particular the lack of deaccenting in (18) raises the same question as Wagner's (16b)/(16c): Why can the noun, whose meaning is clearly salient in these discourses, not be deaccented as given?

5.3.2 Wagner (2012b)

Intuitively, what goes wrong in example (16b) above is that deaccenting the noun (inappropriately) suggests that 'red convertible' truly contrasts (again in an intuitive, non-technical sense) with 'high-end convertible,' which it does not. 'Cheap convertible,' on the other hand, does contrasts with 'high-end convertible,' so deaccenting the N in (16a) is felicitous. This is precisely what Wagner (2006) argues, proposing the constraint in (19):

(19^{CON})   An expression and its alternative(s) must contrast.

Setting technical questions aside until Section 5.3.3, let us call an F-alternative that is contrastive in the sense intended here a TRUE ALTERNATIVE (to the focussed element, or its denotation), and the relation between such alternatives TRUE CONTRAST.

According to (19), whether or not something is a true alternative is decided at the level of the focussed element itself; "high end" is a true alternative of ‹cheap$_F$›, but not of ‹red$_F$›. But the informal discussion in Wagner (2006) already makes it clear that we should rather think of this in the larger syntactic context.[8] Accordingly, the formulation of Contrast contemplated in (15) assumes that whether or not an F-alternative counts as a true alternative is decided *at the level of the F-domain*.

Let us look at the focus structure for the examples in (16), representative for all examples in (16)–(18), starting with the deaccenting case (16a) in Figure 5.1(i), and the non-deaccenting case in Figure 5.1(ii).

Figure 5.1(i) uses stacked F-domains (see Section 4.2), one for the answer-focus on the direct object, one for the local accent-shift within NP (alternatively,

---

[8] Wagner's example is: 'used' is a true alternative to 'new' in the context of 'car,' but not 'boy friend.'

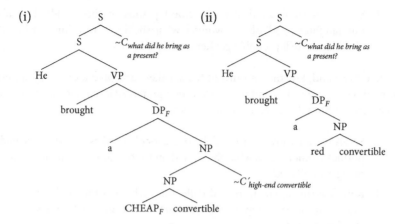

FIGURE 5.1   ‹He bought a Y convertible›, with (i), and without (ii) subdomains/deaccenting.

‹convertible› could be G-marked, along the lines of Section 4.1, in Figure 5.1(i), but the stacked F-domain analysis will be more useful for our expositional purposes). As done occasionally before, the contextually supplied values for the focus variables are indicated in the structure to help comprehension. Assuming that 'high-end convertible' and 'cheap convertible' are true alternatives, the structure in Figure 5.1(i) meets contrast and maximizes on backgrounded constituents by having ‹convertible› backgrounded.[9]

The analogous embedded-F-domain structure would not be possible with ‹red› in place of ‹cheap›, since 'red convertible' and 'cheap convertible' are *not* true alternatives. Rather, the structure in Figure 5.1(ii) must be chosen, in which the only true alternatives needs to be at the root level. On the downside, ‹convertible›

---

[9] One could contemplate having structure (i), rather than that in Figure 5.1(ii), which has ‹convertible› be its own focus domain, without a focus in it:

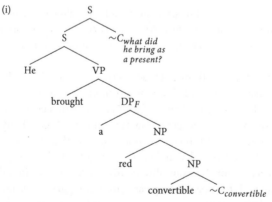

This would make no difference to the intonation (since only Fs are relevant to that). I assume, however, that the NP ‹convertible› does not count as *within* a focus domain if it is identical to the focus domain, and hence does not count as an anaphoric constituent, so that the structure in Figure 5.1(ii) is the official representation of (16c).

in Figure 5.1(ii) is not backgrounded, which is why the structure in Figure 5.1(i) is preferable in the case of ‹cheap›.

This captures the essence of the proposal in Wagner (2012b) (though adapted to our present representational conventions[10]). The basic argument (the contrast between examples (16a) and (16c)), as well as Wagner's intuitive explanation for it (the lack of true contrast between 'red' and 'high-end') seem solid and convincing, and have informed virtually all subsequent work on focus semantics. Arguably, the "anything of the same semantic category is an alternative" view that was virtually universally accepted in the wake of Rooth (1985) is incapable of capturing this contrast, and therefore in need of refinement.

On the other hand, an appropriate reformulation of the F-condition is not easily found, and all current proposals I am aware of raise serious questions of their own. We will turn to these matters momentarily.

Before moving on, however, it is worth pointing out that Wagner's (2012b) proposal to handle these cases—like our adaptation here—crucially relies on *not* having stacked F-markers. That is to say, it is not compatible with Schwarzschild's (1999) idea that every constituent must be GIVEN. To see why, consider the status of the adjective ‹red› in example (16c) (Figure 5.1(ii)): ‹red› is not given (no previous mentioning or other invocation of redness), but it is also not F-marked (for that it would have to be truly contrastive), merely part of an F-marked constituent. Effectively, checking the F-condition only for entire F-domains allows for a third status, other than focussed and backgrounded, namely "part of a focus." (The present adaption of) Wagner's proposal makes use of this by requiring foci to be truly contrastive, and backgrounds to be given, whereas elements within a focus may be either; the F-condition does simply not apply to them, because they are not an "active" part of any F-domain. No such category can exist in a system like Schwarzschild (1999) in which the GIVENness/F-Condition is applied to every constituent in the tree, nor one like Selkirk's (1995b), where every non-F-marked constituent needs to be given.

5.3.3 On the notion of contrast

We have not addressed the question of how to define true contrast, and as I said at the beginning of this section, no entirely satisfactory semantic or pragmatic definition has been forthcoming. Wagner (2006, 2012b) assumes that semantic exclusion is pertinent, and that it is to be looked at at a very local level: a cheap convertible is not a high-end convertible, so 'cheap' and 'high-end' are true alternatives; but a red convertible may be high-end or cheap, so 'high-end' and 'red' are not true alternatives.

---

[10] Wagner's own implementation differs from the present one in various other ways, most notably in that grammar marks G(ivenness), rather than F(ocus). The central condition on the interpretation of G-marking is paraphrased in (i):

(i)   A structure of the form ‹[A B_G]› is well-formed only if there is a (contrasting) alternative A* to A
      s.t. 'A* B' is salient.

Against this view, Katzir (2013) presents examples like (20).[11]

(20)   The people in this club are very particular about the cars they collect. Mary, for example, collects high-end convertibles.
   a. And John collects CHEAP convertibles.
   b. And John collects RED convertibles.

Embedded under ⟨collects⟩, both ⟨cheap⟩ and ⟨red⟩ license deaccenting of ⟨convertibles⟩ in the context of ⟨high-end convertibles⟩. The question is why (20b) is possible. Obviously, if 'red' categorically failed to be a true alternative to 'high-end'—as condition (19) above implies—(20b) should be as impossible as Wagner's original ⟨red convertible⟩ example (16b) above, regardless of the embedding context.

Katzir (2013) argues that the difference can be seen at the clausal level: while bringing a red convertible and bringing a high-end convertible are not true alternatives, collecting red convertibles and collecting high-end convertibles are. To get a sense of this, compare the rather natural example (21a) to the somewhat odd (21b).

(21)   a.   He collects red convertibles, not high-end convertibles.
       b.   #He brought a red convertible, not a high-end convertible.

Collecting red convertibles does not *exclude* collecting high-end convertibles, so Wagner's (2006, 2012b) characterization of true contrast as semantic incompatibility would still exclude (21a). But, following Katzir's lead, '*only* collecting red convertibles' *would* exclude 'collecting high-end convertibles'; whereas, even strengthened in this way, 'only bringing a red convertible' still does not exclude 'bringing a high-end convertible.'

Katzir (2013) further formalizes this intuition using the notion of INNOCENT EXCLUSION (a concept he adopts from Fox, 2007). Roughly speaking, an alternative A to a sentence S can be innocently excluded if "S and not A" does not entail any alternative that S alone doesn't entail already. For example, if we say ⟨John brought a red_F convertible⟩, 'blue' is innocently excludable: 'John brought a red convertible and didn't bring a blue convertible' doesn't entail any alternative of the form 'John brought a x convertible' (except for 'John brought a red/a non-blue convertible,' which already follows from 'John brought a red convertible').[12]

However, 'John brought a red convertible and didn't bring an expensive convertible' entails that John brought a non-expensive convertible, which does not follow from him bringing a red convertible. So 'expensive' is not innocently excludable here.[13]

---

[11] His (20), with ⟨high-end⟩ where Katzir has ⟨expensive⟩, to guarantee minmal contrast with Wagner's example.

[12] To be sure, it is not claimed that e.g. 'John brought a red convertible and did not bring a blue convertible' will *actually* be implied by this sentence (after all, he may have brought two convertibles). Rather this is just a step in determining whether 'blue' and 'red' are true alternatives in this context, which, in a manner of speaking, does not itself leave any marks on the interpretation of the sentence.

[13] The formal definition of innocently excludable is:

In examples with intensional verbs like Katzir's (20b), however, we can inno-cently exclude 'expensive' on the basis of ⟨red$_F$⟩: 'John collects red convertibles and does not collect cheap convertibles' does not entail any additional collection habits on the part of John, in particular, it does not follow that he collects expensive convertibles. Therefore, 'cheap'—as well as 'expensive'—are innocently excludable in (20b), and focussing ⟨red⟩ is legitimate.

To be sure, 'John collects red convertibles and does not collect cheap convert-ibles' does entail something not entailed by 'John collects red convertibles,' namely that he does not collect cheap convertibles. But not collecting cheap convertibles is not an alternative to collecting *red* convertibles; *not* collecting something *never* entails collecting something else, so all of the F-alternatives in such cases are innocently excludable.

To make the following discussion more precise, I will give a formal implemen-tation of this idea in the form of condition (22). Innocent exclusion as defined in Katzir (2013) presupposes that the alternatives in question are all propositional. To still allow our condition to apply to any constituent, condition (22) appeals again to the ∃Clo of the alternatives (recall that the ∃Clo(p) $=$ p if p is already a proposition).

(22^{CON}) CONTRAST $\overset{\mathit{f}}{\sim}$:

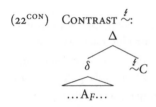

is well-formed if the existential closure of the contextually supplied value of C

    a. entails ∃F-Clo of δ and

    b. *is innocently excludably given* ∃Clo($[\![\,\delta\,]\!]_o$) *and* $\{∃Clo(\alpha) \mid \alpha \in [\![\,\delta\,]\!]_{\mathcal{F}}\}$.

What we now need to convince ourselves of is that examples (16a) and (20b) above meet condition (22), whereas example (16b) does not; structures for these are given in Figures 5.2(i), 5.2(iii), and 5.2(ii), respectively.[14]

The ∃Clo of C in Figure 5.2(i) is 'high-end convertibles exist'; from 'cheap convertibles exist but high-end convertibles don't' we can conclude that there are no high-end convertibles, but that, again, is not (the ∃Clo of) an alternative of ⟨CHEAP$_F$ convertible⟩, so Figure 5.2(i) is predicted to be fine. 'Red convertibles exist, but high-end convertibles do not' entails that non-high-end (red) convertibles exist, which *is* a F-alternative and which does not follow from 'red convertibles exist', so Figure 5.2(ii) is predicted to be unacceptable. Finally 'someone collects red convertibles, but no-one collects high-end convertibles' does not entail anything of

---

(i)   Given an assertion of proposition p with alternatives A, the set of innocently excludable proposi-tions is $\bigcap\{B \mid B$ is a maximal subset of A s.t. $\{\neg p \mid p \in B\} \cup \{p\}$ is consistent$\}$.

                                                                         (cf. Katzir, 2013)

In words: if you start combining p with as many negated alternatives from A as consistently possible, then iff every way of doing so includes $\neg a$, a is innocently excludable.

14 The F-domain in Figure 5.2(iii) excludes the subject, but the result would be the same if the $\overset{\mathit{f}}{\sim} C$ were adjoined to TP instead.

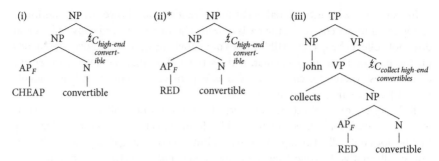

FIGURE 5.2   Structures that innocent exclusion should be applied to.

the form 'someone collects x convertibles' that 'someone collects red convertibles' doesn't already, so Figure 5.2(iii) is predicted to be fine, too.[15]

So this implementation of the Wagner/Katzir system correctly derives the intended effects via the representations in Figures 5.1 and 5.2.[16]

5.3.4 Where and when is focus contrastive?

Anaphoric deaccenting revisited: Wagner's (2012b) cases of noun "re-accenting" in A+N combinations are quite striking and justify the introduction of a notion like true contrast, as formally implemented in the definition of $\overset{\text{\textit{t}}}{\sim}$. But what determines when a focus is to be interpreted via $\sim$, and when it is to be interpreted via the stronger $\overset{\text{\textit{t}}}{\sim}$? Wagner (2012b) explores the most interesting answer to that question, namely that *all* foci are to be interpreted as truly contrastive (by $\overset{\text{\textit{t}}}{\sim}$ in our terms). But if that is the case, why has the universally truly contrastive nature of focus not been realized in other instances? How, in particular, could givenness-deaccenting ("anaphoric deaccenting"), as in example (23) have been explicitly argued *not* to be contrastive (and therefore be different from focussing)?

(23)   (Smith walked in. A minute later,) a police officer arRESted Smith.

---

[15] In particular, it does not follow that someone collects red cheap convertibles, because the collector of red convertibles need not care about the price of their items at all.

[16] Katzir (2013: sec. 2.3) actually applies his F-condition to the entire clause ‹He brought her a red/cheap convertible›, rather than having the DP be a subordinate F-domain; the resulting predictions are the same. However, the entire clause couldn't be the F-domain for the focus on ‹cheap› in example (16a)/Figure 5.1(i) according to present assumptions, because of the first clause of the F-Condition: There is no salient meaning of the form 'he brought a z convertible'. (Katzir, 2013 calls the proposition 'Mary's uncle brought a high-end convertible' an "accommodated expectation," which he seems to assume is sufficient to antecede the focus; we have, however, been assuming that saliency is a more restrictive notion than "expectation"; furthermore, it is unclear in what sense e.g. in Katzir's original example (20) the assertion that Mary collects high-end convertibles should lead to an *expectation* that John, too, collects high-end convertibles.)

According to Wagner (2012b), the first crucial step in addressing this question is to realize that so-called givenness deaccenting typically happens to immediate constituents of the clause; more precisely, it may occur to those and only those (sub-)constituents of a clause that can be scoped to the clausal level at Logical Form. All the examples that show the stronger true contrast requirement have—Wagner (2012b) argues—the element that would be deaccented inside an island, such as a complex DP.[17]

Thus the first step is to realize that structure (24a) is a possible Logical Form, but structure (24b) is not, due to the boldfaced complex NP/DP.

(24)   a.   [a police officer arRESted *t*] Smith
       b.   *[John brought [$_{DP}$a RED *t*]] convertible

The bracketed clause (24a) is then assumed to be the focus projected by the accent on the transitive V. This alone, however, does not yield the right result, at least if we apply condition (22) to (24a), as in Figure 5.3.

'Smith walked in' is one of S's F-alternatives, 'Smith Q'; but from 'Smith was arrested and Smith didn't walk in', we can conclude other properties (=F-alternatives) that Smith has, for example that he stayed outside, which do not follow from 'Smith was arrested.' This informal diagnosis is confirmed if we apply the formal definition of innocent exclusion: 'Smith walked in' is not innocently excludable given that Smith was arrested, and the F-alternative set 'Smith Q.' This confirms the naive intuition that 'walking into the store' and 'being arrested by a police officer' are no more truly contrastive than 'red' and 'cheap.'

Wagner's (2012b) second crucial step, therefore, is to apply a different definition of true contrast to clausal (propositional) F-domains than to all other cases, including that of A+N. According to the propositional definition of true contrast, 'Smith walked in' can be innocently excluded in example (23) as long as 'Smith

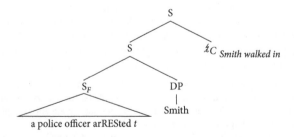

FIGURE 5.3   Applying the true contrast operator after DP raising.

<hr>

[17] I will not attempt to assess the empirical accuracy of Wagner's classification, because in the end, as we will see, the syntactic difference underlying the classification has very little to do with explaining the contrast.

(Wagner, 2012b: 138ff) presents a number of arguments to argue the correctness of his generalization, of which a huge class—the ones involving coordination—seem based on empirically inconclusive data.

was arrested by a police officer and nothing else happened/is the case' entails that Smith did *not* walk into the store. This is not just true for this case, but for any property P, except those where 'P(Smith)' is an entailment of 'a police officer arrested Smith.'[18] Non-clausal constituents, including A+N combinations like ‹red convertible›, on the other hand, follow a different rule in Wagner (2012b): they may contrast with any target A*+N if "everything is an AN" entails "there is no A*N." This works for the standard cases: 'everything is a cheap convertible' entails 'there is no high-end convertible,' but 'everything is a red convertible' does not entail that. Therefore 'cheap convertible' but not 'red convertible' is a true alternative to 'high-end convertible.'[19]

Note that if, instead, we applied Wagner's (2012b) *propositional* condition to the A+N cases, there, too, virtually anything would go: 'everything is a convertible that is red and has no other property' (has no property among the F-alternatives other than those that follow from being red) entails 'nothing is a blue convertible,' but also 'nothing is an expensive convertible,' and *vice versa*. So if 'cheap/expensive/blue/red' are all among the F-alternatives to begin with, any pairing of these is predicted to be truly contrastive. Put differently, Wagner's Contrast Requirement for propositional F-domains, unlike that for non-propositional cases, is, intuitively, not at all contrastive. There are practically no cases it excludes.

In sum, Wagner (2012b) proposes a classificatory diagnostic for when true contrast (in the Katzir, or non-propositional Wagner sense) is required for deaccenting—only for things that cannot move to a clausal level at Logical Form. But crucially then, two very different F-conditions ($\sim$ and $\overset{f}{\sim}$ in present terms), are applied to the two configurations. There is, as far as I can see, nothing about

---

[18] The definitions in Wagner (2012b) are not entirely coherent, but the above is almost certainly what is intended, as is evident from the discussion. Wagner's definition of the exhaustivity operator, his (47), contains an unbound symbol C, which is likely intended to refer to the F-alternatives of the focus to be interpreted. In the definition of his true contrast requirement for propositional constituents—his (48a)—a (likewise unbound) symbol Δ occurs, which should likely refer to the (or a) F-alternatives of the *F-domian*. For concreteness, I assume the intended definition to be equivalent to (i) (where $\oplus$ stands for the standard semantic composition operation applied to meaning in the domains of b and f):

(i) a. $[\![\text{LEA(C)}]\!] = \lambda b.\lambda f.\exists a \in [\![C]\!][\exists FA[FA = \{f' \mid b \oplus f' \in [\![C]\!]\} \,\& \, Exh(b)(f)(FA) \subseteq \neg a]] : b \oplus f$
     b. $Exh(b)(f)(FA) \equiv \lambda w.\forall f' \in FA[[b \oplus f'](w) = 1 \rightarrow [b \oplus f] \subseteq [b \oplus f']]$

The details of what exactly would *not* be innocently excludable remain unclear, since Exh as defined does not apply in the intended way to e.g. generalized quantifiers; but one way or another it will be a rather small class; consistent with that Wagner (2012b) does not contain any examples of sentential F-domains that are excluded by the condition proposed there.

[19] Curiously, this definition also renders 'cheap convertible' and '(cheap) bicycle' truly contrastive (if everything is a cheap convertible, then there are no bicycles); evidently, there must be additional conditions on what may be a contrasting antecedent.

The condition plainly fails in many other cases, among them (i).

(i) No one who KNOWS Kim disLIKES Kim.

'Everyone knows Kim' does not entail that no one dislikes Kim, so this should not be a case of true contrast. Of course, the background in (i) is a direct object, and hence moveable; but I do not see how any permitted form of raising either occurrence of ‹Kim› would produce a form to which the propositional rule could successfully apply.

the syntactic environments which define the two classes from which the difference in F-conditions follows. The association "propositional/moveable $\rightarrow \sim$, non-propositional/non-moveable $\rightarrow \overset{f}{\sim}$" has to be stipulated. This holds regardless of whether $\overset{f}{\sim}$ is spelled out as in Wagner's work (which, however, wrongly rules out cases like Katzir (2013: (20)) or as in Kazir's.

Answer-focus revisited: Apart from standard cases of anaphoric deaccenting, Contrast as defined in (22) also runs into problems with plain answer focus.

(25) (Who arrested Smith?—) JONES arrested Smith.

Intuitively, 'who (arrested Smith)' and 'Jones (arrested Smith)' are not (truly) contrastive. Likewise, formally, the ∃Clo of the question is 'someone arrested Smith' (see Section 3.5.2), but 'Jones arrested Smith and no one arrested Smith' is contradictory, so 'someone arrested Smith' cannot be innocently excludable. This problem applies generally to cases of what we called ELABORATION FOCUS, including examples (26) and (27).[20]

(26) (Someone arrested Smith.—Yeah/Maybe) JONES arrested Smith.

(27) (Shall we bring some wine?—) Yes, let's bring some FRENCH wine.

A tempting response to this problem is to claim that the answer in such cases is indeed truly contrastive, only it does not contrast with the question, but with other potential answers. This line of agument is made explicit, for example, in Wagner (2012b):

> The context [in example (25); DB] makes available a set of propositions of the form ‹x arrested Smith› ... [T]he stress shift can be explained in the same way as we would explain it if the context included the statement ‹Sally arrested Smith›. (Wagner, 2012b: sec. 1.2.6)

Schematically, the argument goes like this:

(28) a question Q denotes the set of its possible answers
      an utterance of any S makes S's denotation salient ('available')
      _____
   so: an utterance of Q makes salient each of its possible answers

Now, note first that, if the same line of argument is to apply to examples (26) and (27), then we have to assume that either these denote sets of propositions, too ('that Sandy arrested Smith', 'that Charles arrested Smith', ...; 'that we bring French wine', 'that we bring German wine', ...), or they otherwise "make available" the corresponding questions, which in turn make available all their possible answers.[21]

---

[20] Example (27) is from Wagner (2012b: sec. 2.4).

[21] This line of argument is taken explicitly for example (27) in Wagner (2012b: 17ff).

Second, and more importantly, there is a problematic equivocation in (28). The conclusion should be that a question makes salient *the set of its answers*, not each element of that set. And for a set of propositions to be salient/"available" is not the same as for the propositions in that set to be salient/"available." For example, an utterance of ⟨*Sally arrested Smith*⟩ makes available the proposition that Sally arrested Smith, and hence allows for deaccenting of a clause expressing that proposition, as one would expect, cf. (29). But the same is not even remotely possible in the other two contexts, (30a) and (31a).

(29) (Sally arrested Smith.—) I REAlly DOUBT that Sally arrested Smith.

(30) (Someone arrested Smith.—)
    a. #I REAlly DOUBT that Sally arrested Smith.
    b. I REAlly doubt that SALLy arrested Smith.

(31) (Who arrested Smith.—)
    a. #I REAlly DOUBT that Sally arrested Smith.
    b. I REAlly doubt that SALLy arrested Smith.

Indeed, as the (b) answers show, ⟨*Who/someone arrested Smith*⟩ does allow deaccenting of ⟨*arrested Smith*⟩, which we take to mean that it makes salient the property of arresting Smith, but not the proposition that Sally arrested Smith.

This exact pattern follows immediately if we assume, as we did before, that utterances in general make salient their ∃Clo, which is 'that Sally arrested Smith' for example (29), and 'someone arrested Smith' for examples (30) and (31), and nothing more (or alternatively: that making a set of propositions salient has the same effect as making their grand union salient).

I take this to mean that the idea that elaboration focus, including answer-focus, is a "covert" type of contrastive focus is not a fruitful one. At the very least, "making a proposition available" in the sense of the quote from Wagner (2012b) would have to be a rather different, weaker, notion from "making a proposition salient" in the sense used throughout this book so far. The situation that would—hypothetically—result is schematized in (32):

           must have an 'available', truly contrastive F-antecedent

(32)   SANdy$_F$ arrested Smith

              must have a *salient* antecedent

(Certainly this is not Wagner's (2012b) position, which set out to argue that givenness deaccenting and answer-focus are all the same phenomenon.)

In sum, imposing a true contrast requirement on focussing, even if properly worked out, works well in A+N cases like Wagner's original examples and Katzir's extended data set, but it wrongly predicts that *all* instances of deaccenting are actually—and contrary to all traditional belief—truly contrastive in the same way. There is as yet no uniform condition that could be successfully applied to all cases.

5.4 Open ends in Alternative Semantics

5.4.1 Focus on semantic functions

Up to now, when we paraphrase the F-alternatives to a VP like structure (33), we use formulations like 'do something to Kim' or 'stand in some relation to Kim'.

(33)   kiss$_F$ Kim

These characterizations, intuitively adequate though they may be, are not borne out by our formal semantics, however. In fact, shockingly, the formalism predicts that the F-alternatives of (33) are the same as those of (34) (with or without stacked F-markers on V and DP).

(34)   [kiss Kim]$_F$

How so? The alternative set of (34) is the set of all properties. A transitive verb like ‹kiss› alone, on the other hand, denotes a function from individuals to properties (also called a RELATION), and so its alternative set is the set of all relations. Now— and this is where intuition and formalism part ways—for any property P, we can define a relation, call it R^P which maps Kim, or every individual at all, for that matter, onto P (we could write this function as $\lambda x \in E.P$).

A *fortiori*, then, for any property $P \in [\![$ [kiss Kim]$_F$ $]\!]_{\mathcal{F}}$, there is R^P (which, being a relation, of course is in $[\![$ kiss$_F$ $]\!]_{\mathcal{F}}$, too) s.t. $R^P(\text{Kim}) = P$, and consequently $[\![$ [kiss Kim]$_F$ $]\!]_{\mathcal{F}} = [\![$ kiss$_F$ Kim $]\!]_{\mathcal{F}}$.[22]

So any arbitrary property, say, to be drinking beer, is an element of $[\![$ kiss$_F$ Kim $]\!]_{\mathcal{F}}$, because we can find, among the F-alternatives to ‹kiss$_F$›, functions which map Kim to the property of drinking beer. Generally, the following holds:

(35)   Fact: If $\left[\!\!\left[\begin{array}{c} A \\ \overset{\frown}{} \\ b_F \quad c \end{array} \right]\!\!\right]_{\mathcal{F}}$ is derived by function application, with ‹b› the functor,

i.e. $[\![$ A $]\!]_O = [\![$ b $]\!]_O([\![$ c $]\!]_O)$, then $[\![$ A $]\!]_{\mathcal{F}} = [\![$ A$_F$ $]\!]_{\mathcal{F}}$

One suspects that this is not a good thing, and indeed we can find cases in which this creates very wrong predictions. For example, (36-i) is predicted to be a good reply on Ali's part to convey what intuitively only (36-ii) can: That Captain Hook told Ali, not Ms Summerset, where the treasure is buried.

(36)   Sam: Captain Hook told Ms Summerset where the treasure is buried.
       Ali:
       (i)   #(No,) he TOLD$_F$ me.
       (ii)   (No,) he told ME$_F$.
       (iii)   (I know,) she TOLD me.

---

[22] The missing half of this proof is straightforward: For any $R \in [\![$ kiss$_F$ $]\!]_{\mathcal{F}}$, $R(\text{Kim}) \in [\![$ [kiss Kim]$_F$ $]\!]_{\mathcal{F}}$.

To see how, pick as an F-alternative to $\langle TOLD_F \rangle$ that function ϕ which maps Ali (the speaker) to the property π of telling Ms Summerset where the treasure is buried. Since π is made salient by Al's utterance, Ali's reply (36-i) should count as a contrastive focus sentence (the problem cannot be the lack of accent on $\langle me \rangle$, as answer (36-iii) shows).

The problem originates with functions like ϕ (or the one that maps Kim to the property of drinking beer) being among the F-alternatives of $\langle kiss_F \rangle$ and $\langle tell_F \rangle$. If the F-alternatives were restricted to the kind of denotations that natural language words can express, the problem would presumably go away.

Embarassingly enough, though, it is not straightforward to define even what a "natural" natural language meaning is. In other words, not only do we allow ϕ as a focus alternative, we cannot even block it as the meaning for a transitive verb.

One can conceive of several directions in which to look for a solution to this problem. One would be to grab the bull by the horns and develop semantic restrictions on the notion "natural word meaning," for example by way of meaning postulates, which somehow enforce that the meaning of a transitive VP depends in an intuitive way on the properties of the object referent. One could then enforce the same restriction on F-alternatives. Essentially F-alternatives would be restricted to the meanings of existing (or randomly missing but possible) words or phrases in the language.

Another would be to assume that something structural restricts F-alternatives. Assume, for example, that $\langle kiss\ Kim \rangle$ means something like 'do something to Kim which is a kissing,' and $[\![\ kiss_F\ Kim\ ]\!]_{\mathcal{F}}$ is really 'do something to Kim which is an X-ing' or 'be in relation X to Kim which affects Kim.' That is, assume that certain parts of the verbal meaning are *not* encoded by the F-marked expression itself (or at any rate not affected by it), and therefore invariant across alternatives.

This route is pursued—for very similar reasons—in Bonomi and Casalegno (1993), which models sentence meanings as event description. Thus the F-alternatives for $\langle Sam\ KISSED_F\ Kim \rangle$ (called the BACKGROUND MEANING in Bonomi and Casalegno, 1993) would literally be 'there was an event (of unspecified type) of which Sam is the Agent and Kim is the Theme.' Under reasonable assumptions about what it means to be a Theme of an event, a beer drinking would probably not qualify (and even if it did, it would still have to be a beer drinking of which Kim is the Theme—whatever that would mean—so at least Kim would have to be salient as well).

The same kind of solution is possible in standard Alternative Semantics as well. Either by adopting the event-based semantics wholesale, or by restricting F-alternatives of transitive verb meanings to relations that entail "agent-hood" and "theme-hood" of their respective arguments in some other way. Since not much hinges on the details of implementation I will not explicate this any further here.

One way or the other, it is probably a good idea to restrict F-alternatives to 'natural' meanings, either at the level of introducing them (that is, restrict $[\![\ E_F\ ]\!]_{\mathcal{F}}$) or at the level of retrieving them (restrict $[\![\ E\ ]\!]_{\mathcal{F}}$ in the configuration $\langle [E \sim C_i] \rangle$).

5.4.2 Givenness distributivity

A question I have not seen discussed in the literature is the one in (37).

(37)   Is givenness distributive?
       If a constituent is given, does that entail that every part of it is given?

On the face of it one suspects that the answer is "yes." After all, how could, say ‹eat beans› be given, without both ‹eat› and ‹beans› being given? Yet there are constructions in which things are not that easy.

(38)   a. (Last year, Kim started learning the piano.) And now SAM wants to learn
           a musical instrument.
       b. (For years now, Kim has refused to learn any musical instrument. And
           now ...)
           (i)   #SAM won't practice piano.
           (ii) SAM won't practice PIANO.
           (iii) SAM won't practice.

Example (38a) reminds us that contrastive focus can work via entailment/hypernymy: 'someone is learning the piano' entails 'someone is (and defeasably: wants to be) learning a musical instrument'.

So in (38b), since 'someone refusing to learn any musical instrument' arguably entails 'someone not practicing piano', we might expect that ‹won't practice the piano› in (ii) is given and could therefore be deaccented. But the judgment is that deaccenting the verb phrase as in example (38b-i) is odd, and that, in particular, ‹piano› should bear a PA, as in (38b-ii).[23]

The problem with (38b) is likely not the inference from 'refuse to learn any musical instrument' to 'not practice', because precisely that inference is needed to explain the felicitous deaccenting in example (38b-iii).

One does not have to look too far for an intuitive explanation for the contrast between (38a) and (38b-i). While ‹won't practice piano› might be given in the context of (38b), ‹piano› itself is not, and therefore cannot be deaccented. This is different in (38a): not only is ‹learn a musical instrument› given (since 'learning the piano' is salient), but so, too, is ‹musical instrument›, being a hypernym of the

---

[23] Other cases in which a given constituent might potentially contain non-given material involve disjunction and tautologies, as illustrated below:

(i)   a. salient: that Kim drove.
      b. ?given?: ‹Kim or Sam drove.›

(ii) a. salient: that Kim drove.
      b. ?given?: ‹Kim drove and Sam drove or didn't drive.›

In these cases, too, the (b) sentence is a logical entailment of the salient proposition in (a), and hence predicted to be given. While this seems implausible, I found it difficult to construct pragmatically plausible examples of this kind which would actually *demonstrate* that this is the wrong prediction, i.e. that disjuncts and tautologies cannot be deaccented without antecedents.

salient 'piano'; likewise in (38b-iii), both ‹won't practice› and ‹practice› are given (by 'refuse to learn any musical instrument').

So example (38b-i)/(38b-ii) appears to be the crucial case: a (technically) given constituent—‹won't practice the piano›—contains a non-given constituent— ‹piano›. And the accenting facts suggest that in this case the given constituent nevertheless needs to contain an accent, in fact the NPA.

How do the various theories of F-interpretation measure up to this kind of case? The accenting on ‹piano› is predicted by a theory like Schwarzschild (1999), or Selkirk (1995b): Since *every* constituent needs to be checked for GIVENness (or givenness, respectively), F-marking on ‹piano› in example (38b) is obligatory— regardless of the givenness status of any constituent containing it. It is, however, unexpected given systems like Rooth (1992b), Wagner (2006, 2012b) or Büring (2012b), which do not use stacked Fs as newness markers and represent example (38b-i)/(38b-ii) above as in Figure 5.4.

As long as 'someone won't practice the piano' is entailed by something contextually salient, these structures should be fine. Indeed, any type of structure that would instead mark ‹piano› as an additional focus, such as those in Figure 5.5, might not meet the F-Condition: 'that someone practices something' is not entailed by anything salient in (38b), unless we take ‹learn any musical instrument›, without the ‹refused to› part, as a possible antecedent.

Even more clearly, ‹practice piano› does not meet any stronger condition on truly contrastive F-domains: no property 'practice x' is salient in the context. Finally, it is far from obvious that the structures in Figure 5.5 have more backgrounded elements than (i) in Figure 5.4, rather than *fewer* (‹piano› is in the background in Figure 5.4(i), but not Figure 5.5(i)), or the same (‹practice› is already contained within a G-marked constituent in Figure 5.4(ii); G-marking itself, as in Figure 5.5(ii) hardly makes it *more* backgrounded).

So adopting the stacked-F assumption—effectively that every constituent is an F-domain—would correctly predict the lack of deaccenting in these downward entailing contexts. But recall from Section 5.3.2 that any true contrast requirement on foci is incompatible with stacked-F systems (since these do not allow for a constituent to be neither given nor F-marked).

What can be done to get the best of both worlds? Since this question has not, to the best of my knowledge, been discussed in the literature, I can only offer some speculations.

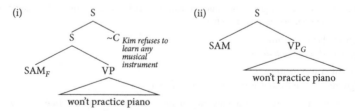

FIGURE 5.4   Unacceptable deaccenting as permitted by Rooth (1992b)/Büring (2012b) (i), and Wagner (2006, 2012b) (ii).

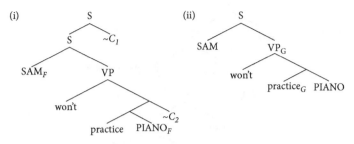

FIGURE 5.5   Impossible F/G-assignments for Büring (2012b), (i), and Wagner (2006, 2012b), (ii).

One route to explore would involve a refinement of the notion of saliency; effectively a salient meaning μ need not make all its entailments salient, or maybe at least not in DE contexts. The effect to be gained is that while 'playing the piano' makes 'playing a musical instrument' salient, 'not practicing' would not make 'not practicing the piano' salient (even though it entails it). This sounds plausible enough, but it is not clear to me that an elaboration of the idea would not, in the end, involve a "saliency check" on every "part" of a salient property, much like (but more obscure than) the Schwarzschildian GIVENness check on every syntactic constituent expressing it.

On the other hand, there may be independent reasons for wanting to adjust what exactly is made salient by an utterance. In some cases, it appears that an utterance makes salient something it does not entail, as in example (39) below, due to Mats Rooth.[24]

(39)   (Yesterday, John was looking for a horse, and today) BILL tried to find one.

The verb ⟨find⟩ in example (39) is deaccented, even though it is not given: someone looking for something does not entail someone finding something (unfortunately). Yet we might want to say that 'looking for something' makes 'finding something' salient, resulting in givenness of ⟨find⟩.

Now, might example (39) not be precisely the case we were looking for earlier, namely a constituent being given, and hence deaccented, while containing non-given material? Note that the representation in Figure 5.6 would indeed license this pattern, due to the fact that 'looking for a horse' arguably does entail 'trying to find a horse' (this, in fact, was Rooth's point with this example.)

This would be in marked contrast to our earlier example (38b), where this kind of structure was—judging by the need to accent ⟨piano⟩—impossible (compare Figure 5.4 to the allegedly legitimate Figure 5.6).

However, the same kind of deaccenting appears possible on ⟨found⟩ in example (40).

[24] p.c. June 9, 2012.

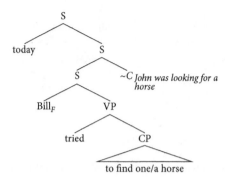

FIGURE 5.6   This structure for example (39) would license deaccenting of VP, including the non-given ⟨find⟩.

(40)   (Dozens of trained policemen and -women were looking for the missing container all night. But in the end,) playing CHILDREN found it.

Crucially, there is no 'try to' in this example. Hence, it is unclear what could license a F-domain here (cf. Figure 5.7), given that 'looking for the container' clearly does not entail 'find the container'.

Again it seems intuitively plausible to think that the context sentence in example (40) makes the property of finding the missing container salient, and thereby licenses givenness and deaccenting of ⟨found it⟩. But there is, in all likelihood, no constituent in that context sentence whose ∃Clo would entail that someone found the missing container, so none of the theories reviewed actually predicts this to be possible.

Where does this leave us? It seems to me that examples like (40) (and maybe (39)) suggest a refinement of what it means to make a meaning salient, since the current definition undergenerates in these cases (not predicting deaccenting where it should). A successful refinement of that notion might at the same time fix some *overgeneration* problems that arise with Rooth/Büring/Wagner-type theories in connection with downward entailing contexts such as example (38b), but that is a mere speculation. If not, these examples remain problematic, unless we return to Schwarzschild's (1999) idea that every node is an F-domain, which seems successful in these cases, but problematic elsewhere (see again Section 5.3).

5.4.3 Focus/background compared to new/given once more

Generally speaking, the theories of focussing reviewed so far regularly entail, implicitly or explicitly, the conjecture in (41).

(41)   BACKGROUND–GIVENNESS CONJECTURE
       Elements in the background are given.

This is most evident in Selkirk's (1995b) and Schwarzschild's (1999) proposals. Backgrounded elements are all and only the ones without F-marking, and the

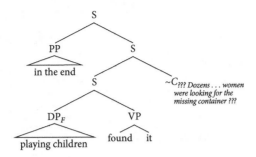

FIGURE 5.7 Deaccenting apparently without any salient antecedent.

licensing conditions in these theories directly entail that F-less elements must be given (due to the fact that the conditions apply to every constituent in a tree).

We discussed two cases in which, potentially, conjecture (41) may not hold in systems in which not every constituent, but only F-domains have to meet a licensing condition,—such as Rooth (1992b)—in Sections 5.4.1 and 5.4.2 above. I argued that the empirical picture there also seems to support (41), even where technically we might predict otherwise.

What would a *bona fide* counter-example to conjecture (41) look like? There are two scenarios to be distinguished. First, that a non-given element remains unaccented because it is in the background of a focus. And second that an element is accented because it is non-given, but yet can be shown not to contribute alternatives to some higher focus domain.

New but unaccented: Neeleman and Szendrői (2004) argue that Superman Sentences like (42) are instances of the first scenario.

(42) Father: What happened?
      Mother: (You know how I think our children should read decent books.
          Well, when I came home, rather than doing his homework), Johnny was
          reading SUPERMAN to some kid.

According to Neeleman and Szendrői (2004), ‹(to some) kid› in example (42) is unaccented because it is in the background of a contrastive focus, ‹Superman›. The example's focus structure is argued to be along the lines of Figure 5.8(i).

The gist of Neeleman and Szendrői's (2004) analysis is expressed as follows:

The discourse status of Mother's reply is complex, as it contains a contrastive focus inside a contrastive focus inside an all-focus sentence. First, her answer tells Father what happened and therefore . . . [TP] must be in focus as a whole. Second, the VP ‹reading Superman to some kid› is contrasted with doing his homework. Finally, the DP ‹Superman› is contrasted with decent books. These three foci share a single phonological marking, namely, the stress on *Superman*. (Neeleman and Szendrői, 2004: 150)

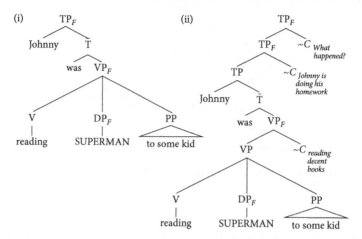

FIGURE 5.8   Superman can run faster than a speeding bullet. But can he background non-given elements?

The tree in Figure 5.8(ii) fleshes this out a little for perspicuity, using annotated F-variables.[25] The crucial point is that ‹to some kid› is not given (and neither is, consequently, the background of the lowest F-domain, VP), yet it is deaccented. In a slogan:

(BON) 'Backgrounding overrides newness'

It is not clear whether Neeleman and Szendrői (2004) would subscribe to BON in general, or only for cases in which the new-yet-backgrounded material occurs within a larger Focus. The more detailed proposal in Féry and Samek-Lodovici (2006: esp. 137ff), which partly builds on Neeleman and Szendrői (2004), clearly entails the more general prediction that, at least within a limited prosodic domain, contrastive focus may generally license deaccenting of new elements. Apart from the original Superman sentence (42) above, they claim Rooth's (1992b) farmer example (‹An AMERican farmer was talking to a CaNAdian farmer.›; see Section 3.1 above) as an instance of BON, as well as examples involving Right Node Raising such as (43) (their (43)), modeled after parallel German examples discussed in detail in Féry and Hartmann (2005).

(43)   Q: What do your friends like?
       A: Ramon likes [CUBAN]$_F$ and Malte prefers [ARGENTINIAN$_F$ music]$_F$.

---

[25] Neeleman and Szendrői (2004) utilize neither F-marks nor F-domains, so the choice of F-domains in particular may not be precisely what they have in mind, but nothing should hinge on this as long as ‹to some kid› is in the background of *some* focus. Neeleman and Szendrői (2004) present examples like this one as an argument against using F-marking in general, but as far as I can see, they are only problematic for theories that *move* foci to a designated clausal position.

In (43), ⟨*music*⟩ is deaccented, ostensibly because it is in the background of the contrastive F-domain ⟨*(prefers) Argentinian$_F$ music*⟩.

Are we to conclude from these examples that conjecture (41) above ("elements in the background are given") is simply wrong and BON is the more accurate generalization? I would caution against this. It still seems rather clear to me that in general, neither free nor associated contrastive foci can license deaccenting of non-given material in their background; witness the examples in (44) and (45).

(44) a. (The store across the street sells refurbished computers, but) # we sell NEW printers.
      b. (This store sells new and refurbished computers, but) # it only sells NEW printers.

(45) a. (George brushes every day, and) # he FLOSSes on the weekend.
      b. (George gargles and flosses every weekday, but) # he only GARGLES on the weekend.

In all these examples I tried to make a contrast as plausible as possible without at the same time having a parallel F-domain (complete with symmetrical deaccenting). The results still are strongly marked.

A similar diagnosis is, I think, warranted for answer focus. Focussing ⟨*candle holder*⟩ in (46)—which is the predicted answer focus—does not license deaccenting of the new adverbial following it.

(46) (What did you buy Kim for christmas? —) I bought Kim a CANdle holder (# at the christmas market.)

In all these cases an (additional) pitch accent on the final NP seems necessary, as would be expected given conjecture (41) above.

So it seems to me that the examples discussed in Féry and Samek-Lodovici (2006) are restricted to a narrowly circumscribed class of constructions, quite likely something like symmetrical deaccenting, though of course more empirical work is required to establish whether that is the correct characterization.

The Superman cases clearly do *not* involve any kind of symmetry or parallelism, but here, too, I would hesitate to draw any radical conclusions before a more comprehensive empirical picture is available. I think structurally parallel cases to Neeleman and Szendrői's (2004) do not in general allow backgrounding of a new element. Some rather marked examples are given in (47) and (48).

(47) (You know how I think our children should read decent books. Well, when I came home, rather than doing his homework, . . .)
      a. #Johnny was reading SUPERMAN to some woman.
      b. #Johnny was reading SUPERMAN in the bathroom.

(48) (I said it is important that you don't hang out with politicians. And yet, at the party, instead of staying in the kitchen,) # you introduced the MAYOR to my uncle.

Perhaps it is significant that the deaccented item in the original Superman sentence (42) above was the noun ‹kid› (rather than ‹woman›, ‹bathroom› or ‹uncle› in (47) and (48)); the context does contain the word ‹children›, and clearly the speaker's kid (and the fact that he is a kid) is salient in it.

In sum, although the empirical evidence is not unequivocal, I will assume for the time being that conjecture (41) above describes the rule, rather than the exception.

Accented but backgrounded: The other case outlined at the beginning of this section—something in the background of a focus that is new and accented—is argued to be found in examples like (49), by Katz and Selkirk (2011).

(49) (Gary is a really bad art dealer. He gets attached to the paintings he buys. He acquired a few Picassos and fell in love with them. The same thing happened with a Cézanne painting.)
So he would only offer that [Modigliani]$_{FOC}$ to [MoMA]$_{New}$.
(I bet the Picassos would have fetched a much higher price.)

‹Only› in example (49) associates with the focus ‹Modigliani›; its F-domain is, presumably, VP, including the PP ‹to MoMA›, which is not given. Katz and Selkirk's (2011) first finding, from a series of production experiments, is that the PP ‹to MoMA› (which is *not* the focus of ‹only›) in this case is produced with a clear pitch accent. Their second finding is that the pitch accent on the contrastive focus, ‹Modigliani› in example (49), is slightly but systematically stronger than that on the following non-given phrase, ‹MoMA› in (49). The implications of the latter finding will be discussed in Chapter 6. What we are interested in now are the implications of the first finding for focus interpretation. The most straightforward conclusion seems to be that in example (49) ‹only› associates with the focus ‹Modigliani› within the F-domain ‹offer that Modigliani to MoMA›. Anticipating some representational devices from Chapter 10, this can be represented as in the tree in Figure 5.9.

The tree in Figure 5.9, however, cannot be the whole story, because it would predict deaccenting of ‹to MoMA›, which Katz and Selkirk (2011) did not generally

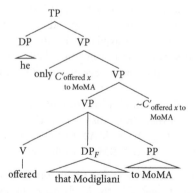

FIGURE 5.9   First step towards representing example (49): mark ‹that Modigliani› as a contrastive focus, which associates with ‹only›.

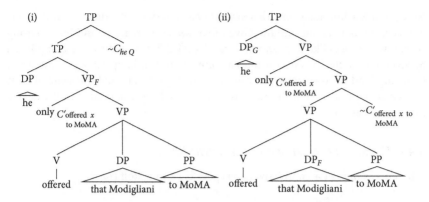

FIGURE 5.10   Either the restriction of ‹only› need not be the value of a F-variable, (i), or focussing alone does not license deaccenting of its background; only G(ivenness)-marking does, (ii).

find (in fact, the tree in Figure 5.9 would represent a kind of Superman sentence, discussed at the start of this subsection, in which a new element would be backgrounded and deaccented; indirectly, then, Katz and Selkirk's (2011) findings provide an argument against the general possibiliy of such sentences).

It is important at this point to realize that the value of the variable C' restricting ‹only›, 'offered x to MoMA,' is not contextually given, since at least the MoMA has, by assumption, not been discussed or otherwise been salient. While this offers an intuitive reason for ‹to MoMA›'s need to be accented, it also raises a red flag about having 'offered x to MoMA' being the value of the F-variable $\sim C'$ in the tree in Figure 5.9, and indeed any F-variable at all: a non-anaphoric F-variable wrongly allows deaccenting of non-given material. Put differently, our choices at this point seem to be: either assume that the variable on ‹only› need *not* be coindexed with a F-variable, or assume that focussing alone does not license deaccenting. These options are represented in Figures 5.10(i) and 5.10(ii).

The value of C' in Figure 5.10(i) could still be constrained by the F-alternative value of its sister, for example it may have to be a subset of it. In that way, we would not lose all connection between ‹only› and prosodic focussing.[26] The tree in Figure 5.10(i) also would not be a case of overfocussing, since no further F-domains within VP could be anaphorically licensed, so this is in fact the minimal focussing compatible with the standard F-conditions. The main drawback of this representation is that it does not account for any special prosodic marking on ‹Modigliani›, since it is, on this account, just part of a regular VP-Focus; so if Katz and Selkirk's (2011) experimental findings turn out to be robust, Figure 5.10(i) does not provide a satisfactory representation to encode them.

The tree in Figure 5.10(ii), on the other hand, distinguishes between the focus ‹the Modigliani›, any given parts (here: only the subject), and the rest, which is

[26] It is tempting to think that this is already implemented, since the value of an F-Variable $\sim C$ is allowed to be a subset of the F-alternatives of its sister. The difference is that it still *also* has to be

backgrounded, but not given. This kind of system reduces the function and effects of focussing to a bare minimum: Given foci (see Section 2.4.2), and "extra strong accenting" in cases like Katz and Selkirk's (2011). All deaccenting is accomplished by givenness alone. This necessitates a complete re-thinking of the pragmatics of focussing (and the question what forces G-making), and though the general lines of such an approach seem clear at this point, I will leave elaboration of the details to a later occasion.

5.4.4 The role of context and world knowledge

A famous example for contrastive focus goes back to Lakoff (1968):

(50)   (She called him a Republican, and then) HE insulted HER.

The contrastive focussing of ‹he› and ‹her› is predicted to be possible if there is a salient target (antecedent) of the form 'x insulted y,' for example that she insulted him. But all the context provides is the proposition that she called him a Republican. Of course, as Lakoff already notes, the very accenting in example (50) conveys that calling someone a Republican does indeed imply insulting them. Put differently, the felicity of contrastive focussing in example (50) hinges on a presupposition which licenses the inference from 'she called him a Republican' to 'she insulted him' (which can then serve as the focus antecedent for ‹HE insulted HER›).

It is because of examples like these that the licensing relation for givenness and focussing is often taken to be, not logical entailment or strict hypernymy/synonymy, but something like CONTEXTUAL ENTAILMENT, CONTEXTUAL IMPLICATION, or ABDUCTIVE IMPLICATION. The obvious idea is that world knowledge or beliefs, both encyclopedic and probabilistic, can provide additional premises on which to base the conclusion from the ∃Clo of a contextually salient meaning to the ∃F-Clo of an utterance. For example, that she called him a Republican, taken together with the unspoken premise that the allegation of Republican allegiances constitutes an insult, logically entails that she insulted him.

---

anaphoric, lest focussing itself (not just the restriction of ‹only›) lose any relation to context. What we are talking about here is more along the lines of (i):

(i)

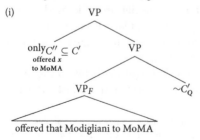

offered that Modigliani to MoMA

Similarly in example (51).[27]

(51) A: They invited Woody Allen as their keynote speaker.
      B: Yeah, they WANted a New Yorker.

The concept ‹New Yorker› can be deaccented as given in example (51) because the individual Woody Allen is made salient by A's utterance, which in turn makes New York and its denizens salient by our encyclopedic knowledge that the famous writer and director is a New Yorker.[28]

A tricky detail not usually discussed in this connection is that it is not straightforward to implement this intuition in terms of privative givenness. Suppose we tried something like definition (52).

(52^{CON}) CONTEXTUALLY BRIDGED GIVENNESS, 1st Attempt
      An expression E is given if there is a contextually salient meaning A so that *shared assumptions of the participants* together with the ∃Clo of A entail the ∃Clo of E.

The reason (52) is inadequate, in fact dangerous, is that by this condition, anything entailed by shared assumptions of the participants alone would also qualify as given. To give a random illustration, assuming that Ali and Bern know that London exists, (52) predicts that they could deaccent ‹London› at any point, regardless of context.

(53) Ali: You should come over for dinner next week!
      Bern: #(Sorry) I'm GOING to London next week.
             (instead of ‹I'm going to LONDON next week.›)

Formally, since the background assumptions include that London exists, the salient proposition that Bern should come over for dinner *together* with the background assumption that London exists entails that London exists, which would make ‹London› given (shared (but not salient) assumptions are printed in gray).

(54)   Bern comes over for dinner
        London exists
        _____

        Bern comes over for dinner and London exists   ⇒ London exists
                                                         (=∃F-Clo(53)-B))

As a first step to solving this conundrum we notice that in (54), givenness is actually met by the shared assumptions alone; the contextually salient meaning has no role to play in it. So maybe condition (55) below would fare better?

---

[27] Based on ex. (29) in Schwarzschild (1999), attributed to Satoshi Tomioka (p.c.) there.

[28] Alternatively one could hypothesize that New York does not gain *bona fide* saliency, but that the mere saliency of Mr Allen satisfies the licensing condition on focussing (i.e. the licensing condition itself is not just entailment but something like "entailment *cum* background knowledge"). Since I do not see any empirical consequences of the choice here, I will continue to equivocate somewhat on this point.

(55^{CON})   CONTEXTUALLY BRIDGED GIVENNESS, 2nd Attempt

An expression E is given if there is a contextually salient meaning A so that shared assumptions of the participants together with the $\exists$Clo of A, *but not alone*, entail the $\exists$Clo of E.

This works fine for example (54), but it also wrongly rules out example (51) above, as shown in (56): that Woody Allen is a New Yorker all by itself entails that New Yorkers exist (=$\exists$Clo(New Yorker); similarly for example (50) above.

(56)   they invited Woody Allen

$$\frac{\text{Woody Allen is a New Yorker}}{\text{they invited Woody Allen, who is a New Yorker}} \quad \begin{array}{l} \Rightarrow! \\ \Rightarrow \end{array} \begin{array}{l} \text{New Yorkers exist} \\ \text{(=}\exists\text{F-Clo(51)-B))} \end{array}$$

Something like condition (55) *would* give the correct predictions at the level of the F-domain. So instead of applying condition (55) above to single words and phrases, we should enforce definition (57).

(57^{CON})   CONTEXTUALLY BRIDGED F-DOMAIN-LICENSING, final

An F-domain is licensed if there is a contextually salient meaning A so that shared assumptions of the participants together with the $\exists$Clo of A, but not alone, entail the $\exists$F-Clo of F-domain.

Examples (58)–(60) review the situation for a clausal F-domain in examples (50), (51), and (53).

(58)   she called him a Republican

$$\frac{\text{calling someone a Republican is insulting them}}{\text{she insulted him}} \quad \begin{array}{l} \text{someone insulted} \\ \Rightarrow \text{someone} \\ \text{(=}\exists\text{F-Clo(50)-B))} \end{array}$$

(59)   they invited Woody Allen

$$\frac{\text{Woody Allen is a New Yorker}}{\text{they invited a New Yorker}} \quad \Rightarrow \begin{array}{l} \text{there was some relation they had to a} \\ \text{New Yorker (=}\exists\text{F-Clo(51)-B))} \end{array}$$

(60)   Bern comes over for dinner

$$\frac{\text{London exists}}{\text{Bern comes over for dinner and London exists}} \quad \not\Rightarrow \begin{array}{l} \text{Bern is in some} \\ \text{relation to} \\ \text{London} \\ \text{(=}\exists\text{F-Clo(53)-B))} \end{array}$$

Now we get the correct results: Licensing the larger F-domains requires both a salient antecedent and an additional premise out of the shared assumptions (gray).[29] What these cases show again, then, is that givenness alone, at least when bridged by contextual assumptions, is not sufficient to license deaccenting. The

---

[29] I still include the 'but not alone' clause because, for example, it may be part of the shared assumptions that (once, somewhere) someone insulted someone, but we do not want that to be sufficient to get the ‹SHE insulted HIM› prosody (without a salient antecedent about some kind of insult).

resulting pattern also has to "fit" in the larger domain. It seems that deaccenting always also involves focussing.

5.5 Chapter summary and outlook

In this chapter I first collected arguments in favor of a strictly discourse-related, anaphoric theory of focus and givenness (Sections 5.1 and 5.2), not least because of the lack of sufficiently precise, workable alternatives. I then turned to what may be described as a laundry list of loose ends for such a theory. Naturally, it is difficult to try to draw any conclusions from that part. In particular, while some of the observations and generalizations seem to favor a reduction of privative givenness to focussing—Sections 5.3 and 5.4.4—others seemed to argue for an even stronger dissociation of focussing and givenness than assumed by standard theories—Sections 5.4.2 and 5.4.3.

Likewise, the idea that the F-condition should include some stronger notion of contrast (which, interestingly, hinges on the idea that deaccenting always involves focussing), while backed up by compelling evidence in some cases (Section 5.3.1), seems to be unsupported in others (Section 5.3.4) (which, incidentally, look like privative deaccenting).

In addition to the phenomena discussed in this chapter, there are at least two types of focussing configurations that are different enough from ordinary focussing (answer, contrast, elaboration) to merit separate mentioning. Since what we know about them at this point does not shed much new light on focus in general, some pointers to the relevant literature will suffice here.

First, so-called POLARITY or VERUM FOCUS, often realized by a single pitch accent on the finite verb as in (61).

(61)   (I really wish you were on my team.—) But I AM on your team!

Generally speaking, polarity focus is used where the propositional content of a sentence is given in its entirety, whereas the fact that it holds true is contrasted with someone's belief or impression that it is not (it is thus the posititve counter-part of narrow focus on ‹not›). For thorough discussion see the seminal Höhle (1992), as well as Gutzmann and Miró (2011), Stommel (2011) and the papers collected in Blühdorn and Lohnstein (2012).

Second, Bolinger (1961) famously discusses a cartoon[30] showing a man upside down, with his feet on the ceiling, in a psychiatrist's office, the psychiatrist saying (62) to the man's wife.

(62)   Our first concern is to persuade the patient that he is a stalagMITE.

[30] From the *New Yorker* (April 14, 1956, p.36).

The striking thing about (62) is that the focussed element is neither a word nor a morpheme, but simply a prosodic foot, ‹mite›. Artstein (2004) convincingly shows that this kind of WORD-INTERNAL FOCUS has all the properties of regular contrastive focus, including the ability to associate with ‹only›, and argues that speakers devise an *ad hoc* interpretation for ‹stalag/stalak›, as a function that maps the expression ‹mite› to the meaning 'Stalagmite' (and the expression ‹tite› to the meaning 'Stalagtite'), and provides a compositional semantics to integrate this into Roothian Alternative Semantics (see Artstein, 2004: for details).

6

Prosodic structure

In this chapter and the next, information structure interpretation and representation will take a bit of a back seat, while we elaborate on the nature of prosodic representations, in particular:

- What elements make up prosodic structures?
- How are prosodic structures derived from, or related to, syntactic structures?
- How does information structure, in particular focus and givenness, influence prosodic structure?

This is not just so as to be more accurate about information structure realization. As will become clear, finer points about prosodic structure have repercussions for information structure interpretation and representation as well.

6.1 Introducing prosodic structure

The picture to be adopted in this book sees prosodic structures basically as in the autosegmental-metrical theory (see e.g. Ladd, 2008: for a brilliant introduction), as consisting of a bracketed metrical grid representing stress and prosodic constituency, associated with an autosegmental representation of tones in the tradition of Pierrehumbert (1980), Liberman and Pierrehumbert (1984) and the intonational part of the TONE AND BREAK INDICES (ToBI) conventions.

With Selkirk (1984, 1995b, 2011; a.o.) and others, we assume that metrical structure is closely related, but not structurally isomorphic, to syntactic structure. There are MAPPING PRINCIPLES (SYNTAX-PROSODY) which relate one to the other. In addition, there are prosody-internal well-formedness principles, which define the class of generally admissible prosodic structures, as well as those principles relating focus and givenness, our current citizens of information structure, to prosody. All of these I will cast in terms of ranked and violable constraints, as used in Optimality Theory (Prince and Smolensky, 1993), to be illustrated momentarily.

Our exclusive interest in this chapter will be with stress patterns, accent patterns, and prosodic phrasing. That is, we will not consider different intonational realizations of what we consider the same underlying metrical structure. Consequently, we will exclusively speak of stress in this chapter, assuming that which stresses get associated with pitch accents, and which shape a certain pitch accent will take, are independently determined.

There are two kinds of prosodic representations regularly employed in the literature: METRICAL STRUCTURE, which represents prosodic units of various sizes (syllable, foot, prosodic word, phonological phrase, etc.) and their stress patterns

Intonation and Meaning. First edition. Daniel Büring.
© Daniel Büring 2016. First published 2016 by Oxford University Press.

(more about which momentarily);[1] and INTONATIONAL STRUCTURE, which also represents certain prosodic units like the intonational and intermediate phrases, but focussed on *tonal* events such as pitch accents and boundary tones.[2]

We will employ a single prosodic representation, which consists of hierarchically ordered prosodic constituents of various sizes (as in metrical structures), the elements of which can be associated with tonal events (as in intonational structure).

6.1.1 Metrical structure: prosodic constituents, heads, and stress

Example (1) illustrates a metrical representation at the word level, as employed in prosodic and metrical phonology.[3]

```
(          ×        )prosodic word
(×    ) ( ×        )foot
(×)( ×) ( ×)  ( × )syllable
```
(1)   in-tro-duc-tion

Example (1) represents three levels or LAYERS of metrical representation. Prosodic units, or constituents, on each layer are indicated by parentheses.

Each prosodic constituent has one metrically strongest element, its HEAD, indicated by a '×'—a BEAT—between the parentheses marking that constituent. For example, the head of the prosodic word ‹introduction› is the foot ‹duction›, and the head of that foot is the syllable ‹duc› (the head of which is the vowel ‹u›). Occasionally the relation 'head of' is understood as transitive, so that for example the syllable ‹duc› will also be called a/the head of the prosodic word ‹introduction› (this is made perspicuous by the vertical alignment of heads in COLUMNS).

As said at the start of the section, the entire metrical representation (i.e. parentheses and beats) is called a BRACKETED METRICAL GRID.

Being the head of a constituent above the syllable (and thus carrying a beat at the level of that constituent) amounts to bearing (a certain amount of) STRESS; for example, bearing word stress is the same as being the head of a prosodic word. Prosodic element A has more/higher stress than prosodic element B (of the same layer, i.e. two syllables, two prosodic words, etc.), if A's column of beats × is taller than B's. If A is the head of C, A bears higher stress than any other element (on the same layer) in C.[4]

---

[1] Other representation formats proposed in the literature include metrical grids, bracketed metrical grids, and metrical trees (see e.g. Halle and Vergnaud, 1987, Hayes, 1995, Liberman and Prince, 1977, Prince, 1983). The prosodic structures employed here are special instances of bracketed metrical grids and as such represent the same information as those.

[2] Structures of the former kind are the primary object of investigation in PROSODIC PHONOLOGY, which often diagnoses prosodic units as the domains for segmental phenomena, and METRICAL PHONOLOGY, which is interested primarily in stress patterns. Structures of the latter kind (intonational structures) are the representation of choice in INTONATIONAL PHONOLOGY.

[3] Adapted from Giegerich (1992: 203).

[4] Formally: A bears more stress than B iff A is the head of the smallest prosodic constituent containing A ("A's mother"), and either (i) A and B are sisters, or (ii) the A's mother bears more stress than B's mother.

Metrical structures like (1) are defined in essential ways by prosody-internal principles: the inventory of primitive elements such as syllables (presumably further analyzed into onset, nucleus, and rime), feet, boundaries, etc., and the set of PROSODIC WELL-FORMEDNESS CONSTRAINTS, which, in purely prosodic terms, define how these can be combined, and hence what is a well-formed prosodic structure. While sometimes morphological information might *influence* metrical structure (e.g. in compounds), metrical structure is not just some annotated form of morphological structure. In fact, as (1) already illustrates, morphological structure—here [[‹introduc›][‹tion›]] (or perhaps [[[‹intro›][‹duc›]][‹ion›]])—and prosodic structure (here: at the foot level) do not even need to be isomorphic. This point may seem trivial at the word level, but it is worth establishing at the outset since it is arguably true for the relation between syntactic and prosodic structure in general (see Taglicht, 1998, for English; Nespor and Vogel, 1986, for general discussion).

6.1.2 Stress and accent

As just discussed, the columns of asterisks in (1) correspond to metrical strength or STRESS. But up to now, I have not clarified what stress actually is, except to say that it is related to, but not the same as, pitch accent. To illustrate the difference once more, ‹introduction› can be produced with one, two, even three, or no pitch accent.

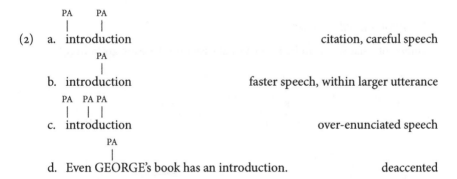

I assume here that in all of these realizations, ‹introduction› has the same metrical structure, (1). While this means that the number of pitch accents is not determined by the stress pattern, there are strict rules on the association of the two. If a constituent contains a pitch accent, its head is pitch accented. Put differently, pitch accents are assigned "from top to bottom": the accent on ‹tro› is only possible if ‹in› is accented, which in turn is possible only if ‹duc› is. In addition, within a prosodic word or any bigger prosodic constituent, there cannot be pitch accents

---

If > represents "bears more stress than," then clause (i) establishes that in (1) ‹in›>‹tro›, ‹duc›>‹tion›, and ‹duction›>‹intro›. By clause (ii), furthermore, ‹duc›>‹in›, and ‹duc›>‹tro›. This accords with the intuitive use of the terms "stronger" or "more stressed."

after the metrically strongest syllable, so no pitch accent on ‹tion›, which follows the strongest syllable ‹duc›; this will be of importance later on. Both these properties are encoded in (3).[5]

(3^{CON})   STRESS-TO-ACCENT (a prosodic well-formedness constraint)
The last pitch accent (if there is any) within a prosodic constituent above the foot is on the head of that constituent.

Note that by (3), being the last pitch accent within a prosodic constituent and being the element with the highest level of stress within that constituent necessarily coincide. We remarked in Chapter 1 that the last pitch accent in a phrase is perceived as the most prominent. By (3), this has now a theoretical counterpart: it *is* the *metrically strongest*.

Is stress, then, simply an abstract notation for potential pitch accent positions? No! Even among unaccented syllables, stress differences are detectable, for example by the presence vs absence of full (unreduced) vowels (see e.g. Hayes, 1995: ch.1). Experimental evidence suggests that in general, higher stress—on accented and unaccented syllables alike—correlates with phonetic parameters such as increased duration, higher intensity, or more careful articulation;[6] these effects are very subtle though and will not play much of a role until Chapter 7. As we will see there, however, even information structure distinctions are sometimes realized by stress, with no involvement of pitch accents.

6.1.3 Intonational structure

Examples of what we mean by intonational structures here are given in (4).[7]

(4)   a.   design improvements and a schedule

    b.   if he can then there's no argument about it

Intonational structure for English typically involves two levels of constituency, the INTERMEDIATE PHRASE (iP), and, above it, the INTONATIONAL PHRASE (IP). An

---

[5] The same logic for accent assignment is argued for e.g. in Pierrehumbert (1980: 37ff).

[6] See a.o. Baumann et al. (2010), Beaver et al. (2007), Cooper et al. (1985), Eady and Cooper (1986), Eady et al. (1986), Xu and Xu (2005).

[7] Examples from the MIT Open Courseware page at http://ocw.mit.edu/courses/electrical-engineering-and-computer-science/6-911-transcribing-prosodic-structure-of-spoken-utterances-with-tobi-january-iap-2006/index.htm, ch.2.8; sound files available there.

intermediate phrase contains at least one PA, written with an asterisk, as in H* (for "high") in (4), and a PHRASE TONE on its right, which determines the pitch on syllables after the final PA. Phrase tones are written with a minus sign, i.e. H– or L– ("high," "low").

An intonational phrase contains at least one intermediate phrase, and a BOUND-ARY TONE to the right, which determines the pitch on the final syllable of the IP. Boundary tones are written with a percent sign, i.e. H% or L%.

In (4) the boundary tones are written as associated with the right IP boundary, and the phrase tone as associated with the right boundary of the iP (which is where they belong phonologically). The latter, however, are actually realized on the entire stretch between pitch accent and boundary, and where necessary (for lack of syllables) *on* the pitch accented syllable. The phonetic realization is thus more transparently rendered in (5), where syllables associated with two different tones are realized as rising (or, in the case of HL, falling).

(5) a. ...improvements   b. ...can   c. ...argument about it.

Structure (5) also indicates, in gray, what the actual pitch contour of these examples would, approximately, look like.

Usually, H(igh) and L(ow) are the only tones assumed. I will turn to the tonal phonology—that is when to choose H, L, or some combination thereof—in Chapter 9. In the present chapter we will usually stay agnostic about the choice of tone, and just write PA (for any starred tones) and, where relevant, T- and T% for phrase and boundary tones.

Intonational phonology does not usually represent metrical heads for iPs and IPs, but it is straightforward, and, as we will see, useful, to import this feature and assume that iPs and IPs, like lower prosodic categories, have a metrically strongest element, the head. Since IPs by definition contain at least one iP, and iPs by definition contain at least one PA, the head of an iP/IP must be the element bearing the final pitch accent in iP/IP, if we assume Stress-to-Accent in (3) above.

(6) if he can then there's no argument about it

Any utterance involves at least one IP (and hence an iP). In short, mono-clausal utterances, iP and IP often coincide, as in (6).[8]

---

[8] Ladd (2008: 114).

```
                                    L–H%
                                     |
         (        H*       H*        \ )IP
         (        |        |         \ )iP
(7)    Could I have the bill please?
```

Where utterances consist of several iPs, as in (6), and several IPs, as in (4a), this means that in such cases, they will have an iP or IP boundary within them.

The presence of an iP boundary can be diagnosed intonationally by the presence of a phrase tone T-, as well as by some amount of FINAL LENGTHENING, that is lengthening of the syllable(s) before the right iP boundary (e.g. on ‹can› in (6)). Analogously, a right IP boundary implies that there is a boundary tone T%, and it, too, leads to (an even greater amount of) final lengthening, and possibly an audible pause. A more subtle cue is the SCALING of pitch accents: within an IP (and perhaps lower prosodic constituents as well), subsequent high tone pitch accents often follow a pattern of relative lowering from one to the next, so called DOWNSTEP. This pattern is reset after an IP constituent boundary, that is, the absolute height of pitch accents after a boundary may be "re-set" to a higher frequency than the previous pitch accents.[9]

All of the above regards the *detection* of iPs and IPs in a given utterance, that is, they may help to assign the correct intonational representation to a recorded utterance. We have not yet addressed the task of *predicting* where within a sentence iP and IP boundaries will occur. There is relatively little work on this question, which in part reflects the fact that intonational phonology is primarily concerned with the question of what intonational structures in a given language may look like, and less with how intonational structures are related to syntactic structures.

The task of predicting prosodic structure takes center-stage, on the other hand, in much work on prosodic phonology, which at the same time is primarily focussed on prosodic phrasing within simple clauses, that is, below the iP level, or, as we will say here PHRASAL PROSODY.

6.1.4 Phrasal prosody

Generally, prosodic structure at the phrasal level (above the prosodic word, below the clause level) is organized just like within the word: Elements at a lower level are grouped into constituents at the next higher level, and one of them becomes the head, bearing maximal stress within that constituent. Which elements are grouped together is in large part determined by syntactic structure, and the crucial question is: how? Or, as it is often put, how is syntax "mapped" onto prosodic structure?

Roughly, we can distinguish two kinds of approaches: Those that assume a limited inventory of prosodic categories above the word level, usually between two and four, and those that use an unlabeled general prosodic phrase, which can be freely stacked, often in very close parallelism to syntactic embedding.[10] We

---

[9] See e.g. Truckenbrodt (2002), Truckenbrodt and Féry (2005) for German.

[10] Representatives of the first class include most work by Elisabeth Selkirk up until the early 2000 years, Hubert Truckenbrodt's work, and most work on the segmental effects of prosodic phrasing

will for the most part use a system of the former kind (but return to the issue in Section 6.3.4).

The main source for the system used here is that developed in Truckenbrodt (1995, 1999, 2006, 2007a), which assumes just one level above the prosodic word level and below the iP, called the PHONOLOGICAL PHRASE (pP). The heads of phonological phrases correspond to PHRASAL STRESSES, and are, in Truckenbrodt's proposal, eventually associated with pitch accents.

Above the pP, Truckenbrodt's prosodic categories coincide with those of intonational phonology, discussed in Section 6.1.3, that is, phonological phrases are contained in intermediate phrases, whose heads are nuclear stresses, and which in turn are contained in—and in case of simple sentences coincide with—intonational phrases. Example (8) is adapted from Truckenbrodt (2007a: ex. (1))

```
    (                    x         )intonational phrase
    (                    x         )intermediate phrase
    ( x        )(        x         )phonological phrase
    ( x        )( x   )( x         )prosodic word
(8)  Beverly  likes  Arkansas.
```

As before, the beats on each level mark the heads of prosodic phrases on that level—there is thus one asterisk between each pair of matching parentheses. Metrical structure being purely relational, it does not matter from a stress point of view that ‹Arkansas› bears four beats of stress rather than three (it does matter that it bears three and not two, since this expresses that it is stronger than ‹Beverly›). The rationale for two layers, rather than one, on top of the phonological phrase is simply the observation that each utterance, even one-word utterances, have, or at least may have, prosodic movements at their right edge which are characteristic of the phrase tone plus boundary tone combinations found at the right edge of IPs. This is translated into the theory by assuming that every utterance, no matter how long or short, comprises the entire hierarchy of prosodic categories, from the syllable (or below) to the IP (or above). We will revisit the details of this in Section 6.3.4.

A more complete prosodic structure for this example would then look as in (9); PA, NPA, and T are of course eventually fleshed out as particular tones (H/L) or combinations thereof (L+H*, L*+H, etc.).

```
                    NPA      T-    T%
                     |             |
    (PA                 x          )intonational phrase (IP)
    ( |                 x          )intermediate phrase (ip)
    ( x        )(       x          )phonological phrase (pP)
    ( x        )( x  )( x          )prosodic word (pWd)
(9)  Beverly  likes  Arkansas
```

in metrical phonology (see e.g. the papers collected in Inkelas and Zec, 1990). The second type is represented by Halle and Vergnaud (1987), Hayes (1995) and Wagner (2005), and much work on rhythm and stress in metrical phonology.

Where intonational phrases contain exactly one intermediate phrase—ostensibly the case in many mono-clausal sentences—we will abbreviate (9) to (10), in which the two layers are fused.

<pre>
    PA   NPA   T–T%
     | | \ |
    (| ×   )_{i/IP}
    (×   )(×   )_{pP}
    (×   )(×)(×   )_{pWd}
(10) Beverly likes Arkansas
</pre>

The accent assignment in (9)/(10) conforms to our STRESS-TO-ACCENT principle in (3); however, (10) is not the only accent pattern predicted to go with the stress pattern indicated; STRESS-TO-ACCENT does not specify a minimal metrical weight or prosodic phrase level to attach a pitch accent to; it optionally allows us to assign an additional pitch accent to the prosodic word ‹likes›, because it is pre-nuclear in its pP ‹(likes Arkansas)_{pP}›.

<pre>
    PA   PA   NPA   T–T%
     | | | \ |
    (| | ×   )_{i/IP}
    (×   )(| ×   )_{pP}
    (×   )(×)(×   )_{pWd}
(11) Beverly likes Arkansas
</pre>

This is intended, because, as discussed in Section 4.4.2, the two-PA pattern in (10) is in free variation with the three-PA pattern in (11).

In allowing structures like (11) I depart from Truckenbrodt (1995), in which it is assumed that pitch accents can only associate with stresses at the p-phrase level (or higher). On that view, the optionality of accenting a transitive verb must correspond to a difference in metrical structure, as represented in (12a) vs (12b).

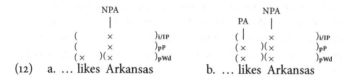

<pre>
              NPA   NPA
               | PA |
    (×   )_{i/IP}   (| ×   )_{i/IP}
    (×   )_{pP}   (×)(×   )_{pP}
    (×)(×   )_{pWd}   (×)(×   )_{pWd}
(12) a. … likes Arkansas   b. … likes Arkansas
</pre>

Similarly, Kratzer and Selkirk (2007) assume that if and only if an element is pitch accented, it is the head of a MINOR PHRASE, a prosodic category below the pP[11] and above the prosodic word; so for them, too, two different metrical structures—rather than just two accent patterns, as assumed here—may realize the same sentence.

Such theoretical disagreements reveal a more fundamental difficulty with phrasal phonology in English, namely that the observable reflexes of pPs—or more generally: phrases above the pWd and below the iP—are primarily pitch accenting, and relative stress between metrical sisters. All approaches sketched in this section converge on these aspects; they predict that ‹likes› is less stressed than ‹Arkansas›, that the latter must carry a PA, and the former may. To adjudicate between them,

---

[11] MAJOR PHRASE in Kratzer and Selkirk (2007).

other than on grounds of theoretical eloquence, we would need a precise theory of the realization of word stress vs phrasal stress independent of accent, or some independent way of diagnosing pP (minor/major phrase) boundaries.[12] Pending a more precise understanding of these matters, we will assume that STRESS-TO-ACCENT as formulated in (3) may assign pitch accents to any level of stress, including word stress, in pre-nuclear position, so that (10) is a possible representation for the three-accent pattern.

This concludes our introduction to the basic building blocks and properties of prosodic structure. In the following sections we will detail how syntax restricts metrical structure (and, mediated by STRESS-TO-ACCENT, intonation), by way of replacing the Toy Rules from Chapter 1 with precise and realistic prosodic constraints.

We will not usually indicate pitch accents in our prosodic representations in this chapter, since their placement can be predicted from Stress-to-Accent (more precisely, the placement of the NPA is predictable, as is the location of potential pre-nuclear accents); similarly for phrase and boundary tones. Where examples are given without prosodic structures, we will continue to use capitalization to indicate pitch accents, usually with no special marking of the nuclear pitch accent (which, again, is predictable).

6.2 Building prosodic structure: phrasal stress and integration

6.2.1 Phrasal stress: WRAP-XP and STRESS-XP

We start with the rules that govern the formation of pPs. Recall that the heads of pPs correspond to phrasal stresses, which in turn are default locations for pitch accents. Therefore the rules locating pP-heads (i.e. phrasal stresses) will be stress-related re-renderings of Step 1 from the Toy Rules in Section 1.2.2 of Chapter 1, namely the original constraints from Truckenbrodt (1995) on which Step 1 was based.

(13^{CON}) WRAP-XP
        Any XP is contained in a phonological phrase.

(14^{CON}) STRESS-XP
        Any XP contains a pP-level stress.

The duo of STRESS-XP and WRAP-XP will be satisfied if a syntactic phrase is aligned on both edges with a pP, as AP is in (15a). AP meets STRESS-XP because it bears a beat at the pP-level; and it meets WRAP-XP because the boundaries of pP do not exclude any part of AP (AP is "wrapped in" pP; pP wraps AP).

The inclusion ("wrapping") of nearby function words is possible, too, since WRAP-XP does not call for an *exact alignment* of XPs and pPs, but is rather satisfied

---

[12] As it is, pP structure resembles foot structure, more than intonational structure. Metrical feet, too, are reflected in relative stress and, indirectly, accent assignment, but have no known boundary correlates.

as long as the XP is *contained*—properly or not—in a pP, as in (15b) (more on the treatment of function words in Section 6.2.4).

$$
\begin{array}{ll}
\begin{array}{l}
(\quad \times \qquad)_{\text{pP}} \\
(\quad \times \qquad)_{\text{pWd}}
\end{array} &
\begin{array}{l}
(\qquad\qquad\quad \times \quad)_{\text{pP}} \\
(\qquad \times \;)(\quad \times \quad)_{\text{pWd}}
\end{array}
\end{array}
$$

(15) a. $[_{\text{AP}}$ orange$]$ b. $[_{\text{DP}}$ every $[_{\text{NP}}$ gate $]]$

In fact an element to be "annexed" into a pP need not be a function word; as long as it is a single X°—and not a phrase, which would itself invoke STRESS-XP—it can be part of a pP whose head is the syntactic head of a different phrase. And in this property lies the key to Truckenbrodt's treatment of integration.

6.2.2 Integration

Head complement structures in general can meet WRAP-XP and STRESS-XP by being wrapped, as it were, into a single pP, as in (16).

$$
\begin{array}{ll}
\begin{array}{l}
(\qquad \times \;)_{\text{pP}} \\
(\quad \times)(\; \times \;)_{\text{pWd}}
\end{array} &
\begin{array}{l}
(\quad \times \qquad)_{\text{pP}} \\
(\quad \times)(\times \quad)_{\text{pWd}}
\end{array}
\end{array}
$$

(16) $[_{\text{XP}}$ X YP$]$ $[_{\text{XP}}$ YP X $]$

In (16), both XP and YP contain a phrasal stress, the head of pP, and they are both wrapped, in pP. This will be the typical metrical structure for PPs, complex NPs with complements, DPs, transitive VPs, and auxiliary+main verb (phrase) combinations, among others (see Section 8.5 for more discussion).[13]

(17) a. $[_{\text{PP}}[_{\text{P}°}$across$]\,[_{\text{DP}}$ the $[_{\text{NP}}$ room$]]]$

b. $[_{\text{NP}}[_{\text{N}°}$ friends$]\,[_{\text{PP}}$ of $[_{\text{DP}}$ the $[_{\text{NP}}$ theater$]]]]$

c. $[_{\text{VP}}[_{\text{V}°}eat]\,[_{\text{DP}}[_{\text{NP}}$sushi$]]]$

d. $[_{\text{T}}[_{\text{T}°}$should$]\,[_{\text{VP}}$laugh$]]$

The alternative structure, which forms two pPs, not only fails to improve in terms of STRESS-XP, it unnecessarily violates WRAP-XP: (18) meets STRESS-XP as well as (17c), but the VP is no longer contained in a p-phrase (it is "split up," rather than wrapped).

---

[13] We assume here that articles and similar elements are not normally prosodic words of their own, since they do not bear any stress and contain reduced vowels (things are different, of course, if they are focussed, hence "normally"). Selkirk (1995a) argues that in fact, they are bare syllables (not even feet), which are directly subordinated to the pP (not the pWd). We parse them into the pWd here for reasons of simplicity (to avoid non-exhaustive parsing in the representations, to be precise), without meaning to dispute Selkirk's analysis.

$$
\begin{array}{l}
(\quad\ \times\ )\,(\qquad\times\qquad)_{\text{pP}} \\
(\quad\ \times\ )\,(\qquad\times\qquad)_{\text{PWd}}
\end{array}
$$

(18)   * $[_{\text{VP}}[_{\text{V}^\circ}\text{eat}]\ [_{\text{DP}}[_{\text{NP}}\text{sushi}]]]$

As noted in Section 6.1.4, STRESS-TO-ACCENT, applied to the structures in (17) yields two "allophonic" accent patterns, exemplified here with (17c).

$$
\begin{array}{ll}
\qquad\qquad\quad\text{PA} & \qquad\qquad\quad\text{PA} \\
\qquad\qquad\quad| & \qquad\quad\text{PA}\qquad| \\
(\qquad\qquad\times\ )_{\text{pP}} & (\quad|\qquad\times\ )_{\text{pP}} \\
(\ \times\ )\ (\quad\times\ )_{\text{PWd}} & (\ \times\ )\ (\quad\times\ )_{\text{PWd}}
\end{array}
$$

(19)   a. $[_{\text{VP}}\text{eat}\ [_{\text{DP}}[_{\text{NP}}\text{sushi}]]]$ b. $[_{\text{VP}}\text{eat}\ [_{\text{DP}}[_{\text{NP}}\text{sushi}]]]$

This is different in head-final structures, illustrated in (19) with the German translation of (19).

$$
\begin{array}{ll}
\qquad\quad\text{PA} & \qquad\qquad\text{PA} \\
\qquad\quad| & \qquad\qquad|\quad\text{PA} \\
(\quad\times\qquad)_{\text{pP}} & (\quad\times\qquad|\ )_{\text{pP}} \\
(\quad\times\ )(\ \times\ )_{\text{PWd}} & (\quad\times\ )(\ \times\ )_{\text{PWd}}
\end{array}
$$

(20)   a. $[_{\text{VP}}[_{\text{DP}}[_{\text{NP}}\ \text{Sushi}]]\ \text{essen}]$ b. * $[_{\text{VP}}[_{\text{DP}}[_{\text{NP}}\ \text{Sushi}]]\ \text{essen}]$

Example (20b) violates STRESS-TO-ACCENT, since it has a pitch accent on ‹e(ssen)›, which is post-head within the pP ‹Sushi essen›. The effect of wrapping verb and object into a single pP is thus much more tangible in head-final structures than in head-initial ones, as it yields *obligatory non-accenting of an open class element in final position* or, put differently, leftward shifting of the NPA.

The effect in head-initial structures is much less noticeable: the optionality of a pre-nuclear pitch accent on the head (which, as discussed before, is perceptually much less prominent and often not easily detected even by trained listeners).

For this reason, the descriptive label "integration" is usually reserved for head-final structures, where it leads to a phrase-final unaccented head, as in (20a). As far as metrical structure goes, though, head-initial and head-final structures are treated exactly parallel (they are wrapped into a single pP, and the complement is metrically stronger than the head), with the accentual difference due to the Stress-to-Accent mapping alone.

Note finally that the integration/wrapping effect is predicted to reiterate with multiple embeddings, as in (21).

$$
\begin{array}{l}
(\qquad\qquad\qquad\qquad\times\qquad)_{\text{pP}} \\
(\quad\times\ )(\ \times\ )\ (\quad\times\qquad)_{\text{PWd}}
\end{array}
$$

(21)   a. $[_{\text{T}}\text{may}\ [_{\text{VP}}\text{eat}\ [_{\text{DP}}[_{\text{NP}}\text{sushi}]]]]$

$$
\begin{array}{l}
(\qquad\times\qquad\qquad\qquad\qquad)_{\text{pP}} \\
(\qquad\times\ )(\ \times\ )(\ \times\qquad)_{\text{PWd}}
\end{array}
$$

   b. $[[_{\text{VP}}[_{\text{DP}}[_{\text{NP}}\ \text{Sushi}]]\ \text{essen}]\ \text{darf}\ ]$
           Sushi   eat   may

That this is indeed the correct result is particularly evident again in head-final structures such as the German (21b). Recall that by STRESS-TO-ACCENT in (3), pitch accents may be associated with word level stresses *before* the pP head, but not after it. Therefore, none of the verbs in a complex head-final VP such as (21b) may bear a pitch accent, shifting the NPA increasingly leftward to the most deeply embedded VP, followed by a—potentially long—string of unaccented verbs.

Truckenbrodt's STRESS-XP and WRAP-XP thus not only handle the general mapping between syntactic XPs and prosodic pPs, they yield the integration effect between a head and its phrasal complement as a side effect.

6.2.3 Non-integration

Integration in head+complement structures contrast with the situation in which a syntactic XP contains two independent phrases YP and ZP, for example in adjunction or coordination structures.

(22) a. $[_{VP}[_{VP}$ work$][_{PP}$ in Sweden$]]$ b. $[_{DP}[_{DP}$ a boy$]$ and $[_{DP}$ a girl$]]$

WRAP-XP could be satisfied here by wrapping the larger XP in one pP:

$$
\begin{array}{llll}
(& &)_{pP} & (&)_{pP} \\
(& \times \quad)(\quad \times &)_{PWd} & (\quad \times)(\quad \times &)_{PWd}
\end{array}
$$

(23) a. $[_{VP}[_{VP}$ work$][_{PP}$ in Sweden$]]$ b. $[_{DP}[_{DP}$ a boy$]$ and $[_{DP}$ a girl$]]$

The problem is that one pP can only have one head, and hence license only one phrase level stress. Whether that stress goes on ‹work› (‹boy›) or ‹Sweden› (‹girl›), it will leave one XP without a p-level stress, in violation of STRESS-XP.[14] Instead, each XP will get its own pP:

$$
\begin{array}{llll}
(\quad \times \quad)(\quad \times &)_{pP} & (\quad \times)(\quad \times &)_{pP} \\
(\quad \times \quad)(\quad \times &)_{PWd} & (\quad \times)(\quad \times &)_{PWd}
\end{array}
$$

(24) a. $[_{VP}[_{VP}$ work$][_{PP}$ in Sweden$]]$ b. $[_{DP}[_{DP}$ a boy$]$ and $[_{DP}$ a girl$]]$

Example (24) is indeed the observed stress pattern in coordination and adjunction structures. This is particularly clear again in head-final structures where adjunctions and coordinations form minimal pairs with head-complement structures (two phrasal stresses vs one).

(25) a. er hat im   ZELT geRAUCHT/# im ZELT geraucht. (German)
      he   has in the tent   smoked
      'He smoked in the tent.'

   b. er hat 'nen JOINT geraucht/# JOINT geRAUCHT.
      he   has a   joint   smoked
      'He smoked a joint.'

---

[14] We assume with Truckenbrodt (1995) that the lower segment of an adjunction structure counts for STRESS-XP.

(26) a. Sie hat an der THEke gestanden. (German)
    she has at the bar stood
    'She was standing at the bar.'

  b. Sie hat an der THEke geSTANden.
    she has at the bar confessed
    'She confessed at the bar.'

(27) a. Er hat sie STÖren sehen. (German)
    he has her disrupt seen
    'He saw her disrupting (someone/something).'

  b. Er hat geHÖRT und geSEHen.
    he has heard and seen
    'He heard and saw.'

Note that the structures (underlying the accent patterns) in (24)–(27) as well as (28) below satisfy STRESS-XP, but violate WRAP-XP, since the higher VP/DP is split up into two pPs. What this tells us is that WRAP-XP may be violated in order to avoid a violation of STRESS-XP. As mentioned at the beginning of this chapter, we assume that WRAP-XP and STRESS-XP, as well as the other constraints to be discussed in this chapter, are all violable in this sense. In the terminology of Optimality Theory, STRESS-XP must OUTRANK WRAP-XP.

Apart from adjunctions and coordinations, the non-wrapped structure will also be found in headed structures with more than one complement, as in the German ditransitive VP in (28).

$$
\begin{array}{lllll}
(& \times &)(& \times &)_{pP} \\
(& \times &)(& \times~)(& \times &)_{pWd}
\end{array}
$$

(28) [$_{VP}$[$_{DP}$ einem Freund] [$_{DP}$ ein Bier] bestellen] (German)
    a-DAT friend a beer order
    'to order a friend a beer'

Here, again, the need for each complement DP to bear phrasal stress (STRESS-XP) outranks the desire for VP to be wrapped (WRAP-XP). In order to predict the correct structure, it has furthermore to be assumed that WRAP-XP is a CUMULATIVE CONSTRAINT, so that it is still preferable to phrase the verb with its closest complement (incurring one violation of WRAP-XP for VP) rather than separately (incurring two).

The same result is presumably empirically adequate for English ditransitive VPs; intuitionistically, ‹friend› in (29a) is stronger than ‹order›, but weaker than ‹beer› (though I am not aware of any empirical study of this).

$$
\begin{array}{llllll}
(& & & \times &)_{i/IP} \\
(& \times &)(& \times &)_{pP} \\
(\times &)(& \times &)(& \times &)_{pWd}
\end{array}
$$

(29) a. order a friend a beer   b. order a friend a beer

That ‹beer› is strongest here will eventually follow from the fact that it bears the sentence-final phrasal stress, as indicated in (29b). The wrapping of ‹order› and ‹a

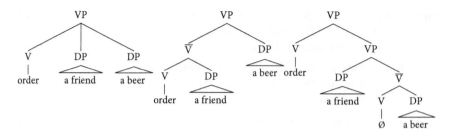

FIGURE 6.1   Different syntactic structures for ditransitive VPs in English (which all yield the same metrical structure).

friend⟩ is compatible with a number of syntactic assumptions about ditransitive VPs in English, including the three given in Figure 6.1.

On either analysis, STRESS-XP makes it impossible to wrap VP (*either* VP, in the third structure) into a single pP. At the same time, nothing encourages mapping the V alone onto a pP, so in the interest of minimizing the amount of WRAP-XP violations for (the top) VP, V will wrap with its closest argument, resulting in structure (29b).

What we have just discussed about phrases containing two disjoint phrases holds *mutatis mutandis* for phrases with three and more XPs in them, for example entire clauses and sentences: a WRAP-XP violation will be incurred for any two XPs, as long as one is not a complement to the other.

This at least holds as long as each XP is eligible for carrying phrasal stress in its own right, that is, as long as it is headed by a non-given, non-backgrounded open class element.

6.2.4 Function words and integration

A functional element in sentence-final position does not bear the NPA in normal pronunciation. Some examples are given in (30)–(32):

(30)   a. I SEE something   b. I SEE her   c. # ... see HER/SOMEthing

(31)   a. I'll eat more than SArah can.   b. # ... Sarah CAN

(32)   a. What did you LOOK at?   b. # ... look AT?

⟨*Her*⟩, ⟨*something*⟩, ⟨*can*⟩, and ⟨*at*⟩ all head their own XP in these examples, so by STRESS-XP we should expect phrasal stress on them. This is particularly clear for the pronoun cases in (30), which clearly do not involve transitive heads.

As Selkirk (1995a) observes, the sentence-final elements in the above examples all have to (in the case of (31) and (32)), or at least may (in the case of (30)) have full vowels, which is taken to indicate that they are prosodic words. The fact that they do not bear phrasal stress then must have to do with their morphological status as function words (rather than with their prosodic status). To keep things simple, we will therefore assume the constraint in (33).

(33^{CON})   P-Stress → X^0_{lex}
Only lexical heads may carry phrasal stress.

P-Stress → X^0_{lex} is violated by the p-stress on ‹some(thing)› in (34), but respected in (34b).

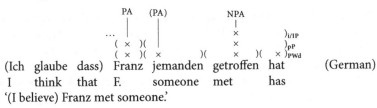

(34)   a. #[$_{VP}$see [$_{DP}$ something]]   b. [$_{VP}$see [$_{DP}$ something]]

The fact that the structure underlying the acceptable stress pattern violates Stress-xp for the DP object furthermore shows that P-Stress → X^0_{lex} must outrank Stress-xp.

P-Stress → X^0_{lex} interacts in the expected way with stressing and accenting in OV structures. First and foremost, integration is blocked, and the final phrasal stress must fall on the V:[15]

(35)   a. etwas   SEhen   b. sie   SEhen   c. # ETwas/   SIE   sehen
           something see   her   see   s.th.   her   see

Furthermore, similar to English VO structures with lexical objects, a pre-nuclear pitch accent on the object seems possible, at least with indefinite pronouns, as in (36).

(36)   (What happened? —

                          PA   (PA)   NPA
                           | | |
                     ... | | ×   )$_{\iota/IP}$
                         (×)(| ×   )$_{pP}$
                         (×)(×   )(×   )(×)$_{PWd}$
     (Ich glaube dass) Franz jemanden getroffen hat   (German)
      I   think   that   F.   someone   met   has
     ‘(I believe) Franz met someone.’

---

[15] Gussenhoven (1983a: 29) proposes a different explanation for (34), according to which quantificational arguments have to form their own pP (F-domain in his terms). The two hypotheses should be easily distinguished, since an indefinite pronoun in final position should be deaccented according to P-Stress → X^0_{lex}, but bear the NPA if it formed its own accent domain. While the former prediction appears to be correct in most cases, cf. example (29a) above, Gussenhoven (1983a) presents (i) in support of the latter.

(i)   I've seen NO-one.

Of course, it is possible that (i) is an instance of narrow object focus, rather than integration (within a broad focus). Generally, sentential negation within a broad focus is preferably realized by ‹not… any…› in English, cf. (ii), whereas ‹…no-one/nothing› seems more felicitous in narrow focus.

(ii)   (Kim behaved weird, don't you think? —)
       a.   I didn't NOTice anything.
       b.   ?#I noticed NOTHING.

If so, (i) might simply not be the right example to test for integration, and it is indeed P-Stress → X^0_{lex} that blocks it with indefinite pronouns in general. Otherwise, whatever the decisive factor is must draw a distinction between ‹no-one› and the rest of the indefinite pronouns.

This is the effect of STRESS-TO-ACCENT, which only blocks accenting *after* the NPA (e.g. on ‹something› in (34b)).

6.2.5 iP-HEAD-RIGHT

The final principle involved in default stress we need to introduce is given in (37):

(37^{CON}) IP-HEAD-RIGHT
Align the head of the intermediate phrase with the head of its rightmost daughter pP.

We have already seen the effect of iP-HEAD-RIGHT in some of the examples in the previous subsections: Where a sentence contains several phrasal stresses, the final one becomes the head of iP and gets to bear sentential stress.

$$
\begin{array}{llll}
& (\times\ )(& & \times\ )(\ \times\ )_{pP} \\
& (\times\ )(\ \times\ )(\ \times\ )(\ \times\ )_{PWd} \\
(38) & \text{Kim ordered a friend a beer}
\end{array}
\quad\Rightarrow\quad
\begin{array}{l}
(\qquad\qquad\qquad\qquad \times\ )_{i/IP} \\
(\times\ )(\qquad\qquad \times\ )(\ \times\ )_{pP} \\
(\times\ )(\ \times\ )(\ \times\ )(\ \times\ )_{PWd} \\
\text{Kim ordered a friend a beer}
\end{array}
$$

Consider a hypothetical 'misalignment' of the iP-head:

$$
\begin{array}{l}
(\qquad\qquad \times\qquad\qquad)_{i/IP} \\
(\times\ )(\qquad \times\ )(\ \times\ )_{pP} \\
(\times\ )(\ \times\ )(\ \times\ )(\ \times\ )_{PWd} \\
(39)\ \#\text{Kim ordered a friend a beer}
\end{array}
$$

The main ill effect of the iP-head placement in (39) would emerge in conjunction with STRESS-TO-ACCENT, (3): In (39), there could not be a pitch accent on ‹beer›, since its phrasal stress occurs post-head in the iP. Thus it is important to align the iP-head to the right (in default prosody).

Note, too, however, that STRESS-TO-ACCENT would also yield the correct accenting pattern if applied directly to the iP-less structure in (38):

$$
\begin{array}{llll}
\text{PA} & (\text{PA}) & \text{PA} & \text{PA} \\
| & | & | & | \\
(\times\ )(& & \times\ )(& \times\ )_{pP} \\
(\times\ )(\ \times\ )(& \times\ )(& \times\ )_{PWd} \\
(40)\ \text{Kim ordered a friend a beer}
\end{array}
$$

This is true for all the structures discussed so far: Since our algorithm independently determines positions for phrasal stresses throughout the sentence, the descriptive notion of nuclear stress (and hence, by STRESS-TO-ACCENT, the NPA) falls out automatically, without the need to evoke a constraint like iP-HEAD-RIGHT, or, for that matter, a structural notion of 'iP-head' at all.

But, as we will see, this is only the case for default prosody. Assuming that there is a structural entity "iP-head" will become crucial in our treatment of information structure in Chapter 7.

Before closing, it should be emphasized that integration structures do not violate iP-HEAD-RIGHT. Consider again a typical example:

```
(                        ×              )i/IP
(    × )(                 ×             )pP
(    × )(    × )(      ×  )(     ×  )PWd
```

(41)   Kim   hat   ein   Buch   bestellt   (German)

K.   has   a   book   ordered

While the head of iP in (41) does not align with the head of the rightmost prosodic word, ‹(be)stellt›, it does align with the head, ‹Buch›, of the rightmost pP, ‹hat ein Buch bestellt›. Thus, the iP is strictly right-headed, in compliance with IP-HEAD-RIGHT. The fact that the head of the pP ‹hat ein Buch bestellt› is not *its* rightmost daughter pWd is irrelevant, since IP-HEAD-RIGHT does not regard the placement of pP-heads (which follows from STRESS-XP and P-STRESS → X^o_{lex}).

6.2.6 Appendix: alternative approaches to the syntax–prosody mapping

In this chapter we opted for what may be called a STRESS-BASED MAPPING between syntax and prosodic structure. There are alternative proposals in the literature, the outlines of some of which I will present in this appendix, namely:

- Edge-based mapping (or occasionally: end-based mapping): Edges of syntactic phrases (of certain kinds) are aligned with edges of prosodic phrases *on one side*, i.e. left edges or right edges (the other edge is determined mechanically so as to partition the string exhaustively into non-overlapping prosodic phrases)
- Isomorphic mapping: syntactic phrases (of certain kinds) are aligned with edges of prosodic phrases on both sides.

As an illustration, consider a ditransitive sentence in English. A syntactic structure and the targeted prosodic structure, as predicted by the system developed above, are given in (42).[16]

(42)   Eliza presented the lady with a flower.

a. [TP [DPEliza] [VPpresented [DPthe [NPlady]] [PPwith [DPa [NPflower]]]]]

```
(                           ×        )i/IP
( ×  )(                  ×   )(       ×    )pP
( ×  )(     ×      )(   ×   )( × )(    ×   )PWd
```
b. Eliza presented the lady with a flower

We will take the pWd level as given in what follows and only indicate pPs and higher categories for the sake of perspicuity.

The pPs in (42) could be derived by an edge-based mapping based on (43).[17]

---

[16] As before, various more complex syntactic structures, including a VP-shell analysis, would yield the same results.

[17] Edge-based mappings were the method of choice in virtually all early work on prosodic phonology, starting with Selkirk (1986).

(43^{CON})   ALIGN-R(XP$_{LEX}$,pP) (for this appendix only)
Align the right edge of every (lexical) XP with the right edge of a pP.

(44) $[_{TP}[_{DP}$Eliza$][_{VP}$presented$[_{DP}$the$[_{NP}$lady$]][_{PP}$with$[_{DP}$a $[_{NP}$ flower$]]]]]$
)pP   )pP   )pP

It is particularly worth noting that there is no boundary between the V and its argument, since there is no *right* XP boundary between them; similarly, there are no boundaries between NPs and determiners and prepositions selecting them. Furthermore, where right edges of several syntactic constituents coincide (like VP, PP, and NP in (44)), a single pP-boundary satisfies (43).
   Now left brackets are inserted so as to exhaustively parse the string into non-overlapping pPs:

(45) $[_{TP}[_{DP}$Eliza$][_{VP}$presented$[_{DP}$the$[_{NP}$lady$]][_{PP}$with$[_{DP}$a $[_{NP}$ flower$]]]]]$
   (   )pP(   )pP(   )pP

The heads of these pPs will be determined in accordance with the following principle of prosodic structure:

(46^{CON})   ALIGN-R(pP-HEAD, pWD-HEAD) (for this appendix only)
Align the head of a pP with the head of the rightmost pWd within it.

The resulting structure is (47).

(47) $[_{TP}[_{DP}$Eliza$][_{VP}$presented$[_{DP}$the$[_{NP}$lady$]][_{PP}$with$[_{DP}$a $[_{NP}$ flower$]]]]]$
   (×   )pP(×   )pP(×   )pP

This is the same pP-structure as in in (42b). Adding a right-headed iP on top of (47) yields (42b).
   Why does edge-based mapping match the results of stress-based mapping so precisely? The reason is that it aligns boundaries, and assigns stress, on the recursive side, that is, on that side on which complements occur relative to their heads. The result is that heads and their complements are not separated, and the complement receives stress. A head final structure, like a German VP, would require the mirror image rules: Align the *left* boundary of XP with pP, and align the pP-head with the *left*most pWd.

(48)   a. $[_{VP}[_{DP}[_{NP}$ Sushi $]]$ essen$]$ 'eat Sushi'   (German)

    b. $[_{VP}[_{DP}[_{NP}$ Sushi $]]$ essen$]$ align (left
       (

    c. $[_{VP}[_{DP}[_{NP}$ Sushi $]]$ essen$]$ close parentheses
       (   )

    d. $[_{VP}[_{DP}[_{NP}$ Sushi $]]$ essen$]$ assign head left
       (×   )

On the stress-based treatment, the left/right choice follows automatically, without the need to parameterize the rules, as discussed in Section 6.2.2. As Truckenbrodt

(1995: ch. 6) argues, this is desirable: While not all languages avoid pP-boundaries between heads and their complements (Bengali apparently does not), those that do invariably assign pP-stress within the complement, not on the head.[18] More crucially, however, mirror image rules like the ones assumed for German VPs above would yield entirely wrong results for head initial structures like PPs (or NPs/APs) in the same language:

(49)   a. [$_{PP}$ im [$_{DP}$[$_{NP}$ Auto]]]   'in-the car'

　　　　　(　　　 (
　　 b. [$_{PP}$ im [$_{DP}$[$_{NP}$ Auto]]]   align (left

　　　　　(　　) (　　　　)
　　 c. [$_{PP}$ im [$_{DP}$[$_{NP}$ Auto]]]   close parentheses

　　　　　(　× 　) (　× 　　)
　　 d. [$_{PP}$ im [$_{DP}$[$_{NP}$ Auto]]]   assign head left

PPs in German, just as in English, form a single pP with the main stress on the complement. They are the prosodic mirror image of German VPs discussed in Section 6.2.2 (or postpositional phrases). Short of assuming different alignment constraints for different syntactic categories, this cannot be captured by an edge-based theory. In short, edge-based mapping can achieve the same effects as stress-based mapping in languages with uniform headedness, if the constraints are adjusted accordingly for the language type. But it seems to fail systematically in mixed languages.

　　Let us now turn to isomorphic mapping.[19] The main difference is that iso-morphic mapping makes extensive use of recursive prosodic structure, while edge-based mapping—like stress-base mapping—"flattens out" structures. As an illustration of isomorphic mapping, assume that every PP, DP, and VP is aligned left and right with a pP, and every TP with an iP (this is for simplicity, and roughly following Féry, 2011, though in our particular case, it wouldn't make a difference if NP were mapped onto a pP as well.) The resulting structure looks as in (50).

(50)　 (　　　　　　　　　　　　　　　　　　　　　　　　　　　　　　　)$_{iP}$
　　　　　　　　 (　　　　　　　　　　　　　　　　　　　　　　　　　　)$_{pP}$
　　　　　　　　　　　　　　　　　　　　　　(　　　　　　　　　　　　)$_{pP}$
　　　　　 (　　　　)$_{pP}$　　　　 (　　　　　　)$_{pP}$　 (　　　　　)$_{pP}$
　　 [$_{TP}$[$_{DP}$Eliza][$_{VP}$presented[$_{DP}$the[$_{NP}$lady]][$_{PP}$with[$_{DP}$ a[$_{NP}$ flower]]]]]

---

[18] A second prediction is that, by alignment constraints like (43), a language could in principle be made to group a head with its specifier, to the exclusion of the complement, say in a Spec-Head-Comp language by aligning *left* XP boundaries with left pP boundaries. Since a lot depends on the specifics of the syntactic analysis, in particular the question of what is a clear example of an overtly realized specifier of a lexical category, we will not pursue this aspect further.

[19] Much work in metrical phonology can be subsumed under isomorphic mapping; see Hayes (1995: ch. 9) for a representative example. These, however, tend not to discuss the relation to pitch accenting and intonation in general. A recent example of what I call isomorphic mapping here, including the assignment of pitch accents, can be found in Féry (2011), though many details of the proposed system remain unclear from that paper.

Structure (50) violates various conditions on bracketed grids that we have silently
been assuming, most prominently something we may call UNIFORM DEPTH: that
each terminal element is dominated by the same number of prosodic phrases. Accordingly, the notion of head assignment, and its ultimate metrical interpretation,
is not straightforward. A "conservative" head assignment—roughly, 'one asterisk
between any pair of brackets on any level'—would result in the structure in (51).

$$
\begin{array}{lll}
(& \times &)_{iP} \\
\quad(& \times &)_{pP} \\
& \times &)_{pP} \\
\quad\quad(& \times &)_{pP} \\
(\quad \times \quad)_{pP} \quad\quad (\quad\quad \times \quad)_{pP} \quad (\quad\quad \times \quad)_{pP} &
\end{array}
$$

(51) $[_{TP}[_{DP}\text{Eliza}][_{VP}\text{presented}[_{DP}\text{the}[_{NP}\text{lady}]][_{PP}\text{with}[_{DP}\text{a}[_{NP}\text{ flower}]]]]]$

Despite its complexity, (51) actually only represents two different levels of metrical
strength, and is thus equivalent to something like (52), where prosodic phrases on
adjacent layers may 'share' a head.[20]

$$
\begin{array}{lll}
(\quad\quad (& \times &)_{pP})_{iP} \\
(\quad \times \quad) \quad\quad (\quad\quad \times \quad)(\quad\quad (& \times &))_{pP}
\end{array}
$$

(52) $[_{TP}[_{DP}\text{Eliza}][_{VP}\text{presented}[_{DP}\text{the}[_{NP}\text{lady}]][_{PP}\text{with}[_{DP}\text{a}[_{NP}\text{ flower }]]]]]$

The crucial observation here is that recursive mapping yields the same relative,
(51), or even absolute, (52), stress pattern as the methods previously employed.
Crucially, however, it derives a lot more right, and in English examples in particular,
left boundaries, namely between any head and its complement, regardless of
directionality. If these boundaries had a definable prosodic interpretation, this
would constitute evidence in favor of such a structure; if they do not, one can
view them either as harmless by-products of the stress assignment algorithm, or
as illicit relics of syntactic structure with no rightful place in prosodic structure
(and hence to be avoided in the ways seen in stress-based and edge-based mapping
algorithms). Clearly, further empirical work is required.[21]

Table 6.1 summarizes the results of our little comparison between the three kinds
of mapping approaches. Given suitable assumptions, all three can presumably
be made to converge on predicted stress patterns, including head–complement
integration; this is so because they all refer to syntactic phrases, rather than heads.

---

[20] One can derive the stress assignment in (52) by simply assigning the minimum number of beats
necessary to ensure (i):

(i)   Each pP/iP has exactly one metrically strongest element.

Details here are murky because all of the more recent work on the mapping of syntax to prosody I am
aware of relies on a purely intuitive understanding of what bracketed metrical grids are, rather than
defining them as formal objects, and the notion of "head" seems particularly vague in formal terms (see
Halle and Verganud, 1987, for an early more formal treatment, if only to get an idea of what that would
entail).

[21] Gussenhoven (2004: ch. 14), while using an edge-based account, derives very complex nested
pP-structures (since frequently both edges are mapped) and presents some metrical evidence for their
specifics, in particular within complex NPs. The reader is referred to that work as an inspiration for one
kind of work that may shed light on whether certain prosodic boundaries exist or not.

TABLE 6.1   A crude comparison of the boundaries created by different types of mapping algorithms.

Mapping Type	Syntactic Xp Boundaries Aligned With Prosodic Boundaries
stress-based	only on recursive side of embedding category
edge-based	only on one side, depending on parametrization of alignment
isomorphic	both sides

Isomorphic and stress-based mapping share the property of automatically projecting directionality of complementation onto the metrical structure, whereas edge-based mapping must rely on directional constraints to achieve the same effect. As discussed, edge-based mapping thus appears to miss a cross-linguistically valid generalization, and runs into difficulties in treating mixed languages, that is, languages in which direction of complementation varies between categories or even lexical items.

Stress-based and isomorphic mapping differ mostly in the amount of "syntactic residue" they create in prosodic structure. Whereas the former eliminates all but the structure necessary to achieve a layered and fully parsed bracketed metrical grid 'on the way to prosody' (via complex mapping constraints), the latter preserves much or all of the, often asymmetrical, embedding of syntactic structure in the prosodic structure and relies on more complex rules mapping prosodic structure to actual prosody, including, presumably, rules that simply ignore a lot of prosodic structure.

It is perhaps worthwhile to emphasize that elements of isomorphic mapping are of course found in *all* of the approaches sketched here, simply reflecting the observation that prosodic structure does, after all, in many ways reflect syntactic constituency. For example, Wrap-xp and Stress-xp (especially when linked by Wrap-xp/Stress-xp-Correspondence as done in Section 6.3.2), are very close in spirit and effect to a rule like "each lexical XP is mapped onto a prosodic phrase." In fact, Selkirk (2011) and subsequent work based on it, sometimes referred to as the Match Theory of syntax–prosody mapping, is built around a family of constraints that require exact matches (i.e. left *and* right alignment) between syntactic and prosodic category type in the by now predictable way (syntactic word↔prosodic word, lexical phrase↔phonological phrase, clause↔intermediate phrase), much like those assumed in our discussion of isomorphic mapping earlier in this Appendix. Still, in a Match Theory, these constraints are severely counteracted by other constraints which, among other things, favor flatter, non-recursive prosodic structures of equal depth. The resulting prosodic structures thus look a lot more like those derived here by the stress-based mapping such as (42b), than ones that are truly isomorphic to syntactic structure, such as (51). The label "isomorphic mapping" is meant exclusively for approaches in which the hierarchical syntactic structure is in fact reflected (more or less) unmitigated in prosodic structure. What we may call Categorial Mapping Constraints like "lexical phrase↔phonological phrase," may occur in isomorphic mapping approaches (where they are mostly or completely unimpeded by counteracting constraints) as well as others, including Selkirk's match theory or stress-based accounts (where they are routinely violated in favor of other constraints, particularly prosody-internal well-formedness constraints).

6.3 Towards more complex stress (and accent) patterns

In this section we will discuss some finer points of English phrasal and sentential intonation. The data here are more subtle and, more often than not, have not been experimentally tested. We will follow the literature in casting our discussion in terms of the relative metrical strength of accented elements. It should be borne in mind, though, that the actual acoustic cues for this may be varied, for example phrasing, lengthening, accent scaling, or accent type. Much in this area needs to be investigated in more detail, and the content of this section should be seen as (even) more speculative than that of the previous sections.

The overarching theme of this section is the idea that—contrary to what we assumed up to now—prosodic structure shows a limited kind of recursion, what Ladd (2008) calls COMPOUND PROSODIC DOMAINS, namely adjacent layers of prosodic phrases of the same type, as shown in Figure 6.2.

6.3.1 Additional levels of phrasing above the intermediate phrase

Speakers can discriminate between different groupings of IPs, as shown in Ladd (1988) for cases involving entire sentences. Two of his examples are given in (53).

(53) a. Warren is a stronger campaigner, and Ryan has more popular politics, but Allan has a lot more money.
      b. Warren is a stronger campaigner, but Ryan has more popular politics, and Allan has a lot more money.

In an experiment reported in that paper, speakers reading those sentences consistently marked each clause as an intonational phrase, that is, they used a complex boundary tune before ⟨and⟩ as well as ⟨but⟩. In addition, however, they marked (and perceived) the boundary before ⟨but⟩ stronger than that before ⟨and⟩: They produced, on average, a longer pause, and realized the first pitch accent *after* the break higher (a phenomenon known as RESET). This, Ladd concludes, suggests the following two groupings:

(54) a. (A and B) but C
      b. A but (B and C)

$$
\begin{array}{llll}
(\quad\quad)_{pWd} & (\quad\quad)_{pP} & (\quad\quad)_{iP} & (\quad\quad)_{IP} \\
(\ )\ldots(\ )_{pWd} & (\ )\ldots(\ )_{pP} & (\ )\ldots(\ )_{iP} & (\ )\ldots(\ )_{IP}
\end{array}
$$

FIGURE 6.2   compound prosodic domains.

But if each of A, B, and C are themselves IPs, the highest prosodic category below the utterance, what could the bracketed constituents correspond to? Ladd's (2008: sec. 8.2.4f) answer is that in such cases, the level of the intonational phrase is recursive:

(55) a.
```
    (                                                      )Utt
    (                                  ) (                 )IP
    (                    )(            ) (                 )IP
      Warren . . . campaigner, and Ryan . . . politics, but Allan . . . money
    (                                                      )Utt
    (                    )(                                )IP
    (                    )(                )(              )IP
```
b.   Warren . . . campaigner, but Ryan . . . politics, and Allan . . . money

Note that this proposal suspends the assumption that each prosodic category level occurs exactly once in each prosodic structure. However, as Ladd points out, there is a very limited kind of recursion here: The same category—the intonational phrase—occurs twice in adjacent layers. I call this "limited recursion" since there is no such thing as, say, a prosodic word or a phonological phrase that contains an intonational phrase; the strict ordering of categories is still preserved. Likewise, the structures proposed in Ladd (1988) still show EQUAL DEPTH: If A and B are metrical sisters, they contain the same number of prosodic levels.[22]

Expanding on the discussion in Ladd (2008), note that—as far as intonation in the narrow sense is concerned—each clausal boundary is associated with exactly one IP boundary tone. The "stacked IP" effect only regards boundary correlates such as length of the pause, final lengthening, and tonal reset. Put differently, only one IP layer—the lower[23]—is associated with the intonational features of an IP, while the ones above it simply indicate prosodic breaks of a higher degree. If this were truly stacking of IPs, one might expect that a "double IP boundary" like that between ‹campaigner› and ‹but› in (54b) could also have a more complex boundary tune—consisting of two, potentially different, T% tones, one for each IP—than a "single IP boundary" like that between ‹politics› and ‹and›.

So an alternative way of looking at Ladd's compound prosodic domains is that what we have here is not recursion of the *intonational category* IP, but of some roughly clause-sized *metrical* category. One way to write this is sketched in (56), where we use ϕ indiscriminately for prosodic phrases, and annotate them with T% where they have the intonational characteristics of an intonational phrase:

(56)
```
    (                                        )φ
    (                             )φ  (       )φ
    (                  )φ T%(      )φ T%(     )φ T%
      Warren...campaigner,   and Ryan...politics,   but Allan...money
```

In what follows, we will further explore the consequence of the idea that this kind of limited recursion is allowed in prosodic structure.

---

[22] Equal Depth is a more general version of Uniform Depth, mentioned in Section 6.2.6—each terminal element is dominated by the same number of prosodic phrases.

[23] It has to be the lowest, since Ladd found that each clause boundary was realized with boundary tones, including the lowest.

6.3.2 Left-branching sub-constituents

Since the metrical structures used so far have a fixed and rather small number of layers, the constraint duo STRESS-XP and WRAP-XP used to map syntactic to metrical structure radically "flattens out" structures. Its workings can be summarized as:

- in a cascade of two or more XPs, each properly containing the next, they form one p-phrase around the highest, and assign p-stress within the lowest;
- where of two or more XPs neither contains the other, each forms it own p-phrase;
- the last p-stress becomes the head of the i/IP.

By "flattening out" I mean that two or more XPs that aren't syntactic sisters routinely end up corresponding to pPs which are metrical sisters. Take for example the complex phrases in (57).

```
                    (                                    ×        )_{i/IP}
                    (      ×     ) (      ×     ) (       ×        )_{pP}
(57)   a.          the   boy   met the  girl     at the teach  -in
       b.          the   boy    ,    the  girl  , and the teacher
       c. (I like)       Nancy  ,         books ,    and bebop
       d.    (an)   unexpected           loud            noise
```

Our constraints predict that the pPs wrapping DP, VP, and PP in (57a) are all metrical sisters. The same holds for the DPs in (57b–57c), and the two APs and NP in (57d). The asymmetry in metrical strength is purely due to prosody-internal reasons, namely the fact that the iP-head is right-aligned. The resulting structure jibes well with the prosodic facts.

In particular, the fact that the last two elements in each sequence—‹met the girl + at the teach-in›, ‹the girl + and the teacher›, ‹books + and bebop›, ‹loud + noise›—on most syntactic accounts form a constituent to the exclusion of the first seems to have no additional prosodic effect.

On the other hand, in the following examples, there seems to be a stronger boundary, informally indicated by $|$, separating the first two elements from the third:

(58)   a. (both) the boy with the pearl $|$ and the teacher
       b. (I like) fancy books $|$ and bebop
       c. (an) unexpectedly loud $|$ noise

The impression is that a left-branching sub-phrase—‹the boy with the pearl›, ‹fancy books›, ‹unexpectedly loud›—is prosodically demarcated, rather than flattened out. The same is regularly seen with complex subjects:

(59)   a. The mayor of Chicago $|$ won their support.
       b. The boy and the girl $|$ won their support.

The break between the head noun ‹mayor› and the PP ‹of Chicago› is weaker than that between subject and VP in (59a); similarly for the break between the two conjuncts in (59b).

These patterns are unexpected: our theory so far predicts the same "flat" prosodic constituency for both these types of syntactic structures, schematized in (60a) (representing (57)) and (60b) (representing (58)/(59)).

$$
\begin{array}{ll}
\begin{array}{l}
(\qquad\qquad \times \quad)_{i/\text{IP}} \\
(\ \times\ )\ (\times)(\times\quad)_{\text{pP}} \\
\text{a.}\ [\ \text{XP}\ [_{\Sigma\text{P}}\text{YP ZP}\ ]]
\end{array} &
\begin{array}{l}
(\qquad\qquad\qquad \times \quad)_{i/\text{IP}} \\
(\qquad \times\ )(\times)(\ \times\ )_{\text{pP}} \\
\text{b.}\ [[_{\Sigma\text{P}}\ \text{XP YP}\ ]\ \text{ZP}\ ]
\end{array}
\end{array}
$$

(60)

Both structures satisfy STRESS-XP for each of XP, YP, ZP, and all higher constituents, and both satisfy WRAP-XP for XP, YP, and ZP, but violate it for all higher constituents, including the complex sub-constituent labeled ΣP in (60a/60b). No asymmetry between the left- and right-branching structures is predicted.

Consider now a prosodic structure for the left-branching configuration in which pP can be recursive:

$$
\begin{array}{ll}
\begin{array}{l}
(\qquad\qquad \times\ )(\ \times\ )_{\text{pP}} \\
(\qquad \times\ )(\times)(\ \times\ )_{\text{pP}} \\
[[_{\Sigma\text{P}}\ \text{XP YP}]\ \text{ZP}\ ]
\end{array} &
\begin{array}{l}
(\qquad\qquad\qquad\qquad\qquad\qquad\qquad \times \qquad)_{i/\text{IP}} \\
(\qquad\qquad\qquad\qquad\qquad \times\quad)(\qquad\qquad \times \qquad)_{\text{pP}} \\
(\qquad\qquad \times\ )(\qquad\qquad \times\ )(\qquad \times \qquad)_{\text{pP}} \\
[[_{\Sigma}\text{the boy with the pearl}][\ \text{and the teacher}]]
\end{array}
\end{array}
$$

(61)

This seems like a promising structure to model cases like (58) and (59) (more on the details in Section 6.3.3). Similar to the cases of IP recursion discussed in Section 6.3.1, it allows for a very limited kind of recursion: A prosodic category "repeats" on adjacent layers.

What would motivate a structure like (61)? It turns out that, unlike in (60b) above, WRAP-XP is satisfied in (61) for ΣP as well, by the initial pP on the higher level. So the additional layer of pP is in fact advantageous in terms of avoiding a WRAP-XP violation, motivating its inclusion, as in structure (61).

Still we have not derived (61) quite yet. Note that (62) meets WRAP-XP even better than (61).

$$
\begin{array}{l}
(\qquad\qquad \times\ )_{\text{pP}} \\
(\qquad \times\ )(\times)(\ \times\ )_{\text{pP}} \\
[[_{\Sigma\text{P}}\ \text{XP YP}]\ \text{ZP}\ ]
\end{array}
$$

(62)

The top-most pP now wraps *each* phrase in the entire structure, including ΣP and, unlike in (61), the entire structure (the unlabeled outermost brackets). So at this point, (62), not the empirically more adequate (61), is predicted to be the outcome.

To force the phrasing in (61), we will follow the spirit of Truckenbrodt and Büring (in preparation) and adopt the following additional restriction:

(63^{CON})   WRAP-XP/STRESS-XP-CORRESPONDENCE

For any syntactic phrase XP, WRAP-XP and STRESS-XP must be met by the same prosodic phrase.

WRAP-XP/STRESS-XP-CORRESPONDENCE is met for ΣP in structure (61) above: the initial pP on the top layer wraps ΣP, and its head is within ΣP. Let us call a pP that meets STRESS-XP and WRAP-XP for a given XP a CORRESPONDENT of XP. ΣP in (61) has a correspondent. Similarly on the lower layer: Each of XP, YP, and ZP contains the stress of the pP that wraps it, and thus has a correspondent. Not so in (62): Even though ΣP is wrapped (by the top layer pP), and stressed (by each of the two initial pPs on the lower layer), it does not contain the stress of the pP that wraps it (which is on ZP). It does not have a correspondent.

WRAP-XP/STRESS-XP-CORRESPONDENCE thus derives the advantage for structure (61) that we have been looking for. Still, one last amendment is required. As it is, (61) and (62) are in fact equally good in terms of WRAP-XP/STRESS-XP-CORRESPONDENCE: While (61) provides a correspondent for ΣP, it does not provide a correspondent for the entire structure. Structure (62), on the other hand, has a correspondent for the entire structure (the top layer pP), but not for ΣP.

A simple way to get the advantage of both structures is by adding yet another layer of prosodic phrasing, as in structure (64):

$$
\begin{array}{llll}
(& & \times &)_{?P} \\
(& \times)(& \times &)_{pP} \\
(& \times)(\times)(& \times &)_{pP}
\end{array}
$$
(64) $[[_{\Sigma P} \text{ XP YP] ZP }]$

In (64), *each* syntactic phrase, including the one corresponding to the unlabeled outermost brackets, has a correspondent. In fact, (64) involves nothing above and beyond what we already have, if we assume that ?P is in fact the intermediate or intonational phrase. That is, if we assume that STRESS-XP and WRAP-XP can be met by *any* kind of prosodic phrase, not just pP.

Summing up at this point: by allowing WRAP-XP to be satisfied by higher layers of structure, i/IP or recursive pP, we can effectively avoid all WRAP-XP violations. WRAP-XP/STRESS-XP-CORRESPONDENCE imposes an additional restriction on this system, which forces intermediate layers of phrasing in structures with complex sub-constituents such as left-branching coordinations or complex subject.

To conclude this section, we will now return to the case of right-branching structures such as those in (57), and their flat prosodic structure (60a), repeated in more detail in structure (65) below.

$$
\begin{array}{lllll}
(& & & \times &)_{i/IP} \\
(& \times &) (& \times &) (& \times &)_{pP}
\end{array}
$$
(65)   a. $[_{IP}[_{DP}$ the boy $][_{VP}[_{VP}$ met $[_{DP}$ the girl]] $[_{PP}$ at the teach-in]]]
        b. $[_{\&P}[_{DP}$ Nancy $][_{\&P}[_{DP}$ books $]$ $[_{\&}$ and bebop]]]
        c. $[_{NP}[_{AP}$ unexpected] $[_{NP}[_{AP}$ loud $]$ $[_{NP}$ noise]]]
            $[[_{XP}$ $][_{\Sigma P}[_{YP}$ $]$ $[_{ZP}$]]]

Note that the minimal prosodic structure in (65) already meets WRAP-XP for all syntactic phrases involved. In particular, ΣP is wrapped in i/IP, and—unlike in the case of left-branching structures—the head of i/IP is by default within ΣP. Thus i/IP is a correspondent for the entire structure, ΣP, ZP, and whatever phrases are embedded in the latter.

The three-layered structure (66) provides no advantage over (65).

$$
\begin{array}{lllllll}
(& & & & & \times &)_{i/\text{IP}} \\
(& \times &) & (& & \times &)_{\text{pP}} \\
(& \times &) & (& \times &)(& \times &)_{\text{pP}}
\end{array}
$$

(66) a. $[_{\text{IP}}[_{\text{DP}}$ the boy $][_{\text{VP}}[_{\text{VP}}$met $[_{\text{DP}}$the girl$]][_{\text{PP}}$at the teach-in$]]]$
   b. $[_{\&\text{P}}[_{\text{DP}}$ Nancy $][_{\&\text{P}}[_{\text{DP}}$ books $][_{\&}$ and bebop $]]]$
   c. $[_{\text{NP}}[_{\text{AP}}$unexpected$][_{\text{NP}}[_{\text{AP}}$ loud $][_{\text{NP}}$ noise $]]]$
      $[[_{\text{XP}}$ $][_{\Sigma\text{P}}[_{\text{YP}}$ $][_{\text{ZP}}$ $]]]$

We can rule out (66) by introducing a low-ranked constraint *STRUCTURE or *RECURSION that penalizes additional structure; crucially WRAP-XP outranks *STRUCTURE, so that a structure that *improves* on satisfying WRAP-XP, like (61) above is unaffected by *STRUCTURE. That way, (66) will be blocked by (65), but (61) will not be blocked by (60b).[24]

To sum up this section, we have made it easier to fulfil WRAP-XP in some ways, but harder in others. By allowing WRAP-XP to be met by i/IP in addition to pP, and by allowing recursion at the pP level, more levels of prosodic structure became eligible to satisfy WRAP-XP. Indeed, if this were all we had done, WRAP-XP would be met almost trivially, as long as there is one all-encompassing prosodic phrase, like i/IP, wrapping everything. By imposing an additional restriction, WRAP-XP/STRESS-XP-CORRESPONDENCE, we make it harder again to meet WRAP-XP. Additional prosodic structure may be required to ensure that a syntactic phrase also contains the *head* of the prosodic phrase that wraps it. Since iP is right-headed, this will generally happen in left-branching structures, such as those in (58) and (59).

The net effect of these changes is to allow for "deeper," more differentiated prosodic structures, as seems adequate for clauses with complex sub-constituents, especially left-branching ones. Such structures also provide additional evidence in favor of limited prosodic recursion, as envisaged by Ladd (2008), discussed in Section 6.3.1, this time at the level of the phonological phrase.

6.3.3 Left-branching and stress equalization

In this section we make explicit an additional assumption made in our discussion of left-branching structures above. For concreteness, (67) and (68) give two detailed instantiations of left-branching structures, previously schematized in (61):

---

[24] The proper functioning of the system relies on the proper ranking of *STRUCTURE/*RECURSION and IP-HEAD-RIGHT. Crucially, we need (ia) to be preferred over (ib):

$$
\begin{array}{ll}
(& \times &)_{i/\text{IP}} \\
(& \times)(\times &)_{\text{pP}} \\
(& \times)(\times)(\times &)_{\text{pP}}
\end{array}
\qquad
\begin{array}{ll}
(& \times &)_{i/\text{IP}} \\
(& \times)(\times)(\times &)_{\text{pP}}
\end{array}
$$

(i) a. $[[_{\Sigma\text{P}}$ XP YP$]$ ZP $]$ b. $[[_{\Sigma\text{P}}$ XP YP$]$ ZP $]$

Structure (ib) violates IP-HEAD-RIGHT, (ia) meets IP-HEAD-RIGHT, but involves more prosodic structure. It is thus crucial that *STRUCTURE/*RECURSION is ranked below IP-HEAD-RIGHT.

```
(                            ×  )IP
(                 ×   )(     ×  )pP
(    ×   )(        ×   )(     ×  )pP
(    ×   )(        ×   )(     ×  )pWd
```
(67) [DP[DP John]and [DP Mary]][VP won]

```
(                                    ×   )i/IP
(                    ×   ) (          ×   )pP
(   ×   )(            ×   ) (          ×   )pP
(   ×   )(            ×   ) ( ×  )(          ×   )pWd
```
(68) [[John]and [Mary]][won [our [support]]]

Note that the VPs ⟨won (our support)⟩ here have two isomorphic layers of pPs
wrapping them. The reason for this is simply that we would not get a well-formed
structure if we didn't "augment" the structure in this way. More specifically, we are
implicitly assuming that prosodic sisters need to be of equal depth: If the subject is
mapped onto a prosodic structure with three layers of phrasing (and accordingly:
three levels of stress), so must be the VP.[25]

Hayes (1995) employs a process called STRESS EQUALIZATION in similar circumstances, whereby one phrase—like ⟨(won)$_{pP}$/(won our support))$_{pP}$⟩ in (67)/(68)—
gets an additional level of structure and stress, in order to be equal in prosodic
structure to a more complex constituent to its left. This is done by "inserting" a layer
of prosodic structure. We assume that something like Hayes' Stress Equalization is
available in order to guarantee equal depth.

For illustration, suppose we want to derive the metrical structure for (69):

(69) John and Mary won our support.

By STRESS-XP and WRAP-XP, the VP here would be predicted to have the structure
in (70).

```
(                      ×   )pP
(   ×   )(             ×   )pWd
```
(70) [VP won [DP our [NP support]]]

But this cannot directly be concatenated with the subject (71), which—by the
reasoning just developed in Section 6.3.2—has one more level of structure:

```
(                 ×   )pP
(    ×   )(        ×   )pP
(    ×   )(        ×   )pWd
```
(71) [DP[DP John]and [DP Mary]]

In order to get a well-formed prosodic structure for (69) as a whole, (70) needs to
be augmented by one layer:

[25] Equal depth is guaranteed in a framework which adheres to the Strict Layer Hypothesis. But now
that we allow for recursion in prosodic structure, this is no longer the case.

```
       (                          ×    )pP
       (                          ×    )pP
       (     ×   )(               ×    )pWd
(72)   [ won [ our [ support ]]]
```

This now matches the complex subject ⟨*John and Mary*⟩ in prosodic complexity, and we get (73a), and the accent pattern in (73b).

```
       (                                              ×    )i/IP
       (                          ×     ) (            ×    )pP
       (     ×    )(              ×     ) (            ×    )pP
       (     ×    )(              ×     ) (  ×   )(    ×    )pWd
(73)   a.  [ [ John ] and [ Mary ]][ won [ our [ support ]]]

           PA              PA        (PA)         NPA
       (    |              |                       |     )i/IP
       (    |              |    ) (                 |   × )pP
       (    ×    )(             ×    ) (            ×    )pP
       (    ×    )(             ×    ) (  ×   )(    ×    )pWd
       b.  [[ John ] and [ Mary ]][ won [ our [ support ]]]
```

6.3.4 Excursus: free recursion?

In Section 6.3.1 we speculatively suggested that it might be advantageous to give up the fixed link between prosodic categories and intonational categories, so that the former, but not the latter, may be recursive. Taken to the extreme, we may assume that there is only one type of prosodic phrase, call it ϕ, which is freely recursive. Intonational categories like iP and IP may more or less freely align with ϕs at any level, the only restriction being that if a ϕ-level is realized by intonational phrases, it must dominate a ϕ-level realized as intermediate phrases.

So for example, instead of (74a), we would have (74b), where $\phi\%$ means "a prosodic phrase whose right edge is aligned with a boundary tone," $\phi-$ "a prosodic phrase whose right edge is aligned with a phrase tone," and $\phi*$ "a prosodic phrase whose head is aligned with a PA" etc.

```
          )IP          )ϕ%
          )iP          )ϕ-
          )pP          )ϕ*
(74)  a. ...)pWd   b. ...)pWd
```

Using this notation we can not just translate standard structures as in (74), but also describe non-standard structures such as (75) (or (56) above):

```
       (                                                    ×   )ϕ-%
       (                        ×    )ϕ   (                  ×   )ϕ
       (    ×   )ϕ*  (          ×    )ϕ*  (                  ×   )ϕ*
       (    ×   )pWd (          ×    )pWd (  ×   )pWd(        ×   )pWd
(75)   the boy       and the girl        won      their support
```

Structure (75) involves what we called recursive pP levels above. Note, too, that we can now officially write $\phi-\%$ to mean that iP and IP are co-extensional, that is, our former abbreviatory notation i/IP is now an official theoretical construct. By the same token, we may write things like (76a), instead of (76b), for the citation form.

$$
\begin{array}{ll}
 & (\ \times\ )_{\text{IP}} \\
 & (\ \times\ )_{\text{iP}} \\
 & (\ \times\ )_{\text{pP}} \\
(\ \times\ )_{\phi*\text{-}\%} & (\ \times\ )_{\text{pWd}} \\
\end{array}
$$

(76)   a. girl   b. girl

Lastly, by loosening the connection between metrical structure and intonational structure, we can account for certain instances of "intonational allophony." For example, (77) is an alternative realization (out of several) for the same metrical (not prosodic!) structure as (75):

$$
\begin{array}{lllll}
(& & & & \times\ )_{\phi\%} \\
(& & \times\ )_{\phi\text{-}} & (& \times\ )_{\phi\text{-}} \\
(& \times\ )_{\phi} & (& & \times\ )_{\phi} \\
(& \times\ )_{\text{pWd}*} & (& \times\ )_{\phi} & \times\ )_{\phi} \\
\end{array}
$$

(77)   the boy   and the girl   won   their support

In (77), the subject is intonationally realized as an intermediate phrase by a phrase tone on ‹girl›, whereas in (75) there is no phrase tone here. Furthermore, and independently of that, (77) has a pitch accent on the verb, while (75) does not. The two intonational patterns are schematized in (78a) (=(75)) vis-à-vis (78b) (=(77)):

$$
\begin{array}{lll}
\text{T*} & \text{T*} & \text{T*T--T\%} \\
| & | & |\ | \\
\end{array}
$$

(78)   a. the boy and the girl won their support

$$
\begin{array}{lll}
\text{T*} & \text{T*T--\ T*} & \text{T*T--T\%} \\
| & |\ |\ \ | & |\ | \\
\end{array}
$$

b. the boy and the girl won their support

The constraints as defined here are compatible with such structures. In the following, we will stick to the more conservative assumption that pP, iP, IP, etc. are *bona fide* categories of prosodic structure, with a limited amount of recursion permitted.

6.3.5 Right-branching structures

We have seen in Section 6.3.2 that complex left branches yield more articulate prosodic structures. For right-branching structures we continue to predict a flat structure. It has been argued, however, that such structures routinely have more complex stress patterns. Hayes (1995) for example claims the following pattern as natural for the sentence ‹John bought five black cats›, which is strictly right-branching (Hayes' metrical grids for this example is not bracketed, but see below):

$$
\begin{array}{lllll}
 & & & & \times \\
 & \times & & & \times \\
 & \times & & \times & \times \\
 & \times & \times & \times & \times & \times \\
\end{array}
$$

(79)   John bought five black cats

Hayes argues that this stress pattern, except for the nuclear stress on ‹cats›, is not determined based on the syntax-to-prosody mapping, but by prosodic principles alone. In other words, the only structurally determined aspect of this stress pattern would be something very flat like (80).

```
                              ×
    ×     ×     ×     ×     ×
(80) John bought five black cats
```

The additional accents in (79) are purely rhythmic in nature, basically imposing a regular rhythmic pattern on the pre-nuclear material (note that the pattern in every line is a regular iteration of "stress"–"no stress").

This is in principle compatible with the system developed in this chapter. What is needed is a "late" operation of structure addition which can apply purely rhythmically, on condition that it does not change the relative stress between heads and non-heads within a phrase (which here merely amounts to ‹cats› being strongest).

What is less clear is the actual metrical structure of the stress pattern in (79). If we want to continue assuming exhaustive parsing above the level of (the lowest) pP, the only structure compatible with the stress pattern in (79) is (81).

```
(                              ×  )ɪ/ɪP
( ×  )(                         ×  )pP
( ×  )(            ×  )(         ×  )pP
( ×  )( ×     )( × )( ×  )( ×  )pP
(81)  John bought five  black cats
```

Note that according to (81), ‹bought five› is a pP, although it is of course not a syntactic constituent. Its sole raison d'être is to provide for an additional level of stress on ‹five›.

Curiously all our syntax-to-prosody mapping constraints are met in (81); in particular, each syntactic XP—‹[_{AP} black], [_{NP} black cats], [_{DP} five black cats], [_{VP} bought five black cats]› and ‹[_{DP} John]›—is contained in a pP (WRAP-XP) with a head in XP (STRESS-XP,WRAP-XP/STRESS-XP-CORRESPONDENCE). Still, obviously more work is required to determine if (81) is indeed the/a correct structure for ‹John bought five black cats›, and if so by what principles or operations it is licensed. Suffice it to say at this point that the prosody of right-branching structures in English need not be as flat as predicted by our official rules, but that apparently the attested patterns all preserve any differences in metrical strength predicted by them.

7

Prosodic structure and information structure

We are now ready to combine the detailed and more realistic picture of prosodic structure developed in Chapter 6 with our earlier insights about the effect of information structure on prosody.

7.1 Focus

In Section 2.3 of Chapter 2 we described the effect of focus as in condition (1), our adaptation of Truckenbrodt's (1995) modification of a rule proposed in Jackendoff (1972).

(1^{OLD}) F-Realization Condition
For any F-domain D, the final accent in D lies in a focus of D.

We will now replace condition (1) by its final incarnation, (2), (which is closer in various aspects to Jackendoff's and Truckenbrodt's original proposals[1]).

(2^{CON}) Focus Realization
The highest stress within a F-domain D falls on a focus of D.

Condition (2) captures the effect of (1) within the prosodic setting developed so far. To see that, let us start with cases in which the F-domain is identical to the entire sentence. Then condition (2) requires that the focus contain the strongest stress in the sentence, that is: the head of i/IP. And by Stress-to-Accent, the head of i/IP

---

[1] The original formulations are given in (i) and (ii):

(i) Focus
If F is a focus and DF is its domain, then the highest prominence in DF will be within F. (Truckenbrodt, 1995: 107)

(ii) If a phrase P is chosen as the focus of a sentence S, the highest stress in S will be on the syllable of P that is assigned the highest stress by the stress rules. (Jackendoff, 1972)

(i) uses "prominence" rather than "stress," but is otherwise identical to (2). (ii) differs from both merely in that it lacks the relativization to F-domains, i.e. it takes the domain of the focus to invariably be the entire sentence.

Intonation and Meaning. First edition. Daniel Büring.
© Daniel Büring 2016. First published 2016 by Oxford University Press.

will bear the last pitch accent in i/IP. So in this roundabout way, FOCUS REALIZATION in (2) derives that the focus must contain the NPA.

The abstract rationale behind this effect can be summarized simply as follows: By FOCUS REALIZATION, focus entails maximal stress, and by STRESS-TO-ACCENT, maximal stress entails the final pitch accent. We will now turn to some of the finer points of this.

7.1.1 How to reassign sentential stress: head misalignment vs de-phrasing

In a sentence with focus on the subject, FOCUS REALIZATION can in principle be satisfied—that is, the i/IP head/NPA be brought within the subject—in two ways: By "shifting" the i/IP head to the left, in violation of IP-HEAD-RIGHT, as in (3a), or by omitting post-focal p-phrases, in violation of STRESS-XP, as in (3b).

(3)   (Who ate pumpkin?—)

```
         (    ×           )ᵢ/IP
         (    ×     ) (          ×      )ₚₚ
         (    ×     ) ( ×  )(      ×      )ₚwd
     a. [ JONES ]ꜰ [ ate [ pumpkin ]]              i/IP-head misalignment

         (    ×           )ᵢ/IP
         (    ×           )ₚₚ
         (    ×     ) ( ×  )(      ×      )ₚwd
     b. [ JONES ]ꜰ[ ate [ pumpkin ]]               VP de-phrased
```

By STRESS-TO-ACCENT, both of these structures result in the NPA on the subject, and no accent on the verb or object, which is the correct outcome.

(Note that, perhaps contrary to appearances, (3b) does not violate IP-HEAD-RIGHT at all; in fact, since there is only one pP within i/IP, IP-HEAD-RIGHT is trivially met. (3b)'s only fault lies with its failure to provide for phrasal stress on the object or the VP; recall the discussion of IP-HEAD-RIGHT in integration structures at the end of Section 6.2.5.)

We can thus choose one outcome or the other by adjusting the relative ranking of IP-HEAD-RIGHT and STRESS-XP. Ranking IP-HEAD-RIGHT higher than STRESS-XP yields dephrasing, as in (3b), ranking STRESS-XP higher than IP-HEAD-RIGHT results in iP-head misalignment.

We will assume the latter option, iP-head misalignment, for English here (though the former is likely correct in other languages).[2] I will review four arguments for the choice here; a fifth argument will come from the phenomenon of second occurrence focus, to be discussed in Section 7.3.

Length effects: What we may expect to find in structures like (3a) are prosodic reflexes of the pP boundary between subject and VP, as well as of the phrasal stress—though not accent—on the object. Jun and Fougeron (2002) note in passing that in English (unlike French) the VP in a subject focus sentence is not signifi-

---

[2] Dephrasing was assumed for English in Büring and Gutiérrez-Bravo (2001) and Büring (2001a, 2001b), following the analysis of focus in Chichewa in Truckenbrodt (1999); iP-head-misalignment was assumed in Samek-Lodovici (2005).

cantly shorter than in the same sentence under default accenting. Assuming that both phrasal stress and boundaries result in lengthening, omission of a pP and its concomitant p-stress in (3b) should result in such a shortening. Since this is not the case, they conclude that English omits accents (i.e. shifts the iP head leftward), but does not omit phrases or stresses.

Alignment effects: Likewise in passing, (Hayes and Lahiri, 1991: 68) note that the *right* boundary of a focussed element can serve as the point of alignment for a phrase tone (their (31), notation and presentation slightly amended):

(4)   ('North Carolina' is monomorphemic?!—No,)

       H*   L⁻   L%
       | | /
   [TIpperary]_F is monomorphemic.

The fall after the pitch accent on ⟨Ti-⟩ does not extend across the entire sentence, but "levels off near the end of the main stressed word" (ibid.). Assuming that phrase tones like L- in (4) do not associate with PWd boundaries, there must thus be a higher prosodic phrase boundary at the end of ⟨Tipperary⟩.[3]

Relative strength effects: Studies such as Huss (1978) have shown early on that speakers can distinguish pairs like ⟨IMport⟩/⟨imPORT⟩ even in the absence of F_0 excursions (i.e. without pitch accenting). That is, word stress is detectable in the absence of pitch accenting. The same is true, I suspect, for phrasal stresses.

   Note that according to structure (3b) above, neither the verb nor the object bear phrasal stress, merely word stress, whereas according to (3a) the object still has more stress than the verb. I actually think that a contrast in stressing is detectable in a normal pronunciation of, for example, (5):

(5)   (Who wants to order pumpkin?—) JONES wants to order pumpkin.

Even without any pitch accents in VP, ⟨pumpkin⟩ seems metrically stronger than ⟨order⟩ in (5). To make this intuition a little more tangible, compare (5) to (6).

(6)   (Who wants to order something?—) JONES wants to order something.

Since ⟨something⟩ is a function word it doesn't bear phrasal stress (see Section 6.2.4); the metrical structure of VP in the question is thus (7a), as opposed to (7b).

```
        (×                )pP      (       ×      )pP
        (×    ) (×         )pWd     (×     ) ( ×    )pWd
(7)  a.  order something      b.  order pumpkin
```

---

[3] Hayes and Lahiri (1991) do not label the phrase in question, nor does (Pierrehumbert, 1980: sec. 2.6), where this is presented as an argument for the distinction between (in present terms) T- and T%. Note however that, as with Norcliffe and Jaeger cases, the alternative to postulating a p-phrase boundary here would be to allow iPs without pitch accents.

To my ear, the answer in (6) still has a detectably different stress relation between verb and object (namely strong V–weak O) than in (5) (weak V–strong O).[4] Such a difference in post-focal stress could not be accounted for if all phrasal stresses were deleted after the iP-head.

Phrasing effects: Norcliffe and Jaeger (2005) found that speakers systematically mark prosodic boundaries after the NPA, as becomes evident when the location of boundaries serves to disambiguate. Their sentences showed particle/preposition ambiguities such as in (8).

(8) The Vikings won over their enemies.
    a. (Heartless violence led to a bloody victory.)
       The Vikings [won] [over their enemies].

    b. (Gentle persuasion led to a friendly settlement.)
       The Vikings [won over] [their enemies].

As brought out by the lead-in sentences, there can be a major syntactic constituent break between ‹won› and ‹over›, or between ‹over› and ‹their›. The corresponds to a difference in prosodic structure, roughly as in (9).[5]

$$
\begin{array}{llll}
(& & \times &)_{i/IP} \\
(& \times \quad) (\times) (& \times &)_{PP} \\
\end{array}
$$

(9) a. the vikings won over their enemies   (=(8a))

$$
\begin{array}{llll}
(& & \times &)_{i/IP} \\
(& \times \quad) (\quad \times \quad) (& \times &)_{PP} \\
\end{array}
$$

    b. the vikings won over their enemies   (=(8b))

Norcliffe and Jaeger embedded sentences like (9) in contrastive focus contexts, as in (10), which trigger deaccenting of the entire ambiguous stretch.

(10) (A: Heartless violence led to a bloody victory./Gentle persuasion led to a
        friendly settlement.
     B: So the Romans won over their enemies?)
     A: No, the VIKINGS won over their enemies.

They found that even in this post-nuclear position, and hence in the absence of pitch accents in the ambiguous region, the lengths of the rimes (here ‹(w)on› and

---

[4] Similarly in (i):

(i) a. Who ate pumpkin?—JOHN ate pumpkin.
    b. Who ate something?—JOHN ate something.

My intuition is in fact that ‹John› is longer in (ib) than in (ia), and that that is the case because in (ib) (but not (ia)), ‹John› and ‹ate› are adjacent p-level stresses, and hence spaced out evenly using something like the "silent demibeats" of Selkirk (1984).

[5] To explain the phrasing of the VP by WRAP-XP, it would suffice to assume that ‹over their enemies› is a VP adjunct in structure (9a), and that ‹their enemies› is extraposed in structure (9b). Nothing hinges on this, though.

‹(ov)er›) differed significantly depending on which construal was intended (i.e. ‹won› longer and ‹over› shorter on the V+PP construal (9a), and *vice versa* on the V+PRT+DP construal (9b)).

Norcliffe and Jaeger (2005) conclude that these lengthening effects are best accounted for by postulating a prosodic phrase boundary higher than a PWd after the NPA. Deleting all post-focal boundaries would obviously make such an analysis impossible and fail to provide an explanation for the contrast Norcliffe and Jaeger (2005) found.[6]

From the four arguments just discussed, we conclude that early NPAs in narrow focus constructions are the result of shifting the iP-head to a non-rightmost pP daughter, as in structure (3a) above, not of dephrasing post-focal material. The pitch accent "shift" is simply a consequence of STRESS-TO-ACCENT applied to the resulting metrical structure.

7.1.2 Accent assignment within the focus

FOCUS REALIZATION in (2) above makes no mention of *where* within a bigger focus the strongest stress should fall. Our earlier constraint (1), explicitly stated that the last default pitch accent within the focus was to be the NPA of the focus domain. In the present set-up this follows, because default stress assignment, governed by STRESS-XP and WRAP-XP will proceed as usual within (and, if we follow the arguments made in Section 7.1.1, after) the focus; crucially, the same must be true for iP-HEAD-RIGHT, that is the iP-head is still aligned with a phrasal stress as far to the right as possible *while respecting FOCUS REALIZATION*.

To illustrate, both iP-head alignments in (11) are compatible with FOCUS REALIZATION, since the focus is the entire subject ‹Jones and Keats›.[7]

(11)   (Who ate pumpkin?)

```
        (              ×                    )i/IP
        ( × )(       ×   )(        ×        )pP
        ( × )(       ×  )( × )(    ×        )PWd
a.     Jones and Keats ate pumpkin.
        ( ×                                )i/IP
        ( × )(       ×   )(        ×        )pP
        ( × )(       ×  )( × )(    ×        )PWd
b. # Jones and Keats ate pumpkin.
```

But in (11b), there are two pPs (and thus p-stresses) between the head of iP and its right edge, while in (11a) there is only one: (11a) meets iP-HEAD-RIGHT as well as possible, given the demands of FOCUS REALIZATION. Technically, this means

---

[6] Norcliffe and Jaeger point out that this phrase could be an iP, provided one is willing to give up the standard dictum that iPs must contain at least one pitch accent. Obviously, the facts they measured do not provide any insights into this question, but assuming pPs, as we do here, achieves this effect while maintaining that iPs have to contain pitch accents.

[7] Note incidentally that the theory does not predict an additional layer of pP in the structures in (11), even though we have a case of a complex subject here, similar to those discussed in Section 6.3.2. But because the iP-head is shifted thanks to FOCUS REALIZATION in (11), WRAP-XP/STRESS-XP-CORRESPON-DENCE—condition (63) in Section 6.3.2—is met for the subject DP in (11). Additional structure would bring no advantage here.

that ɪP-Head-Right, like Wrap-xp (cf. Section 6.2), is a cumulative constraint: minimizing the number of pPs between the head and the right boundary of iP is important.

Generally, Focus Realization works in all its simplicity because rather than stating everything relevant for assigning stress in a focus sentence, it merely states what is *specific* about stress in a focus sentence (or really: focus domain), leaving the rest of the work to the same principles that are active in default prosody. In other words, Prosodic Inertia: default prosody is maintained as much as possible under focussing.

7.1.3 Focus Realization *effects below the iP-level*

In the previous chapters, the effect of (2), Focus Realization, (and its predecessors) was formally captured by a two-step procedure: one that deleted any post-focal pitch accents (within the focus domain), another that assigned pitch accent to the focus in case there wasn't one by default. The latter was necessary to capture cases like those in (12), in which an element which does not carry phrasal stress (or, by the rules from Chapter 1, no default pitch accent) is focussed.

(12) a. (Who is Kim visiting?—) Kim is visiting ME.
      b. (Does Holm want to sell sushi?—)

        Nein, Holm will   Sushi ESSEN.   (German)
        no   H.   wants sushi eat
        'No, Holm wants to EAT sushi.'

In the current setting, this effect will follow from Focus Realization, too, which forces the iP-head to align with the focus. We assume that the head of an iP can only align with the head of a pP, and that generally, columns of stresses have to be continuous (the Continuous Column Constraint, cf. e.g. Hayes, 1995: 34). Thus, (13a) is not a possible prosodic structure for (12a), only (13b) is: Focus Realization effectively forces the re-alignment of a p-phrase head onto the focus.[8]

```
         (                    ×  )i/IP
         ( × )(      ×            )pP
         ( × )(      ×      )( × )PWd
(13)  a. * Kim is visiting  me]]

         (                    ×  )i/IP
         ( × )(               ×  )pP
         ( × )(      ×      )( × )PWd
      b.   Kim is visiting  me]]
```

The structure for (12b), (14a), will force amendments at the level of the p-phrases, too, here: addition of a p-phrase (compare to (14b), repeated from Section 6.2.2, example (20a)), effectively "undoing" integration.[9]

---

[8] I assume that auxiliaries and modals like ‹will› in (14a) are not pWds of their own, but nothing hinges on that. See also Selkirk's (1995a) discussion of phrase initial function words in English.

[9] Note that shifting the pP-head to the final pWd, analogous to (13b), would leave the object ‹sushi› without phrasal stress, yielding an additional Stress-xp violation. Since we saw above that Stress-xp must be ranked above Wrap-xp, the two-pP structure is preferred in case of focus on a transitive head.

```
(                              ×      )i/IP
(      ×   )(           ×   )(    ×    )pP
(      ×   )(           ×   )(    ×    )PWd
```
(14) a.   Holm   will   Sushi   essen_F]]
           H.   wants sushi   eat

```
      ...        ×              )i/IP
      (          ×              )pP
      (          ×   )(    ×    )PWd
```
b. ... [_VP[_DP[_NP Sushi]] essen]

What these examples show along the way is that Focus Realization must out-rank not only iP-Head-Right, but also P-Stress → X^o_{lex} (for (13b)) and Wrap-xp (for (14a)). In general, as we will see, there is no evidence for thinking that Focus Realization is dominated by any of the constraints discussed in this book.

Summarizing, Focus Realization may not only force leftward shifting of the iP-head, corresponding to our previous Step 1a toy rule of post-focal accent deletion, but also calibrations at lower levels of prosodic structure, including addition and relocation of phrase stress, corresponding to our previous Step 1b toy rule of accent addition.

The reason Focus Realization subsumes both is that, rather than stating a procedure to create the correct prosodic structure, it merely describes the well-formed output: highest stress on F. How this is achieved is solely governed by independent syntax–prosody constraints such as Stress-xp and Wrap-xp and prosody-internal constraints, such as iP-Head-Right or the Continuous Columns Constraint.

7.1.4 iP-heads and focus

Focus Realization is formulated in purely relational term ("highest stress"); but even though it does not directly refer to the head of iP, the following corollary holds (ignoring recursive pP-layers for the moment).

(15)   Corollary: In any F-domain with more than one pP, Focus Realization can only be met by assigning iP-level stress.

Corollary (15) holds because among two or more pP-level stresses, none can be the highest, unless it is at the same time the head of a higher prosodic category, namely iP. (In principle, if a focus domain consists of only one pP, Focus Realization could be met as long as the focus contains the head of that pP, and thereby the highest stress.)

Corollary (15) is unremarkable if we assume that any utterance comprises one or several iPs and hence iP-heads; this seems to be a common assumption, given the hypotheses that each utterance obligatorily contains every level of prosodic structure, and that every prosodic phrase must have a head. Some authors, notably Katz and Selkirk (2011), however, have proposed that focus-less utterances do not have a metrically strongest element; they do not have an iP-head. An iP-head is only present in order to guarantee, in present terms, a metrical asymmetry among pP heads, as required by Focus Realization (as per corollary (15)).

The system developed in this chapter is compatible with such a position (though it does not rely on it). As remarked in Section 6.2.5, the assignment of stress and accents in default prosody does not rely on the presence of an iP-level stress. Only FOCUS REALIZATION, in most cases, does.

7.1.5 Pre-nuclear accent shift

As discussed in Section 6.3.2, complex NPs, including NPs modified by adjective phrases (APs) show a stress pattern that is plausibly analyzed using a recursive pP-structure. To recap, a DP such as ‹an American farmer› gets the default metrical structure in (16).

$$
\begin{array}{llllll}
(& & & & \times &)_{pP} \\
(& & \times &)(& \times &)_{pP} \\
(& & \times &)(& \times &)_{pWd} \\
\end{array}
$$

(16)   [$_{DP}$ an [$_{NP}$[$_{AP}$ American][$_{NP}$farmer]]]

To fully predict (16) (as well as the structures given in Section 6.3.2), we first have to supplement one more principle, namely one that ensures that the head of a complex pP like ‹American farmer› in (16) is on the rightmost daughter. Condition (17) achieves this.

(17^{CON})   COMPLEX-PHRASE-HEAD-RIGHT
Align the head of a prosodic phrase dominating pPs with the head of its rightmost daughter.

Condition (17) is a generalization of our earlier iP-HEAD-RIGHT, which applies to any prosodic phrase that dominates pPs, that is, iPs or higher pPs in recursive p-structures.[10]

We are now in a position to see what goes on in smaller F-domains such as discussed in Section 3.1.3 of chapter 3; the pertinent examples are repeated here.

(18)   a.   An AMERICAN farmer met a CANADIAN farmer.
       b.   An AMERICAN farmer took a CANADIAN farmer to a BAR.

---

[10] Condition (17) does not apply to pPs that dominate pWds only. Recall that head-final integration structures generally involve left-headed pPs, as in (ia).

$$
\begin{array}{ll}
\begin{array}{lll}
(& \times &)_{pP} \\
(& \times)(\times)_{pWd} \\
\end{array}
&
\begin{array}{lll}
(& & \times)_{pP} \\
(& \times)(\times)_{pP} \\
(& \times)(\times)_{pWd} \\
\end{array}
\end{array}
$$

(i)   a. [$_{VP}$ DP V]   b. [$_{VP}$ DP V]

With the advent of recursive pP structures, (ib) emerges as a competitor, which, like (ia), meets STRESS-XP and WRAP-XP for DP and VP. If (ia) involved a violation of some constraint pP-HEAD-RIGHT, integration would never happen, since structure (ib) would be favored. As it is, (17) is not violated on either structure, so nothing will tip the scale in favor of (ib). A constraint *STRUCTURE, no matter how low, will then favor (ia), as desired.

As argued in Chapter 3, ‹American› and ‹Canadian› are focussed here, contrasting with each other in the F-domain NP or DP. Crucially, the domain of the focus cannot be the entire sentence, as that would include the target of contrast.

By Focus Realization this means that the adjectives have to bear the highest stress within the NPs containing them. The following structures are predicted to underlie the accent patterns in examples (18a) and (18b).

```
       (                                          ×                    )i/IP
       (                  )(                       ×                    )pP
       (        ×    )( ×  )(                       ×    )(   ×          )pP
       (        ×    )( ×  )(      × ) (            ×    )(   ×          )pWd
(19)   [DP an American[ farmer]][VPmet [DP a Canadian [NP farmer]]]
               └──────────────┘                      └──────────────┘
                  F-domain                               F-domain
```

```
       (                                                          ×  )i/IP
       (        ×             ) (                        )(         ×  )pP
       (        ×    )( ×     ) (             ×    )(  ×  )(         ×  )pP
       (        ×    )( ×     ) (   ×    )(   ×    )(  ×  )(         ×  )pWd
(20)   [[DPan American[farmer]][VPtook [DPa Canadian[NPfarmer]][PPto a bar]]]
             └──────────────┘                 └──────────────┘
                F-domain                          F-domain
```

Recursive pP-structure here allows us to reconcile the requirements of Focus Realization with those of Stress-xp: The backgrounded NP ‹farmer› can receive phrasal stress (and thus satisfy Stress-xp) and yet be less stressed than the AP (as demanded by Focus Realization) at the higher pP layer.[11]

The main lesson to take away from these examples is that structural principles like Complex Phrase-Head-Right, as well as information structural principles like Focus Realization, apply in any prosodic constituent with more than one

---

[11] Note as an aside that the following structures are *not* predicted to be possible:

```
       (                                ×              )i/IP
       (         ×        )(            ×              )pP
       (       ×    )( ×  )(   ×)(      ×    )(   ×    )pWd
(i)  a. [DP an American[ farmer]][VPmet[DP a Canadian[NP farmer]]]
       (                                          ×  )i/IP
       (         ×        )(            ×        )(  ×  )pP
       (       ×    )(×    )(  × )(     ×    )(   ×    )(  ×  )pWd
     b. [DP an American[ farmer]][VPtook[DP a Canadian[NP farmer[PPto a bar]]]]
```

(ia/b) satisfy Focus Realization just like structures (19) and (20) in the main text. In fact, (ia/b) encode virtually the same metrical strength relations as (19) and (20). By virtue of that they also lead to the same accent patterns, in particular, ‹farmer› is post-nuclear in the pPs ‹American/Canadian farmer› and thus doomed to remain accent-less. What, if any, prosodic differences are expected between (i) and (19) is in fact unclear. It may therefore be desirable to allow for both, or employ a representation which does not even distinguish them formally.

Theoretically, however, (19) is forced upon us by two decisions made earlier: first, to allow pP-recursion for the sake of avoiding Wrap-xp/Stress-xp violations, which in turn was motivated by the prosodic facts discussed in Section 6.3.2. Second, to assume that focus in the sentential domain leads to head-misalignment, rather than post-focal dephrasing, cf. Section 7.1.1; technically this means that Stress-xp is ranked higher than ip-Head-Right or its successor Complex-Phrase-Head-Right in (17), which in turn means that pPs will be constructed on all syntactic phrases, even ones following the head of their mother prosodic phrase.

Given the lack of conclusive evidence for the existence of structures like (i), we will be content to assume that focussing of non-final XPs at any prosodic level involves recursive pP structure, as in (19).

daughter, not just at the sentential level. This is easy to overlook in simple examples of the ‹Kim loves Sam› type, in which the only metrical asymmetry is between the nuclear stress (head of i/IP) and everything else.

7.2 Givenness

7.2.1 Nuclear deaccenting

In Section 2.3 of Chapter 2 we characterized the effect of givenness on accenting as in (21).

(21^{OLD})   G-Realization Condition

A G-marked constituent does not contain the nuclear accent, unless forced by the F-Realization Condition.

How can we adopt it to the stress-based setting we are developing now? It is easy to see how to drop the "unless forced by the F-condition" part from (21); we simply need to assume that (21) is a violable constraint, and, crucially, that it is ranked below Focus Realization. Thereby, if a focus contains only given elements, (21) effectively runs empty.

As discussed in previous chapters, (21) intentionally refrains from saying that given elements must not be accented, since they regularly are in pre-nuclear position. In present terms, being given should not be incompatible with bearing pP-level stress.[12] It should only be incompatible with bearing nuclear stress. We will encode this in a somewhat roundabout way, for reasons that will become clear momentarily.

(22^{CON})   Givenness Realization

If the strongest stress in a prosodic constituent π is on a given element, π itself is given.

By condition (22), if the head of an iP is on a given element, the entire iP must be given.[13] In a typical instance of givenness deaccenting, this is of course not the case:

(23)   (Why don't you have some French toast?—)
     a.   #I've forgotten how to make French TOAST.
     b.   I've forgotten how to MAKE French toast.

‹Toast› in (23a) bears the NPA, which entails that it is the head of iP. Since ‹(French) toast› is given, Givenness Realization in (22) could only be met if the entire iP, and hence the entire sentence ‹I've forgotten how to make French toast› were given, too. Since it is not, (23a) is ruled out as a violation of Givenness Realization, as desired.

---

[12] As it is under e.g. Féry and Samek-Lodovici's (2006) Deaccent Given.

[13] This way of talking presupposes that a prosodic phrase (rather than a syntactic one) can be given. We assume that a prosodic phrase is given if every syntactic element whose prosodic realization is contained in it is given.

In (23b), the iP-level stress is on ‹make›, which is not given. Therefore, GIVENNESS REALIZATION is satisfied vacuously. We assume that GIVENNESS REALIZATION is ranked below FOCUS REALIZATION (so as to allow for foci that are entirely given, as said above), and above all other prosodic constraints. Therefore, givenness deaccenting will be achieved in the same ways focussing is achieved, for example by iP-head misalignment in (23b). Contrast this with (24).

(24)   (Why don't you have some French toast?—) French TOAST is HIGH in SAturated FATS.

Here, ‹toast› can bear a pitch accent, equal in metrical strength to those on ‹high› and ‹saturated›, which suggests that ‹French toast› forms a pP in (24); since ‹French toast› is itself given, GIVENNESS REALIZATION is met: ‹toast›, which is given, is the head of the equally given pP ‹French toast›. The head of iP (sentential stress) in (24), on the other hand, is ‹fats›, which is not given, so here, too, GIVENNESS REALIZATION is met. Since there are no other constraints that would counteract STRESS-XP for the DP ‹French toast›, it is thus predicted to be treated equally to the non-given XPs following it, in particular to be accentable, as desired.

It is important to note that this reasoning hinges on relative stress alone, not on the category distinction between pP and iP. Given elements may, under the right circumstances, bear even iP stress, as in example (25) (the inverse case, where a given element may not even bear an accent in pre-nuclear position, will be discussed in Section 7.2.2).

(25)   (What happens if Sam talks to Kim?—) If Sam talks to KIM, we're in big TROUBLE.

Generally, if a constituent big enough to be realized as an iP is repeated *verbatim*, it can be realized with a full-blown prosodic structure, including an NPA, as indicated by the small caps on ‹Kim› in (25). This is compatible with GIVENNESS REALIZATION, since the entire iP within which the given element ‹Kim› bears maximal stress, ‹if Sam talks to Kim›, is indeed itself entirely given.

Example (25) is in fact just another instantiation of our earlier observation that the given–new distinction is frequently neutralized in pre-nuclear position, if we assume that there is a prosodic domain in (25) which encompasses the entire sentence, call it the UTTERANCE PHRASE, and whose head is on ‹trouble›. This would entail that the accent on ‹trouble› is also perceived as more prominent than that on ‹Kim›, which seems at least plausible.[14]

---

[14] It also seems to me that there is an asymmetry between (25) and its mirror-image version (i):

(i)   (What happens if Sam talks to Kim?—) We're in big TROUBLE if Sam talks to Kim.

If there can be pitch accents in the ‹if›-clause at all, these have to be different from those in the ‹if›-clause in (25). There is also a clear sense in which the pitch accent on ‹trouble› in (i) is the most prominent in the utterance. It seems tempting to say that the entire ‹if›-clause in (i) appears not just post-focally (as it doubtlessly does), but also in a significant sense post-nuclear, namely in the hypothesized Utterance

7.2.2 Pre-nuclear deaccenting

Just like FOCUS REALIZATION is applicable in F-domains smaller than a clause (Section 7.1.5), so is givenness deaccenting. Again, we need to look at complex structures that involve recursive p-phrasing. Consider the text in (26).

(26) (The company acknowledges that there are "problems" in Ogoniland.) Pictures of the region show poorly maintained, above ground pipelines that crisscross villages, some even through people's homes.

A natural way of pronouncing the subject of the second sentence in (26) involves deaccenting the DP ‹the region›. Intuitively, this is a case of anaphoric deaccenting, due to the fact that ‹the region› is understood to refer to Ogoniland, and hence given. The prosodic domain of deaccenting is the DP, not the clause containing it (which has further pitch accents, at least on ‹pipelines› and ‹villages›). The crucial bit of metrical structure would thus look as in (27).

$$
\begin{array}{llll}
(& \times & &)_{pP} \\
(& \times &)(& \times &)_{pP} \\
(& \times &)(& \times &)_{pWd}
\end{array}
$$

(27)   [$_{DP}$ [$_{NP}$ pictures] [$_{PP}$ of the region]]

Since the pP ‹of the region› is post-nuclear within the higher pP, it cannot, by STRESS-TO-ACCENT, receive a pitch accent: it is deaccented.

Let us see then how, in turn, the metrical structure in (27) comes about: ‹the region› bears the strongest stress within the pP ‹of the region› in (27), which is compatible with GIVENNESS REALIZATION, (22), since that entire pP is given (moreover, pP stress is encouraged by STRESS-XP). But ‹the region› cannot bear the main stress of the complex pP ‹pictures of the region›, as this would violate (22): that entire phrase is *not* given. Hence the head of the higher pP is shifted leftward onto the (non-given) pP ‹pictures›, in violation of COMPLEX PHRASE-HEAD-RIGHT, but in accordance with the higher ranked GIVENNESS REALIZATION.

It is instructive to compare (26) to (28).

(28) (The company acknowledges that there are "problems" in Ogoniland.) The Nigerian region is infamous for poorly maintained, above ground pipelines . . .

Here ‹Nigerian region› need not be unaccented and indeed is likely to form a complex pP analogous to structure (16) above, despite the fact that, like ‹the region› in (26), it is given. This is so because the pP ‹the Nigerian region› does not itself bear the strongest stress within any larger constituent, so GIVENNESS REALIZATION, (22), does not apply here. The given noun ‹region› in example (28) *does* bear the

Phrase, leading to a systematic reduction in the realization of all following stresses. On such a view, *any* size of prosodic phrase could be pre- or post-nuclear, when embedded within an even larger utterance.

strongest stress within a larger constituent, ⟨the Nigerian region⟩, which, however, is also given, meeting GIVENNESS REALIZATION.

We pointed out this type of fact in our discussion earlier in Section 7.2, as well as in Chapter 2: givenness is commonly "neutralized" in non-final position. We can now refine this statement: givenness deaccenting may be observable whenever a given element occurs final in *some* complex prosodic domain, including in complex pre-nuclear domains, as in (26).

To sum up, GIVENNESS REALIZATION makes sure that a given constituent cannot receive the highest stress within a domain that contains non-given elements. Simplifying a little, given elements must not be metrically *stronger* than non-given ones. Like FOCUS REALIZATION, GIVENNESS REALIZATION must be ranked above the constraints responsible for default prosody, but crucially below FOCUS REALIZATION itself, to allow for given foci.

7.3 Second occurrence focus

In Section 7.1 we reviewed some evidence for the existence of post-nuclear prosodic phrasing, as well as different levels of stress. The next step is to ask whether variations in these can be triggered not just by lexical and syntactic factors, but also by information structure related factors, in particular focus.

On the face of it, this may seem a hopeless endeavor: We hypothesized earlier that focus always bears the NPA, and if that turns out to be true, then by definition we cannot expect to find post-nuclear focal prosody.

However, it has been noted in the literature for some time that under certain conditions, elements that should be foci by semantic and pragmatic criteria are completely unaccented. This phenomenon has been christened SECOND OCCURRENCE FOCUS. A classic example from Hajičová et al. (1998) is given in (29).

(29)   (Everyone already knew that Mary only eats vegetables.)
        If even PAUL_F knew that Mary only eats vegetables_F,
        (then he should have suggested a different restaurant).

The ⟨if⟩-clause in (29) has two foci, ⟨Paul⟩ and ⟨vegetables⟩. We know they are foci because the particles ⟨even⟩ and ⟨only⟩ are focus sensitive, and their meaning contribution changes depending on what in the sentence is focussed (see Chapter 10). In (29) the resulting meanings are that Paul is the least likely person to know what Mary eats (⟨even⟩), and that vegetables are the only thing Mary eats (⟨only⟩), which means that, semantically at least, ⟨Paul⟩ and ⟨vegetables⟩ are foci. But surprisingly, only ⟨Paul⟩, but not ⟨vegetables⟩, in example (29) is marked by a pitch accent.

Crucially, however, the focus on ⟨vegetables⟩ in example (29) *is* prosodically marked (and perceived as prominent), despite the absence of pitch accents, primarily, once again, by longer duration. First suspicions to this effect can be found in Rooth (1996b) and Bartels (2004), which have been systematically confirmed for English in Beaver et al. (2007) and Jaeger (2004), and later for German in Baumann et al. (2010) and Féry and Ishihara (2009).

We take this marking to be the prosodic realization of stress, just as we did in Section 7.1. Second occurrence focus, then, provides us with a very direct argument in favor of formulating Focus Realization in terms of stress in (2) at the start of this chapter, rather than directly in terms of pitch accenting, as in earlier chapters: if *stress* is the primary realization of focus, it is entirely expected that focus may sometimes be realized by stress *and* accent, other times by stress only. If *accent* were the primary realization of focus, we should expect stress to be the optional element in focus realization. Instances where focus is realized by stress, but not accenting, would require an additional "backup" theory of focus-to-stress to account for them, leaving any parallels between the accented and accent-less realizations without a principled explanation.

This also jibes well with what Ladd (1996, 2008: ch. 7) refers to as the general Stress First View. The Stress First View hypothesizes that syntactic structure and information structure are mapped onto a hierarchical *metrical* structure, which represents first and foremost the relative metrical weight or stress of syllables (and, in the case of the bracketed grid, as used here, prosodic constituency), just as we did in this chapter and chapter 6. Pitch accents, and intonational events in general, are then associated with this metrical representation by largely or perhaps exclusively phonology-internal principles such as Stress-to-Accent. See also Ladd (1996, 2008: ch. 7.2) for an extended argument for this view.

7.3.1 The basic generalization and how to derive it

Let us now turn to the question under what circumstances a focus ends up unaccented (but stressed). When do we find second occurrence focus? Büring (2013/15) ends with a general characterization of when second occurrence focus occurs, which, using theoretically neutral terminology, can be rendered as in generalization (30):

(30) Generalization about Second Occurrence Focus
      If the domain of a focus F is completely given, and follows the last focus whose domain is not completely given, F is realized by stress, but not accent (i.e. as a second occurrence focus).

Let me illustrate this with a variation on example (29) above.

(31) (Sorry, I didn't know that Carter only likes GREEN vegetables.—)
      But McDUFF knew that Carter only likes green$_{SOF}$ vegetables.
      (So why didn't that knucklehead speak up!?!).

Figure 7.1 gives the structure for this example. The domain of the focus ⟨green$_F$⟩, is marked by ∼C_2 adjoined to the embedded verb phrase VP*. The "same" variable C_2 occurs as an implicit argument of ⟨only⟩, representing the fact that ⟨only⟩ excludes "liking vegetables of other colors than green," that is, it excludes the F-alternatives to VP*. We say that the focus on ⟨green⟩ associates with the particle ⟨only⟩: the properties ⟨only⟩ excludes are the F-alternatives of ⟨green⟩'s F-domain (more

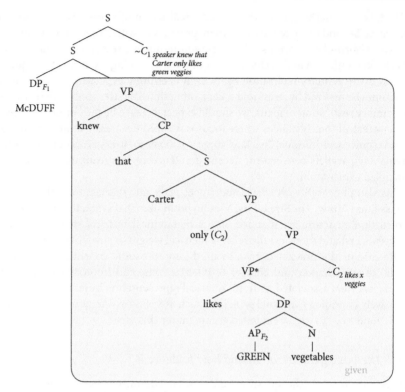

FIGURE 7.1   Structure for a typical Second Occurrence Focus example; the given part of the tree is boxed in darker gray.

precisely: those F-alternatives that are in the F-antecedent of that domain; see Chapter 10 below for thorough discussion).

Generally, we can diagnose the F-domain of an associated focus with the help of the focus sensitive element it associates with: the F-domain of an associated focus, say ⟨green$_F$⟩ in (31), is the sister of that element, ⟨only⟩ in the case of (31).

The crucial bit is that that F-domain, VP*, is completely within the given sub-tree, and hence generalization (30) above correctly captures that ⟨green⟩ is realized as a second occurrence focus.

It is not sufficient if only the (would-be) second occurrence focus—for example ⟨Davis⟩ in example (32)—is given.

(32)   (Davis invited Moody's entire family.)
    a.   But MOOdy only invited DAvis.
    b. #But MOOdy only invited [Davis$_{SOF}$]$_G$.
    c. #But MOOdy ONLy invited Davis$_{SOF}$.
    d. #But MOOdy ONLy inVITed Davis$_{SOF}$.

Nor is it sufficient that the associated focus is contained in *some* given constituent.

(33)   (Davis' kid invited all the kids on the block.) But Evans' kid…
       a. only invited DAvis' kid.   b. # ONLY invited [Davis'$_{SOF}$ kid]$_G$.

Finally, the focus sensitive expression associating with a second occurrence focus, ⟨only⟩ in example (34), does *not* need to be given:

(34)   (The kids really likes their exotic vegetables and their fish, don't they!—)
       Unfortunately, they ONLY [like exotic$_{SOF}$ vegetables]$_G$.
       (Local veggies would be so much cheaper.)

Evidently, then, the second occurrence focus configuration cannot be described in terms of F- and G-placement alone (since F is (part of) a given constituent both in examples (31) and (34), where not accenting the focus is acceptable, and in examples (32) and (33), where it is not). Rather what is crucial seems to be the relation between the entire F-*domain* and givenness, as stated at the outset in generalization (30).

   In Büring (2013/15) I argue that generalization (30) can in fact be derived from general principles of how focus and givenness are realized in English. Adopting the line of argument there to the terminology used in this book, the crucial ingredients are repeated below:

(35)   FOCUS REALIZATION
       The highest stress within a F-domain *D* falls on a focus of *D*.

(36)   GIVENNESS REALIZATION
       If the strongest stress in a prosodic constituent π is on a given element, π itself is given.

(37)   STRESS-TO-ACCENT (a prosodic well-formedness constraint)
       The last pitch accent (if there is any) within a prosodic constituent above the foot is on the head of that constituent.

Consider again example (31), repeated as (38).

(38)   (Sorry, I didn't know that Carter only likes GREEN vegetables.—)
       But McDUFF$_F$ knew that Carter only likes green$_{(SO)F}$ vegetables
       _____
                                                    F-domain
       _____
                                                    F-domain
       (so why didn't that knucklehead speak up!?!).

Suppose, contrary to fact, that the focus ⟨green⟩ were realized by the NPA in the sentence. This would presuppose, by STRESS-TO-ACCENT, (37), that ⟨green⟩ is (part of) the prosodic head (head of iP) of the sentence. But on the other hand, ⟨green⟩ is given, so by GIVENNESS REALIZATION, (36), the entire sentence would need to be given if ⟨green⟩ bears its NPA, which clearly it is not. This seems to explain why ⟨green⟩ cannot bear the NPA.

But of course we know that GIVENNESS REALIZATION can be over-ruled by FOCUS REALIZATION. So we cannot claim that FOCUS REALIZATION is violated in (38) (‹green› does not bear nuclear stress) because of GIVENNESS REALIZATION (‹green› being given), since we have direct evidence—completely given foci (recall Section 2.4.2 of Chapter 2)—that FOCUS REALIZATION outranks GIVENNESS REALIZATION and not the other way around.

What is crucial instead is that the F-domain of ‹green› is just the VP ‹like green vegetables› (see also Figure 7.1), and that *within that F-domain* FOCUS REALIZATION *is met*, as long as ‹green› bears higher stress than ‹likes› and ‹vegetables›—the other elements in that domain. The required stress pattern is schematized in Figure 7.2.

‹McDuff›, on the other hand, has a legitimate claim to bearing the highest stress in the *sentence* (by FOCUS REALIZATION, (35)), since *it* is a focus with a sentential—that is: maximal—F-domain. By STRESS-TO-ACCENT, (37), ‹McDuff› must bear a pitch accent, and anything else—being post-nuclear—must not.

In sum, a structure in which ‹McDuff› bears the NPA, and ‹green› bears maximal stress in its VP, but no pitch accent, complies with FOCUS REALIZATION, (35), GIVENNESS REALIZATION, (36), and STRESS-TO-ACCENT, (37), while one in which ‹green› is accented, or in which ‹vegetables› bears higher stress than ‹green› (as it would in default prosody) does not.

Note that it is not crucial for this analysis what the full prosodic structure of example (38) is, as long as it preserves the relative metrical strengths shown in Figure 7.2, and thereby guarantees that ‹McDuff› must, and ‹green› cannot be accented. Applying default prosody as much as possible, the predicted full structure is that given in Figure 7.3.

Now let us compare (38) and Figure 7.1 with example (33), where an accent-less realization of ‹Davis› is impossible. The syntactic structure for that example is given in Figure 7.4.

Here, ‹Davis› meets FOCUS REALIZATION, but only by violating GIVENNESS RE-ALIZATION: FOCUS REALIZATION requires ‹Davis› to bear the strongest stress in its F-domain, VP, even though VP as a whole is not given, in violation of GIVENNESS REALIZATION. Crucially, there is no higher F-domain in Figure 7.4 that would require the sentential stress to be elsewhere, so by Prosodic Inertia, it will be aligned with the last accented element in the sentence, ‹Davis›.

One might object at this point that predictions would be different if one assumed instead that ‹Evans'› or ‹Evans' kid› were a contrastive focus, as illustrated in Figure 7.5.

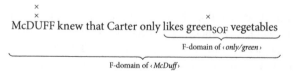

FIGURE 7.2   The crucial metrical relations for example (38).

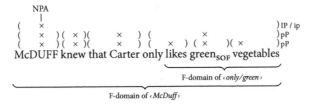

FIGURE 7.3 Full prosodic structure for example (38).

(Davis' kid invited all the kids on the block.) But . . .

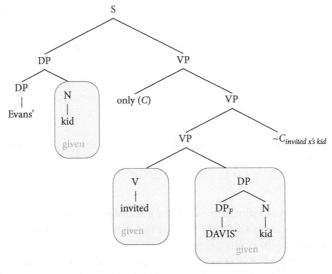

FIGURE 7.4 A focus within a given constituent will not be realized as second occurrence focus if the domain of the focus is bigger than the given element (note that while *invited* and ‹Davis' kid› are each given, ‹invited Davis' kid› is not).

According to that structure, ‹Evans› is a focus with sentential domain and thus should bear the highest stress in S; furthermore, since ‹Evans› and ‹Davis› are F-marked, the F-alternatives to the sentence should be 'that x's kid invited y's kid';[15] they meet the F-Condition, since it is salient that Davis' kid invited all the kids on the block.

But note that according to this reasoning, ‹Davis› is in fact not just a focus of ‹only›, but also of the root-level ~. Only that way will the relevant F-alternatives be 'that x's kid invited y's kid,' rather than 'that x's kid invited Davis' kid.' But if ‹Davis› is a focus of the root ~, then by FOCUS REALIZATION it is eligible to bear the highest

---

[15] In case one is worried about the presence of ‹only›, it can be assumed that ‹only› is in fact F-marked, too. This may predict the intonation in (i), but that one is just as unacceptable in the context given.

(i) EVANS'$_F$ kid ONLY$_F$ invited Davis' kid.

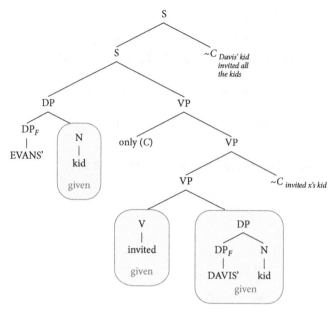

FIGURE 7.5   If ⟨*Evans*⟩ is a root level focus, then so is ⟨*Davis*⟩, and the prosodic net result will be the same.

stress in that domain (the entire sentence), and since a later NPA is preferred over an earlier one by IP-HEAD-RIGHT, ⟨*Davis*⟩, not ⟨*Evans*⟩, is predicted to bear the NPA under the analysis in Figure 7.5, too.

If on the other hand, ⟨*Davis*⟩ were *not* a focus of the root ∼, there would be no salient antecedent (of the form 'that *x*'s kid invited Davis' kid') to license the variable *C*; the structure would fail to meet the F-condition. So the structure in Figure 7.5 is either not appropriate pragmatically in the given context, or if it is, it correctly yields the NPA on ⟨*Davis*⟩, just like the structure in Figure 7.4.

One might still feel uneasy about the fact that, according to this, the representation in Figure 7.5 is vague, in that it is not clear whether ⟨*Davis*⟩ is a focus of the root ∼*C* or not. This kind of vagueness will generally arise where one focus is c-commanded by more than one ∼. For this reason (among others), Büring (2013/15) opts for a system of indexed foci, so that the two options can be notationally distinguished, along the lines of Figure 7.6 (see Section 10.5 on how to formally interpret indexed foci).

7.3.2 Further aspects of second occurrence focus

Büring's (2013/15) account of second occurrence focus, as well as our adaptation of it here, makes further interesting predictions. In particular, certain patterns of focussing are predicted to be ineffable on any stress/accent assignment. One such example is (39), due to Roger Schwarzschild (p.c. and 2006: 142f).

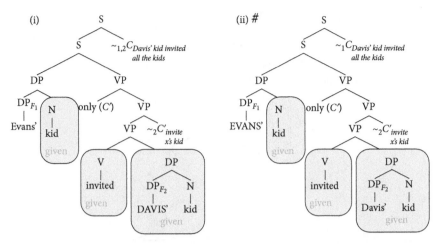

FIGURE 7.6 Indexed Fs, along the lines of Büring (2013/15). Structure (i) needs C to be valued with something like 'x's kid (only) invited y's kid' and yields NPA on ‹Davis›; structure (ii), which would predict second occurrence focus on ‹Davis› and the NPA on ‹Evans›, needs C to be valued with a proposition like 'x's kid (only) invited Davis' kid', which is not salient in the context given (in (33)), hence the hash mark.

(39) What food will Renee only eat in Paris?
    a. #She'll only eat crêpes in PARIS.
    b. #She'll only eat CRÊPES in Paris.

Response (39a) seems to answer the wrong question, whereas (39b) wrongly 'has poor Renee surviving on a strict diet of crêpes during her Parisian sojourns!' (Schwarzschild, 2006: 143). The diagnosis seems simple: whatever ends up with the NPA is interpreted both as the answer focus and as the focus associated with ‹only›, but that is infelicitous in the context, which requires them to be different (‹crêpes› as answer focus, ‹Paris› as associated focus).

In the context of our present discussion, however, we should ask: Why can ‹Paris› not be a second occurrence focus? It is given, within the background of the answer focus, and follows the answer focus. So why not accent ‹crêpes› and merely stress ‹Paris›?

The assumptions made so far, already provide the answer to this question. Consider the syntactic structure for this example in Figure 7.7.

‹Crêpes› is the answer focus, which means it is associated (and, if only for convenience, coindexed) with the root-level $\sim$. Therefore, it should, by FOCUS REALIZATION, (35), contain the highest stress in S, and ultimately the NPA. At the same time, ‹(in) Paris› is the focus of ‹only›/$\sim_2$, so, again by FOCUS REALIZATION, Paris should contain the highest stress in VP. Obviously, this cannot be, because VP contains ‹crêpes› as well, so that both ‹crêpes› and ‹Paris› would have to bear the highest stress in VP. As Rooth (2009: 25) vividly puts it: 'This would be comparable to the tallest mountain in North America being in Alaska, while the

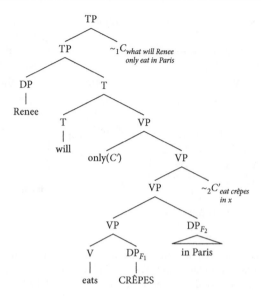

FIGURE 7.7   Tree for the ineffable answer to the question in example (39).

tallest mountain in the Americas is in Colorado.'[16] Therefore, as long as FOCUS REALIZATION is strictly inviolable, it follows that this kind of configuration cannot be realized at all: A focus with a broad domain (‹crêpes› in example (39)) cannot be contained within a second, smaller F-domain.

Unless, that is, it is at the same time a focus of that smaller domain, as in example (40):[17]

(40)   (One should only wear hats outside, just like) one should only wear SWEAT pants at HOME.

On (40)'s most plausible reading, ‹at home› associates with ‹only›, but it is at the same time a free, contrastive focus (along with ‹sweat pants›), as represented in Figure 7.8.[18] This means that ‹at home› simultaneously satisfies FOCUS REALIZATION for the F-domains VP and TP.

---

[16] As one would expect, this effect is not restricted to answer focus. The contrastive focus example (i) from (Büring, 2013/15) can, as noted there, only constitute "an indecent offer."

(i)   I think you're more intelligent than everybody else, but that doesn't mean I only want to TALK to you.

But there should be a perfectly innocent reading, on which ‹only› associates with ‹you›, while ‹(want to) talk› would be a free focus. The unavailability of that reading for (i) can again be blamed on the fact that the sentential free focus ‹talk› is within the domain of the would-be associated focus ‹you›.

[17] Büring (2013/15): ex. (45).

[18] As Max Prüller (p.c.) pointed out to me, it is not clear how the value of C' in Figure 7.8 would be salient in the context. I have to leave this question for further research.

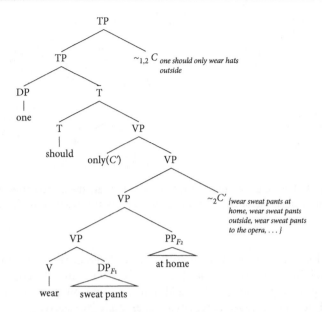

FIGURE 7.8 ‹*At home*› has to be a doubly associated focus, lest we cannot explain how it, rather than ‹*sweat pants*›, qualifies as sentential focus and bearer of the NPA.

To render the generalization precisely, then, we have to say that the linearly last focus inside a F-domain must be bound within that F-domain.[19]

7.3.3 Open questions

Parallel to ineffable examples like example (39) (‹*Renee will only eat crêpes in Paris*›), we find perfectly well-formed examples like Rooth's (1992b) classic in (41a), or Büring's (2013/15) (41b).

(41)   a. People who GROW rice generally only EAT rice.
       b. (I only have a credit card.—That's quite alright,) we only ACCEPT credit cards.

Plausible representations for these examples are given in Figures 7.9(i) and 7.9(ii).

These examples are structurally parallel to example (39) (cf. Figure 7.7): the free focus ‹*eat*$_{F_1}$›/‹*accept*$_{F_1}$› is contained in the domain, but not a focus, of ‹*only*›/$\sim_2$. But (41a) and (41b) are perfectly acceptable with the free foci maximally prominent, also within what ought to be the F-domain of ‹*only*›.

---

[19] Note that in Figure 7.8, F1 is within the $\sim_2$ domain, but not linearly last. In Figure 7.1, ‹*green*› is the last focus in the root domain, $\sim C_1$, but it is bound within that domain by the lower $\sim C_2$.

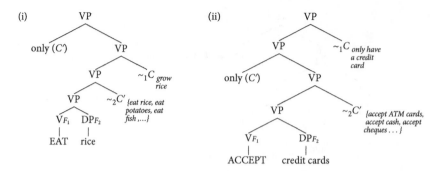

FIGURE 7.9   In both these examples, the free focus F1 bears the highest stress within the domain of the associated focus, ~2, in violation of FOCUS REALIZATION for that domain.

It is unclear at present what precisely the crucial difference between example (39) above[20] and those in (41) is. Rooth (2009: 26ff) assumes that the crossed configuration is generally good, and that additional, presumably prosodic, factors are responsible for the degraded acceptability of example (39) above.

As opposed to that, I assumed in Büring (2013/15: sec. "Prosodic Focus Domains") that the crossed configuration is generally ineffable, but that short intervening focus strings like ‹eat› or ‹accept› allow for some kind of prosodic restructuring to rescue this configuration, while metrically heavier strings like ‹eat crêpes› do not. Yet another possibility is that the crucial difference is whether *only* the free focus occurs between ‹only› and its focus, as in examples (41a) and (41b), or the free focus plus some of its background, as in example (39). Clearly this question merits future attention.

7.3.4 Outlook

On a speculative note, it seems likely to me that future investigations will unearth more cases of information structure-related stress-phenomena in post-nuclear positions. It seems to me, for example, that there is a noticeable difference in the pronunciation of ‹the brakes/Brakes were engaged› between (42a) and (b), even if in both the NPA is put on the matrix verb, as indicated (to facilitate that reading one has to assume that the happy couple's last name in (42b) is Brake):

(42)   a. (At this point the automatic brake system had already kicked in, but) we hadn't REalized that the brakes were engaged.

   b. (At this point, they had already decided to get married, but) nobody had TOLD us that the Brakes were engaged.

---

[20] . . . and equally infelicitous examples like it, see Büring (2013/15: exx. (61)f).

Intuitively, ‹brakes› in (42a) is stronger than ‹engaged›, whereas in (42b), ‹engaged› sounds as strong, or stronger than ‹Brakes›.

This contrast parallels the one seen between these clauses when they are pronounced *with* accents in all-new contexts.

(43)   (Newspaper headlines:)
    a. Committee Reports: Southfork train derailed because the BRAKES were engaged.
    b. Trial Part 15: Witness reveals to stunned jury that the BRAKES were enGAGED.

This is the difference between an integrated, (43a), and a non-integrated, (43b), intransitive clause. In Section 8.5.2 of Chapter 8 it will be argued that non-integrated intransitive sentences may involve a TOPIC boundary between the subject and the predicate. Whatever the underlying information structural reason for this distinction may be, it seems to manifest in terms of relative stress (and perhaps phrasing) in the post-nuclear domain, not unlike second occurrence focus.[21]

7.4 Summary

In this chapter and Chapter 6 I have introduced a concept of prosodic structure which goes beyond pitch accent assignment and which in particular includes prosodic constituency as well as differentiated degrees of stress; these two are tightly interlocked: each prosodic constituent contains exactly one element which bears more stress than all others. The relation between stress and pitch accenting is governed by a single principle, STRESS-TO-ACCENT, which is operative at every level of prosodic structure. I then showed how the effects of information structure discussed so far, focus and givenness, can be superimposed on such a prosodic model.

The added complexity in prosodic structure has several consequences. First, it allows for a more differentiated and thus potentially more accurate description of prosodic reality, especially in sentences with complex sub-constituents.

Second, it is essential in capturing post-nuclear prosodic phenomena, in particular second occurrence focus, which by definition cannot be accent-related.

Third, it allows us to appreciate that principles that relate information structure to prosody—FOCUS REALIZATION and GIVENNESS REALIZATION in our case—apply at various levels of prosodic representation. Their basic effect is simple, and exclusively regards the assignment of maximal stress within a domain. Operating at all levels of phrasal prosodic organization, however, they yield rather com-

---

[21] The claim that information structure may influence the (im)possibility of integration does not undermine the argument made in Section 4.4.2 that it is independent of focussing. The effect of the putative topic marking is orthogonal to the question of focussing: the earlier argument was that integration in the background of an F-domain can not be accounted for by rules of F-projection; this is unaffected by whether or not there can be additional topic marking in the background.

FOCUS REALIZATION[p.164], GIVENNESS REALIZATION[p.173],

STRESS-TO-ACCENT[p.136], WRAP-XP/STRESS-XP-CORRESPONDENCE[p.157]

$$\bigvee$$

STRESS-XP[p.141], P-STRESS $\rightarrow X^0_{lex}$ [p.147]

IP-HEAD-RIGHT[p.148], COMPLEX-PHRASE-HEAD-RIGHT[p.171]

$$\bigvee$$

WRAP-XP[p.141], *RECURSION[p.159]

FIGURE 7.10   The ranked constraints used in Chapters 6 and 7 with page references to their definitions.

plex prosodic patterns, which are beyond the predictive reach of simple accent-assignment algorithms.

Following virtually all of the more recent literature on the topic, we have used ranked violable constraints to illustrate the basic mechanisms connecting prosodic structure, syntactic structure, and information structure, as well as those defining the basic inherent properties of prosodic structure. Figure 7.10 summarizes the constraints used and their relative ranking as established.

One advantage of using ranked violable constraints is that this allows for a rather straightforward modeling of a central property that has emerged in the previous chapters: that information structure realization principles, general principles of syntax-to-prosody mapping, as well as prosody-internal well-formedness constraints mingle. For example, the placement of nuclear stress/pitch accent, primarily the result of the prosody internal principles IP-HEAD-RIGHT and STRESS-TO-ACCENT, crucially builds on, and thus empirically reflects in part, the effects of the mapping constraints STRESS-XP and WRAP-XP, which determine the assignment of boundaries and stresses in general, nuclear and pre-nuclear. The realization of focus and givenness, in turn, while driven by the specific constraints FOCUS REALIZATION and GIVENNESS REALIZATION, hinges in essential ways on default prosody as determined by the aforementioned constraints, modeling the observation that focus/givenness prosody still preserves in large part features of default prosody. In other words, each constraint, including in particular the ones related to default prosody, continues to be active even when in part "overwritten" by higher ranked information structure realization constraints like FOCUS REALIZATION and GIVENNESS REALIZATION, that is: Prosodic Inertia.

8

More on focus/givenness realization

In this chapter we will delve deeper into various aspects of focus realization. In particular, the discussion in Section 8.1–8.3 concerns languages other than English and its fellow Flexible Accent Languages (discussed in Chapter 2). The goal, however, is not to give a typological overview of focus realization, or to arrive at a cross-linguistically applicable theory of it,[1] nor to review the sizeable literature on the syntax of focussing.[2] Rather I will concentrate on cases in which phenomena of focus realization appear to, or are argued to, have direct repercussions for the overall theory of intonational meaning.

In Sections 8.4 and 8.5 we return to the Germanic languages to discuss some of the finer points about focus realization, in relation to syntax (Section 8.4) and other information structural categories (Section 8.5).

8.1 Italian: two focus types and no givenness

The case of Italian is instructive for various reasons: First, it appears that Italian shows no givenness deaccenting. Second, Italian seems to realize corrective focus, perhaps contrastive focus in general, very differently from answer focus, perhaps elaboration focus in general.

8.1.1 Clause-final focus only

To set the stage, we start by noting the most famous property Italian displays in regard to information structure realization: regular answer focus can only be realized clause-finally; an early, *in situ*, focus is highly marked, if not unacceptable in such contexts.[3]

---

[1] Contributions to this endeavor include Büring (2009), Drubig (2003), and collections like Lee et al. (2007), Molnár and Winkler (2006), Rebuschi and Tuller (1999) among others.

[2] As initiated in Rizzi (1997), see e.g. Benincà and Munaro (2010), Cruschina (2012); Cruschina and Remberger (to appear), Frascarelli and Hinterhölzl (2007), and the references therein for recent overviews.

[3] Example minimally adapted from Samek-Lodovici (2005: 688).

Intonation and Meaning. First edition. Daniel Büring.
© Daniel Büring 2016. First published 2016 by Oxford University Press.

(1) (Who laughed? —)

    a. Ha riso   GIANni.   b. * GIANni ha   riso.   (Italian)
       has laughed G.   G.   has laughed
       'Gianni laughed.'

This behavior, which Italian shares (by and large) with several other languages (closely related ones—Spanish and Catalan—as well as unrelated ones—Tangale), is often explained along the following lines, after the seminal proposal for Spanish in Zubizarreta (1998): Like English, Italian needs to place the nuclear stress within the focus (i.e something like FOCUS REALIZATION from Chapter 7). But unlike in English, the prosodic rules of Italian do not allow for the nuclear stress to occur anywhere but clause final (though see Section 8.1.3 for a substantial qualification of that claim); instead, Italian "sacrifices" canonical word order so as to bring the focus to the right clause boundary, where it can receive the proper nuclear accenting by default prosody. If the mountain (NPA) will not come to the prophet (focus), the prophet must go to the mountain.

The same type of explanation likely carries over to OV-languages with strictly pre-verbal focus positions such as Hindi/Urdu, Malayalam, or Turkish. In neutral sentences, these languages have the main stress on the immediately preverbal element (usually the direct object), presumably an effect analogous to integration. Thus, the focus position, though not strictly peripheral, coincides with the neutral main stress position.

The Italian type of failure to change default prosody for purposes of information structure marking in itself does not shed any new light on the interpretation of focus, but it provides crucial background for the two properties of Italian to be discussed next.

8.1.2 Lack of givenness accenting

It has been observed anecdotally that, much unlike English and other Germanic languages, Italian does not deaccent given material in nuclear accent position, as in (2) and (3).[4]

(2) Le   inchieste   servono a   mettere a   POSTO cose   andate
    the investigations serves   to   put   to   place things gone
    fuori POSTO.   (Italian)
    out of place
    'The investigations are helping to put back in order things that have gone out of order.' (lit.: # '... out of ORDER')

---

[4] Example (2) is a quote from former Italian president Scalfaro, reported in Ladd (2008: 233); example (3) courtesy of Vieri Samek-Lodovici (p.c.).

Cruttenden (2006) finds more or less systematic lack of deaccenting in this kind of case in French, Italian, Spanish, Swedish, and probably (some varieties of) Arabic, but not or less so in Albanian, English, German, Greek, Lithuanian, Macedonian, and Russian. Re-accenting, as Cruttenden calls it, seems also commonly attested in variants of English such as Indian English, Caribbean English, and others; see Brown (1983), Cruttenden (1993, 2006), and the references in note 11 below.

(3) Q: (Cosa ha fatto la mamma di Gianni quando ha sentito
        what has done the mother of G.   when   has heard
        del   suo incidente?)
        of   his accident
        'What did John's mother do when she heard about his
        accident?'
    A: Ha [chiamato GIANNI]$_F$
    A': *Ha [CHIAMATO Gianni]$_F$
        has called   G.
        'She called Gianni.'

Swerts et al. (2002) systematically investigate this phenomenon, which, following Cruttenden (1993, 2006) is called RE-ACCENTING, in a production experiment, finding conclusive confirmation.[5] When naming a shape of a certain color (in an instruction to another subject to move a card with that element on it), zero out of eight Italian speakers deaccented the color word, even in a context where a different shape of the same color had just been named.

(4)   (PREVIOUS MENTION: rettangolo nero —) triANgolo NEro
                            rectangle black — TRIangle BLACK

    unattested: triANgolo nero

In sharp contrast, eight out of eight Dutch speakers in the same setting do deaccent the second word (the noun naming the shape in Dutch) where only the first is contrastive in the context (Dutch thus behaving like its Germanic cousin English).[6]

(5)   (PRECEDING: gele   vierkant —) BLAUwe vierkant   (Dutch)
                    yellow square — BLUE   square

    unattested: BLAUwe VIERkant, blauwe VIERkant

As discussed in Section 7.2.2 above, givenness deaccenting occurs in pre-nuclear position in English as well. Again, this is different in Italian, as the contrast between the English (6a), where ‹Laden› is deaccented, and the Italian (6b), with regular pre-nuclear accent on ‹Laden›, shows.[7]

(6)   (Bin Laden has successfully avoided capture for nearly five years.)
    a. It's NOT CLEAR that [the SEARCH for [Bin Laden]$_G$] is STILL going ON.
    b. Non è chiaro che la ricerca di Bin Laden sia ancora in
       not is clear that the search of Bin Laden be still   in
       corso.
       progress

---

  [5] As with the term 'deaccenting', 're-accenting' suggests removal (and in the case of 're': restitution) of pitch accent; the term, however, should be understood purely descriptively.

  [6] See Swerts et al. (2002: Table II, 638).

  [7] The English example is reported in Selkirk (2007: 37), its Italian translation and description of its prosody is taken from Bocci (2013). I thank Silvio Cruschina for bringing Bocci's example to my attention.

A straightforward way to interpret these observations and results is to assume that givenness (but not focus) is irrelevant for the grammar of Italian and languages like it; in "feature speak," Italian has F-markers but no G-markers. This in turn implies, obviously, that givenness and focus must be grammatically distinct phenomena; analyses which formally unify them, like those for English discussed in Chapters 3 and 4, are "too successful," since they are ill-equipped to tease the two apart in a case like Italian.

On the other hand it seems tempting to relate the lack of givenness deaccenting to the general inability of Italian to move the NPA away from the right clause boundary, mentioned in connection with focussing in the previous subsection. Indeed this connection is quite commonly made in discussion of re-accenting as well as inflexible stress languages.[8] Concretely, we may tell a story along the following lines: It is syntactically impossible to re-order the DP+P and N+AP cases so as to have the non-given element in final (=accented) position: *⟨POsto fuOri⟩, *⟨NEro triANgolo⟩. And it is prosodically impossible to shift sentential stress leftward, so as to deaccent the given elements: *⟨fuOri posto⟩, *⟨triANgolo nero⟩. The only remaining possibility is to just *ignore* givenness and apply default prosody within the PP/DP.

Part of what makes this line of reasoning attractive is that it leaves room for givenness effects where syntax permits. It is well known that major constituents, if given, are frequently left and right dislocated in Italian, and right dislocation appears possible *only* with given constituents.

Similarly, pronominalization/cliticization often seems to serve to avoid re-accenting a given element; it is in fact preferred over re-accenting in case a given element occurs within a broader focus, (7A′) vis-à-vis (7A).[9]

(7) Q: Cosa ha fatto la mamma di Gianni quando ha sentito del
        what has done the mother of G.   when   has heard   of
        suo incidente?
        his accident
        'What did John's mother do when she heard about his accident?'
     A:??[Ha schiaffeggiato GIANNI]$_F$
     A′: [Lo ha schiaffeggiato]$_F$.
         him has slapped
         'She slapped John.'

This suggests that the GIVENNESS REALIZATION may be overruled where it would require accent shift, but is otherwise alive and well in the language (I thank Silvio Cruschina (p.c.) for helping me get clearer on this point). Put differently: the syntactic treatment Italian inflicts upon given major constituents, dislocation, has

---

[8] Valldují (1990), Valldují and Zacharski (1993), Ladd (2008: 235), Swerts et al. (2002: 651).

[9] Data and judgments in (7) courtesy of Vieri Samek-Lodovici (p.c.); note the contrast with example (3) above, where pronominalization is possible (⟨Lo ha chiamato.⟩), but not strictly preferred. Samek-Lodovici suggests that re-accenting (rather than pronominalizing or dislocating) in (3) is possible only on an understanding (and with an intonation contour signaling) that calling Gianni is a very obvious thing for his mother to do in such a situation.

the systematic side effect of removing them from positions of sentential stress, just as though they were subject to GIVENNESS REALIZATION. Assuming that givenness (say in the form of G-marking) is absent in the grammar of Italian leaves this completely unexplained.

Lastly, looking at the survey in Cruttenden (2006), it appears that there is at least a tangible correlation between re-accenting and a fixed accent position. In particular, I am not aware of any clear flexible accent languages that lack givenness deaccenting, though clearly more work is needed here.

However, the Italian case is more intriguing, and hence more interesting from a theoretical point of view, than that: deaccenting, or nuclear accent shift to the left, *is possible* sometimes, for example in sub-constituent answer foci, metalinguistic corrections, and, somewhat marginally, direct contrast.[10]

(8) (How many cherries have you given to Mary?—)
     Ho   dato   a   Maria TRE   ciliegie
     have.1sg given to Mary   three cherries
     'I gave THREE cherries to Mary.'

(9) (Che   cosa ha   comprato Gianni, di   rosso?)
     what   has   bought Gianni   of   red
     'What red object did Gianni buy?'
     Gianni ha   comprato un capPEllo rosso.
     G.   has   bought   a   hat   red
     'Gianni bought a red hat.'

(10) Non ho   detto CAsa   bianca, ho   detto COsa   bianca.
     not have said   HOUSE white,   have said   THING white
     'I didn't say white HOUSE, I said white THING.'

(11) ?Adesso faccio   scorrere il   TUo   bagnetto.
     now   make-1SG   run   the YOUR bath
     'Now I'll run YOUR bath.' ("spoken to a child whose baby brother had just had his evening bath"; Ladd, 2008: 235)

These examples show that we cannot assume an absolute ban on accent shift. In particular, even for elaboration/answer foci, as in examples (8) and (9), deaccenting of the noun is possible: examples (4) and (9) above form a near-minimal pair. This, then, provides evidence in favor of dissociating givenness and focussing after all: (9), just like the other cases in (8) through (11), is a clear instances of narrow focus on the accented word. For Swerts et al.'s (2002) re-accenting cases (4), on the other hand, it seems plausible to think that the entire DP ‹triANgolo NEro› is focus (given the experimental setup, in which one person is telling another which card to move next, which seems to imply the question 'Which card shall the addressee move next?'), and what we witness is failure of givenness deaccenting *within* a focus

---

[10] Examples from Samek-Lodovici (2005: 704), Brunetti (2004b: 84), Ladd (2008: 233/235), respectively. Ladd (2008: 233) also gives examples of contextual deaccenting of predicate nouns and adjectives, as well as main verbs when preceded by a stressed auxiliary; see his (37). Perhaps these are polarity foci, though Ladd does not give a context, so it is hard to say.

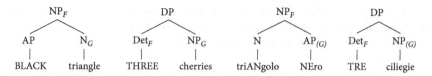

FIGURE 8.1   Narrow F and G-within-F may yield the same accent pattern in English, but perhaps not in Italian?

(likewise Ladd's (2) is unlikely to have narrow focus on ‹posto›). The hypothesized information structure markings are shown in Figure 8.1.

If Italian has no G-marking (or alternatively: G-marking is ignored/overruled by the rules of default prosody), then the difference between examples (2) and (4) comes down to that between narrow focus *with* concomitant deaccenting, (8)–(11), and wide focus with*out* focus-internal givenness deaccenting, examples (2) and (4). The difference between English and Italian would simply be that English, but not Italian, utilizes G-marking. The contrast between (4) and (9) (and the other cases in the respective classes they represent) can be made sense of.

Note that on this rather simplistic picture there is no connection any more between the lack of givenness deaccenting and the lack of clause-medial *in situ* focus in Italian (the former being due to properties of G-marking or G-realization, the latter to prosodic properties). We can, however, still loosely tie these two properties together. Suppose for that sake that there are several independent factors at play in Italian (as well as other languages): IP-HEAD-RIGHT, urging the NPA on the rightmost word in the clause, FOCUS REALIZATION, requiring the NPA within the focus, and GIVENNESS REALIZATION, which prohibits the NPA on given elements, familiar from Chapters 6 and 7. In addition assume a constraint CANONICALORDER, which is violated by dislocations and other kinds of constituent order rearrangements like object–subject orders (Grimshaw's, 1997, STAY). If we rank these forces (e.g. in the way customary in Optimality Theory), the two languages come out as in ranking (12) below.

(12)   a. English: FOCUS REALIZATION, CANONICALORDER ≫ GIVENNESS REALIZA-
          TION ≫ IP-HEAD-RIGHT
       b. Italian: FOCUS REALIZATION ≫ IP-HEAD-RIGHT ≫ GIVENNESS REALIZATION
          ≫ CANONICALORDER

On a view along these lines, both types of lack of deaccenting in Italian—no post-focal deaccenting, remedied by rearranging constituent order as much as syntactically possible, minimal NPA shift plus deaccenting otherwise; and no focus-internal givenness deaccenting, remedied by simply not realizing givenness—are due to the high ranking of the prosodic constraint IP-HEAD-RIGHT in that language.[11]

---

[11] We could of course still model a language that has one property without the other. The ranking in (ia) would give us a language which realizes backgrounding as well as givenness by constituent order

Note that the preceding musings are not just a digression into prosodic typology. Suppose it turns out that we are correct in our suspicion that Italian treats givenness deaccenting very differently from background deaccenting. Then this would provide a *prima facie* argument in favor of keeping these two notions distinct in the theory. In particular, the very existence of such a case (Italian, if we are on the right track) poses a challenge to theories like Schwarzschild (1999) or Büring (2012b) which subsume givenness under focussing, or Wagner (2010), which reduces focussing to G-marking.

Yet, this need not be the only possible conclusion. Alternatively, the hypothesized Italian pattern could also be derived by an adjustment to the options regarding focus *representation*. If Italian simply did not allow for embedded F-domains, the observed effect would, by and large, be the same: sentential (or generally: non-subordinated) F-domains realize their focus, but the effects of sub-focussing/givenness within a focus disappear because there are in general no embedded F-domains (incidentally, there also seem to be no multiple foci in Italian, which may be connected to the lack of recursive F-domains on this view). Again, to tease these options apart, we need a more thorough picture of the data than currently available.[12]

The Italian deaccenting facts might be instructive in other regards as well. As Ladd (2008: 236ff) observes, Italian puts the NPA in broad focus on indefinite pronouns where Germanic languages would deaccent them.

(13) a. Ho sentito qualCUno.   b. I HEARD someone.
      I   heard   someone

This may be interpreted as an indication that the deaccenting of indefinite pronouns in the Germanic languages should be analyzed as a case of givenness

---

variation ("generalized Italian"), while ranking (ib) describes a language in which everything remains *in situ* and backgrounding is achieved by post-focal deaccenting, while givenness is simply ignored ("Italianized English").

(i) a. FOCUS REALIZATION ≫ GIVENNESS REALIZATION ≫ IP-HEAD-RIGHT ≫ CANONICALORDER
     b. FOCUS REALIZATION, CANONICALORDER ≫ IP-HEAD-RIGHT ≫ GIVENNESS REALIZATION

The latter case might be actualized in Hawaiian Pidgin and Indian and Caribbean English (Vanderslice and Pierson, 1967, and Gumperz, 1982, as cited in Ladd, 2008: 232), though the data available are not conclusive regarding the focussing/givenness distinction.

What ranking the constraints allows us to express is that givenness still has *some* role to play in Italian, though a less important one than focus. A system along these lines also excludes a language in which for example focus would be exclusively realized by rearranging constituents, and givenness exclusively by shifting the NPA; rather, any language is predicted to have a "primary" method of achieving information structure effects (syntactic rearrangement in the case of Italian), and, possibly, a "last resort" one (NPA shift), modeled by the relative ranking of the markedness constraints responsible (i.e. IP-HEAD-RIGHT ≫CANONICALORDER in Italian). Both FOCUS REALIZATION and GIVENNESS REALIZATION can independently be ranked so as to achieve their goal via both, via the primary only, or not at all, but never via the Last Resort Way only.

[12] Another analytical option, suggested to my by Vieri Samek-Lodovici (p.c.) is to assume that Italian has embedded F-domains but no givenness deaccenting. This presupposes that English has in fact both, something we did not consider in Chapter 4, but which is assumed in Féry and Samek-Lodovici (2006).

deaccenting (analogous to epithets and full lexical phrases), rather than structural non-accenting of function words (analogous to pronouns, which are cliticized, and hence unaccented in Italian as well).

Another difference noted by Ladd is that Italian completely prohibits focus-driven manipulation of word stress (see Section 5.5), including in number sequences. It is not at all obvious that this fact could be correlated to the other instances of Italian re-accenting. At least on the face of it (and according to Artstein's 2004 analysis) shifting an accent within a word is unlikely to be triggered by givenness, since it appears to be an instance of contrast without meaning, which is to say: It seems more palatable to think that ‹BRItannic› contrasts with ‹TItanic› than to think that ‹tan(n)ic› is given. If the correlation between re-accenting and lack of word stress shift turns out to be systematic, though, one should probably attempt to adapt Artstein's analysis accordingly. Again, this is a case in which typological data can inform our theory of information structure interpretation, rather than just its realization.

8.1.3 Clause-initial (and clause-medial) focus

Turning to another relevant property of information structure realization in Italian, there is a set of cases in which focus can be realized by an early NPA, complete with post-focal deaccenting. Examples of such FOCUS FRONTING are given in (14).[13]

(14) a. La felpa,   l'ha   vinto Gianni.
         the sweatshirt it has won   G.
         'Gianni won the sweatshirt'

      b. No, [la maglietta]$_F$ ha   vinto Gianni.
         no   the T-shirt   has   won   Gianni

(15) a.   Che cosa ha   vinto Gianni?
           what thing has   won   G.
           'What did Gianni win?'

      b. ??[La maglietta]$_F$ ha   vinto Gianni.
           the T-shirt   has   won   Gianni

As (15) shows, regular answer focus is generally highly marked or even unacceptable in this position (but rather occurs right-peripherally, see beginning of this section).[14] The precise characterization of what kind of foci may occur in this

---

[13] Examples (13)/(14) from Brunetti (2004b: 99).

[14] Torregrossa (2010) notes that left-peripheral answer focus "is acceptable in contexts in which [the questioner] expects [the questionee] to have bought something unusual," as in (i) (his (70)).

(i) (Che cosa hai   comprato?—) Il PAne ho   comprato.
      what thing have-2SG bought   the bread have-1SG bought

Torregrossa hypothesizes that in such a case "the function of the CF is ... to negate all the propositions asserting that the speaker bought something unusual" (2010: 20).

Cruschina (2012) argues for a similar characterization of early foci in Sicilian (see esp. his ch. 2.4.1).

clause-initial position is not clear from the literature, but certainly corrections as in (14) are a prominent candidate, as are, according to É. Kiss, questions like (16), which have a precisely limited domain of possible answers.[15]

(16)   A: Chi di voi due ha rotto il vaso?
          'Who of you two broke the vase?'

        B: MARIA ha rotto il vaso.
           Maria has broken the vase

É. Kiss proposes that generally, left peripheral focus in Italian is *contrastive*, in the sense that it has to "select an individual from a closed set of known candidates" (É. Kiss, 1998, p. 269), which would be the target of a correction (‹la felpa› in example (14b)), and the alternative(s) not chosen in the answer in the context of a question like (16a). This is reminiscent of the individual case in Rooth's (1992b) proposal, in which a contextually salient meaning has to be an *element* (rather than a subset) of the F-alternatives.

Brunetti (2004a), Frascarelli (2000), and Gryllia (2009) provide convincing evidence that early foci in Italian are not semantically exhaustive—unlike preverbal foci in Hungarian (see Section 8.2). A left peripheral focus can be associated with additive particles like ‹anche› or ‹persino›, 'even'/'also'.[16]

(17)   a. [Anche un cappello]$_F$ gli   ha comprato Maria.
              also   a   hat   him-DAT has bought   M.
           'Maria also bought him a hat.'

        b. [Persino un cappello]$_F$ gli   ha comprato Maria.
              even   a   hat   him-DAT has bought   M.
           'Maria even bought him a hat.'

Gryllia (2009: sec. 3.3) reports that twelve out of twelve native speakers judged sentence (18b) to be an entailment of (18a) (Gryllia's (37)).

(18)   Hai   comprato un paio de pantaloni a Bill e   Stella?
        have-2SG bought   a   pair of trousers   to B. and S.
        'Did you buy a pair of trousers for Bill and Stella?'

        a. Ho   comprato un paio di pantaloni a Gianni e   a Maria.
           have-1SG bought   a   pair of trousers   to John and to Mary
           'I bought a pair of trousers for John and for Mary.'

        b. [A Gianni]$_F$ ho   comprato un paio di pantaloni.
           to John   have-1SG bought   a   pair of trousers
           'For John, I bought a pair of trousers.'

If the early focus ‹a Gianni› in (18b) were exhaustive ('it was Gianni I bought pants for'), the sentence should be incompatible with (18a). Likewise, the sentences in

---

[15] É. Kiss (1998: example (73)).

[16] Examples (15b/c) from Brunetti (2004a). Gryllia (2009) and Cruschina (2012) provide similar arguments for Greek and Sicilian, respectively.

(17) should be contradictory (compare ‹It was (*even) a HAT that Mary bought for him›).[17]

Whatever the precise requirements for focus fronting in Italian may be, what is relevant for our subject matter is that these facts suggest a *grammatical* distinction between two types of focus, say contrastive focus and non-contrastive (elaboration and answer focus), a distinction we have not found clear evidence for in English.

One important fact to keep in mind is that while the left peripheral position in Italian may be reserved for contrastive foci, it is not *obligatory* for them. Corrections and narrow contrastive foci may be realized in the post verbal, right peripheral position as in (19) as well.[18]

(19) a. Ha   telefonato   [Maria]$_F$, non Piero.
           has telephoned   M.   not   P.

      b. (CONTEXT: You gave the winner a T-shirt)
         No. Abbiamo   dato   al   vincitore   una   MEDAGLIA.
         no   have-1PL   given to the   winner   a   medal
         'No. We gave the winner a medal.'

In other words, occurring left peripherally is a sufficient, but not necessary condition for a focus to be interpreted contrastively.[19]

Brunetti (2004b, 2006, 2009) proposes an alternative explanation for the contrast between left peripheral focus and right peripheral focus in Italian. According to those works, the left peripheral position is in fact compatible with *any* kind of focus. However, in case an answer/elaboration focus moves there, ellipsis of the core clause becomes near-obligatory. In other words example (15b) above is degraded because its "proper" realization would be ‹la maglietta›, or more precisely the structure in (20).

(20) (Che   cosa   ha   vinto   Gianni?—) [La   maglietta]$_F$ ~~ha~~   ~~vinto~~
       what   thing has won   G.?   the T-shirt   has   won
       ~~Gianni.~~
       G.

---

[17] In both these respects, Italian early focus contrasts with Hungarian preverbal focus, which does not tolerate additive particles, and creates a contradiction in sequences like (18), see Szabolcsi (1981) and É. Kiss (1998) among others.

[18] Examples (115) from Brunetti (2004b: 133) and Samek-Lodovici (2005). See the discussion in López (2009: esp. pp.55ff), though, where left peripheral focus is claimed to be obligatory in corrections.

[19] Various researchers have proposed that contrastive *in situ* foci move to the left peripheral position in covert syntax, which would yield a 1-to-1 correspondence between position and focus type. I know of no evidence, however, which would *syntactically* distinguish contrastive and non-contrastive, right peripheral, foci in Italian (see e.g. Frascarelli, 2000: ch. 3, for thorough discussion of that point).

Samek-Lodovici (2006, 2009) on the other hand, presents extensive arguments for unifying the other way around, i.e. that early foci in Italian are in fact clause-final foci, (optionally) followed by right-dislocated material. The question why this option is marked for answer/elaboration focus is not discussed in those papers. On the other hand, Brunetti's discussion of that question is, as far as I can see, unaffected by the syntactic analysis of early foci.

This of course raises the question why ellipsis should not be obligatory in the cases of contrastive focus we have discussed above. Brunetti's answer is that ellipsis is possible only if the background of the focus is identical to the background of some previous utterance (Brunetti, 2004b: 113); where this condition is met, ellipsis becomes (near) obligatory, rendering the clausal version highly marked. This is guaranteed to be the case in answer focus, where, by assumption, everything but the ‹wh›-phrase in the question is background (‹ha vinto Gianni› in example (20) below) and can therefore license (and force) ellipsis of the main clause in an answer with left peripheral focus.[20]

Crucially, Brunetti (2004b) points out, foci in corrections with left peripheral focus are marked just like answer foci, if, as in (21) (her (59)), the focus in the target is the same as in the correction.

(21)   Gianni ha vinto [la FELpa]$_F$.
        'Gianni won the sweatshirt.'
        a.   No, [la maGLIETta]$_F$.
        b. ??No, [la maGLIETta]$_F$ ha vinto Gianni.

A typical case of left peripheral focus in Italian, then, is one in which the foci do not "match," in which case ellipsis is not obligatory, and in fact becomes impossible, as in example (22) below.

(22)   a.   La felpa, l'ha vinto [Gianni]$_F$.
              'Gianni won the sweatshirt.'
        b.   #No, [la maglietta]$_F$.
        c.   No, [la maglietta]$_F$ ha vinto Gianni.
              no the T-shirt has won Gianni

If the target of correction is a canonical SV(O) sentence, its focus cannot be on the subject, which means that a correction of anything but the object will yield a left peripheral focus, too, cf. example (23):[21]

(23)   a.   Paolo ha vinto [la felpa]$_F$.
              'Paolo won the sweatshirt.'
        b.   #No, [Gianni]$_F$.
        c.   No, [Gianni]$_F$ ha vinto la felpa.

---

[20] This leaves examples like É. Kiss' example (16) above to be explained, which do not force ellipsis. Brunetti assumes that in such questions, the ‹wh›-phrase, being contextually linked ("D-linked"), is not a focus, and hence the foci in question and answer do not match:

(i)   a.   Chi di voi due [ha rotto il vaso]$_F$?
       b.   [Maria]$_F$ ha rotto il vaso.   (Brunetti, 2004b: (80), 117)

Alternatively one might argue that the focus in the question is just ‹chi›, not ‹chi di voi›, which would probably suffice to interrupt the matching relation required here.

[21] Brunetti (2004b: (61)); see also the discussion in Samek-Lodovici (2006: 849ff).

It is worth noting that the condition on ellipsis that Brunetti proposes (identity of background between antecedent utterance and focussed utterance) is an unusual one. All focus-related rules we reviewed thus far (and virtually all I am aware of in the literature) are "one-way only": they relate the F-alternatives of an utterance to the *content* of an antecedent utterance or otherwise salient meaning—never to the information structure of that antecedent. IS-symmetrical rules, especially across sentences, as proposed in Brunetti's work, seem highly unusual in this light.

At the same time, if data like example (21) (and in particular the contrast to example (22)) are systematic, it shows at the very least that "contrastiveness" is not even a sufficient condition for left peripheral focus in Italian, substantially weakening the case for contrastive focus as a grammatical category.

In sum then, Italian provides *prima facie* evidence for two distinctions not easily seen in the English data: That between backgrounding and givenness deaccenting, and between contrastive and non-contrastive focus (or something like those). If these cases turn out to be solid (and more systematic empirical investigation is certainly needed here), they should inform our theories about focus/givenness representation and interpretation in English as well. The resulting theory might end up recognizing three distinct features, F, G, and CF for contrastive focus (or some sort of feature system which can yield at least these categories), with potentially different prosodic and syntactic realizations.

I have also sketched interpretations of the data that may yet be compatible with a more parsimonious view of focussing, that is, with using a single grammatical marker F only. Either alternative needs more work, both in establishing the relevant generalizations, and modeling the semantic concepts behind the classification. Italian and languages like it should certainly play a central role in such future investigations.

8.2 Hungarian

Hungarian is famous in studies of information structure because it seems to provide a rather direct mapping of information structure functions like topic and focus to syntactic positions. The picture is, as we will see, more complicated, but, like Italian, it can indicate directions in which a theory of information structure representation and interpretation should probably be refined.

A distinguishing feature of Hungarian is a designated preverbal focus position. Apart from linear order, the presence of an element in that position can be diagnosed, in many instances, using verbal morphology: if certain preverbs, like ‹be›, 'in,' in (24), follow, rather than precede the finite verb, the F-position is filled.[22]

(24) Be-mutattam   Jánost   az   unokahúgomnak.   (Hungarian)
      in-showed-1SG J.-ACC   the   niece-my-DAT
      'I introduced John to my niece.'   (neutral)

---

[22] Example from Horvath (2010: 1352).

(25) Q: Kinek mutattad be Jánost? ('To whom did you introduce John?')
    a. [az   unokahúgomnak]$_F$ mutattam   **be** Jánost
       the   niece-my-DAT   showed-1SG in John-ACC
       'I introduced John to my niece.'

    b. *[az   unokahúgomnak]$_F$ **be**-mutattam   Jánost
       the niece-my-DAT   in-showed-1SG John-ACC

We will take this diagnostic and the existence of a designated position for granted here.

Starting with the seminal work in Szabolcsi (1981), there has been general agreement that elements in the focus position are interpreted exhaustively, and that sentences with that position filled have an existential presupposition. Both of these effects appear to be non-cancelable and are thus taken to be semantic entailments, rather than pragmatic implicatures. Put differently, sentences with a filled F-position in Hungarian have essentially the semantic properties of English cleft sentences, rather than intonational focus sentences in English.

What makes Hungarian very different from English is that both contrastive focus and answer focus virtually obligatorily have to occupy the F-position, whereas the status of answer foci *in situ*, that is, post-verbally as in (26b), is at best controversial.[23]

(26) Kivel   beszélt   Zeta?   (Hungarian)
     who-INSTR speak-PAST-3SG Zeta
     'Who did Zeta speak with?'
    a. EMÖKÉVEL   beszélt.
       Emöke-INSTR speak-PAST-3SG
       'He spoke with EMÖKE.ÁŢ'
    b. *Beszélt   Emökével.
       speak-PAST-3SG EmÖke-INSTR

The pertinent generalization seems to be something along the lines of (27).

(27^{GEN}) GENERALIZATION ABOUT HUNGARIAN FOCUS
      If a (pragmatic) focus is compatible with the properties of the F-position, it must occur in the F-position.

The hedge "if it is compatible" is important here, because, as, for example, Horvath (2000: 201) shows, an answer focus in preverbal position is strictly *im*possible if the general semantics of the answer is incompatible with the exhaustivity implied by the F-position, as in (28b).[24]

---

[23] Example and judgments from Puskás (2000: 72). É. Kiss (1998) argues that foci can appear *in situ* (i.e. post-verbally) as well as in in the preverbal position, and that rather, the structures involving a preverbal focus are akin to English clefts. According to Szendrői (2001), however, foci cannot generally occur *in situ*.

[24] More examples of this sort can be found in Horvath (2010: 1356).

(28)   Q: Kit   hívtak   meg?   (Hungarian)
            who   invite   PRT
            'Who did they invite?'

       a.   Jánost   hívták   meg.
            J.-ACC   invited   PRT
            'They invited John (and no one else).'

       b.   *Jánost   például   hívták   meg.
            John-ACC   for-example   invited   PRT
            'They invited John, for example/among others.'

       c.   Meghívták   *(például/többek   kőzött)   Jánost
            invited-they   for-example/others   among   John-ACC
            'They invited John, for example/among others.'

If, as in this case, an interpretation of the focus as Exhaustive Identification is made impossible, for example by adverbs like 'among others' as in (28b), an answer focus has to appear post-verbally, that is *in situ*.[25]

But if movement of foci is not truly obligatory in Hungarian, why is it that nevertheless foci appear in the preverbal F-position whenever possible? Or put differently: Even if the main effect of the F-position is semantic exhaustivity, or if all foci that are to be interpreted exhaustively have to be moved to that position, why is it that contrastive focus and even answer focus so urgently needs to be encoded with *grammatical* exhaustivity? After all, English has a cleft-construction, too, and yet using it in a focus construction, even one that is to be understood as exhaustively identifying (e.g. answering the question ‹Which team won the tournament this year?›) is at best optional.

A plausible and intriguing answer to this question is proposed in Kriszta Szendrői's work (Szendrői, 2001, 2004, 2006), according to which movement to the preverbal position is driven by prosody. The preverbal position receives the unmarked sentence stress in Hungarian, and thereby provides a perfect placement for phrases that are, or contain, the focus. Taken together with the exhaustivity facts, the picture that emerges can be described as follows: Hungarian focus—like English and Italian focus—wants to be realized by sentential stress; sentential stress is (most cheaply) acquired in the preverbal position; independently, that preverbal position is grammatically associated with an exhaustive interpretation; therefore, foci will be realized in that position, provided the intended interpretation is at least compatible with exhaustivity.

Szendrői (2001, 2003) presents additional evidence for this idea. If the preverbal position remains empty, sentential stress falls on the (uninverted) particle+verb complex. Such a sentence can be interpreted as VP focus, as narrow V focus, or as polarity focus.

---

[25] Another instance of this are foci associated with ‹még›, 'even', which cannot be moved to the F-position either (unlike foci associated with ‹csak›, 'only'). Arguably, this is so because the additive semantics of 'even' (which, roughly, presupposes that a more likely alternative is true as well) is incompatible with exhaustifying the focus; see Horvath (2010: 1355, ex. (21)) for discussion and illustration.

(29) A   kalapját   a   nö   [LE VETTE az   elöszobában]$_F$.
her hat-ACC the woman   off took   the hall-in
'The woman took her hat off in the hall.'   (Szendrői, 2003: 41)

(30) Péter FEL-OLVASTA a   Hamletet   a   kertben   (nem pedig
Peter PREV-read   the Hamlet-ACC the garden-in (not rather
úszott).
swam)
'Rather than swim, Peter read Hamlet in the garden.'[26]

(31) De, én ODA VITTEM a   levelet.
But I   PREV took   the letter-ACC
'But, I TOOK the letter (, I didn't bring it).'   *or*

'But, I DID take the letter there.'   (Szendrői, 2001: 56)

Note that these examples, similar to broad focus examples in Italian, suggest that it is not a syntactic position, but a prosodic property that is crucial for focus realization. On this view, term focus and polarity/V/VP focus in Hungarian share this crucial property (containing main sentential stress), whereas they do not share—in any obvious way—the same syntactic position.

The preceding discussion of Hungarian does not merely illustrate another strategy of focus realization, but rather has a point to make about focus representation and interpretation. É. Kiss (1998) proposes that Hungarian should be analyzed as distinguishing between what she calls IDENTIFICATIONAL FOCUS and INFORMATIONAL FOCUS. The former is interpreted exhaustively (and with an existential presupposition), while the latter is not. And crucially, identificational focus requires placement of the focus in the preverbal focus position, while informational focus does not (and, in the absence of such a requirement, stays post-verbally). This view implies that grammar distinguishes the two types of focus (since placement rules make reference to them), and that it is the identificational focus feature that triggers the exhaustive interpretation, or put differently: that there is a grammatical sub-category of focus, the identificational one.

While this is certainly an adequate and plausible way of modeling the Hungarian facts, it is not the only one. An analysis along the lines of Horvath's proposals, as sketched above, avoids postulating two different grammatical focus types. An identificational focus is simply a focus which also sits in an exhaustifying position. Combined with Szendrői's idea that the preference for preposing focus is actually due to prosodic, rather than syntactic factors (for which she provides further convincing evidence), the facts come out equally well, perhaps better, without distinguishing two types of focus.

The point is a subtle one, and it does not challenge any of É. Kiss's (1998) distinguishing diagnostics. But it is relevant in the context of our discussion, because

---

[26] From Kenesei (2006: 153), based on Kenesei (1998); Kenesei actually claims that ‹fel›, ‹Hamletet›, and ‹kertben› bear "primary stresses" (p.152); the capitalization here follows Puskás (2000: 96). I have adjusted the gloss so as to make it clearer that the contrast is with swimming, not swimming in the garden.

it suggests that Hungarian might not, on closer inspection, provide evidence for two variants of focus so much as for the interaction of one kind of focus with other factors.

It should also be noted that even if we adopt the idea of identificational focus, either as a descriptive or as a theoretical concept, its scope is quite different from that characterizing what we discussed under the label contrastive focus in Italian in Section 8.1. Identificational focus does not fit in with a taxonomy that distinguishes, say, answer focus, contrastive focus, elaboration focus or corrective focus, but cuts right across them (it seems to comprise instances of all of them, but only if compatible with exhaustive interpretation).

8.3 Outlook: focus, sentential stress, and verb adjacency

We have seen in our discussion of Italian in Section 8.1 that constituent order effects of focus, in particular answer focus, though quite different on the surface, may well be related to the way flexible accent languages, discussed in Chapter 2, realize focussing: Marked word order—like accent shift—generally results in the focussed element containing the final pitch accent—as required for example by FOCUS REALIZATION.

The case of Hungarian preverbal focus at first glance seems to be much more similar to the left peripheral focus in Italian, since it clearly involves dislocation of the focussed element in most cases. However, it is also striking that the main stress position in Hungarian, like in Italian, coincides with the focus position, including in cases where no focus movement has taken place and the verb bears main stress, signaling for example VP focus.

It is tempting to think, then, that aligning the focus with the main stress position is a universal strategy of focus realization, at least for languages that have a clearly identifiable main stress position. Languages differ as to whether the main stress position is flexible (English and other flexible accent languages), and if not, whether it coincides, in a neutral constituent order sentence, with an argument position (Italian and similar languages) or a head position (Hungarian), necessitating different kinds of constituent order "adjustment."

There is reason to be cautious about such a generalization, however. The most extensive study of a language that seems to clearly defy the "focus↔main stress" correlation is Koch's (2008) discussion of Nɬʔkepmxcin (Thompson River Salish). As Koch shows, the nuclear stress in Nɬʔkepmxcin is right peripheral, yet focus is invariably realized at the left edge of the clause, adjacent to the verb (Nɬʔkepmxcin is VSO). As far as positional focus goes, Nɬʔkepmxcin behaves perfectly regularly: V-, VP- and S-focus are all realized by canonical order, whereas object- and subject-focus involve marked constituent orders.[27]

---

[27] Koch's examples (11), (18), (25), (30), and (33) (2008: 67–72).

(32) (What happened?)   (Nⱡʔkepmxcin)
    ʔéx xeʔ čax̣-t-ø-és   ⱡn-sx̣áẏwi   e   swúxʷt
    PROG DEM clean-TR-30-3TS DET IsG.PS-husband DET snow
    '[My husband was cleaning up the snow]ꜰ.'

(33) [describing pictures of a woman, Michelle]
    χʷúẏ xeʔ ƛ̣xʷ-úm tk   χʷʔít tk   snúye.
    FUT DEM win-MDL OBL.IRL much OBL.IRL money
    'She's [gonna win lot of money]ꜰ.'

(34) (What is the woman doing to the cow?)
    ʔé   xeʔ kʷúp-ø-ø-es   e   smúⱡec e   mósmos.
    PROG DEM push-TR-30-3TS DET woman DET cow
    'The woman's [pushing]ꜰ the cow.'

(35) (Who ate some bread this morning?)
    ŋcéweʔ   e   ⱡaʔx̣áns te   seplíl ⱡ   snwénwen.
    1SG.EMPH DET eat   OBL bread DET morning
    '[I]ꜰ ate some bread this morning.'

(36) (What did you make to drink this morning?)
    Kápi   xeʔ e   n-s-cw-úm   ʔeⱡ   e
    coffe DEM DET   1SG.POSS-NOM-make-MDL   and   DET
    n-s-Púqʷeʔ   ⱡ   snwénwen.
    1SG.POSS-NOM-drink DET morning
    'I made [coffee]ꜰ to drink this morning.'

Crucially, Koch (2008) shows that (34) and (35), and (36) show the same overall intonational pattern as the earlier sentences. In particular, the rightmost content word is accented, whether it is part of the focus as in examples (32) and (33) or in the background, as in (34) and (35), and (36). In other words, while focus is aligned to the left, the NPA is on the right.

Other languages, too, suggest that sometimes adjacency to (or identity with) the predicate (rather than main stress) is a precondition for focus interpretation. Western Bade, an SVO language, has to place foci post-verbally. Crucially, however, subject focus is realized as VSO, not VOS (Western Bade, like Tangale below, treats all ‹wh›-phrases like foci, so questions will be used where the literature did not provide declarative narrow focus exampes).[28]

(37) gafa-n ke   viiridgwarən   (Western Bade)
    caught who giant rat
    'Who caught a giant-rat?'

At least on the face of it, this makes it seem as if Western Bade marks focus by adjacency to the verb, rather than right peripherally (though of course closer inspection may reveal that the object in example (37) is right-dislocated), which

[28] Examples (37) and (38) from Kidwai (1999: 234 and 216).

in turn is unexpected if what underlies the focus position were a (peripheral) main stress position. Note that in this regard, Western Bade is different from Italian, where only right-dislocated elements may follow a (post-verbal) focussed subject, or Tangale, another SVO language, which truly appears to place foci right peripherally, and where, accordingly, a subject focus is realized in VOS, not VSO, order.

(38) a. wad Billiri nuŋ dooji?   (Tangale)
          go   B.   who tomorrow?
          'Who will go to Billiri tomorrow?'

      b. tui worom mono shire
          ate beans my   she
          'SHE ate my beans.'

In sum, although many languages—including Italian and Hungarian—can be beneficially analyzed based on the "focus↔main stress" correlation, this seems problematic in other cases, such as Nɬʔkepmxcin or Western Bade.

On the other hand, there still is, to my mind, a striking commonality to all the languages touched upon in our discussion. There appears to be exactly one grammatical position ("position" understood in a broad sense), call it the FOCUS REALIZATION POSITION (FRP) which may host narrow foci, but is also part of any broad focus (VP, S). In Italian (and Spanish, Tangale, …), this is the VP-final position, in Hungarian the left most position in the main clause (i.e. the focus position, or the fronted verb, or the preverb+verb complex), in Western Bade the post-verbal position, and in Hindi/Urdu (Malayalam, Turkish, …) the preverbal position. In Nɬʔkepmxcin, the FRP is the left-peripheral, or predicate, position.

Furthermore, a broad focus must not only include the FRP, but also have otherwise "normal" constituent order (thus, Italian SVO may be clausal focus, but VOS may not).

In many cases, the FRP can arguably be identified with the default main stress position, its focus affinity by some principle like FOCUS REALIZATION, and the constituent order effect by some version of CANONICALORDER (or, if you will, SYNTACTIC INERTIA, for example prohibition of spurious reordering movements). Nɬʔkepmxcin, and perhaps Western Bade, militate against generalizing this attractive type of analysis. The next weaker analytical option would be to parameterize the notion of what defines the FRP (i.e.—for the time being—stipulate it for each language), and have FOCUS REALIZATION align the focus with whatever characterizes the FRP in a given language. Coupled with prosodic/syntactic inertia, this would yield the kind of empirical picture described in this subsection.

What seems crucial, to my mind, is that such an analysis, whatever its details, implements the apparently systematic parallelisms between the realization of narrow foci, and that of focus *exponents* of wide foci (i.e. that element within a wide focus which bears the main stress). This parallelism, it seems to me, is not readily captured by approaches that involve a specific *syntactic* focus position.

8.4 A note on Nuclear Stress Rules

Chomsky and Halle (1968) proposed a Nuclear Stress Rule (NSR), which derives a stress pattern for any given syntactic tree on a purely structural basis. The empirical validity of their rule has been questioned subsequently, for example in Bierwisch (1966, 1968), Schmerling (1976), Liberman and Prince (1977), Gussenhoven (1983a), and many others. Most of these works propose to replace Chomsky and Halle's (1968) NSR by rules which create (at least partially) prosody-based stress patterns. The algorithms utilized in this book—both the simple accent-based approach used in Chapters 1–4 and the more nuanced stress-based approaches from Chapters 6 and 7—are properly characterized as belonging to that group of proposals.

A slightly different direction is pursued in Selkirk (1984, 1995b) and Gussenhoven (1983a), which derive the default accent pattern as the all-focus pattern: default accenting is simply the accenting of a sentence that is all-focus and contains no given elements. I argued that such an approach misses an important generalization: that the same prosodic defaults apply within all-new and all-given constituents (including all-given foci), and therefore opted against that strategy in this book.

A more direct descendant of Chomsky and Halle's (1968) NSR that still enjoys considerable popularity was proposed in Cinque (1993), and substantially refined in Zubizarreta (1998). Both works develop algorithms that directly predict the location of the main stress from syntactic structure (Cinque) or syntactic structure plus argument structure (Zubizarreta). The basic idea in Cinque's (1993) proposal is that main stress falls on that head which is syntactically the most deeply embedded one; in transitive sentences, that is almost always a head within the direct object DP (its head, or the head of a nominal complement within the object DP). In this regard, Cinque's proposal improves on, for example, Chomsky and Halle's (1968), which invariably predicts main stress on the last lexical element: In OV languages, main stress is predicted to fall on the *pre*verbal object (the head of which is more deeply embedded than the V head).

Truckenbrodt's (1995) Stress-xp/Wrap-xp-based account, which we adopted in this book, shares this advantage of Cinque's proposal; it, too, predicts that among nested phrases, the most deeply embedded one bears the phrasal stress (of the prosodic constituent that wraps those phrases). However, the Stress-xp/Wrap-xp-based account is much more *local* than Cinque's NSR. Depth of embedding is only predicted to be crucial for main stress assignment where phrases properly contain one another. Among phrases which are disjoint, relative metrical weight is determined purely linearly; for example, in a ditransitive sentence, the final argument will bear the main stress, regardless of anything else; except, if there is an adverbial phrase following it, *that* phrase is predicted to be assigned main stress, and so forth. This is so because among phrasal stresses, the strongest stress is simply the last.

There are at least two clear advantages to this way of doing things: Cinque's (1993) NSR does too little, and it does too much. It does too little because it only predicts the nuclear stress within a tree, but no pre-nuclear stresses. But crucially,

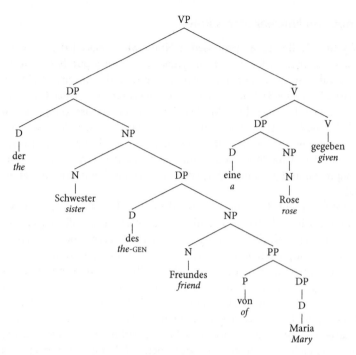

FIGURE 8.2   No matter how deeply embedded the penultimate argument, it will never get to bear the nuclear stress (*pace* Cinque, 1993).

the regularities of pre-nuclear stress assignment are in essential ways the same as those of nuclear stress assignment (a point made especially forceful for example in Gussenhoven, 1983a: and discussed in detail in Section 6.3 of Chapter 6); in particular do we find integration effects. Once something that takes care of these pre-nuclear phrasal stresses is added to Cinque's (1993) system, it is likely to make the main stress assignment part, the NSR, redundant.

Cinque's (1993) NSR does too much in that it predicts "weight effects" between disjoint phrases, such as those in example (39):[29]

(39)   Der   Peter   hat   der   Schwester   des   Freundes   von   Maria   eine
        the   P.   has   the   sister   the-GEN   friend   of   M.   a
        Rose   geschenkt   (German)
        rose   given
        'Peter gave the sister of the friend of Maria's a rose.'

Casual inspection of the structure of example (39), given in the tree in Figure 8.2, reveals that—regardless of finer details of the syntactic analysis—‹*Maria*›

---

[29] Example from Truckenbrodt (2006: 575), where it is used to make the same point as here. The earliest version of this argument I know of is given in Jacobs (1991/2a: note 19).

is more deeply embedded than ⟨Rose⟩, predicting main stress on ⟨Maria⟩. But this prediction is wrong: the main stress has to fall on ⟨Rose⟩, regardless of the syntactic complexity of its co-arguments. Note that the problem here is that the relation between ⟨Maria⟩ and ⟨Rose⟩, on Cinque's account, is treated just like that between, say, ⟨Rose⟩ and the verb ⟨gegeben⟩: more deeply embedded. What *ought* to set them apart is that ⟨(the) Rose⟩ is within the projection of V (and hence both can be content with just one accent), but ⟨the sister of . . . Maria⟩ is not part of the projection of ⟨Rose⟩, therefore they will each get an accent (the later one becoming nuclear). Again, Cinque's rule fails because it is (wrongly) focussed on the question who gets to bear *the* main stress, rather than just who gets to be *a* phrasal stress.[30]

As far as I know, no language has been reported to display the kind of weight effect predicted by Cinque's algorithm. That is to say, there are no examples of languages in which the out-of-the-blue main stress position in a sentence can be shifted between two immediate constituents just by adding or subtracting levels of embedding, while keeping the overall syntactic structure the same.

Is this a fundamental flaw of Cinque's (1993) proposal, or could it somehow be fixed? Presumably the answer depends on what "fundamental" means. The fix, it seems obvious, is to do what Truckenbrodt (1995) does: strictly limit the role of embedding to predict that between a head and an argument, phrasal stress will fall on the argument. And leave the rest to a purely linear NSR (such as I/IP-HEAD-RIGHT). This solves both (fundamental?) problems with Cinque's (1993) proposal: it derives pre-nuclear stresses, and it excludes wrong prediction involving "weight effects" such as in example (39) below.[31]

---

[30] Cinque (1993: 269) notices a similar problem with specifiers in English, such as in ⟨the man from Philadelphia's hat⟩ (wrongly predicted main stress on ⟨Philadelphia⟩). He proposes to restrict the field of "competitors" (for the title of "most deeply embedded head") to the "recursive" side of the language. Considering that the original motivation of the proposal was to avoid independent reference to the headedness of the phrase (which is of course just the inverse of the "recursive side"), this is already an unattractive move. But as Truckenbrodt's example (39) shows, it does not address the underlying problem.

Incidentally Cinque (1993) never explores cases that would reveal this, even in English, such as ⟨the [conquest of the Persian empire][by Alexander]⟩ (translated from Jacobs, 1991/2a: 15).

[31] Zubizarreta's (1998) proposal, too, can be interpreted as an implementation of that idea: If among two syntactic sisters, one selects the other, the selectee must be more prominent (=argument integration; in Zubizarreta, 1998). If there is no selection between the sisters (=adjunction), the right sister must be more prominent (C-NSR; technically, the C-NSR is based on asymmetrical c-command, rather than linear order, hence effectively depth of embedding; but that work adopts a proposal popular at the time of its writing due to which asymmetrical c-command corresponds directly to left-to-right order, so that effectively the C-NSR always picks out the rightmost element). This correctly places the main stress in the same cases that Truckenbrodt's (1995) does, but still says nothing about pre-nuclear stresses.

An independent question seems to be whether the improved version needs to refer to an independent prosodic structure, as Truckenbrodt (1995) does, or could in principle be based on assigning stress to syntactic nodes, as envisaged by Cinque (1993). To my mind, the latter position makes sense only as part of a general program to eliminate prosodic structure entirely. In the light of the facts discussed in Chapters 6 and 7, I do not presently see how such a program could have any hope of success.

8.5 Integration revisited

In this section, I discuss more properties (and quirks) of integration, mostly for completeness' sake.

8.5.1 Some more cases of non-integration

In our discussion of object integration in Chapter 6 we discussed a number of configurations in which objects and verb systematically fail to integrate: if the object is a function word (including indefinite pronouns), or if object and verb have different information structural status—given object and non-given verb, or focussed verb and backgrounded object.[32]

There are at least two more well-known factors that may prevent integration. First, as discussed in Gussenhoven (1983a: 7.3), generic objects systematically fail to integrate. The following minimal pairs illustrate.

(40) a. If you want your CARpets cleaned (call this number).
      b. If you like your CARpets CLEAN (use this product).

(41) Wenn man in   die USA einreisen will,   muss man ...   (German)
      if   one into the US   enter   wants, must one
      a. ... VORstrafen   ANgeben. b. #... VORstrafen angeben.
             prior convictions list   prior conv. list
      'If you want to enter the US, you have to list any prior convictions/#you have to list some prior convictions.'

(42) a. Wenn du   KINDer dabei hast (bekommst du   einen
         if   you   children with   have   get   you   an
         extra   Teller).
         additional plate
         'If you have children with you (you get an extra plate).'
      b. Wenn du   KINder ANlügst (verlieren sie   das Vertrauen).
         if   you   children to-lie   lose   they the trust
         'If you lie to children, they won't trust you.'

I did my best to construct examples which could plausibly occur even when carpets, children, or priors are not salient (which, otherwise, would explain the lack of integration). It truly seems that genericity is an independent anti-integration factor.

Second, also discussed in Gussenhoven (1983a), quantified DPs do not integrate, as seen in (43) (based on Gussenhoven's examples).[33]

---

[32] Technically speaking, a narrowly focussed object or a non-given object and a given verb also do not qualify as integration, but rather present instances of givenness deaccenting and post-focal deaccenting. But since these sound the same as integrated structures, they are of less interest to us.

[33] My impression is that ‹both›, ‹neither›, ‹each›, ‹all›, ‹most›, ‹exactly n›, and ‹no› behave like ‹everyone›; ‹some, a› and unmodified numerals, on the other hand, form integrating subjects.

(43) (all new)
    a. The PRISoners have escaped!
    b. #EVerybody has escaped!
    c. #Every PRIsoner has escaped!

Presumably both generics and quantified DPs can be argued to be "anaphoric" or "topical" in the sense to be discussed in Section 8.5.2, and therefore their resistance to integration is part of a broader generalization. In the alternative, one would stipulate a constraint like (44).

(44) MAP-QPHRASE-PP
    Align the left and right edge of a generic or strongly quantificational phrase with the left and right edge of a phonological phrase.

Ranked sufficiently high (above WRAP-XP in particular), this constraint will block integration by *fiat*. Another option, is to assume that generic and quantificational phrases occupy (at some level of syntactic representation) a VP-adjoined or otherwise VP-external position (as advocated in one form or another in Kratzer, 1995; Diesing, 1992; de Hoop, 1992), so that STRESS-XP/WRAP-XP treat them like adjuncts, rather than complements.

8.5.2 Intransitive subject integration

So far we have only seen cases of object integration in transitive sentences. But the phenomenon is also found with subjects in intransitive sentences like (45), as discussed most famously in Schmerling (1976).[34]

(45) a. (What's new?—) Your MOTHER called.
    b. (Why is the water brown?—) The PIPES are rusty.

However, unlike object integration, which is found in basically any transitive VP, subject integration seems impossible in many cases. Examples (45a) and (45b) contrast with examples like those in (46).

(46) a. (What's the commotion?) JOHN is YOdeling.
    b. (Why did they interrupt the performance?) An ACTor was CRYing.
    c. (Any reactions to her latest escapades?—) Her FANS WORry.

This pattern is the neutral one. The subjects in example (46) do not need to be given (or the VP narrowly focussed) for this pattern to emerge. ‹JOHN is yodelling›, ‹An ACTOR was crying›, and ‹Her FANS worry› are interpreted as narrow subject foci.
    Importantly, the distinction between intransitives that do integrate, and those that do not does *not* correspond to the unaccusative-vs-unergative distinction:

---

[34] As well as Kraak (1970), Fuchs (1976, 1980, 1984), Allerton and Cruttenden (1979), Gussenhoven (1983a), and Faber (1987), among many others.

example (45a) above shows integration with an unergative verb, while (46c) is a case of non-integration with an unaccusative. Likewise, the non-integrating activity verb in (46a) above minimally contrasts with the integrating one in example (47) (although similar examples in German are discussed as early as Krifka, 1984: sec. 3.1, it is worth reiterating this point, since it is regularly ignored in the literature[35]).

(47)   (What's that noise?—) A DOG is barking.

Descriptively, subject integration is basically obligatory with highly collocative forms, verbs of appearance and disappearance, and "verbs expressing misfortune" (see Allerton and Cruttenden, 1979):[36]

(48)   a. A TRAIN arrived.
       b. Our DOG's disappeared.
       c. My WALLET is missing.
       d. Your COAT's on fire.

But then what predicts the default accent choice in intransitive sentences? I think it is fair to say that no reliable correlate has been identified in the literature as of yet. The following discussion will review some ideas and proposals, and in the course of that, point out some more generalizations, but not propose an answer either. What is important to keep in mind, again, is that all cases to be discussed involve wide-focus, or all-new, sentences in which neither the subject nor the predicate is given. This rules out analyses in terms of givenness deaccenting or focussing, at least as long as these are to be understood even vaguely in the sense used in this book.

In the typological literature, the choice of accent pattern is often related to the THETIC (integrated) vs CATEGORICAL (non-integrated) distinction (Brentano, 1874; Kuroda, 1972; Sasse, 1987; Ladusaw, 1994; thetic and categorical are what Brentano and others call MODES OF JUDGMENT). According to Kuroda, Sasse, and others, in a categorical statement, the argument is first "presented," and then the predicate is predicated of it. In a thetic sentence, on the other hand, the entire argument+predicate complex is presented as an unseparated whole.

---

[35] Irwin (2011), Kahnemuyipour (2009), Legate (2003), Zubizarreta and Vergnaud (2006), to name just a few recent publications.

Hoskins (1996) and Irwin (2011) provide experimental results in defense of the correlation between integration and unaccusativity. However, as Hirsch and Wagner (2011a, 2011b) show, the effects these studies found are likely explained by factors such as animacy, and disappear once these are controlled for.

[36] Verhoeven and Kügler (2015), in a study on German intransitive sentences, find that, in all-new contexts, (intransitive) passive sentences are strongly preferred with the integrated pattern, while either pattern is acceptable with (active) unergatives, as long as the verb is not, in their terms, highly predictable (i.e. verb and subject have a high degree of collocation, in which case integration is preferred). While these results suggest that passive→integrated is a reliable generalization (and unergative→non-integrated is not), this does not entail anything about the relevance of unaccusativity. Taking all the evidence together, it simply seems that unaccusatives do not behave like passivized verbs when it comes to integration. See also the references in note 35.

The crux in using these notions in a formal account of integration is of course to clarify what it *means* to "present an argument" and then to "make a statement about it." Unless we can tie them to other aspects of the overt discourse, these labels are little more than re-codings of the terms "integrated" and "non-integrated."

Nevertheless, one can make tentative connections between some of the observations listed above and the intuition behind these characterizations of thetic and categorical statement. For example, those verb types that strongly favor integration (thetic sentences) include verbs of appearance and coming into existence. It is plausible to think that one cannot present the argument of such a verb prior to, and independently of, asserting its appearance or coming into existence. Put simply, while it sounds natural to paraphrase ⟨*John is yodeling*⟩—as the answer to 'What happened?'—as 'there is John, and he is yodelling,' it seems odd to paraphrase ⟨*a TRAIN arrived*⟩ in the same context as 'there was a train, and it arrived.'

For another example, perhaps being "presented in isolation" (as a categorical subject) is only possible for a subject whose referent can be anchored to the discourse independent of the property ascribed to it by the predicate. Thus the discourse new, non-integrated subject ⟨*an actor*⟩ in example (46b) above may still be said to be anchored to the performance mentioned in the previous sentence. Accordingly, the likewise discourse-new DP ⟨*a child*⟩ in example (49) is more prone to integration (theticity), since a performance does not automatically involve children, and thus serve as an "anchor."

(49) (Why did they interrupt the performance?) A CHILD was crying.

Jäger (2001) formalizes some of these ideas. According to that paper, the subject in categorical sentences denotes a TOPIC, and topic-hood is what blocks integration (which otherwise is the structural default). Simplifying Jäger's (2001) proposal considerably, a topic is an individual or event which is either anaphoric, or anaphorically related via bridging. DPs that denote topics include DPs denoting old discourse referents (many proper names, definites), but also indefinites on a "partitive" reading, broadly construed (⟨*performance*⟩—⟨*an actor*⟩). In thetic sentences, on the other hand, *the event described by the verb* is the topic, that is, anaphorically related to a previously introduced event (e.g. by spacial or temporal proximity); the subject, not being topical, can integrate with its predicate.

One prerequisite for a thetic sentence, then, is to have a predicate describing an event that is located in space or time, that is, typically an eventive predicate, not a stative predicate or an individual level predicate; this prediction seems borne out. A prerequisite for a categorical sentence, on the other hand, is a subject that is— directly or via bridging—anaphoric.

Still, there is a considerable residue. The subjects in examples (45a) and (45b) above as well as examples (50a) and (50b) can all be claimed to be anaphorically related by bridging, yet they integrate.

(50) a. (Out of the blue) Your COAT is on fire!
      b. (John has a house in the country side.) But the ROOF is leaking.

I think it is not implausible to think that, nevertheless, the topic in these sentences is not the subject referent but rather the addressee in example (50a), the house and the pipes in examples (50b) and (45b), respectively, or the situation in example (45a) above. The point is that the relevant notion of topic is not *reducible* to anaphoricity in Jäger's (2001) sense, and thus a formal account of the thetic–categorical distinction is, still, wanting.

In this book we took WRAP-XP and STRESS-XP to be essential for deriving integration as part of default prosody. But subject integration does not immediately follow from these constraints: subjects in English are VP-external, so WRAP-XP has no "desire" to put subject and VP in the same prosodic phrase. And STRESS-XP cannot be satisfied for VP by an accent on the VP-external subject. If we want subject integration to be the structural default, just like object integration, we need to adjust the system. What is instructive in this connection is that, independently, integration is "preserved" under movement, as observed first for examples such as (51) from Bresnan (1971).

(51)   How many LANguages do you speak?

If we assume that subjects, too, originate VP-internally, we can explain subject integration analogously to Bresnan's example (51). For concreteness, I will assume (52).

(52^{CON})   CHAIN CONTAINMENT
    A phrase α is (for the purposes of WRAP-XP and STRESS-XP) contained in a phrase β if β contains α or a trace of α.

Condition (52) rather directly derives that (intransitive) subjects behave just like (direct) objects when it comes to integration. What about the non-integration cases? If we follow Jäger's (2001) general idea that non-integrating subjects are topics, we have to add something to the system that blocks integration with topics, such as (53).

(53^{CON})   MAP-TOPIC-PP
    Align the left and right edge of a topic with the left and right edge of a phonological phrase.

Condition (53) does not say anything about how topic-hood is *represented*, and I will remain agnostic about that. Options include phrase structure distinctions, for example by assuming that all and only topical subjects occupy, at some level of representation, a VP-external position (Jäger, 2001; Kratzer and Selkirk, 2007),[37] or via a dedicated feature "topic" or "informationally autonomous" (Schmerling, 1976; Jacobs, 1991/2c, 1999). Either kind of distinction can be referenced by the rules that

---

[37] It would arguably be more elegant to derive the prosodically non-integrated status of topics directly from their adjunction status, as done in the papers cited. Given the assumptions made in this section, this route is not viable, since definition (52) effectively preempts reference to surface structure position.

construct prosodic structure, in particular condition (53), and thus successfully encode the difference.[38]

To be sure, the above is a stand-in for a theory of non-integration/categorial sentences, rather than a theory itself. The important conclusion for now, it seems to me, is that the question whether subject integration takes places or not is related to pragmatics and/or information structure, but not to focussing or givenness as understood here, nor, in all likelihood, argument structure (unaccusative vs unergative).

8.5.3 Special cases of object integration

As hinted at in the previous section, integration need not be strictly local. The generalization seems to be that as long as only given elements occur between the nuclear stress and the verb, integration is possible.[39] An early discussion of this pattern is found in Gussenhoven (1983a), using examples (54) and (55).

(54) (out of the blue)
    a. Our DOG's disappeared.
    b. Our DOG's mysTERiously disapPEARED.
    c. #Our DOG's mysteriously disappeared.

(55) (Talking about mysteries:) Our DOG's mysteriously disappeared.

An intervening adverbial blocks integration—(54b), not (54c)—which is otherwise possible with ‹disappear›—(54a). If, however, the adverbial is itself given (and subject and verb are not), integration "across a distance" is possible again—example (55).

---

[38] It seems to me that there are no arguable *syntactic* correlates to the two subject positions postulated by the accounts that assume a phrase structural distinction. This is unlike the case of, say, existential vs non-existential indefinite objects, for which linear order in German or case in Turkish may well be independent correlates (Diesing, 1992; Hoop, 1996; Kratzer, 1995); and of course much unlike the unergative–unaccusative distinction, for which there appear to be many independent correlates.

[39] Put differently: the argument has to carry the NPA of a prosodic phrase containing the verb. What this excludes, in particular, are cases in which another accented phrase intervenes between the verb and its accented argument. Thus, the neutral pronunciation for the question how many languages a linguist should speak has PAs on the preposed object, the subject and the verb, as in example (ic); the alternative PA patterns either indicate givenness of—example (ia)—or contrastive focus on ‹linguist›.

(i) a. How many LANguages should a linguist speak?
    b. How many LANguages should a LINguist speak?
    c. How many LANguages should a LINguist SPEAK?

This generalization was in essence captured already in Gussenhoven's (1983a) original Sentence Accent Assignment Rule (SAAR), which allows domain formation by a focussed predicate and its focussed argument across any kind of unfocussed material. In particular ‹you› in example (51) above, being a function word, does not itself need to form an accent domain; ‹a linguist› in example (i), on the other hand, is a lexically headed phrase and neither given nor backgrounded, which means it has to form the head of an accent domain. If that happens, however, ‹speak› can no longer be part of the same accent domain as its internal argument ‹how many languages›, so that integration is structurally blocked.

Under such favorable circumstances, even TRANSITIVE SUBJECT INTEGRATION may occur, as in the German example (56) (from Jacobs, 1988), or the English (57).

(56) (Wo   hast du   denn das   tolle Armband her?)   (German)
      where have you then the   great bracelet from
      'Where did you get that great bracelet?'

      Das   hat GERDA mir   geliehen.
      the-ACC   has G.   me-DAT   loaned.
      'Gerda lend it to me.'

(57) (He looks sad. What's the matter?—) His WIFE left him.

These cases all behave as we would expect, given something like (52) above; in particular, the element that bears the nuclear stress originates within the projection of the integrating head, and intervening material is given and may thus stay unaccented.[40]

We now turn to some surprising cases, in which one or both of these conditions is violated, but integration is still possible. First, consider the examples in (58).

(58) a. Your COAT is on [$_{NP}$ fire].
      b. My CAT is [$_{AP}$ sick].
      c. I met a MAN [$_{RelCl}$ that [$_{TP}$I [$_{VP}$ knew]]].
      d. They gave me BOOKs [$_{S}$to [$_{VP}$ read]].

While all of these meet the description of integration, they are not predicted to integrate, given what we said so far—unless we assumed that the accented DP was internal to each of the bracketed phrases at some point in the derivation. While the plausibility of such an analysis may differ from case to case ((58d), for example, could be analyzed via head-raising), note in particular that ‹your COAT› in (58a) would have to be internal to the DP/NP ‹fire› (not just the PP ‹on fire›) for this instance of integration to be analyzed as involving a head and its internal argument, which strikes me as less than plausible.

Similar problems are raised by unaccented secondary predicates as in example (59) (from Winkler, 1997) and—perhaps as a special case of this—directional argument PPs as in example (60) (Uhmann, 1991).[41]

(59) a. They painted the WINDows [$_{AP}$shut].

      b. Sie   haben sich die   FÜSse platt gelaufen.   (German)
         they   have   self the   feet   flat   walked
         'They walked their feet flat.'

---

[40] The details of this are worked out in Truckenbrodt and Büring (in preparation); in particular, we also need to invoke WRAP-XP/STRESS-XP-CORRESPONDENCE, discussed in Section 6.3.2.

[41] Examples like these are noted in Winkler and Göbbel (2002), Jacobs (1991/2c: 22), von Stechow and Uhmann (1986: 315ff), Krifka (1984).

(60) a. Wir   müssen   noch   das   HEU   ins   Trockene   bringen.
        we   must   still   the   hay   into the   dry   bring
        (German)
        'We still need to get the hay to a dry place.'

    b. Er   hat   ein   LOCH   in   die   Wand   gehauen.
       he   has   a   hole   in   the   wall   knocked
       'He knocked a hole into the wall.'

In all of these cases, both the main verb (⟨*painted/gelaufen/bringen/gehauen*⟩) and the secondary predicate or directional PP (⟨*shut/flach/ins Trockene/in die Wand*⟩) remain unaccented. By the logic of the WRAP-XP-based approach we are using, this should only be possible if either the accented DP were the structural internal argument to *both* predicates, or in the alternative, if it were the internal argument to the secondary predicate/the PP, which in turn were the internal argument of the main verb. Neither of these assumptions jibes too well with the selectional relations and constituency facts in these examples.

What other analytical options do we have? We could, under the combined weight of these problematic cases, abandon the structural head–complement approach to integration in favor of one that utilizes a broader concept of "predicate–argument structure," which would encompass all these cases without any commitment to phrase structural parallelism.[42] In a nutshell, STRESS-XP and WRAP-XP would have to be replaced by something like STRESS ARGUMENT+PREDICATE and WRAP ARGUMENT+PREDICATE.

Another possibility is to stick with purely syntactic configurations, but still replace the notion of "XP" with some more flexible domain. To illustrate this strategy, a look at Kahnemuyipour's (2003; 2009) analysis of Persian will be instructive.

Persian, like other OV-languages, often shows main stress on the preverbal object. However, in a number of cases, neutral stress systematically appears to the *left* of that, leaving the object unstressed. Examples of this with main stress on an indirect object and a measure adverb are given in examples (61a) and (61b), with main stress indicated by underlining.[43]

(61) a. Ali   <u>ye   tup</u>   be   Hassan   daad.   (Persian)
       Ali   a   ball   to   Hassan   gave
       'Ali gave a ball to Hassan.'

    b. Ali   <u>xeyli</u>   sib   dust   daare.
       Ali   a lot   apple   friend   has
       'Ali likes apples a lot.'

---

[42] This is most likely the route envisioned in Gussenhoven (1983a), and it is formalized syntactically in Winkler (1997); Büring (2012a) explores how to combine this line of analysis with a prominence based model of focus realization like the one we use in this book.

[43] Kahnemuyipour's (2009: (43a), 93 and (26c), 86). Example (62) is his (37a), p.91.

Similar to example (61b) above, manner adverbs take the unmarked main stress in intransitive sentences, leaving the verb (phrase) unstressed.

(62) Ali <u>sexaavatmandaane</u> komak kard.
      Ali generously   help   did
      'Ali helped generously.'

The generalization Kahnemuyipour argues for is that sentential stress in Persian is assigned to the leftmost element within (a specific projection of) the verb phrase. There are at least two ways of implementing this: In a prosodic account, the verbal projection in question is mapped onto a single phonological phrase, whose head is the leftmost prosodic word within it (Kahnemuyipour, 2003). In a syntactic account, main stress is assigned to the syntactically "highest" phrase within that verbal projection (Kahnemuyipour, 2009).

Note that, unlike in the cases of integrated secondary predicates and directional PPs in examples (59) and (60) above, cases like (61a), (61b), and (62) are problematic for a predicate–argument approach to integration just as much as for the head–complement approach. However, the latter, being based essentially on syntactic notions, is more naturally modified to accommodate the Persian kind of data than the former. Essentially, Persian replaces STRESS-XP with something like STRESS VP (or, following the syntactic analysis in Kahnemuyipour, 2009, English STRESS AspectP with STRESS MannerP). In the same vein, examples (59) and (60) above could be captured by using something like STRESS V*P, where V*P stands for some verbal projection that contains the verb, directionals, and at most one argument (this is essentially the line taken in Kratzer and Selkirk, 2007).

To my mind, Truckenbrodt's (1995) head–complement analysis of integration constitutes the most interesting variant of a STRESS DOMAIN-X approach: it utilizes the most general version of STRESS, STRESS-XP, but more importantly, it truly *explains* the prosodic headedness of integrated prosodic domains (i.e. the placement of the main stress) on purely structural grounds (most deeply embedded head); accounts like Kahnemuyipour (2009) and Kratzer and Selkirk (2007), on the other hand have to invoke independent conditions (similar to linear head-alignment) for this purpose.

However, this buys them the freedom to capture (if perhaps not explain) integration within just about any syntactic domain, as appears to be required for Persian, and the English and German cases discussed in the examples in (58) and following.

In any event it should be kept in mind that the proposals discussed here also share a substantial amount of common ground. They all define the default accent/stress domain in phrase structure related terms (XP, VP, MannerP, ...). They also share the crucial assumption that, once accent domains are formed (or stress is assigned), sentential stress is a purely linear matter (the rightmost accent domain in the case of Germanic as well as Persian), without further regard to hierarchical structure, or argument structure (which is where they crucially differ from approaches like Cinque, 1993 or Zubizarreta, 1998, discussed in Section 8.4).

9

The meaning of tones

In Chapter 6 and 7 we have seen arguments for the "stress first" position, according to which stress (i.e. relative metrical strength) is the primary realization of focussing, non-givenness, etc. Pith accents, on this view, are assigned mechanically to stressed positions.

This chapter reviews work on the meaning of tone *choice*, that is, interpretive consequences of using a high, rather than a low accent, or a rising rather than a falling tune, etc. Though on the face of it, the stress-first view might seem as if it is bound to ignore such aspects of intonational meaning, the two are actually compatible. This will be illustrated programmatically in Section 9.1; I then turn to more specific proposals about tone meanings made in the literature.

9.1 Intonational morphemes and text-to-tune alignment

To start with an example, colloquial Italian, like many languages of the world, can mark yes-/no-questions using only intonation; that is to say, there is no syntactic difference between declaratives and polar interrogatives, nor any special particle to mark the latter.

(1) Laura viene   con noi   (Italian)
     L.   come.3SG.PRE.IND with us
     'Laura is coming with us.' or 'Is Laura coming with us?'

If we represented stress/accent positions only, (1) would simply be ambiguous; however, with a rising right boundary, (1) is unambiguously a yes-/no-question, while with a falling right boundary it is a declarative.[1]

To model this, one would assume INTONATIONAL MORPHEMES or autosegments. For our toy case, the falling boundary means 'I am a declarative (add my content to the common ground)'; and the rising boundary means 'I am an interrogative (set the current goal of the common ground to finding out if my content is true or not)'. Either morpheme may (right)-attach to the root clause; its pragmatic/semantic content operates on the meaning of the sentence radical (e.g. a

---

[1] Example from Velupillai (2012: 353); see also Maiden and Robustelli (2000).

Intonation and Meaning. First edition. Daniel Büring.
© Daniel Büring 2016. First published 2016 by Oxford University Press.

TABLE 9.1   Declarative and polar interrogative tunes/
intonational morphemes in Bengali and Campinas
Brazilian Portuguese.

	'I am a declarative'	'I am a question'
Bengali	H* L⁻ L%	L* H⁻ L%
Campinas BP	H+L* L%	L+H* L%

proposition).[2] Its realization is a H–L% or L–H%, respectively, in the prosodic structure. We will illustrate this in more detail for English in Section 9.2.1.

Now let us look at a slightly more complicated case. Very often, the question/assertion distinction is intonationally (and only intonationally) marked not just by the final boundary tone, but by an entire TUNE, consisting of pitch accent(s) and boundary tones. Bengali, for example, marks yes-/no-questions by a low NPA, followed by a rise–fall; neutral declaratives, on the other hand, have a high NPA followed by a fall (Hayes and Lahiri, 1991). Brazilian Portuguese in the Campinas area realizes a yes-/no-questions by a L+H* rising NPA followed by a low boundary L%, whereas the otherwise identical declarative has a falling H+L* NPA followed by a low boundary L% (Truckenbrodt et al., 2009). To a first approximation, we could write the pertinent morphemes as in Table 9.1.

Semantically, the intonational morphemes in Table 9.1 still operate on clausal meanings. But their realization is no longer just at the boundary of the corresponding prosodic unit, the intermediate/intonational phrase—whence the starred tones in (1).

In such a case, it is assumed that the abstract tune associated with the intonational morpheme ALIGNS WITH, or is LINKED TO, the prosodic structure in an autosegmental way: the pitch accent goes to the head of the intermediate phrase (= the nuclear pitch accent), the boundary tone goes to the right boundary of the IP, and the phrase tone associates with the syllables in between. This is illustrated for Bengali in Figure 9.1(i).

What about the other phrasal stresses, the ones that precede the nuclear stress? According to Hayes and Lahiri (1991), these are uniformly linked to L*H⁻ tunes, in the way shown in Figure 9.1(ii).[3] Each phonological phrase that precedes the one containing the nuclear stress is associated with an independent L*H⁻, see Figure 9.1(iii); the tune gets repeated however many time necessary to "cover" the pre-nuclear stretch.

---

[2] Likely, the meaning of the tune is, in many cases at least, a conventional implicature, rather than part of at-issue meaning. That is, the falling version of example (1) still denotes the proposition that Laura is coming with us, rather than 'add the proposition that Laura is coming with us to the common ground', whereas the 'add to the common ground' is part of the non-at-issue content of the sentence. See Gutzmann (2008) for a detailed implementation of this idea.

In the case of y-/n-question marking, on the other hand, things are likely to be different: we want the question to *denote*, rather than somehow imply, a question meaning.

[3] Hayes and Lahiri (1991) assume that phrase tones, which they write as T_p, align with the right edge of phonological phrases; no additional intermediate phrases are assumed.

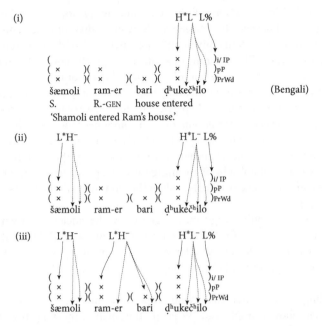

FIGURE 9.1 Stress-to-Tune ("Text-to-Tune") linking, exemplified with Bengali (adapted from Hayes and Lahiri, 1991: esp. 55f and 78).

This kind of picture has been observed for many languages: What is intuitively identified as the "same" tune consists of a NUCLEAR TUNE (or for short: NUCLEUS), which is obligatory and comprises the NPA and everything after it up to and including the final boundary, and a pre-nuclear part, sometimes called the HEAD, which takes care of any pre-nuclear accents and boundaries, and can be reiterated as many times as necessary (or not used at all), depending on how much pre-nuclear material there is.

What we just sketched for the case of Bengali is an example of a HOLISTIC approach to interpreting intonational contours, that is, one that assigns a meaning to an entire tune, possibly one comprising several pitch accents.[4] It would be misguided, on this view, to ask what the meaning of, say, the H* on ‹dʰukeĉʰilo› in Figure 9.1 is, since the meaning of the tune as a whole is 'I am a declarative,' and it is applied to the meaning of the entire clause, not just the element marked by pitch accents; the form-side of the declarative morpheme could thus be written as something like (L*H⁻)* H*L⁻L% (where the star after the parentheses means 'zero or more repetitions of what is in the parenthesis,' the so-called KLEENE STAR); the individual components are just phonemic, with no meaning of their own.

A COMPOSITIONAL approach, as opposed to that, would assign meanings—and thus award morphemic status—to smaller units than entire tunes. The work of

---

[4] This terminology—including the antonymous COMPOSITIONAL—is used, among others, by Pierre-humbert and Hirschberg (1990).

Baumann and Grice (2006) and Röhr and Baumann (2010, 2011), to be discussed in Section 9.3.3, illustrates this category. Here, individual pitch accents are taken to signal the discourse status (given, inferable, new, . . .) of the individual word or phrase they occur on. The meaning of a tune is simply the sum of the meanings of the pitch accents (and possibly boundary tones) that occur in it.

What the smallest meaning-bearing units in a compositional approach are differs from analysis to analysis. In particular, in the case of bi-tonal accents (H+L, L+H etc.) it may be each pitch accent, or each component tone (e.g. the meaning of L+H* is composed of the meaning of L and H*); or it could be the tonal sequence on the one hand, and the alignment on the other (e.g. the meanings of L+H* and L*+H each "contain" a basic meaning for L+H, plus a meaning for "align the right tone with the stressed syllable"/"align the left tone with the stressed syllable," respectively[5]).

Conversely, one could assign meanings to, say, the nucleus as a whole, and a separate one to the head (in the sense introduced just above), but neither to the tune as a whole, nor to any smaller parts of it. In other words, the "holistic–compositional" opposition is best thought of as a matter of degree, rather than a binary one.

Accordingly, rather than classifying proposals as holistic or compositional, we will, in what follows, simply ask: "What are the smallest meaning-bearing units?" Separate from that, we will ask the question "What is the semantic argument of the purported morphemes?" For example, the choice between assertion and question is clearly a sentence-level meaning. Anything that involves a whole statement ('p is taken for granted', 'p is unexpected' . . .) is a clause-level, or propositional meaning (because only statements/propositions can be taken for granted, be surprising, etc., though see Section 9.3.1 below). Whether or not something is given, or salient, on the other hand, is a phrase-level meaning, as constituents of any size and category may be given.

We would hope to find a comforting parallelism between the prosodic domain on which an intonational morpheme is realized, and the kind of meaning it has: Individual pitch accents correspond to phrasal meanings, but entire tunes, or Intonational Phrase boundaries correspond to clausal or sentential meanings. This would seem to be the zero hypothesis, and it is likely to be what Pierrehumbert and Hirschberg (1990) have in mind in the following quote:[6]

Our idea of the compositionality of tune meaning is based upon a hierarchical model of phonological domain, in which the scope of interpretation of tones is the node to which they are attached. So, the components of tune—pitch accents, phrase accents, and boundary tones—are each interpreted with respect to their distinct phonological domains. Pitch accents, phrase accents, and boundary tones each operate on a (progressively higher)

---

[5] Truckenbrodt et al. (2009)

[6] Assuming that "being interpreted with respect to/over" and "operate on" a phonological domain all mean the same thing, something like: "The meaning of a tone/intonational morpheme is a function whose domain corresponds to the semantic class of the meaning of the prosodic domain it associates with."

domain of interpretation. Not only is each of these types of tone interpreted over a distinct domain, but each contributes a distinct type of information to the overall interpretation of a tune. (Pierrehumbert and Hirschberg, 1990: 286)

As we will see, not all analyses that have been proposed (and, as I will argue, not even Pierrehumbert and Hirschberg's, 1990, own) fit neatly into this picture of perfect correspondence.

In what follows, I will review the most influential proposals on the interpretation of tones from the literature, starting with the boundary tones and then moving on to accents. A word of warning is in order at the start. With very few exceptions, work on tone and tune choice is much less rigorous and formalized than the work on stress/accent *placement* reviewed so far in this book. Even though there is a rich literature mostly meant for the purposes of aiding foreign language learning and teaching, in particular in the so-called 'British School' (Crystal, 1969; Kingdon, 1958; O'Connor and Arnold, 1973; Schubiger, 1958; a.o.), more systematic investigations are few and far between. The seminal work on English, outlining very clearly what the project is, is without a doubt Pierrehumbert and Hirschberg (1990); unfortunately, the bulk of the subsequent literature has been content with repeating Pierrehumbert and Hirschberg's (1990) judgments, generalizations, and even examples, but very little has been done in the way of making their ideas precise, or systematically investigating the generality of the meanings proposed in that paper in the 25 years since it appeared.

Naturally, I will, in what follows, present those works that do go beyond Pierrehumbert and Hirschberg's (1990) in some detail. However, given how much in that paper has *not* been significantly improved upon, I will also provide a rather detailed discussion of the preliminary and informal proposals in that paper itself, pointing out what I see as the main desiderata for future work.

9.2 Boundary tones

9.2.1 Rising vs falling declaratives

In English, as in many other languages, declarative sentences can be used as requests for a "yes"/"no" answer, much like polar interrogatives. Thus examples (2a) and (2b) below—where the final question mark indicates rising intonation—can be used as requests for information, and are interchangeable, in many contexts, with polar question, examples (2c) and (2d).[7]

(2) a. That's a persimmon? b. You're leaving for vacation today?
     c. Is that a persimmon? d. Are you leaving for vacation today?

An analysis that suggests itself for this case is to assume that a SENTENCE RADICAL, that is, a neutral encoding of the sentence's content—for example the proposition

---

[7] Examples from Gunlogson (2001).

that the addressee is leaving for vacation today—is embedded under either an assertive or an interrogative operator, yielding two different illocutionary meanings. For concreteness, assume that the assertive operator ASS instructs the addressee to add the sentence radical to the common ground, whereas the interrogative operator INT instructs the addressee to set the question whether or not the sentence radical is true as the current question under discussion. This is sketched in (3).

$$\text{L\%}$$
$$|$$
(3^{DEF}) a. $[\![\text{ ASS }]\!] = \lambda p \in D_t.$ add p to the common ground

$$\text{H\%}$$
$$|$$
b. $[\![\text{ INT }]\!] = \lambda p \in D_t.$set $\{p, \neg p\}$ as the current question under discussion

As indicated, ASS and INT are lexically specified as low and high boundary tones, respectively, which associate with the text in an autosegmental manner, as sketched in (4).

(4^{CON}) Associate T% with the right boundary of the smallest intonational phrase containing the material that contributes to the meaning of p.

(3a) and (3b) are thus intonational morphemes whose meaning operates on propositions, and whose phonological forms are autosegments, namely boundary tones. Analyses of rising declaratives along these lines have been proposed in Gussenhoven (1983b), Pierrehumbert and Hirschberg (1990), and Bartels (1999) among others. Note in particular the pleasing correspondence between meaning and realization: The functions denoted by ASS/INT operate on sentence (radical) meanings (propositions, we assumed), and their realization targets the boundary of the prosodic counterpart of a sentence, the intonational phrase.

Gunlogson (1999, 2001), too, assumes that the meaning of IP-final rise and fall operate on sentence meanings, but argues for a more fine-grained distinction than just that between assertions and polar questions. Gunlogson argues that both rising and falling declaratives are assertions (whence the title "True to Form"), but that their update potential is different: While the falling declarative commits the *speaker* to the truth of the sentence, the rising declarative *commits the addressee*. On that view, rising declaratives are semantically distinct from both falling declaratives and polar interrogatives.

The point of departure for this idea is a meticulous study of contexts in which rising declaratives and polar interrogatives are not exchangeable (or at least not without clear changes in appropriateness or speaker's meaning), some of which are given in examples (5) and (6) below.

(5) [on a tax form]
    a. During the tax year, did you have income from a foreign trust?
    b. #During the tax year, you had income from a foreign trust?

(6) [on a health insurance form] Are you married? If so . . .
    a. . . . does your spouse have health insurance?
    b. #. . . your spouse has health insurance?

As Gunlogson observes, rising declaratives express a clear bias for the truth of the proposition they express ("the yes-answer"), which makes them unsuited for neutral questions and questions whose presuppositions depend on hypotheticals; other contexts in which this bias is unwarranted (and hence rising declaratives, but not polar interrogatives, sound odd) include exam questions, explicit deliberations about open questions, requests for advice, self-addressed deliberative questions, and alternative questions, among many others (Gunlogson, 2001: 14ff).

At the same time, rising declaratives may be *more* appropriate than polar interrogatives where a complete absence of bias is implausible or impossible, either due to world knowledge, as in example (7), or due to linguistic material, like the adverbial ‹of course› in example (8).[8]

(7) [at a restaurant]
    a. Hello! My name is Carl? I'll be your waiter tonight?
    b. #Hello! Is my name Carl? Will I be your waiter tonight?

(8) a. The manager has of course been informed?
    b. #Has the manager of course been informed?

Gunlogson concludes that rising declaratives, unlike polar interrogatives, do express a commitment to the propositional content of the sentence, but that this commitment is the addressee's, rather than the speaker's. Roughly, the speaker of, for example, (8) says 'I take it you are committed to the claim that the manager has been informed (and that that is a matter of course)'. This immediately explains why rising declaratives are particularly apt to ask for confirmation, as in (9B).

(9) A: I can give you a ride!
    B: You have a car?

On the other hand, since a rising declarative commits one participant, the addressee, to the truth of the sentence, while at the same time the speaker explicitly refrains from committing to it (as they could by using a falling declarative), the context becomes *biased* in favor of the truth of the sentence.[9] This explains their infelicity in contexts like exams or forms, where neutrality is required.

Formally, Gunlogson models a context as including two sets of public commitments $\langle cs_{spkr}, cs_{addr} \rangle$, the speaker's and the addressee's (the usual common ground of Stalnaker, 1978, being the intersection of those). The meaning of the fall and rise are

---

[8] Examples from Gunlogson (2001: 18), based on similar ones in Hirschberg and Ward (1995) and Huddleston (1994).

[9] Gunlogson (2001: 29f) formally defines a dialogue context as bias towards a proposition p if p is a commitment of one, but not both participants, and neither is committed to 'not p'.

functions from propositions to functions from contexts to contexts, such that the
following holds (where $\downarrow$S and $\uparrow$S are falling and rising declaratives, respectively):

(10^{DEF}) for any context $\langle cs_{spkr}, cs_{addr} \rangle$, declarative sentence S,

      a. $\langle cs_{spkr}, cs_{addr} \rangle + \downarrow S = \langle cs_{spkr} + S, cs_{addr} \rangle$

      b. $\langle cs_{spkr}, cs_{addr} \rangle + \uparrow S = \langle cs_{spkr}, cs_{addr} + S \rangle$

So like Gussenhoven (1983b), Pierrehumbert and Hirschberg (1990), and Bartels
(1999), Gunlogson (1999, 2001) associates intonational phrase boundary tones with
operations on sentential meanings. The main difference is that Gunlogson does
not equate rising declaratives with polar interrogatives, but rather assumes a cross-
classification: declaratives can be falling or rising, and so can (polar) interrogatives.
Both interrogativity and intonation have independent meanings, which are combined compositionally and yield, among other things, the difference between the
use conditions for polar interrogatives, rising declaratives, and "ordinary" falling
declaratives.[10]

9.2.2 Phrase tone meanings

Pierrehumbert and Hirschberg (1990, henceforth PH), in keeping with their radically compositional project, assign individual meanings to each of the phrase tones,
L^- and H^-, and each of the boundary tones, L% and H%. Accordingly, there cannot
be, on their model, a meaning for rising or falling nuclei *per se*.

PH claim that an H^- phrase tone "indicates that the current phrase is to be taken
as forming part of a larger composite interpretive unit with the following phrase,"
(1990: 302) whereas an L^- phrasal tone "emphasizes the separation of the current
phrase from a subsequent phrase" (1990: 302).

This echoes earlier observations such as in O'Connor and Arnold (1973):

All statements associated with . . . falling nuclear tones sound *definite* and *complete* in the
sense that the speaker wishes them to be regarded as separate items. For example, if we
say [(11a)] we are treating each of these three attributes as being a complete and separately
interesting feature of the man;

(11)   a. He was tall\ dark\ and hand\some.

      b. He was tall/ dark/ and hand\some.

but if we say [(11b)] we are linking the three together into a single, composite picture.
(O'Connor and Arnold, 1973: 47; notation adapted)

While intuitively plausible, O'Connor and Arnold's (1973) characterization begs the
question what it means to treat attributes as "complete and separately interesting" vs
as "a single, composite picture." What about Pierrehumbert and Hirschberg (1990)?
Here, too, we would like to know what it *means* to be an "interpretive unit," and
what concrete predictions this makes.

---

[10] For further elaboration of Gunlogson's proposal see also Steedman (2007, 2014).

While PH do not provide a more precise characterization either, they do give some examples of minimal pairs, including (12)–(14).[11]

(12) Is a disjunction exhaustive (H⁻), or giving two of many (L⁻)?

H*   H⁻ H*   L⁻   L%
| | | | /
a. Do you want apple juice or orange juice.

(exhaustive: or nothing at all?)

H*   L⁻ H*   L⁻   L%
| | | | /
b. Do you want apple juice or orange juice.

(...or something else)

(13) Is there a causal (or otherwise) connection between the conjuncts (H⁻) or not (L⁻)?

H*   H* H⁻   H*   H*   !H* L⁻L%
| | | | | | /
a. I opened the door and the rain poured down.

(causal: 'no sooner did I...')

H*   H* L⁻   H*   H*   !H* L⁻L%
| | | | | | /
b. I opened the door and the rain poured down.

(neutral)

(14) implicit conditional reading favored (H⁻) or not (L⁻)

H* H⁻   H* L⁻L%
| | | |/
a. Eat another cookie and I'll kill you.

(if...then)

H* L⁻   H* L⁻L%
| | | |/
b. Eat another cookie and I'll kill you.

(and then...)

While the contrasts here seem reasonably clear, we should ask whether they can indeed be traced back to a single interpretive source. According to PH, the choice of H⁻ in examples (13) and (14) leads to what we may call an "asymmetric" interpretation of ⟨and⟩ ('and thus,' 'and because of that,' see PH, 1990: 304), but unfortunately they do not elaborate on the connection between being an "interpretive unit" and the asymmetric construal. Perhaps we could say that plain logical "A and B" is equivalent to separate assertions of "A" and then "B," whereas on a causal interpretation neither part can be asserted without the other (and while "and then," a possible interpretation in (14b), is also asymmetric, it still entails the separate assertion of both conjuncts). But what about (12) on this view? According to PH, the speaker "emphasizes," through the use of H⁻, that the two kinds of juice "form an entity, namely, the set of available juices" (PH, 1990: 302). Presumably the term "entity" here relates back to "interpretive unit" in the earlier characterization of H⁻'s meaning, but where earlier we were talking about two propositional meanings, we are now talking about two ontological kinds or individuals (apple juice and orange juice) being the extension of a specific individual concept ("the juices available"). Perhaps it is possible to give content to the notion "be taken as

---

[11] Pierrehumbert and Hirschberg (1990: 302ff) continuations/labels mine; I added a !H* pitch accent on ⟨down⟩ in example (13), which makes the example sound more natural to my ears.

forming part of a larger composite interpretive unit" so that indeed it naturally subsumes these two cases; certainly at present, a true unification of the uses of H⁻ along these lines is no closer than at the time of O'Connor and Arnold (1973).

Truckenbrodt (2012) departs from PH's proposal for the meaning of phrase tones in two important respects. First, he proposes that H⁻ generally "puts up" a proposition as a question. This essentially follows Hirschberg and Ward's (1995) analysis of the so-called HIGH RISE, H* H⁻ H%. They propose that this contour is used to "elicit information about whether the hearer can relate [the] propositional content [of the sentence ending in the high rise; DB] to information in the hearer's . . . belief space" (Hirschberg and Ward, 1995: 410). Concretely, in (15) ((3) in their paper), the speaker is (implicitly) asking: 'Have you heard of that place?' (Note that the sequence H⁻H% is phonetically realized as a further rise, as indicated in (15).)

(15)   Chicago radio station DJ: Good morning Susan. Where are you calling from?

H* H⁻H%
Caller: I'm calling from SKOKIE

The second half of Truckenbrodt's proposal is that H⁻ may put up for questioning a contextually salient proposition. This may be, as in Hirschberg and Ward's (1995) case, a proposition like 'you (the addressee) can relate what I said to what you know' (or, idiomatically: 'you know what I'm talking about'). But it may also be the propositional content of the sentence directly, which results in a raising declarative of the sort Gunlogson (2001) analyzed (see Section 9.2.1 above).

Truckenbrodt's (2012) analysis carries over well to questions. First, since H⁻ puts up *one, maximally salient* proposition, it does not work well in constituent questions, whose denotation is a set of propositions and therefore fails to make one particular proposition more salient than the others. This addresses an old conundrum about the intuition that H⁻ signals "questioning" in general: Why would it do so in yes-/no-questions but not ‹wh›-questions? The answer, Truckenbrodt argues, is that yes-/no-questions contain but a single proposition, so H⁻ can unambiguously put that proposition up for questioning (the question is thus doubly marked, as it were: by the syntactic form, and by the H⁻ tone).

The contrast between single- and multiple-proposition questions comes out particularly nicely in disjunctive polar questions. While the string (16) is generally ambiguous between an alternative question reading ('which one of those did you go to?') and a yes-/no-question ('did you go to either one?'), a contour ending in H⁻ as in (16a) only allows for the latter; the alternative question requires a low phrase tone, (16b) (Truckenbrodt, 2012: 2050).

L* H⁻H%   H* L⁻L%
(16)   Did you go to Berlin or Potsdam?   a. Potsdam?   b. Potsdam?

This is so because the alternative question, not unlike a ‹wh›-question, makes equally salient *two* propositions ('you went to Berlin,' 'you went to Potsdam'), whereas the yes-/no-question does only one ('you went to Berlin or Potsdam'), and hence allows for an H^- tone.

Note that the interpretative difference at stake in (16) is quite different from that in Pierrehumbert and Hirschberg's (1990) similar example (12) above (‹*Do you want apple juice or orange juice?*›). In the ‹juice› example, the distinction is whether other drinks are available or not; presumably, either variant is a yes-/no-question. Also note that in Pierrehumbert and Hirschberg's (1990) example, the H^-/L^- contrast occurs in the first disjunct, whereas in Truckenbrodt's (2012) (16) it is in the second. It is unclear what predictions Truckenbrodt (2012) makes for the phrase tone in first coordinates, because it is not clear whether only the propositional content of the first conjunct is a candidate for the being "put up" by H^-, or both. Generally, it is not clear what the "H^- puts up a proposition for questioning" account has to say about Pierrehumbert and Hirschberg's (1990) cases (12)–(14).

Another concern is whether Truckenbrodt's (2012) idea that the proposition associated with H^- is given contextually is not too permissive. Truckenbrodt proposes to restrict the choice using the notion of "uniquely salient": "an antecedent proposition for H^- is a uniquely salient proposition *put up for question by the speaker*" (2012: 2051, emphasis in original). It seems to me, however, that this equivocates between "having been put up," "being put up," or "be intended to be put up." If H^- itself is *doing* the putting up, it cannot at the same time refer to the proposition that is *being* put up.[12] Presumably the intention here is that the proposition "put up for question" must be identifiable for the addressee, as would be the case for those propositions directly denoted by the sentence, for example in yes-/no-questions or rising declaratives.

But for the general case, including the "you know what I'm talking about" implication in examples of the ‹Skokie› variety, (15), it is not clear what makes the one proposition "uniquely salient," and would, on the other, exclude a similar proposition in, say, example (16) below (e.g. "do you know why I'm asking this?"), potentially resulting in an alternative question for the H^- version (16a).

9.2.3 Boundary tone meanings

As with H^-, most analyses of H% (and analyses of rising nuclei more generally) elaborate in one way or another on the idea that a high right boundary signals "openness" or "incompleteness," whereas a low boundary signals finality. The paradigm case of H% are of course simple yes-/no-questions and rising declaratives, or utterances like (17) which otherwise "clearly convey[s] that there is more that could or should be said" (PH, 1990: 307).

---

[12] In Section 3.2 of Truckenbrodt (2012) it is suggested that it is a *presupposition* of H^- that the speaker is putting a salient proposition "up for question." That presupposition in turn may be accommodated, thereby "establish[ing] a speech act" (2012: 2053). This is not the subject of the concern I raise in the main text, though. The question is not whether the "putting up" is done by assertion, implicature or accommodation, but how to identify the content to be/have been put up.

$$L^-H\%$$
|/
(17)   So, I guess there's just nothing more to say.

According to Pierrehumbert and Hirschberg (1990) "the choice of boundary tone conveys whether the current IP...is to be interpreted with respect to some succeeding phrase or whether the direction of interpretation is unspecified," and "indicates that S[peaker] wishes H[earer] to interpret an utterance with particular attention to subsequent utterances" (1990: 305). Since the notion of "interpreting with respect/particular attention to" is not further clarified, it may be best to look at examples again. One such case involves pronoun interpretation; apparently, backwards anaphora in the second sentence of (18) is facilitated if the sentence ends in H%, thereby signaling that the third sentence is relevant to the interpretation of the second.[13]

(18)   My new car manual is almost ...

$$L^- \boxed{H\%} \qquad L^- \boxed{L\%}$$
| / | /
a. ...unreadable. It's quite annoying.

(1st and 2nd sentence form unit, excluding 3rd; ‹it› likely the manual from 1st sentence)

$$L^- \boxed{L\%} \qquad L^- \boxed{H\%}$$
| / | /
b. ...unreadable. It's quite annoying.
I spent two hours figuring out how to use the jack.

(2nd sentence interpreted w.r.t. third: ‹it› likely 'that speaker spent two hours ...')

In other cases, the pertinent relation seems to have more to do with some form of hierarchical discourse structure. It is instructive in this connection to look at example (19), in which the third sentence is interpreted as summing up the first two.

$$L^-H\% \qquad L^- \boxed{H\%/L\%} \qquad\qquad\qquad\qquad L^-L\%$$
|/ |/ |/
(19)   George likes cake. He adores pie. He'll eat anything that's sweet and calorific.
                     (1st and 2nd sentence provide evidence for 3rd)

As indicated, (19) could be realized with either L% or H% at the end of the second sentence. According to Pierrehumbert and Hirschberg (1990), the H%-on-‹pie› variant in (19) signals that the second clause (as well as the first) are interpreted w.r.t. the third, which summarizes them, or is motivated by them (1990: 306f); the L%-on-‹pie› variant, on the other hand is motivated by the second clause being the final element in the list of observations motivating the third. Note that this suggests

[13] Examples (18a) and (18b) summarize Pierrehumbert and Hirschberg's (1990) (59) and (60), (19) their (61) and (64).
    Since PH assume that L% simply leaves the "directionality unspecified," it is presumably the (lack of) H% in the second sentence that is crucial for the contrast. Note that even in (18a), where ‹it› refers to the car manual, there is no sense in which the *first* sentence should be interpreted "relative to" the second, so it is not clear what motivates H% on ‹unreadable› in (18a).

that L% does have a function, or more carefully: that there is a discourse-structural function—closing a list—that may motivate the use of L%.

Concentrating on the latter kind of case (signaling grouping and hierarchical structure), assume that it is a necessary condition for the use of H% that the unit so marked is part of a larger, yet incomplete unit. L% on the other hand marks completion of a larger group, if there is one. Representing the rhetorical structure of (19) as in (20), S_1 and S_2 form a group—the evidence for the generalization in S_3—as do all three sentences—a claim about George's sweet tooth.

(20) $((S_1 \, S_2) \, S_3)$

evidence for

In this situation, the boundary between S_2 and S_3 qualifies for the use of either boundary tone: L% for signaling the end of the sub-group ($S_1 \, S_2$), or H% for signaling the incompleteness of the larger group. The boundary between S_1 and S_2 on the other hand is marked by H%, since both groups are incomplete, and no group (other than the trivial group consisting of S_1 alone) is being completed at this juncture (see Hobbs, 1990: for a similar reinterpretation of examples like these).

In contradistinction to PH's account, this does not require us to assume that S_1 is "interpreted with respect to" S_2 in example (19) in order to explain its H% boundary tone; S_1 and S_2 are simply equal (and independent) constituents in a larger group. For cases like (18a), it suffices to assume that a pronoun preferably finds its antecedent within its minimal group; this not only eliminates reference to the somewhat nebulous notion of "interpreted with respect to," it also goes some way towards explaining why H% is the preferred boundary on ‹unreadable› in (18a).

9.2.4 Interim summary: phrase and boundary tone meanings

The proposals I reviewed in this section have a number of tenets in common. All of them assume that phrase tone and boundary tone meanings—PBTMs, for short—operate on clausal meanings, that is, propositions. As said initially, this lends itself to a formalization in terms of intonational morphemes which combine with clausal constituents and are realized on the intermediate or intonational phrase corresponding to that constituent—where "correspondence," in the papers reviewed, is basically the tacit assumption that iPs and IPs map one-to-one onto syntactic clauses or at least something that has propositional content, though certainly more should be said here.

Whereas Gunlogson's (2001) proposal can by design apply to entire sentences only (since the PBTM changes, if you will, the utterance's speech act potential), the other proposals allow, at least in principle, for PBTMs to apply to non-root clause meanings as well—owing of course to the obvious fact that phrase and boundary tones are not limited to sentence/utterance boundaries.

Almost all proposals assume that the proposition PBTMs operate on the propositional content of the clause they attach to. The notable exception here is Truckenbrodt (2012), who, partly following Bartels (1999), assumes that PBTMs operate on a contextually provided proposition which may, but does not have to, be identical to the propositional content of the clause that realizes the corresponding tones. It bears noting at this point that none of the studies reviewed finds any reasons to assume that PBTMs operate on, or otherwise have access to, the F-alternatives of their clauses.

If we try to approach the kind of meanings attributed to PBTMs, we find a preponderance of speech act related meanings. This is, naturally, most clearly seen in those proposals that attempt at least a moderate amount of formal precision: For Gunlogson (2001), the PBTM is what turns a propositional sentence meaning into a context change potential (i.e. a function that updates speaker and addressee commitments); similarly, Truckenbrodt (2012) assumes that PBTMs may directly inject new questions into the discourse (though, unlike in Gunlogson's proposal, they do not change the sentence's basic (kind of) meaning in the process).

For Pierrehumbert and Hirschberg (1990), on the other hand, PBTMs mostly appear to have a structuring function, as we have seen, signaling if and where iPs and IPs should or should not be interpreted as "units." PH often phrase their meanings in terms of instructions (to the addressee) or intentions (of the speaker), though it is not clear to me whether this should be thought of as the PBTMs literal *meaning*, or simply the description of the likely effect their structuring function is going to have on discourse participants. This latter perspective I illustrated at the end of Section 9.2.3, where I attempted to re-render the alleged meanings of L% and H% in purely structural terms.

A common theme in all works I am aware of is to relate the PBTMs to the prototypical intonation of different sentence types or illocutionary types. The clearest example is the association of a rising boundary with simple yes-/no-questions. But such associations are not without problems. For example, though it is usually recognized that a simple "rise=question" fails to explain the systematic *dis*preference for a rise in constituent questions, Truckenbrodt (2012) seems to be the only source to offer a systematic explanation for this (see Section 9.2.2).[14]

Furthermore, in many cases the intonation of a sentence type appears more grammaticalized than pragmatic. (21) provides an illustrative minimal pair from German.

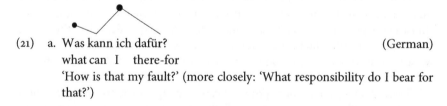

(21)   a. Was kann ich dafür?   (German)
         what can I   there-for
         'How is that my fault?' (more closely: 'What responsibility do I bear for
         that?')

---

[14] PH argue that "other directedness" is not a plausible candidate for the meaning of H% because it would wrongly predict H% to be common in ‹wh›-questions. However, as far as I can see, their alternative suggestion, see Section 9.3.1, is subject to the same objection: if a yes-/no-question "dominates" its answer (and hence is interpreted "with respect to it") because "the satisfaction of the intention underlying [the answer] contributes to the satisfaction of the intention underlying [the question]" (PH, 1990: 306), then why isn't the same true for *constituent*-questions? Why should participants' intentions in constituent-question–answer exchanges be any different from those in polar-question–answer exchanges?

b. Kann ich was dafür?
   can I   s.th.there-for
   'Is that my fault?'

Examples (21a) and (21b), rhetorical questions both, express very much the same message: 'look, it isn't *my* fault'. Yet, in its ‹wh›-question incarnation (21a) it ends in a typical fall (the rise here would make an echo question), while expressed as a polar question, it shows the equally typical rise (while a fall would sound plain odd).

Independent of the particular analysis of the meaning of H%/L%, examples like these show that at least in some cases, pragmatics alone is unlikely to be the determining factor for the choice of boundary tune. It is, to my mind, an open question to what extent we should assume that the boundary tones *contribute* meaning in such cases; in the alternative, PBTMs, where they are in meaningful opposition on the same lexical and syntactic material, may be historically derived from grammaticalized uses such as the rise in yes-/no-questions, but not themselves active in those. Put differently, it may not be an accident that a PBTM denoting "openness" adopted a question tune as its realization, but synchronically, no PBTM is attached to the (grammatically determined) rising tune in, say, yes/no questions.

9.3 Accent tone(s)

I now turn to proposals regarding the interpretation of different pitch accents, or for short: PITCH ACCENT MEANINGS (PAMs). As we will see, the meanings at stake here are even more elusive than those discussed in the previous sections, and my discussion will often be inconclusive and even focussed on negative points.

The examples in this section are exclusively drawn from English and German, which, together with Dutch, are pretty much the only languages whose different pitch accents have received much attention. This is certainly due in large part to the language bias on the part of the researchers involved; however, it also seems to me that the extreme variety of accents and boundary tones found in English (and, though to a somewhat lesser extent, other Germanic languages) is rather exceptional cross-linguistically. Many other languages appear to have a much smaller inventory of tones, and more rigorous rules about when to pick which (see e.g. the papers in Hirst and Cristo, 1998).

9.3.1 Paradigmatic accent tone choice

When it comes to the meaning of different pitch accents, one overwhelmingly frequent observation is that high pitch accents convey "newness," while low pitch accents tend to convey "oldness." For example, while (22a) would be a perfectly normal, informative answer to the question, (22b) (from Pierrehumbert and

Hirschberg, 1990: 292) suggests that the speaker's "desire for a Pavoni espresso machine is already mutually believed" (ibid.).

(22)   (What would you like for your birthday?)

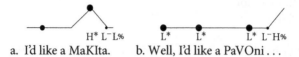

H* L⁻L%   L*   L*   L* L⁻H%
a. I'd like a MaKIta.   b. Well, I'd like a PaVOni . . .

Even before going into the details, we can already address a number of important points using these examples. First, ‹Pavoni› in example (22b) is clearly a(n answer) focus, so even if it is "old," this is not the same as being in the background in the sense of focus/background theories such as those discussed in Chapters 2 and 3 and following. Nor is ‹Pavoni› in (22b) *given* in the sense used there: while it may be *known* that the speaker has a Pavoni-wish, this is certainly not *salient* before the answer is given (see Chapter 5, esp. Sections 5.1.3 and 5.4.4). This point is particularly relevant since it also holds the other way around: The low pitch accent on ‹like›, a part of the background, in example (22a) could be replaced by a H* with no loss in coherence; in short, not all background accents are low (and not all low accents are in the background).

It is also important to emphasize that the use of low pitch accents is not the same as deaccenting. While it may sometimes be hard to reliably distinguish a completely accent-less post-focal word stress, or phrasal stress, from a L* pitch accent, this difference can nevertheless be appreciated for example if there is a following rise; in (23a) the pitch rises continuously from the NPA on ‹not› to the high boundary, whereas in (23b) the rise does not start until the second pitch accent on ‹exam›, which, accordingly, is heard as nuclear.

L*   H⁻H%
(23)   a.   You did not pass your exam last week?

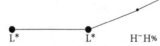

L*   L*   H⁻H%
b. You did not pass your exam last week?

Though the contrast may be subtler, the difference is perceptible in (24), too: in (24a), the L⁻ phrase tone affects the material after ‹not›, whereas in (24b), the pitch drop is more gradual, interpolating between the high and the low PA.

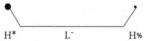

H*   L⁻   H%
(24)   a.   You did not pass your exam last week?

    H*   L* H⁻   H%
    b. You did not pass your exam last week?

Next, let me add a point about the semantics. According to the compositional program endorsed by PH and others, especially the idea that "pitch accents, phrase accents, and boundary tones each operate on a (progressively higher) domain" (recall the discussion in Section 9.1 above, especially the quote at the end of the section), we should expect PAMs to operate on something smaller than an intermediate phrase, for example the accented word or the phonological phrase it heads (see Chapter 6). However, when discussing PAMs, PH consistently refer to the meaning of the entire clause they appear in: what is new in (22a) is the proposition that the speaker wants a Makita, and what is old in (22b) is the proposition that the speaker wants a Pavoni. There is no sense in which ‹Pavoni› alone is "old" or ‹Makita› new. This is evident empirically: An H* is entirely appropriate on a given focus, as long as the proposition expressed by the answer as a whole is new.

(25)   (What did they use to demolish the Makita factory?—) Why, (they used)
         H*
         |
       MaKItas, of course.

The situation here is not unlike that with focus. While you can perhaps *mark* a focus all by itself, you can only *interpret* it with respect to its background. The same goes here: If PH speak about "instantiating variables," there has to be something to instantiate them *in*, and that is a formula representing the background. Hence the meaning of the pitch accents, too, operates on propositional meanings, nothing smaller.

One last remark before we delve deeper into the various proposals: The alert reader will have noticed that examples (22a) and (22b) above do not form a minimal pair, in the sense that the only relevant difference between them would be that one has an H* pitch accent where the other has an L*; rather they feature different nuclear *tunes*, H*L⁻L% vs L*L⁻H%. Unfortunately this situation is rather common in the literature. This may be a simple oversight, or a reflection of something deeper. In many cases it looks as though the composition of tunes is subject to something like an obligatory contour principle (OCP):[15] If it ends in a high boundary, the nuclear pitch accent is low, if it ends in a low boundary, the NPA is high, etc. But it should be clear that this, too, is not obviously compatible with the compositional approach to intonational meaning, or at least would introduce

---

[15] For the origin of this principle in phonology see Leben (1973), and the discussion in Odden (1986); Hayes and Lahiri (1991) argue, for example, that Bengali sentential tunes are strictly subject to the OCP.

TABLE 9.2   PH's decomposition of pitch accents into anchoring point (alignment) and movement

TONAL ANCHOR POINT	MOVEMENT	none	rise L+H	fall H+L
	MEANING	—	scale	inference
H*	new, predication	H*	L+H*	H*+L
L*	no predication	L*	L*+H	H+L*

a major complication in investigating them (essentially, only the first tone in any tune could be trusted to be what it appears to be on the surface).

Pierrehumbert and Hirschberg (1990):   Pierrehumbert and Hirschberg's (1990) treatment of H* and L* falls squarely within the group of approaches just discussed. Although about a dozen different characterizations of the exact meaning or effect of the accents are given in that paper, they all converge on H* signaling that something should be added to the common ground, whereas L*, while "emphasizing" the element so marked, does not advocated its addition to the common ground—for example because it is already in there. L*, in PH's words, marks the absence of "predication."

As for the bi-tonal pitch accents, PH compose their meanings from the choice of main, starred tone plus the direction of movement; in particular, a rising pitch accent is said to "convey the salience of some scale" (1990: 294), while a falling pitch accent signals the presence of an inference path. The resulting cross-classification is shown in Table 9.2.

It is important to mention that the effects of bi-tonal pitch accents on the actual pitch contour is not what one might expect; in particular, the L in both H+L pitch accents is a mid-level tone, and all bi-tonal pitch accents have the additional (or, in the case of H*+L: sole) effect that a following H⁻ or H* are DOWNSTEPPED. Rather than discussing the exact nature of the rules responsible, I will give the contours in the examples that follow.

Examples involving a scale (L+H) are the UNCERTAINTY CONTOUR L*+H L⁻ H%, discussed in detail in Ward and Hirschberg (1985) and illustrated in PH's example (26), where it signals "uncertainty about whether being a good badminton player provides relevant information about degree of clumsiness" (PH: 295), and (27), which invokes a scale of kissable body parts (PH: 296).[16]

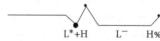

L*+H   L⁻   H%

(26)   A: Alan's such a klutz.   B: He's a good badminton player.

---

[16] While it seems intuitive to sense an "uncertainty about whether being a good badminton player provides relevant information about degree of clumsiness" (Ward and Hirschberg, 1985a: 295) (by hypothesis conveyed by the trailing H tone of the PA), it is less clear in what sense example (26) below does not involve a predication; it seems that the speaker could use (26B) to give new information to the addressee.

(27)   A: I wonder if they're supposed to be married.
       B: No, I don't think they're married.

L+H* L⁻H%

If they were married, he wouldn't be kissing her hand.

Turning to the falling contours, H*+L is distinguished from plain H* only in that it downsteps following H tones. In the Tone and Break Indices (ToBI) notation, this is annotated as a plain H*, with an exclamation point, '!', on the following, downstepped, H tone. Minimal pairs are given in (28) and (29) (the gray line represents the BASELINE, i.e. the speaker's lowest register for an L tone; I added it to make it perspicuous that the tunes in (29) end at a *mid*-level).[17]

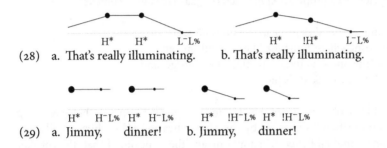

```
         H*      H*     L⁻L%              H*     !H*    L⁻L%
(28)  a. That's really illuminating.  b. That's really illuminating.
```

```
      H*    H⁻L%  H*  H⁻L%      H*    !H⁻L%  H*  !H⁻L%
(29)  a. Jimmy,   dinner!    b. Jimmy,    dinner!
```

Compared to the non-downstepped variants, the (b) examples are said to convey "stylization" or "a pedagogical flavor"; to the best of my understanding, this derives from the "inference path" required by PH, in the sense that the addressee is (supposed to be) not surprised by the occurrence of the utterance. In this connection, PH recall an observation made in Ladd (1978) according to which H*+L followed by H L% is inappropriate for "calling out a real emergency" as in example (30).

H* !H⁻L%
(30)   [to warn occupants in burning building] # Fi-re!

Hobbs (1990):   Hobbs (1990) presents a short comment on Pierrehumbert and Hirschberg's (1990) paper in which he proposes a number of small modifications. Perhaps most interesting in the present context, Hobbs's paper attempts to flesh out further what it may mean for a PAM to operate on the meaning of a single

---

[17] (28) from Veilleux et al. (2006: ch. 2.6, 6), (29) from Pierrehumbert and Hirschberg (1990: 299). The labeling for the downstep examples in the latter paper would be as in (i).

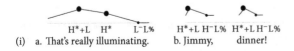

```
          H*+L   H*    L⁻L%      H*+L H⁻L%  H*+LH⁻L%
(i)   a. That's really illuminating.  b. Jimmy,    dinner!
```

constituent, claiming that "every morpheme ... conveys a proposition" (1990: 313). But what kind of a proposition could that be, and how is "conveying" related to "denoting"? In the only example discussed in Hobbs (1990), the meaning of ‹George likes pie› is symbolized as (31).

(31) $(\exists e, x, y)Present(e) \land like'(e, x, y) \land George(x) \land pie(y)$

‹George› is said to convey **George**(x), the common noun ‹pie› to convey 'pie(y) for some possible or nonspecific entity y' (Hobbs, 1990: 313). But evidently, **George**(x) is not a proposition, nor even a formula denoting one (it appears to be a formula that denotes a truth value or a proposition relative to a variable assignment, but which?). Interpreted charitably, we might rerender this as in (32), where the pronouns could be interpreted as in dynamic semantics, so that we can obtain something close to a proposition for each of (32a–32d) and a context.[18]

(32)   a. some event takes place in the present, and
       b. it is one where someone likes something, and
       c. he (the one who likes something) is George, and
       d. it (the thing liked) is pie

Much like PH, Hobbs assumes that H* means 'speaker privately believes p'—p being the proposition "conveyed" by the phrase bearing H*—which entails that p is not (yet) a mutual belief. L* simply means the opposite of that: the speaker does not privately believe p, which means either the speaker does not believe p at all, or not privately, that is, p is already *mutually* believed. This covers cases of L* marking known information (e.g. the ‹Pavoni›-example, (22b) above), as well as cases expressing doubt or downright disbelief, such as Pierrehumbert and Hirschberg's (1990) example (33) (their (4)):

(33)   A: Here's your roast beef, sir.

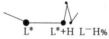

       L*   L*+H L⁻H%
       B: I'm having beef (But I'm a vegetarian. There must be some mistake.)

Note at this point that it is crucial that H* means '(only) speaker believes p' rather than 'p is true,' for otherwise L*—its negation—would mean that p is false, which is incompatible with the use of L* for mutually shared information (the ‹Pavoni› case, (22b) above). Strictly speaking this means that a speaker could also utter a declarative sentence denoting p which they are simply agnostic about (i.e. do not believe, but consider possible). Presumably, this case does not occur because, therefore, there simply would be no point in uttering that sentence in the first place.

---

[18] Strictly speaking we could obtain a set of world–assignment pairs by incrementally updating the given information state with these formulae.

Hobbs (1990) does not discuss questions, but his proposal may carry over in the following way: Suppose a ‹wh›-question also "conveys" certain propositions, as in (34).

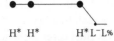

H* H*   H*L⁻L%

(34) Who closed the fridge?
   a. an event took place in the past, and
   b. it was someone closing something and
   c. that (the thing closed) is the fridge

One could argue now that any or all of these propositions is privately believed by the speaker and hence qualifies for marking by H*. In a yes-/no-question, on the other hand, it seems unlikely that any of the propositions in the question would be assumed by the speaker at all, so they would have to be accented L*, if at all.

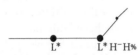

L*   L* H⁻H%

(35) Did you close the fridge?
   a. an event took place in the past, and
   b. it was someone closing something and
   c. that (the thing closed) is the fridge and
   d. (s)he (the person closing the fridge) is the addressee.

Whether or not this works for alternative questions, which often bear H* PAs (see e.g. example (16b) above), depends on how we rig up their component propositions. On the face of it, ‹Would you like TEA, or COffee?› would seem to include the propositions that what the addressee likes was tea, and that it was coffee; obviously the speaker should not be taken to believe both of these. If, on the other hand, we could ascribe something like (36) to an alternatives question, things might work out.

(36) a. there is an event, and
   b. it is a wanting of something by someone, and
   c. he (that someone) is the addressee, and
   d. it (the thing wanted) is one of two things, and
   e. tea is one of them, and
   f. coffee is the other

The speaker now could be claimed to privately believe that the speaker does want something, that it one of two things, and that tea is one of those two, and coffee the other. Hence, H* would be fine to mark these.

Hobbs (1990) also attempts a (de)compositional account of bi-tonal PAs. A leading tone, modifying the same "conveyed" proposition p as a starred tone, relates

p to the *addressee's*—incorrect—private beliefs: H+L* '. . . should mean something like "You might think that this is new information [the H part; DB], but it's actually not new [the L part; DB]",' while L+H* means 'you thought this was not new (i.e. it is already agreed on, or false), but it is (i.e. new and true)' (Hobbs, 1990: 316). The meanings of H+ and L+ are thus "related" to those of H* and L*, respectively.

But let us inspect this latter meaning a little closer. Recall that 'p is new' really is supposed to stand for 'speaker privately believes p' (i.e. the hearer does not (yet)), and its negation means 'either we both believe p, or the speaker does not hold a belief that p.'[19] The sentence thus comes out meaning (37).

(37)   L+ you (wrongly) believed that either
      (i)   we both believe p, or
      (ii) I do not hold a belief that p, whereas
    H* I believe p, and you do not (yet)

Examining the meaning expressed by L+, evidently the addressee cannot be taken to believe both (37i) *and* (37ii), so they must believe exactly one of them. Can it be (37i) the addressee is taken to believe? Hardly: unless the addressee were wrong about their own beliefs (# 'you wrongly thought you believed this, but only I do'), they could only be wrong about their belief that the speaker believes p; but that belief is exactly what is asserted by the speaker using H*, so they could not claim that to be a wrong belief on the part of the addressee. So the addressee can really only be taken to (wrongly) believe (37ii): that the speaker has no belief that p. In other words, contrary to what Hobbs claims, the use of L+ adds nothing about the addressee's previous attitude towards p, only about the speaker's.

All L+ says is that 'you thought I did not have a belief that p'; as far as the addressee's own attitude towards p is concerned, L+H* says the exact same as plain H*: that the addressee did not have a belief that p yet (i.e. they may believe not p, or simply be agnostic about p).[20] The meaning Hobbs wants for L+—'you believe that not p'—is simply not at all related to the proposed meaning of L*.

The proposed meaning for H+L* is more coherent, but it is not clear that it explains the examples Hobbs discusses. L*, recall, means 'either this is a mutual belief of ours, or I do not believe it.' Given that H* means 'I believe it, but you don't,' H+ presumably means 'you think that I believe it, and that you don't ($\equiv$that it is my private belief),' yielding (38) as the meaning for H+L*.

(38)   you (wrongly) thought this was my private belief, but either I do not believe it, or we both do

---

[19] I am using the cumbersome circumlocution 'not hold a believe that p' rather than 'not believe that p' to avoid the negation raising a reading of 'not believe.' The negation of 'speaker believes p' is 'speaker either believes not p, or has no opinion on whether p.'

[20] We assumed above that a *speaker* simply would not utter a sentence entailing p unless they thought that p was true (or maybe downright false, but not 'perhaps true, perhaps false'). But of course for the *addressee* to simply not know whether p is true or not makes perfect sense, so there is no reason to "strengthen" 'you do not believe that p' to 'you believe that not p.'

The first example of H+L* Hobbs discusses is (39) from Pierrehumbert and Hirschberg (1990:300f).

(39)   [mother-in-law to daughter-in-law during a disagreement about why her grandchild woke up]

H*H+L* !H⁻L%
She's teething.

A predicted interpretation is 'you thought only I believed this, but you did, too'. This is a bizarre thing to assert, implying, as it does, that the mother of the baby is wrong about her own beliefs (she thought she did not believe the baby is teething, but she actually does). This, however, seems to be what Hobbs has in mind, saying that "the speaker is suggesting that the hearer knows or should have known [that the baby is teething; DB] and its relevance" and "the information seems to be new, whereas in fact it is inferable from mutual knowledge and thus given" (1990: 316). But how does it "seem to be new," when in fact Pierrehumbert and Hirschberg (1990: 300) say that "the mother-in-law advanced a *mutually known fact* as the correct explanation" (my emphasis)? Worse, Hobbs's analysis equivocates between "knows" (the actual prediction) and "should have known" (what might be correct for the example), even though the second implies the negation (!) of the first.

Additionally, according to (38), example (39) should be useable to assert 'you thought I (but not you) believed the baby is teething, but I do not,' that is, it should be able to entail that the speaker does not have a belief that the baby is crying. Such a reading clearly does not exist.

It does, though, seem to be the kind of meaning Hobbs attributes to B's reply in example (40) (1990: 316):

(40)   (A: Yours is a Freudian account.)

H+L*
B: It's not a Freudian account. (It's a cognitive account.)

Here it seems plausible on the face of it, that A is saying 'it is not my *private* belief that it's a Freudian account, because it is not my belief at *all*.' The trick is that the 'it's not my belief at all,' contributed by L*, is applied to the proposition *below* the negation. But then, by parity of reasoning, a negated sentence should never be able to bear a H* account, as that would claim that the speaker does believe the negated proposition, a prediction that strikes me as clearly wrong.

Moreover, the H+ in (40) should express that A, the addressee, (wrongly) believes that it is B's private, non-shared belief that the account is a Freudian one. But A has just asserted that the account is Freudian, so B obviously cannot take A to think that this belief is A's private one. There is no role for the leading tone to play in this example.

Similar criticisms may be directed at other aspects of Hobbs's proposal: H as a trailing tone (T*+H), phrase tone (H⁻) and boundary tone (H%) always means the same, namely openness or incompleteness; L is the *absence* of incompleteness marking (Hobbs, 1990: 317f); this predicts potentially conflicting interpretations for "mixed" sequences such as H⁻L%, L*+H L⁻, etc., but no clear predictions about how and under which circumstances this is possible are made by the theory. Generally, while Hobbs's paper seems to adhere more strictly to the letter of a compositional approach than Pierrehumbert and Hirschberg (1990), it does not succeed in arriving at even the same descriptive generalizations, and several of its "compositional reductions" appear to rely on imprecision and equivocation more than true decomposition.

9.3.2 Accent alignment in German

Studies on the interpretation of accent alignment—that is: whether a peak (or trough) is reached before, early in, in the middle of, at the end of, or even after the stressed syllable—are closely related to those on accent shape, but they potentially point to very different intonational morphemes (or phonemes). An important example is Kohler's (1991) studies on German, which distinguishes early, medial, and late peaks. In an early peak, the peak is on the pre-nuclear syllable; this, Kohler argues on the basis of extensive questionnaire tests, marks an established fact or final statement. A medial peak has the peak within the accented syllable, and indicates that something is new, possibly open for discussion, and finally a late peak, occurring at or after the end of the accented syllable adds additional emphasis and a sense of surprise or indignation (1991: 157ff, esp. 160). The different peaks are schematized, using one of Kohler's examples, in (41a), (41b), and (41c).

(41)   a. sie hat (ja) geLOgen   (German)

she has PRT lied[21]

'(Once a liar, always a liar. This goes for Anna as well:) She lied.'

b. sie hat (ja) geLOgen
'(NOW I understand:) She lied!'

c. sie hat (ja) gelogen
'(Oh!) She lied!'

---

[21] Kohler (1991) initially included the particle ‹ja› in his stimuli, but then removed it in a second experiment, due to the suspicion that the meaning of ‹ja›—roughly "as is known"—might scoot the

The parenthesized lead-ins in the glosses are not just there to convey a feel for the interpretation to non-German speakers, but are the translations of the actual contexts used by Kohler in an identification test, used to establish that naive subjects do indeed clearly prefer one of the three peak alignments in each of the contexts, while (sometimes quite strongly) rejecting the others.

The autosegmental annotations in (41) are taken from Grice et al.'s (2005) German ToBI (GToBI) rendering of Kohler's three peak types. What are three different alignments of the same high pitch accent, consisting of L+H+L, for Kohler, are three different pitch accents in GToBI. A theoretical question at stake here is: Are there three distinct categories, or is it a continuum of "degree of surprise" or something along these lines?

Towards answering the first question Kohler (1991) synthesized several series of stimuli in which the pitch peak "moves" from early to late in 30ms increments, and then asked German speakers where in the series they perceived a change, the idea being that a continuous category should lead to a more or less even distribution of perceived changes, while a categorical distinction should yield clusters of perceived changes. Based on perception data from 73 subjects, Kohler (1991: 130) concludes that at least the "early-peak–vs–non-early-peak" distinction is categorical; data for the "medial-peak–vs–late-peak" distinction are less clear (Kohler appears to lean towards a categorical interpretation here as well).

A further question then is whether there are three elementary pitch accent morphemes, H+!H* (or "high and early"), (L+)H* ("high and medial") and L*+H ("high and late"), or four: "high", "early", "center", "late", where the meaning of the complex pitch accent is composed of the meaning of "high" plus one of the other three. Another way of putting this question is: Is pitch alignment morphemic (associated with its own, independent meaning), or phonemic (distinguishing accents of different meanings, without itself having a meaning)? The former perspective would predict that at least L (or H–L–H) should show parallel pragmatically and intonationally different variants; regrettably, I am not aware of any studies that address this point.

9.3.3 Paradigmatic accent choice in German

In the discussion so far, I have repeatedly pointed out that the intonational meanings proposed operate on the propositional content of the sentence, or, in the case of Hobbs (1990), sub-propositions thereof. Also, these meanings, to the extent that they are rendered precise enough to make such an assessment, all relate to the doxastic aspect of the context. That is to say, they relate to concepts like "(mutually) believed," "surprising," etc. As pointed out, these meanings are thus very different from the kind assumed for focussing and givenness, which apply to any kind of meaning (names, properties...) and do typically refer not to beliefs of the participants, but to contextual saliency, previous mention, etc.

A notably different approach to PAM is pursued in Baumann and Grice (2006), Röhr and Baumann (2010, 2011), and other papers by what we may christen the

interpretation towards an "established fact" interpretation; the final results are not affected by the difference.

TABLE 9.3   Various accessibility relations and pitch accent types tested in Baumann and Grice (2006), Röhr and Baumann (2010, 2011). The examples are my reasonably faithful transpositions of the German examples discussed in those papers.

(i)		
	given	Tom just bought a **banana**. He puts the **banana** in his pocket.
	synonymy	She had bought **garbanzo beans** [...] She cooked the **chick peas**.
	textually displaced	Django ordered a **whisky**. [...] Django drank the **whisky**
	scenario	I got on a **bus** yesterday. [...] The **driver** was drunk.
	converseness	John had a great **teacher**. [...] He really supported his **student**.
	hypernym–hyponym	Ole was a talented **sportsman**. [...] The press loved the **tennis player**.
	hyponym–hypernym	Ole was a talented **tennis player**. [...] The press loved the **sportsman**.
	whole–part	Jo loved his new **book**.[...] The boy flicked through the **pages**.
	inferentially accessible	Jo is going to visit the **monkeys** in the zoo. [...] He packs the **banana**.
	new	What would you like?—I'll take the **banana**.

(ii)			nuclear accent					
no accent	pre-nuclear accent		H*	!H*	L*	H+L*	L+H*	H+!H*

"Cologne School." Here PAMs are hypothesized to related directly to givenness, or more generally the ACCESSIBILITY status in the sense of Ariel (1999, 2001), Chafe (1976), Clark (1977); Clark and Haviland (1977), Gundel (1996); Gundel et al. (1993), Prince (1981), among others. This, clearly, is a prototypical case of a compositional account on the level of pitch accent types—PAMs operate on the meaning of the DP that bears the accent; and, as just said, it also explores an entirely different *kind* of PAM.

Between the various papers just cited, which I will collectively refer to as the A(ccessibility) S(tatus) approaches, correlations between the accessibility status listed in (i) and the accent types listed in (ii) of Table 9.3 are tested for in German, using various perception and production experiments.[22]

While the authors generally conclude that the accent choice is indeed systematically correlated with AS, it is worthwhile looking at the results more closely.

Baumann and Grice (2006) tested the relations in Table 9.3, except "given" and "new," in order to see whether listeners prefer a nuclear H*, H+L*, or no accent (i.e. deaccenting) on the second DP. Their first finding was that throughout the eight conditions, their subjects preferred H+L* over H* accents, arguably a consequence of the fact that all DPs bore *some* relation to a previous DP, or, as Pierrehumbert and Hirschberg (1990) might put it, there is an "inference path."[23]

---

[22] Unfortunately, some of the accessibility relations potentially interact with coreference. In particular, the examples of Given, Synonymy, and Hyponymy/Hypernymy also show coreference, as does, by happenstance, that of Converseness, albeit with a different DP. See Baumann and Riester (2010) and Riester (2008) for an insightful discussion of how to separate out these factors by distinguishing what they call r(eferential)-givenness from l(exical)-givenness.

[23] The H+L* pitch accent in German goes essentially all the way down to the bottom of the speaker's range, unlike the English H+L* in Pierrehumbert and Hirschberg (1990), in which the L* is a mid-level tone. That latter accent is transcribed as H+!H* in GToBI.

TABLE 9.4   Preferences from the perception experiment in Baumann and Grice (2006: 1650).

ACCESSIBILITY RELATION	PITCH ACCENTING PREFERENCES	DEACCENTUATION PREFERENCE
converses	no accent ≫ H+L* > H*	highly preferred
part–whole	no accent ≫ H+L* ≫ H*	
synonymy	no accent ≫ H+L* > H*	
hyponym–hypernym	no accent ≫ H+L* ≫ H*	
hypernym–hyponym	no accent ≫ H+L* > H*	
textually displaced	H+L*=no accent ≫ H*	
whole–part	H+L* ≫ H*=no accent	
scenario	H+L* ≫ H*=no accent	dispreferred

≫ indicates "highly significant preference" (*p* < .005), > "significant preference" (*p* < .05), = "no significant difference."

The different accessibility relations fell into three groups, as shown in Table 9.4. Clearly, the core of the high correlation Baumann and Grice (2006: 1650) found between type of accessibility relation and type of pitch accent is the distinction between "no accent" and "some accent," whereas the preference for one actual accent type, H+L*, over the other, H*, is not correlated with the different accessibility relations. Assuming that 'whole-part' and 'scenario' behave like non-given (but inferable) DPs, and the rest like given ones would suffice to explain all rows but 'textually displaced'. And for those, it seems as though subjects were essentially split between treating them as given (no accent) or as new (accent).

Röhr and Baumann's (2010) production experiment included 'new' and 'given' as accessibility relations, as well as 'textually displaced' (called 'textually accessible' there) and 'inferentially accessible' vis-à-vis the accent types H*, (H+)!H*, (H+)L*, prenuclear, and no accent. Importantly, pre-nuclear accents in the type of examples they use means that the nuclear accent has "shifted" rightward from its default position, as in (42a), to an otherwise unaccented (namely integrated, see Sections 4.4, 6.1, and 8.5 above) element, as in (42b).

(42)   a.
	NPA	

a. Er steckt die BaNAne ein.   b. Er steckt die BaNAne EIN.
   he packs the banana   in
   'He packs the banana.'   (German)

As discussed in Sections 4.4 and 6.1 above, this type of accent shift forces an interpretation of ‹banana› as given or backgrounded, and of ‹ein› as new and (part of a) focus, for example 'he PACKS it, the banana'. Since accents on pre-nuclear backgrounded or given elements are in many cases optional, this means that no accent and prenuclear accent form—under the assumptions made in this book—a natural class opposite all NPA cases.

Röhr and Baumann's (2010) data clearly support this classification. New DPs get (nuclearly) accented close to 95 percent of the time, and given ones with a close antecedent barely more than 10 percent (bearing no or a pre-nuclear pitch accent the rest of the time); textual accessible—given/coreferential but with several sentences in between—are (re)accented in only slightly less than 20 percent of the subjects' productions.

As for the inferentially accessible DPs, those get accented a little over 45 percent, which probably means that they are treated as either given or new more or less by chance.[24]

What about the different NPA types? Generally, H* was the most frequent NPA type across all categories, a puzzling divergence from Baumann and Grice's (2006) findings discussed earlier. On the other hand, DPs with a literal antecedent—given and textually displaced—show an L* about twice as often as the two other types (22 percent of nuclear pitch accents for textually displaced, 19 percent for given vs 8/10 percent for new and inferentially accessible, though keep in mind that the overall numbers for the given/textually displaced DPs are much lower). This again points to a more likely use of L* for "old" material, and H* for new material; it also supports the idea that inferentially accessible DPs, where nuclearly accented at all, are treated like new DPs (i.e. vastly prefer H pitch accents). On the other hand, we should keep in mind that NPAs on given elements make up only 10 percent of given DPs in the first place (recall that all theories we discussed in Chapters 2 and 3 categorically exclude such accentings), of which L* and H+L* account for 40 percent. As discussed in Section 9.3.1, it may sometimes be difficult to decide whether a phrase in sentence-final position is deaccented or has a low PA. So it may also be that a significant portion of purportedly L* pitch accents on given and textually accessible DPs are in fact just deaccented (and stressed).

While the relative frequency of NPA types among the given/textually displaced DPs is basically identical (H*>H+L*>L*>H+!H*>!H*>L+H*), the "second favorite" NPA type (after H*) between 'new' and 'inferentially accessible' is different: inferentially accessible DPs show early peaks—H+L* and H+!H*—in just over 40 percent of NPAs, whereas new DPs prefer medial peaks, though less clearly (after H* at 43 percent of all NPAs, we see 15 percent L+H* and 13 percent !H*, while the early peaks each hover around 10 percent).

The same contrast was found even more clearly in a perception experiment in Röhr and Baumann (2011), in which subjects were asked to judge "whether the target word in a test sentence sounded as if it was (rather) known or unknown" (2011: 3). Responses distinguished between three groups of marking: pre-nuclear accent or no accent as most known, H+L*, H+!H* and L* in the middle, and H* and !H* as least known.

It seems, then, that early peak accents do in fact signal DPs that are inferentially accessible, though not *vice versa*: high pitch accents seem completely unobjectionable on any of the categories.

Where does this leave us? First of all, it seems that the overall pattern of when a DP must or must not bear the NPA follows quite precisely the predictions of the

---

[24] As can be seen in the example of inferentially accessible DPs in Table 9.3, these are presented with a definite article, so that subjects had to interpret ‹the banana› with no prior mention of bananas or even fruit at all (only monkeys). The accommodation required to meet the uniqueness requirement of the definite determiner probably facilitates accommodating ‘banana’ as a salient concept. It would be instructive to test examples of inferential accessibility with indefinites or categories other than DP.

kinds of theories discussed earlier in this book: New DPs must bear the NPA (if not followed by another new phrase), given DPs must not. Pitch accenting a final predicate or particle is effectively tantamount to deaccenting the final DP, again just as predicted. Pre-nuclear DPs with and without pitch accents are by and large interpreted the same in terms of givenness. This is not an insignificant result, given the frequently made claim that pitch accenting and givenness are in principle one-to-one; relating givenness (and focussing) to the NPA, as we did in Chapters 1, 2, is the empirically more appropriate model.

The (non-)accenting of textually displaced DPs also fits rather well with the theoretical picture drawn earlier: The tendency to re-accent increases with distance to the antecedent, but not dramatically.

When we look at the NPA choice—the topic of this chapter—the results are less clear cut. There does seem to be a generalization that early peak accents signal that a DP is known, or inferentially related to earlier material, while plain new DPs strongly lean towards medial peak accents, first and foremost H*. From this, in turn, we may conclude that—at least in German—a distinction between early and non-early pitch accents is grammatically relevant, whereas the component morphemes postulated in Pierrehumbert and Hirschberg (1990)—rise and fall—and Hobbs (1990)—H* vs L*, H+ vs L+, +H vs +L—do not seem useful here.

All of the papers discussed here that pursue the AS approach conclude that an accessibility scale, including new and given as endpoints, aligns with a "prominence lending" scale with H* NPA and 'no accent' as endpoints. The interpretation of the results I offered here does not draw that conclusion. Rather, the data profit, in my view, from factoring out the question of NPA vs not NPA first, and then comparing pitch accent types within the NPA group only. Within that, there does seem to be an effect of early peak accents as signaling something like inferential accessibility. From that perspective, new/given (including textually displaced) do not belong within the same scale as, say, inferentially accessible. Rather, the former is reflected in the accent *pattern*, while the latter may influence the *shape* of the individual accents.

9.3.4 Another interim summary

In this section I surveyed a number of approaches to pitch accent meaning. As for the *kind* of meanings denoted by pitch accent (or the morphemes they realize), we saw two major kinds of approaches: Those under which tone meanings relate to the doxastic states of the discourse participants; and those under which (at least pitch accents) relate to the discourse accessibility status of concepts. Although these are often lumped together, I would argue that we should pay attention to the difference (see also Section 5.1.3 above): on the doxastic approaches, tone choice and accent placement are essentially orthogonal to one another: One regards common and individual knowledge and the update thereof, the other regards contextual salience (givenness) and contrast (focus). For the AS approaches, on the other hand, the interpretations of different pitch accents overlap significantly with the interpretation of pitch accent distribution.

Regarding the question of holistic vs compositional approaches, we can now formulate the empirical questions at stake in a more succinct manner: First, is the meaning of complex pitch accents derived from the meanings of the simple tones involved (the same meanings they would have as simple pitch accents)? Second, is the meaning of the nuclear pitch accent freely combinable with individual phrase and boundary tones, or does the entire "nuclear tune" form a unit? And third, is the choice of pre-nuclear accents indeed independent of what other accents occur in the intermediate phrase?

At the risk of disappointing the reader, I would not venture any guesses on the answers to those questions, for at least two reasons: First, what is notably absent from every study surveyed here are studies of intermediate phrases with more than one pitch accent. But it is those that could potentially provide strong arguments in favor of a compositional approach: accent types should "mix and match" even within the same intermediate phrase, depending on the doxastic or accessibility status of each individual accented item; the absence of such variability would in turn suggest a more holistic approach.

A second reason for extreme caution is the fact that the proposed tone meanings we have seen are, for the most part, mere *sketches* of meanings, often so vague as to make it impossible to make any clear predictions. Especially in the case of Pierrehumbert and Hirschberg's (1990) proposal, it is not even clear to me that the meanings proposed could in principle apply to non-clausal meanings (which would be a precondition for testing the independence of pitch accents within a single phrase), since they all seem to be characterized in terms of predications and refer to propositional meanings (obtained by combining predicate(s) and arguments).

Given all this, it seems to me that a case for a compositional analysis has yet to be made, on all three counts mentioned above.

9.4 Theme/topic vs rheme/focus accents

One tonal distinction that has received considerable attention in the literature is that between intonation marking focus and intonation marking CONTRASTIVE TOPICS.

An early discussion of this distinction can be found in Jackendoff (1972: sec. 6.7), who distinguishes a high pitch accent followed by a fall completed by a final fall in pitch, from the same high-PA-plus-fall completed by a final *rise* in pitch; Jackendoff identifies these with the A- and B-accent of Bolinger (1965), respectively, and even though this identification may actually be problematic, the A-/B-labels have continued to be used in much of the subsequent literature. According to Jackendoff, the plain fall ("A-accent") marks a focus inside something akin to the traditional notion of COMMENT, while the rise-fall-rise ("B-accent") marks an "independent variable," which corresponds closely to what is now mostly called (contrastive) topic. This is illustrated in (43), which attempts to reproduce example (6.145) from Jackendoff (1972).

(43)   A: Well, what about Fred, what did he eat?

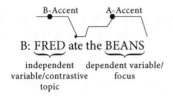

B: FRED ate the BEANS

independent   dependent variable/
variable/contrastive   focus
topic

Vilkuna (1989) and Büring (1997b), among others, assume that a sentence may consist of either background and focus (order irrelevant), or a contrastive topic (CT),[25] a background, and a focus, where the CT is a sub-part of the background (it may also cover the entire background).

An even closer adaption of Jackendoff's taxonomy is found in Steedman (2000a, 2000b, 2007, 2014), who proposes that a sentence is divided into a theme and a rheme, within each of which there can be foci, marked by accents (Steedman, 2014: does not use the term focus in this connection, but e.g. Steedman, 2000a does), a position largely adopted in Büring (2003).

According to (Steedman 2014: 27), H*, H*+L, L*, and H+L* only occur within the rheme, while L+H* and L*+H can only occur within the theme.[26] The boundary between theme and rheme is marked by a L⁻H% phrase/boundary tone. This is illustrated in (44) with an example from Steedman (2000a: 659).

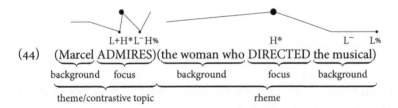

(44)   (Marcel ADMIRES)(the woman who DIRECTED the musical)

background   focus   background   focus   background

theme/contrastive topic   rheme

For terminological consistency, I will use the term Contrastive Topic (CT) throughout the discussion to follow. CT marking requires a pitch accent; we can utilize this property to help diagnose CTs: if an otherwise unaccented element, like a pronoun, is to be a CT, this is particularly noticeable.

(45)   (Who do they want to kick out?—) SHE$_{CT}$ wants to kick ME$_F$ out.

I will return to the prosody of CTs in a moment, after outlining its meaning at least in broad strokes; for the time being, I will simply use the marker CT.

The answer in (45) suggests a continuation along the lines of '...whereas someone else wants to kick so-and-so out.' Compare this to the same example with double focus.

---

[25] I use this term for consistency here. Contrastive topics are simply called topics in Vilkuna (1989), and sentence topics in Büring (1997b).

[26] Steedman (2014) will be discussed in what follows, representing the entire series of Steedman (2000a, 2000b, 2007, 2014) and, to a lesser extent, Steedman (1991).

(46) (Did you kick her out?—) SHE_F kicked ME_F out!

Example (46) is interpreted as 'it was her who did the kicking out, it was me who got kicked out.' Example (45), where ‹she› is a CT, on the other hand, implies that *others* want to do some kicking-out as well.

In Büring (2003) I argued for the following view: Whereas F relates a declarative sentence to alternative propositions, CT+F relates it to alternative questions. In (45), the alternative propositions say things like 'she wants to kick George out,' 'she wants to kick Marcy out,' etc., whereas the alternative questions are 'Who does Bob want to kick out?,' 'Who does Kim want to kick out?,' etc. The alternative propositions are other conceivable answers to the question 'Who does she want to kick out?,' so by the pragmatics of questions they will likely be interpreted as false: she doesn't want to kick George/Marcy . . . out, only the speaker.

The alternative *questions*, on the other hand, are not excluded in any way; rather at least one must be pertinent to the conversation. This is the case in (45): The original question was who they want to kick out. Given that the answer is limited to *her* intentions, there must be other relevant people—the other members of the group referred to by ‹they›—for whom it is pertinent to ask: Who does *(s)he* want to kick out?

This basic idea can be implemented via an extension of Alternative Semantics for focus from Chapter 2, 3, and 5, which derives from a sentence like (45), repeated in (47) below, the set of F-alternatives, (47a), as well as the set of CT-ALTERNATIVES, (47b):[27]

(47) SHE_{CT} wants to kick ME_F out
    a. F-ALTERNATIVES: the set of propositions like 'she wants to kick x out,' for some individual x
    b. CT-ALTERNATIVES: the set of question meanings like 'Who does y want to kick out?,' for some individual y

I will write S^{CT+F} for a sentence containing CT+F (analogously for F+F, F, etc.), and $[\![S^{CT+F}]\!]_O$, $[\![S^{CT+F}]\!]_F$, and $[\![S^{CT+F}]\!]_{CT}$ for its ordinary meaning, F-, and CT-alternatives, respectively.

Most formal proposals for the interpretation of CT agree that one of the questions among the CT-alternatives is currently relevant and not answered by the sentence containing CT itself.[28] Following the presentation in Büring (2016) (which in turn is a slight variation on Büring, 2003), I will assume (48) to be the rule for interpreting CT.

---

[27] See Büring (2003: sec. 12.1) for how to do that, Büring (1997b: sec. 3.3) for details.

[28] See Hara and van Rooij (2007), van Rooij (2010), and Tomioka (2009, 2010). Not all of these assume CT-alternatives to be sets of questions, but the gist is still the same. See the more detailed comparison in Büring (2016).

(48) CT-INTERPRETATION RULE (CIR)

For a sentence S^{CT+F} to be felicitous, there must be at least one question meaning in S^{CT+F}'s CT-value which is

    a. currently pertinent, and   PERTINENCE

    b. logically independent of $[\![\, S^{CT+F}\,]\!]_O$, and   INDEPENDENCE

    c. identifiable.   IDENTIFIABILITY

The requirements on S^{CT+F} introduced by the CIR should be understood as conventional implicatures triggered by the presence of CT marking. Applied to (47), (48) requires that speaker and hearer can identify at least one question instantiating 'Who does y want to kick out?' which is pertinent and independent of (47) itself. In a context in which it was asked who X wants to kick out, X being some group, there are at least as many pertinent questions as there are members of X. If one knows who the members of X are, one can identify the questions about them. And only one of those questions is resolved by—i. e. not independent of—the answer ‹*She wants to kick me out*› (namely 'Who does she want to kick out?'); the other questions ('Who does Jeanne want to kick out?'...) are independent of that answer, meeting (48).

Note that (48) is *not* met in (46) (‹*Did you kick her out?*—SHE *kicked* ME *out!*›). If ‹she› were a CT (and ‹me› a focus), (48) would require that there is at least one question like 'Who did y kick out?' which is pertinent to the conversation *and logically independent of (i.e. not resolved by) the answer*. But this is not the case: What we are interested in is whether he kicked her out, or she him. Answering that she kicked him out resolves this issue completely, in violation of the CIR in (48), in particular Independence, (48b).

Crucially, failure to meet (48) does not mean that (46) is infelicitous, only that it cannot be a CT+F structure. As stated above, it does have a well-formed structure on which both ‹she› and ‹me› are F, to which (48) simply does not apply.

In the following subsection I will illustrate and briefly discuss some of the standard uses of CT discussed in the literature, using the blueprint of the CIR.

9.4.1 A brief natural history of contrastive topics

Partial answers: Answers to multiple ‹wh›-questions, or single ‹wh-question› containing plurals, typically allow CT+F answers:

(49) a. (Which guest brought what?—) FRED$_{CT}$ brought the BEANS$_F$.

     b. (Where do your siblings live?—) My SISTER$_{CT}$ lives in STOCKHOLM$_F$.

The CT values of the answers in (49) are 'What did x bring?' and 'Where does your x-sibling live?', respectively. Given the more general questions about the guests/siblings, we can see how the CIR in (48) is met: The questions in $[\![\, (49a/b)\,]\!]_{CT}$ are obviously pertinent, and independent of the answers in (49).[29]

---

[29] Languages with topic-marking morphemes like Korean ‹-nun› or Japanese ‹wa› likewise use these markers, together with intonational prominence, in such discourses (see Lee, 1999; Uechi, 1998; a.o.)

Shifting topics

(50)   a. (Will Bo come to school today?—) YESTERDAY$_{CT}$ he was SICK$_F$.
     b. (Where did Fritz buy this book?—) BERTIE$_{CT}$ bought it at HARTLIEB$_F$'s.

The CT-questions here are 'How is/was Bo on day x?' and 'Where did x buy this book?.' Which of them are pertinent? For (50b), the very question overtly asked is pertinent and not resolved by the answer. Similarly, for (50a) the question how Bo is today is pertinent, since its answer will indicate whether he will come to school today. (Note that we do not aim to answer the question why the answers in (50) are *relevant* to the question in particular, but only why they can bear the CT+F pattern they do.)

Purely implicational topics

(51)   (Where was the gardener at the time of the murder?—) The GARDENER$_{CT}$ was in the HOUSE$_F$.

In this case, the answer directly resolves the question that was asked. But the CT indicates additional questions: Where was the chauffeur? The cook? Are they pertinent? Quite plausibly 'yes' in a case like (51), where the questioner is easily construed as trying to find the murderer. This is not always the case, of course, compare (52).

(52)   (Where did Thomas Mann write *The Beloved Returns*?—)
    # MANN$_{CT}$ wrote it in [LOS ANGELES]$_F$.

The odd implication of the CT-marking on ‹Mann› is that someone else might have written the novel elsewhere, which defies word knowledge.
    Purely implicational topics as in (51) show that CT-marking does not necessarily just "echo" something that is in the context already, but may itself contribute, possibly by way of accommodation, the notion that more questions are pertinent at this point. Conversely, the CT marking on, for example, ‹the gardener› in (51) can be omitted without loss of coherence. But without it, there is no implication of other suspects (via other questions). So here the speaker is making a choice as to whether to indicate the presence of other questions prosodically or not.

(i)   (Who did what?—)
    [JOE-**nun**]$_{CT}$ ca   -ko   SUE-**nun**   nol-assta.   (Korean)
    Joe CT   sleep   and   Sue CT   play PAST

(ii)   (Dare   -ga   pop   star   -o   sitteita   no?—)   (Japanese)
    who   -NOM   pop   star   -ACC   knew   COMP
    [Onna   -no   pop   star   -**wa**]$_{CT}$ Mary   -ga   sitteita   yo.
    female   -PRT   pop   star   **wa**   Mary   NOM   knew   PRT
    'Who knew the pop stars?—The female pop stars, Mary knew.'

Ineffability: In some cases, CT marking appears impossible, regardless of context. One such case from German is (53).[30]

(53) #ALLE$_{CT}$ Politiker   SIND$_F$ korrupt.   (German)
     all   politicians are   corrupt

Without CT-marking (but retaining F on the finite verb), (53) would be perfectly well-formed. But CT-marking on the determiner ‹alle› leads to unacceptability (even though ‹alle› can be CT-marked under other circumstances, as we will see momentarily). Why is that?

Assuming that F on a finite verb signals polarity focus, the F-alternatives of (53) are that all politicians are corrupt, or that they are not. This means that the CT-alternatives are questions like 'Are Q politicians corrupt?', where Q is some determiner.

Now note that none of these questions are independent of (53)'s assertion: If all politicians are corrupt, that logically entails the answers to 'Are most/some/the…politicians corrupt?', namely: 'Yes.' In other words, independently of actual context, (53) cannot possibly meet the CT-Interpretation Rule (48), specifically Independence, (48b), and hence is ungrammatical (or "unpragmatical," if you like).

If we change the example slightly, CT+F is possible again:

(54)   a. EINIGE$_{CT}$ Politiker   SIND$_F$ korrupt.   (German)
        some   politicians are   corrupt

     b. ALLE$_{CT}$ Politiker   sind ETWAS$_F$ korrupt.
        all   politicians are   a little   corrupt

The CT-alternatives of (54a) are the same as in (53), but since the sentence itself neither entails nor precludes that all, or most, politicians are corrupt, these will be unresolved (and potentially pertinent) questions. In (54b), with the added degree expression, CT-alternatives are 'How corrupt are Q Politicians?', that is questions that could be answered by ‹Only a handful are totally corrupt› or ‹Some are not at all corrupt›. And while the latter is again resolved by (54b)'s assertion, the former, for example, is not. There are thus unresolved (and potentially pertinent) questions among the CT-alternatives, as required by CIR.

Scope inversion: If a S^{CT+F} is structurally ambiguous between a construal on which it violates the CIR—along the lines just discussed in the previous subsubsection—and one on which it does not, CT marking will effectively disambiguate the sentence towards the latter. A case in point is sentence (55), with CT+F marking as indicated, which can only mean that not all politicians are corrupt. Without CT marking, the dominant, perhaps only reading is that all politicians are non-corrupt:[31]

---

[30] Büring (2003: 534).
[31] From Jacobs (1984), analysis following Büring (1997a).

(55) ALLE_CT Politiker   sind NICHT_F korrupt.   (German)
      all   politicians are   not   corrupt
      'Not all politicians are corrupt.'

The same can be observed for example in Hungarian (from Gyuris, 2002: 80): (56) only has the 'not . . . everybody' reading, although quantificational elements in Hungarian usually have a preference for surface scope:

(56) MINDENKI_CT NEM_F ment el.   (Hungarian)
      everybody   not   went PREFIX
      'It is not the case that everybody left.'

Let us focus on the available construal first: The sentence asserts that not all politicians are corrupt, and its CT-alternatives will be 'Is it false that Q politicians are corrupt?', for example 'Is it false that many politicians are corrupt?' This question is not resolved by the assertion, and it is plausibly pertinent, meeting the CIR.

On the other construal, the sentence says that all politicians are un-corrupt, with CT-alternatives like 'Are Q politicians corrupt?' But since the sentence asserts that none of them are, any such question is resolved by the assertion alone. As was the case with (53), this construal of (55) cannot possibly meet the CT Interpretation Rule (48). But in (55), unlike in (53), there is a second construal which *is* (or can be) felicitous, so that the sentence is acceptable, though not ambiguous, with CT+F marking.

9.4.2 Single CT and F+CT

In all the cases discussed so far, CT occurred as part of a 'CT-followed-by-F' pattern (CT+F, for short). English (but not German) additionally has a rise–fall–rise (RFR) pattern—L*+H L⁻ H% in MaeToBI notation—which can occur sentence finally, that is, without a following F:[32]

(57) a. (Will Uncle Michael and Aunt Carolyn be coming to the rehearsal dinner?—) They're INVITED_RFR.
      b. (What about the beans? Who ate them?—) FRED_F ate [the BEANS]_RFR

For both the "sole RFR" and the "F+RFR," the interpretive parallels with CTs are striking. For example RFR on ⟨all⟩ in (58)[33] disambiguates the otherwise scope

---

[32] See a. o. Ward and Hirschberg (1985); Pierrehumbert and Steele (1987); Hirschberg and Ward (1991); examples from Bolinger (1982: 507) and Jackendoff (1972: 261).

[33] From Ladd (1980: 146). I notate the final R at the end of sentence here, indicating that it is not part of the pitch accent on the prominent word—⟨all⟩ in (58)—but a rise at the right edge of the intonational phrase.

ambiguous string towards the 'not all' reading, much like CT+F on ‹alle . . . nicht› ('all . . . not') did in (55) above:[34]

(58)   ALL$_{RF}$ the men didn't go$_R$.

Furthermore, RFR may occur in partial answers and shifting topics, similar to the cases discussed in Section 9.4.1:[35]

(59)   a. (Can Jack and Bill come to tea?—) BILL$_{RF}$ can$_R$.
       b. (Did you feed the animals?—) I fed the CAT$_{RFR}$.
       c. (Do you want a glass of water?—) I'll have a BEER$_{RFR}$.

Such examples can be assimilated to the CT analysis sketched above, assuming that the CT alternatives here are alternative yes-/no-questions, for example 'can x come to tea?' in example (59a), or 'did q men go?' in (58).[36] In the alternative, one could assume with Constant (2006, 2012) that the accent in RFR is a focus, and that RFR operates on the (propositional) F-alternatives, conventionally implicating the existence of independent, relevant, and yet unresolved statements among them.[37]

The main difference between RFR and CT+F, as noted in Constant (2012: 430), is that the single peak RFR pattern cannot occur in a last answer (Constant 2012: ex. (76)), while a parallel CT+F pattern is possible.

(60)   (Can Elizabeth and Persephone come over tomorrow?—)
       ELIZABETH$_{RF}$ can$_R$.
       a. #PERSEPHONE$_{RF}$ can$_R$
       b. PERSEPHONE$_{CT}$ can TOO$_F$.

---

[34] Again, Japanese stressed ‹wa›, and Korean stressed ‹nun›, the pragmatics of which appear very similar to English and German CT marking, can appear without an accompanying focus, yielding scope disambiguation: (Lee, 1999; Hara, 2008; Oshima, 2008; Tomioka, 2009)

(i)   MINNA-WA   ko-nakat-ta.   (Japanese)
      everyone-CT   come-NEG-PAST
      'Not everyone came.'

(ii) MOTU -NUN o   -ci   anh -ass -ta   (Korean)
      all   CT   come PRT   not PAST DEC
      'Not all of them came.'

[35] O'Connor and Arnold (1973: 173), Ladd (1980: 153), examples (16) and (19).

[36] Strikingly, parallel German cases appear to have a focus on the finite verb or negation, as in (55) above, which—by standard F semantics—yields the meaning of a yes-/no-question as the focus value. Generally, German does not allow for CT (or RFR) without a following F, so one can hypothesize that German here chooses an F-marking—on the finite verb—which yields the same result that a CT-only/RFR sentence would (see Büring, 2003: 532).

[37] Again, 'independent' here means neither entailed nor contradicted by the RFR-marked sentence itself. Weaker conditions which merely require alternatives that are compatible (but possibly redundant, such as Wagner 2012a: 24, (46)), or non-redundant (but possibly known to be false, such as Oshima 2008: 7, (17)), or simply not equivalent to S^{RFR} (e.g. Ludwig 2008: 391, (19)) will systematically fail to derive the desired result.

As Ward and Hirschberg (1985) note, the RFR contour seems to "implicate uncertainty" in a way CT in general does not.

9.4.3 Representation and interpretation of CT

In Steedman's (2000a: 659) example (44) above, repeated below, CT is marked on an intonational phrase, by a complete tune which is aligned with the focal accents within it, as well as the boundary.

(61)

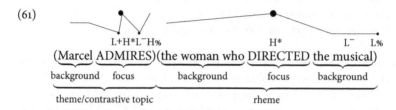

L+H*L⁻H%   H*   L⁻   L%
(Marcel ADMIRES)(the woman who DIRECTED the musical)

background   focus   background   focus   background

theme/contrastive topic   rheme

The CT-alternatives would, accordingly, be 'who does Marcel adore?', 'who does Marcel plagiarize', 'who does Marcel despise?', etc. (assuming, if only for simplicity, that focus and comment coincide). Alternatively, Büring (2003), argues that—as with focussing/deaccenting within a broader focus—the focussing within the CT does not influence the CT-alternatives, which in (44) results in a quite unrestricted set of questions like 'who does John love?', or 'who did the tiger see?' (which, naturally, contains all of Steedman's questions). Example (62) is given in support of this view.

(62)   (Where will the guests at Ivan and Theona's wedding be seated?—)
        [FRIENDS and RELATIVES of the couple]꜀ₜ will sit [at the TABLE].
        (Reporters have to sit at the back.)

Here it looks as though 'where will the reporters sit?' is the alternative question, which would only be a CT-alternative if the entire subject DP, rather than ‹friends and relatives› where to introduce alternatives. On the other hand, one could argue that the pertinent alternative here is 'other guest of the couple', which would be consistent with the claim that only foci within the CT get to introduce alternatives.[38] Since not much seems to hinge on this, I will leave this issue open here.

   A more substantial difference, to my mind, is the question of what derives, sloppily speaking, the ‹wh›-part in the CT-alternative questions. According to Steedman (2014) and earlier works, it is always the entire rheme which is replaced by a variable, whereas Büring (1997b, 2003) assumes that the semantic focus which influences the CT-alternatives may be a proper sub-part of the rheme. Thus CT-alternatives for (63) would be as in (63a) according to Steedman (2014), but as in (63b) following Büring's (2003) proposal.

---

[38] This might well be what Steedman (2014: 21f) has in mind when discussing this example, though I would not want to vouch for that.

(63) (Where did Muller buy that brulee torch?—Don't know...) SMITH$_{CT}$
      bought it on the WEB$_F$.
      a. what did x do?
      b. where did x buy their brulee torch?

Note that the constellation (and the positions) here is the opposite of that within
the CT above: (63a) (Steedman) is the less specific super-set of (63b) (Büring). I
believe that the examples of ineffability—(53), repeated in (64)—strongly argue for
the latter position here. The incoherent example (64a) contrasts with the perfectly
natural (64b).

(64) a. #ALLE$_{CT}$ Politiker   SIND$_F$ korrupt.   (German)
         all   politicians are   corrupt
      b. ALLE$_{CT}$ Politiker sind koRRUPT$_F$.   (Some may be felons, even.)

As indicated, (64b) points towards other properties that politicians may have, that
is, questions like 'what holds of most/many/some politicians?' This is the predicted
result if AP, VP (or whatever category is the sister to the thematic subject ⟨alle
Politiker⟩) were F-marked. But (64b) and (64a) have identical CTs, which means
they also have identical rhemes, distinguished only by the foci within those rhemes.
So according to Steedman's position, both should have the same CT-alternatives,
'what property does/do x have?', whereas for Büring (2003), the only CT-alternative
in (64a) is 'are n politicians (not) corrupt?', which accounts for the infelicity of CT-
marking, since the answer to that question is entailed by, and hence not logically
independent of, the question (64a) answers.[39]

So the assumption that only the focus within the non-CT part of the sentence
introduces alternatives has the advantage that it leads to a direct explanation of
the ineffability cases (as well as the scope inversion cases, see Section 9.4.1), while
no such explanation is forthcoming if CT-alternatives are derived by introducing
rheme-alternatives wholesale, as done in Steedman (2014).

The reason I wanted to clarify these properties in some more detail is that they
point towards important differences between the kind of intonational meanings
assumed for CT vis-à-vis the other kinds discussed in this chapter. First, the
semantics of CT operates on alternative values, not the ordinary meaning, of the
sentences they occur in, whereas all other intonational meanings discussed in this
chapter operate on the ordinary meanings of the constituents they mark (or, in
the case of Truckenbrodt, 2012, a single contextually salient meaning), orthogonal,
as it were, to the interpretation of focussing (this holds regardless of whether

---

[39] Note that for Büring (1997b, 2003), these CT-Alternatives only result if ⟨alle⟩ alone, not ⟨alle
Politiker⟩, is CT-marked. In the alternative, we would actually have an argument here for Steedman's
(2014) position that CT-alternatives are derived from the F-alternatives of the theme, or, put differently,
that Büring's CTs are the counterpart of Steedman's foci *within the rheme*, rather than the rheme itself.
As noted in the main text, it is not easy to tease these positions apart, and not much appears to hinge
on it.

F-alternatives are relevant within the rheme only—Büring's (2003) position—or within the theme only—Steedman's (2014)—or both).

Second, the interpretation of CTs in terms of alternative questions has to happen on a level higher than the CT-marking itself, that is an entire clause, at least if the above conjecture, that the F-alternatives within the rheme are relevant for their calculation, is correct. That is, CT-meaning cannot be computed on the meaning of the CT-marked constituent alone, but only on a larger "CT-domain," analogous to F-domains. This again is different for the intonational meanings proposed elsewhere, and the CT-interpretation argued for in Steedman (2014).

9.4.4 Realization of CT

Discussions such as Steedman (2014) center around cases in which CTs are realized in a separate Intonational Phrase ending in L⁻ H%. It is likely, though, that they are often realized less elaborately, say, as an intermediate phrase.

The other identifiable component, according to Steedman (2014) and others before him, is the use of rising accents—L+H* L*+H—as opposed to plain H* and falling ones (note that these are the 'scale-evoking' accents in Pierrehumbert and Hirschberg, 1990).[40]

How reliable are these prosodic distinctions? Hedberg and Sosa (2007) coded recordings of a TV talk show for information structural category, among them focus, contrastive focus, and contrastive topic (plus old, or "ratified" topic, and new, or unratified, topic), and, independently, 210 of these (42 of each IS category) for intonation, using a slightly modified ToBI system. They were interested in whether (contrastive) topics are reliably differentiated from foci by intonation. They found absolutely no correlation between occurrences of the entire tune (L+)H*L⁻H% and CTs (rather, these were almost exclusively found on foci). As for pitch accent type, their data show that L+H marked CTs are twice as common as L+H marked neutral foci (12:6); however, no corresponding discrepancy is found among the H* accents (24:28, or 1 CT for every 1.16 foci).[41] Generally, CT were found to be marked H* twice as often as L+H. Whether this result is due to inadequate criteria for the coding of IS categories, or should lead us, in the words of Hedberg and Sosa (2007: 119), to "deny that there is any prosodic category as distinctive as a 'topic accent' as opposed to a 'focus accent' " must remain open for further investigation.

---

[40] Steedman (2014), Vallduví and Engdahl (1996), Gundel (1999), and Gundel and Fretheim (2004) all opt for L+H*, whereas Pierrehumbert (1980) assumes H*; where phrase and boundary tones are discussed, they are unequivocally L⁻H%.

[41] H* is the aggregate of Hedberg and Sosa's (2007) H*, H*+L and H*+!H. Pooling plain foci and contrastive foci, the differences get even smaller (.71 L+H foci for each L+H CT, 1 H* CT for every 1.04 H* foci).

The table in this note shows how many instances of each accent type were coded as CTs, Focus and contrastive focus, respectively (missing % were coded as non-contrastive topics).

	H*(+L/!H)		L+H*		L*+H		(H+)L*		no acc.	
contr.topic	24	22%	10	24.4%	2	40%	1	5%	5	14.7%
plain focus	28	25.7%	6	14.6%	0	0%	8	40%	0	0%
contr.focus	23	21.1%	11	26.8%	0	0%	7	15%	1	2.9%

Braun (2005, 2006) reports on a number of production and perception experiments on German CTs. These studies compared the accent on a clause initial subject in a contrastive condition like (65a), to a non-contrastive condition like (65b).

(65)   a. Malaysia and Indonesia are neighboring countries in the South China Sea. [...] In Indonesia, tourism is very important and many people work in this sector. **The Malaysians** *live off of agriculture.*

       b. Many Europeans don't know much about Malaysia. [...] Malaysia is not a highly technological country. **The Malaysians** *live off of agriculture.*

While the perception experiments did not yield clear results, the production experiments showed three significant differences between the contrastive and non-contrastive condition: in the contrastive condition, the initial constituent (‹the *Malaysians*› in (65)) was longer, had a higher pitch excursion and a later peak. In both conditions, the high peak was reached *after* the stress syllable, which means neither qualifies as a proper L+H* according to GToBI labeling conventions, so it is not uncontroversial how to analyze the difference qualitatively.

In addition, (!)H+L* is the preferred nuclear accent (i.e. the accent on ‹*agriculture*› in (65)) after a CT by more than two to one, whereas (!)H* and (!)H+L* were used equally frequently in the non-contrastive condition.

In contradistinction to the English (L+)H*L⁻H% pattern, German CTs are not usually characterized as intonational, or even intermediate, phrases of their own. Rather, they are frequently described as a HAT or BRIDGE pattern, that is, as involving no significant pitch drop, and no further pitch accents, between the rising CT accent and the falling focus accent.[42] This is schematized in (66) for an example from Mehlhorn (2001), similar to example (55) above.[43]

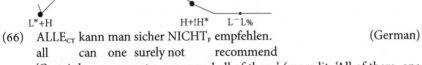

L*+H   H+!H*   L⁻L%

(66)   ALLE_CT kann man sicher NICHT_F empfehlen.   (German)
       all   can   one surely not   recommend
       'Certainly one cannot recommend all of them.' (more lit: 'All of them, one certainly cannot recommend.')

While Braun (2005, 2006) found equally few hat patterns in the contrastive and non-contrastive conditions, Mehlhorn (2001, 2002) finds them regularly in speaker's productions of various kinds of CT contexts. As in Braun's studies, the rise at the beginning of the hat pattern is also characterized by a larger pitch excursion

---

[42] Büring (1997b), Féry (1993), Grabe (1998), Jacobs (1983), Wunderlich (1991).

[43] Example originally from Jacobs (1997), annotation mine; in particular, other authors variously use H+L* or H*+L instead of H+!H* for the final accent in the hat pattern, as used here. Similar "hat" contours are apparently found also in Hungarian (Molnár, 1993, 1998) and Russian (Zybatow and Mehlhorn, 2000).

and significant lengthening of the accented word. In a subsequent perception experiment, Mehlhorn (2001, 2002) furthermore found that listeners perceive CT accents as "highlighting," but perceive no comparable highlighting with pre-nuclear accents in non-CT examples.

Summing up this subsection, it seems extremely difficult to pinpoint the exact realization of contrastive topics in English or German, though at least for the latter, there do seem to be decisive clues. This may be due to individual variation, imperfect test design, or the fact that the theoretical proposals lump together what ought to be different categories, that is, that what is described as CT is not really a unified category, and therefore lacks a uniform realization.

9.5 Chapter summary

In this chapter we have seen some strong arguments for the significance of boundary tone or tune choice, and proposals to model their meanings. For other tone choices, arguments and proposals are less convincing. While the CT-vs-focus distinction seems intuitively and pragmatically rather solid, and has seen various formal modelings, its prosodic realization, or even its existence as a natural prosodic class, is far from clear. Other purported intonational meanings are rather well-defined prosodically, but lack a sufficiently precise characterization of their meaning.

Even though autosegmental analysis of the Pierrehumbert (1980)/ToBI style has proven extremely useful in the 35 years since its inception, it seems prudent to bear in mind that the phonemic, let alone morphemic status of the tones and distinctions it assumes is very much in need of confirmation. In fact, quite a few of the empirical studies I reviewed suggest that aspects such as alignment, length, and height of excursion might play more of a role in distinguishing intonational meanings than these systems can conveniently encode.

Finally I want to point out that there are other aspects to do with tone choice which I have not dealt with in this chapter. Among those are the relative scaling of accent height: when does one high tone downstep with regard to a preceding one, when does it upstep, and when are such down/upstep patterns reset? Truckenbrodt (2002, 2004, 2007b) and Truckenbrodt and Féry (2005), for example, argue quite convincingly that upstep and its reset provide solid cues to prosodic phrasing and the structural relations between phrases (roughly, downstep signals that accents are "intermediate phrase mates," while reset signals a phrase boundary, with the amount of reset proportional to how many levels of phrases are closed at a given juncture).

I also did not discuss studies on how the relative scaling of pitch accent height within a phrase might aid in the recognition of focus size (e.g. that an upstepped nuclear pitch accent may signal narrow focus), or type (contrastive vs elaboration, etc.). I suspect that these phenomena do not strictly speaking relate to tone choice; rather, they seem to regard different phonetic *realization* of the same underlying accents, a topic that, for reasons of space, I cannot discuss in this book.

10

Association with focus

Jackendoff (1972: ch.6.5) coined the term ASSOCIATION WITH FOCUS (AwF) to capture the semantic dependency of "words such as ‹even›, ‹only›, and ‹just›" (1972: 247)—as well as later in that section, ‹merely›, ‹simply›, ‹truly›, and ‹hardly›—on intonational properties of the sentence they occur in. Unlike in the cases discussed up until now in this book—which are usually called FREE FOCUS—focus in connection with these elements (called ASSOCIATED or BOUND) FOCUS appears to have an effect on the *truth conditions* of a sentence.

This effect on the truth conditions can be appreciated introspectively in examples like (1).

(1) a. Kim only brought Harry's BOOK to the meeting.
     b. Kim only brought HARry's book to the meeting.

If Kim brought Harry's book and comb, example (1a) is false, but example (1b) may be true; if Kim brought Harry's and Jo's book, example (1b) is false, but example (1a) may be true. Leaving out ‹only› in both sentences makes them truth-conditionally equivalent (though of course they still convey different emphases).

Given that, plus the fact that the only discernible difference between examples (1a) and (1b) is the placement of the NPA, which in turn we have now had ample opportunity to see, is intimately related to grammatical focus, the obvious conclusion is that ‹only› (and, as we will see ‹also›, ‹even›, and many of their synonyms in English as well as other languages) are FOCUS SENSITIVE: They use information about the focus in fixing their contribution to the truth conditions of a sentence.

Due to its truth-conditional impact, association with focus was the first phenomenon involving intonation that caught the attention of formal semanticists; whereas highlighting, emphasis, and discourse appropriateness could safely be relegated to realms outside the responsibility of grammatical theory (such as pragmatics), AwF undeniably falls within the responsibility of semantics proper, and therefore is in need of semantic analysis (plus, as Jackendoff, 1972, discusses at length, the relation between ‹only›, ‹even›, etc. and their focus is subject to strict syntactic constraints, some of which we will discuss in Section 10.4.2, arguing for a treatment in terms of grammatical rules as well). Many of the tools we introduced in our treatment of free focus, particularly the use of alternatives and Alternative Semantics, in fact originate in analyses of association with focus.

This chapter gives an overview of the basic facts around associated focus and focus sensitive elements, as well as their modeling. We will not, however, attempt

Intonation and Meaning. First edition. Daniel Büring.

to do justice to the vast literature on the precise lexical meanings of particular focus sensitive expressions, which is outside the scope of this book.[1] As is good custom by now, we start by introducing some terminology. Elements whose truth-conditional meaning differs depending on focus (‹only›, ‹even›, etc.) are called FOCUS SENSITIVE ELEMENTS (FSEs). Another common name, at least for the core class including ‹only› and ‹even› (whose syntactic category is somewhat mysterious) is FOCUS PARTICLE or FOCUSSING PARTICLE. We will not use these terms, however, since they may invoke the connotation that these particles are themselves focussed, or somehow accomplish the focussing of other elements, which they do not; they simply depend on focus for their interpretation (and, as I will suggest in Section 10.3, focus, even when associated, still serves its normal pragmatic functions).

ASSOCIATION WITH FOCUS is the descriptive term for the relation between an FSE and the focus it semantically relates to (a focus associates with an FSE, and the FSE associates with a focus). Sometimes an associated focus is also called a bound focus. Lastly, the syntactic scope/c-command domain of an FSE occasionally coincides with the focus it associates with (‹only KIM$_F$›), but more often with a constituent *containing* that focus (‹only eat DARK$_F$ chocolate›). It is therefore imperative not to automatically equate the scope of a FSE with its focus (much less call it that), nor—to be safe—with the domain of that focus (though it is arguable that the c-command domain of an FSE and the domain of the focus it associates with are generally, perhaps always, identical; see Section 2.2 for the notion of F-domain).

10.1 Focus Sensitive Elements

The contribution of focus to the meaning of FSEs like ‹only› can be modeled using the familiar F-alternative sets. The VPs in example (1) above, repeated in (2), have as their F-alternatives properties like {brought Harry's book, brought Harry's bike, ... } and {brought Joe's book, brought Frida's book, ... }, respectively. The FSE ‹only› then relates the F-alternatives and the ordinary denotation of its complement; roughly, ‹only VP› will denote the set of individuals that have the property denoted by VP, but not other properties from VP's F-alternatives.

(2)   a. Kim only brought Harry's BOOK to the meeting.
      b. Kim only brought HARry's book to the meeting.

‹Only› (like ‹merely›, ‹just›, ‹exclusively›, and similar FSEs) is called an EXCLUSIVE FSE, since it excludes other alternatives. The FSE ‹also› (like ‹even, additionally›, and ‹too›, among others), on the other hand, is an ADDITIVE particle, since it requires that one of the alternative properties holds in addition. Thus example (3)

---

[1] Beaver and Clark (2008), Herburger (2000), Ippolito (2007, 2008), Toosarvandani (2010), Geurts and van der Sandt (2004), Wilkinson (1996), Guerzoni (2003), Klinedinst (2005), Jacobs (1983) ...

is true only if apart from bringing Harry's book (literal meaning), Kim brought someone else's book.

(3)   Kim also brought HARRY's book to the meeting.

Let us now explore the semantics of FSE and the constructions they appear in in more detail, using the most studied, ⟨only⟩, as an example. As a blueprint for the meaning of VP-attached ⟨only⟩ we can use definition (4):

(4^{DEF})   ⟨DP only VP⟩ is true if
    a. $[\![$ DP $]\!]_{\mathcal{O}}$ has the property $[\![$ VP $]\!]_{\mathcal{O}}$, and
    b. $[\![$ DP $]\!]_{\mathcal{O}}$ has no other property from a certain set of properties Π

Condition (4a) simply requires that a sentence with ⟨only⟩ implies the truth of the parallel sentence without ⟨only⟩ (often called its PREJACENT), which is straightforward and hence of little interest to us here. Condition (4b), which we may call the EXCLUSION CLAUSE, is the crucial meaning contributed by ⟨only⟩, of which three aspects will be discussed in particular now: first and foremost, how to fix Π, the Q(UANTIFICATION)-DOMAIN of ⟨only⟩, in particular in relation to focus; second, the exact formulation of the exclusion; third, how to generalize this to cases where ⟨only⟩ attaches to categories other than VP, in particular to DP.

It seems plausible to simply equate Π, the Q-domain in definition (4b), with $[\![$ VP $]\!]_{\mathcal{F}}$, the F-alternatives of ⟨only⟩'s sister. The problem with such a move, however, is that this set will often be too comprehensive. While it may be arguable that in example (2b) above (⟨Kim only brought HARry's book⟩) Kim indeed brought no one else's books at all, an analogous unrestricted exclusion seems much too strong in example (5a) (Rogers does not know her own mother??!!), and downright impossible to be true in example (5b) (surely, Holmes breathed, occupied a certain place in a certain room, looked at something, etc., etc.).

(5)   a. Rogers only knows [the DRUMmer]$_{\mathrm{F}}$.
      b. Holmes only [SMILED]$_{\mathrm{F}}$.

So the Q-domain for ⟨only⟩ should at best have to be a proper subset of $[\![$ VP $]\!]_{\mathcal{F}}$, yet it cannot just be *any* subset of $[\![$ VP $]\!]_{\mathcal{F}}$. To see why, consider the hypothetical definition (6).

(6)   INADEQUATE MEANING FOR ⟨DP only VP⟩
      There is a non-empty set $\Pi \subseteq [\![$ VP $]\!]_{\mathcal{F}}$, $\Pi \neq \{[\![$ VP $]\!]_{\mathcal{O}}\}$, and $[\![$ DP $]\!]_{\mathcal{O}}$ has no property in the set of properties Π (other than perhaps $[\![$ VP $]\!]_{\mathcal{O}}{}^{2}$)

---

[2] Note that the qualification in parentheses is not really necessary, since for any non-empty $\Pi \subseteq [\![$ VP $]\!]_{\mathcal{F}}$ that is not $\{[\![$ VP $]\!]_{\mathcal{O}}\}$ there is a Π', namely $\Pi \backslash \{[\![$ VP $]\!]_{\mathcal{O}}\}$, that yields the same truth conditions.

Definition (6) above would in effect mean that ⟨*only*⟩ should make a true sentence as long as it can exclude *some* F-alternative of its complement, which is overly permissive. For example, we would likely want to conclude from example (7) that Kim did not bring Lillith's book.

(7) (Kim was supposed to bring both Harry's and Lillith's book to the meeting. But) Kim only brought HARRY's book.

But no such thing follows, under definition (6), which would predict (7) to be true as long as there is *some* person, any person at all, whose book Kim did not bring, which is almost certainly the case. Similarly, example (5a) above would be true unless Rogers knows absolutely every person there is, when in fact it is plausibly judged to be false in case Rogers also knows the singer, the guitar player, or the percussionist.

The crucial insight here is that while it is too restrictive to identify the Q-domain of an FSE with the F-alternatives of its sister, it is too permissive to just existentially quantify over it. The best we can do is to include a mechanism that is, at least in principle, capable of narrowing the exclusion domain, while still generating truth conditions that are stronger than those expressed by existential quantification in definition (6) above; the exclusion domain should be a contextual variable, an anaphor, restricted, but not fixed, by the semantics of ⟨*only*⟩ and the focus semantic value of its complement.

So our final definitions will be those in (8) and (9).

(8^{DEF}) $[\![$ DP only(C) VP $]\!]_{\mathcal{O}} = 1$ if
  a. $[\![$ DP $]\!]_{\mathcal{O}}$ has the property $[\![$ VP $]\!]_{\mathcal{O}}$, and
  b. $[\![$ DP $]\!]_{\mathcal{O}}$ does not have any properties in $[\![$ C $]\!]_{\mathcal{O}}$
  c. where
    (i) $[\![$ C $]\!]_{\mathcal{O}} \subseteq [\![$ VP $]\!]_{\mathcal{F}}$ and
    (ii) $[\![$ C $]\!]_{\mathcal{O}}$ is a DOMAIN SET for $[\![$ VP $]\!]_{\mathcal{O}}$

(9^{DEF}) DOMAIN SET:
  for any set of meanings C, meaning $\mathcal{O}$, s.t. $\mathcal{O} \in D_\tau$ and $C \subseteq D_\tau$ for some type τ, set C is a DOMAIN SET for $\mathcal{O}$ iff
  a. C is non-empty, and
  b. all elements in C are logically independent of $\mathcal{O}$

I have separated out the specific truth conditional meaning of ⟨*only*⟩, definition (8), from the conditions on its Q-domain, definition (9); as we will see, definition (9) can be used as a general definition of Q-domains for FSEs. A "logically independent" property in the sense intended in clause (9b) is any property P which is, informally speaking, neither entailed nor contradicted by the literal meaning (see definition (20) in the appendix for details). This excludes $[\![$ VP $]\!]_{\mathcal{O}}$ and all of its hyponyms from the Q-domain, so that for example ⟨*Holmes only started to SMILE*> could not, in any context, be falsified by Holmes moving his lips.[3]

Definition (8) gives the truth conditions for a sentence containing ‹*only*›, not the meaning for ‹*only*› itself. As far as that is concerned, the general Alternative Semantic framework offers two possibilities for formulating the lexical semantics of ‹*only*›. The first is a syncategorematic rule along the lines of definition (10), a minimal adjustment of definition (8).

(10^{DEF}) $[\![\, \text{only(C) VP} \,]\!]_O$ is the property that holds of all x s.t.
    a. x has the property $[\![\, \text{VP} \,]\!]_O$,
    b. x does not have any properties in $[\![\, C \,]\!]_O$
    c. where
        (i) $[\![\, C \,]\!]_O \subseteq [\![\, \text{VP} \,]\!]_F$ and
        (ii) $[\![\, C \,]\!]_O$ is a Domain Set for $[\![\, \text{VP} \,]\!]_O$

This definition is syncategorematic because it requires access to the F-alternatives of ‹*only*›'s complement, $[\![\, \text{VP} \,]\!]_F$, an object not otherwise available to the semantic composition rules; put differently, we cannot, in this way, give a meaning for ‹*only*› alone ($[\![\, \text{only} \,]\!]_O = \dots$).[4]

The other possibility, proposed in Rooth (1992b), is to simply coindex the Q-domain variable C with the argument of a squiggle operator, as in structure (11).

(11)

    only(C_1)   VP

           VP $\sim C_1$

This allows us to remove all reference to the focus semantic value from the lexical meaning of ‹*only*›, paving the way for a categorematic definition of its meaning.

---

[3] Commonly, ‹*only*›'s exclusion clause is written as something along the lines of "for all properties P in the Q-domain, if the subject has P, P follows from $[\![\, \text{VP} \,]\!]_O$." This automatically excludes $[\![\, \text{VP} \,]\!]_O$ and its hyponym from being relevant alternatives, even if they should be in the Q-domain, and is otherwise equivalent to clause (8b).

But note that this makes it harder to enforce that the Q-domain contain any "substantially different" property from $[\![\, \text{VP} \,]\!]_O$, since the requirement that it contain at least one element (other than $[\![\, \text{VP} \,]\!]_O$) could now be met by any number of properties entailed by $[\![\, \text{VP} \,]\!]_O$. So in order to make sure that the universal quantification does not run empty, we still need the notion of logical independence, in which case we might as well keep the exclusion clause simple.

[4] The variable C need not, in principle, be part of this definition. One could change the syntax to that in (ia), with ‹*only VP*› interpreted as in (ib).

(i) a. C b. $[\![\, \text{only VP} \,]\!]_O =$
         only VP $\lambda C.\lambda x.[\![\, \text{VP} \,]\!]_O(x) = 1 \,\&\, \neg \exists p[p \in [\![\, C \,]\!]_O \,\&\, p(x) = 1]$,
                                 provided that $[\![\, C \,]\!]_O$ is a Domain Set for $[\![\, \text{VP} \,]\!]_O$

We continue the more standard syntax in definition (8) in the main text.

(12^{DEF}) $[\![$ only $]\!]_\mathcal{O} = \lambda \mathcal{C}_{\{\langle e,t \rangle\}}.\lambda p_{et}.\lambda x_e.$

      a. $p(x)$ is true,

      b. x has none of the properties in $\mathcal{C}$, and

      c. $\mathcal{C}$ is a Domain Set for p

A type in braces, like $\{\langle e,t \rangle\}$ in definition (12) is an *ad hoc* notation for a *set* of meanings, here a set of meanings in D_{et}; generally, $D_{\{\tau\}} = \text{POW}(D_\tau)$ (the POWER SET of D_τ) for any regular (i.e. non-$\{...\}$) type τ. This will be used for F-alternatives throughout: Generally type $\{\tau\}$ is the type of the focus semantic value of an expression of type τ.[5]

If ‹*only*› is truly F-sensitive, and we will review arguments that it is in Section 10.3, the presence of a $\sim C$ immediately below ‹*only*›, and coindexation of C with ‹*only*›'s Q-domain variable in structure (11) must be obligatory; Rooth (1992b: 111f) calls this the "intermediate theory," since a lexical entry can still indirectly require access to a focus semantic value (by way of requiring a coindexed $\sim C$). If this were optional, we would have what Rooth (1992b: 108ff) calls a "strong theory," on which ‹*only*›'s Q-domain is contextually supplied (by the anaphoric Q-domain variable), while the relation to focus is a side-effect of—optionally—coindexing the Q-domain variable with an F-variable (i.e. one introduced by $\sim$). We will return to the choice between these options in Section 10.3.

Assuming a denotation for ‹*only*› along the lines of definition (12), let us finally turn to the question of ‹*only*›'s semantic category. As mentioned at the outset of this section, ‹*only*› may attach to other syntactic categories than VP, most notably DP.

(13)   Meyers noticed only the FOOD.

DP-initial ‹*only*›, too, associates with a focus within its syntactic sister. This seems trivial in a case like (13), but with complex DPs, a clear semantic effect of focus can be discerned.

(14)   a. Only young DOGS can learn this trick.

        b. Only YOUNG dogs can learn this trick.

Example (14a) excludes that other animals can learn this trick (either *all* other animals, or just other young animals, depending on the size of the focus, see Section 10.2), whereas (14b) excludes that other (presumably old) *dogs* can learn this trick.

We will allow for ‹*only*› to attach to any category of a conjoinable type (see Section 3.5.2 above), that is a type that "ends in" t. To achieve this, we start with a propositional meaning for ‹*only*›, definition (15) below, from which the other

---

[5] Since we are using type t for the type of propositional expressions, i.e. $D_t = \{0,1\}^W$, it would be disingenuous to use a functional type like $\langle\langle e,t\rangle,t\rangle$ for focus semantic values, since the usual set/characteristic function equivalence does not hold with this definition of D_t. Furthermore, whereas regular denotations may be partial functions, modeling presuppositions, this would be a useless possibility when characterizing F-alternative sets.

meanings are derived by definition (16) (recall that t is the type of propositions, not truth values; s is the type of possible worlds, that is, $D_s = W$, and $D_t = \{1,0\}^W$).

(15^{DEF}) $[\![$ only $]\!]_O = \lambda C_{\{t\}}.\lambda p_t.\lambda w_s.$ all propositions in C are false in w, and
  a. $p(w)$ is true, and
  b. C is a Domain Set for p

(16^{DEF}) if Ω is a denotation for ‹only› (‹also›,...) of type $\langle\{\tau_1\}, \langle\tau_1, \tau_1\rangle\rangle$, with τ_1 any conjoinable type, then so is
  $\lambda C_{\{<\tau_2,\tau_1>\}}.\lambda p_{\langle\tau_2,\tau_1\rangle}.\lambda x_{\tau_2}.\Omega(\{a(x) \mid a \in C\})(p(x))$

See the appendix for demonstration.

Appendix: We now show how to apply definition (16) to the meaning in (15) to derive denotations for ‹only› that may attach to VP, (17), transitive verbs, (18), and generalized quantifiers, (19).

(17) **VP-‹only›:** instantiate Ω in definition (16) with the meaning for ‹only› in (15) (type $\langle\{t\}, \langle t, t\rangle\rangle$), and τ_2 with e:
  a. $\lambda C_{\{(et)\}}.\lambda p_{(et)}.\lambda x_e.[\![$ only $]\!]_O(\{a(x) \in D_t \mid a \in C\})(p(x))$
  b. $\lambda C_{\{(et)\}}.\lambda p_{(et)}.\lambda x_e.\lambda w_s.$ all propositions $a(x), a \in C$, are false in w, and
    (i) $p(x)(w) = 1$, and
    (ii) $\{a(x) \in D_t \mid a \in C\}$ is a domain set for $p(x)$

(18) **V$_{\text{tr}}$-‹only›:** now instantiate Ω with (17b) (type $\langle\{\langle e,t\rangle\}, \langle\langle e,t\rangle, \langle e,t\rangle\rangle\rangle$), and τ_2 with e again:
  a. $\lambda R_{\{(e,et)\}}.\lambda r_{(e,et)}.\lambda y_e.[(17b)](\{b(y) \in D_{<e,t>} \mid b \in \mathcal{R}\})(r(y))$
  b. $\lambda R_{\{(e,et)\}}.\lambda r_{(e,et)}.\lambda y_e.[\lambda C_{\{(et)\}}.\lambda p_{(et)}.\lambda x_e.\lambda w_s.$ all propositions $a(x), a \in C$, are false in w, and
    (i) $p(x)(w)$ is true, and
    (ii) $\{a(x) \in D_t \mid a \in C\}$ is a domain set for $p(x)$
  $](\{b(y) \in D_{<e,t>} \mid b \in \mathcal{R}\})(r(y))$
  c. $\lambda R_{\{(e,et)\}}.\lambda r_{(e,et)}.\lambda y_e.[\lambda p_{(et)}.\lambda x_e.\lambda w_s.$ all propositions $a(x), a \in \{b(y) \in D_{<e,t>} \mid b \in \mathcal{R}\}$, are false in w, and
    (i) $p(x)(w)$ is true, and
    (ii) $\{a(x) \in D_t \mid a \in \{b(y) \in D_{<e,t>} \mid b \in \mathcal{R}\}\}$ is a domain set for $p(x)$
  $](r(y))$
  d. $\lambda R_{\{(e,et)\}}.\lambda r_{(e,et)}.\lambda y_e.\lambda x_e.\lambda w_s.$ all propositions $a(x), a \in \{b(y) \in D_{<e,t>} \mid b \in \mathcal{R}\}$, are false in w, and
    (i) $r(y)(x)(w)$ is true, and
    (ii) $\{a(x) \in D_t \mid a \in \{b(y) \in D_{<e,t>} \mid b \in \mathcal{R}\}\}$ is a domain set for $r(y)(x)$
  e. $\lambda R_{\{(e,et)\}}.\lambda r_{(e,et)}.\lambda y_e.\lambda x_e.\lambda w_s.$ all propositions $b(y)(x), b \in \mathcal{R}$, are false in w, and
    (i) $r(y)(x)(w)$ is true, and
    (ii) $\{b(y)(x) \in D_t \mid b \in \mathcal{R}\}$ is a domain set for $r(y)(x)$

(19) **Generalized Quantifier** ‹*only*›: instantiate Ω in definition (16) with the meaning for ‹*only*› in (15) again (type $\langle\{t\},\langle t,t\rangle\rangle$), and τ_2 with <e,t>:

    a. $\lambda\mathcal{G}_{\{\langle\langle e,t\rangle,t\rangle\}}.\lambda g_{\langle\langle e,t\rangle,t\rangle}.\lambda P_{\langle e,t\rangle}.[\![\,only\,]\!]_{\bigcirc}(\{a(P)\in D_t\mid a\in\mathcal{G}\})(g(P))$

    b. $\lambda\mathcal{G}_{\{\langle\langle e,t\rangle,t\rangle\}}.\lambda g_{\langle\langle e,t\rangle,t\rangle}.\lambda P_{\langle e,t\rangle}.[\lambda C_{\{t\}}.\lambda p_t.\lambda w_s.$ all propositions in C are false in w, and

        (i) $p(w)$ is true, and

        (ii) C is a Domain Set for p

    $](\{a(P)\in D_t\mid a\in\mathcal{G}\})(g(P))$

    c. $\lambda\mathcal{G}_{\{\langle\langle e,t\rangle,t\rangle\}}.\lambda g_{\langle\langle e,t\rangle,t\rangle}.\lambda P_{\langle e,t\rangle}.[\lambda p_t.\lambda w_s.$ all propositions in $\{a(P)\in D_t\mid a\in\mathcal{G}\}$ are false in w, and

        (i) $p(w)$ is true, and

        (ii) $\{a(P)\in D_t\mid a\in\mathcal{G}\}$ is a Domain Set for p

    $](g(P))$

    d. $\lambda\mathcal{G}_{\{\langle\langle e,t\rangle,t\rangle\}}.\lambda g_{\langle\langle e,t\rangle,t\rangle}.\lambda P_{\langle e,t\rangle}.\lambda w_s.$ all propositions $a(P), a\in\mathcal{G}$, are false in w, and

        (i) $g(P)(w)$ is true, and

        (ii) $\{a(P)\in D_t\mid a\in\mathcal{G}\}$ is a Domain Set for $g(P)$

Note, incidentally, that the Domain Set relation will always end up being checked on (sets of) propositions, so that we can define the notion of logical independence straightforwardly as

(20^{DEF}) LOGICAL INDEPENDENCE

    for any two propositions p_1, p_2, p_1 is logically independent of p_2 iff p_2 entails neither p_1 nor the negation of $p_1(\neg[p_1\subseteq p_2]\ \&\ \neg[p_1\subseteq W-p_2])$

10.2 Probing focus size with Focus Sensitive Elements

Given their truth conditional effects, FSEs can be a useful tool—in addition to questions and contrastive targets—for diagnosing the exact location and size of a focus, independent of intonation. The different types of FSEs in turn lend themselves to different aspects of such a diagnosis.

10.2.1 Detecting maximal focus size: <also>

Using the resources developed in Section 10.1, we can render the denotation of ‹*also*›, to a reasonable approximation, as in definition (21):

(21) $[\![\,also\,]\!]_{\bigcirc} = \lambda C_{\{t\}}.\lambda p_t.\lambda w_s.p(w)$ is *true*, and

    a. C is a Domain Set for p, and

    b. some proposition in C is true in w

(I give only the propositional meaning here, from which all other required types of meanings can be derived by definition (16) above.) Given this kind of additive semantics, the focus associated with ‹*also*› co-determines the kind of thing that has to hold in the context. Particularly, the narrower that focus, the more specific that contextual requirement will be.

For an illustration, note that example (3) above, repeated in (22), is not true if Kim just brought Harry's book and Sam's computer. Kim *has* to have brought someone else's *book*.

(22)   Kim also brought HARRY's book to the meeting.

This clearly indicates that the focus in example (22) is on ‹Harry›, not on ‹Harry's book› (to which Sam's computer would be a legitimate alternative). Thus the additional truth conditional meaning introduced by ‹also› serves as a probe into the actual size of the focus.

That the focus in example (22) is necessarily narrow, on ‹Harry› and nothing else, is actually predicted, if we assume—along with all of the literature that I am aware of—that the relation between an associated focus and accenting is the same as between free foci and accenting: The focus associated with ‹also› must be a constituent within which ‹Harry› receives the last pitch accent by default accenting (i.e. by and large it is the rightmost content word). The only such constituent is the possessive DP ‹Harry's› itself.

This is different in example (23) below. Here, the NPA bearing ‹book› is rightmost within the NP ‹book› and within the DP ‹Harry's book› so a focus ambiguity is predicted.

(23)   Kim also brought Harry's BOOK to the meeting.

And indeed, (23) is clearly true if, apart from Harry's book, Kim brought Sam's computer, but no other possessions of Harry's, to the meeting. In other words, we can confirm, using ‹also›, that the restrictions on F-projection with associated focus parallel those observed in free focus examples.

Strictly speaking, we can not confirm semantically that narrow focus on ‹book› is an option in example (23). Whenever the sentence is true on its narrow focus reading—Kim brought something else of Harry's—it is also true on its wider, DP-focus reading—Kim brought something else, period. But in order to confirm that there is a narrow focus reading, we would need a scenario in which *it* is true, but the wider focus reading is false, which is impossible using just ‹also›. In general, ‹also› can be used to detect what the *maximal* size (the widest F-projection) of a focus based on a given accent pattern is (because that gives us the least specific restriction on what else has to hold true), but not what its minimal size is.

10.2.2 Detecting minimal focus size: <only>

As one might suspect, this is different for exclusive particles like ‹only›. Consider again example (1a), repeated here.

(24)   Kim only brought Harry's BOOK to the meeting.

If the focus were narrow, on ‹book› only, example (24) should be judged true as long as Kim refrained from bringing other things of Harry's; she might have brought other, non-Harry-related things, like Sam's computer. If the focus could only be wider, on ‹Harry's book›, the sentence should be false as long as she brought anything else whatsoever. Generally, speakers agree that example (24) *can* be judged true, even if Kim brought Sam's computer, so it looks as if we can confirm here that the focus may be narrow. Generally, due to its excluding semantics, ‹only› should be a good tool to detect the *minimal* size of focus based on an accent pattern (whereas it cannot tell us anything about the maximal size).

It might seem rather moot to discuss a probe to detect minimum focus size for a given accenting: while quite arguably there are cases in which an accent on a particular terminal cannot project focus beyond a certain constituent (which underlies the entire concept of F-projection rules, see Section 4.4 above), and for which a *maximum* size detector such as ‹also› is useful, there are no known claims to the effect that, ever, the focus indicated by an accent could *not* be as small as the accented word itself (or even smaller, see Section 5.5 above). As we will see in Section 10.5.1, however, it is in some cases crucial to find out whether a focus is narrow or not, so we should keep ‹only› in our toolbox, if only perhaps for just that occasion.

10.3 FSE and pseudo-FSEs

10.3.1 Strong, weak, and intermediate theories of AwF

We have already touched, in Section 10.1, on the question of how an FSE gets access to the F-alternatives of its complement. Following Rooth (1992b: sec. 9) we distinguished imaginable theories according to their restrictiveness or predictive strength. Rooth's complete taxonomy of terms is given in (25), explicated to the best of my understanding.[6]

(25)   **Weak theories:** Focus semantic values are freely available to semantic composition, just like ordinary semantic values. Focus sensitivity is just a property of the lexical meaning of certain words.

---

[6] It is clear what the technical difference between weak and intermediate theories is: the latter always require a ~ to get focus semantic values to interact with the compositional semantics (reducing, along the way, the number of syncategorematic rules needed to one, the rule interpreting ~). It is less clear, what empirical consequences this has, if in turn specific lexical items like ‹only› can subcategorize, as Rooth puts it, for a contextual variable plus its coindexing with an F-variable. I assume in (25) that at least the use of ~, unlike direct lexical access to focus semantic values (as in a weak theory), entails that focus is *also* anaphoric, though this is not the case in the technical implementation Rooth gives (see in particular def. (42) in Rooth, 1992b: 95). In Rooth (1996c: 214), at least, the requirement that a variable introduced by ~ have a "discourse antecedent" is imposed as an additional condition, suggesting that this need not always be the case. In that case, weak and intermediate theories may turn out to be empirically indistinguishable. Since what matters for us here is the difference between weak and intermediate theories, on the one hand, and strong theories, on the other, we will not dwell on this distinction further.

Intermediate theories: Focus semantic values are always mediated through the use of $\sim$, complete with the restrictions on it: foci require an F-variable, which needs to be contextually valued, etc. However, certain lexical items may, as a lexical property, require coindexation of their Q-domain variable with a nearby F-variable

Strong theories: The only use focus semantic values are ever put to is pragmatic focussing, modeled by $\sim$. There are no truly FSE, and no (obligatory) association with focus.

Adopting a weak or intermediate theory implies a significant change in what we might call the basic conception of compositional semantics: that the ordinary (truth-conditional) meaning of a complex expression is determined based on the ordinary meanings of its parts (and their mode of combination). Weak and intermediate theories instead allow an FSE to "look at" its sister's F-alternatives (in addition to its sister's ordinary meaning).

In strong theories, there are no FSEs, only context-sensitive elements. The only element that can ever "associate" with focus is the squiggle, or put more neutrally: the only effect focus can have on meaning is in the form of a contextual appropriateness condition like GIVENness. There is only free focus.

Given that the existence of free focus and its pragmatic effects is uncontroversial, the most parsimonious theory would appear to be one that eliminates bound focus entirely, reducing its effect to free focus effects. This would be a strong theory of focus in general, in the sense of (25).

10.3.2 On strong theories

There are various attempts in the literature to pursue a strong theory of focus. They all assume that ‹only›, ‹also›, etc. are in fact *context sensitive*, not focus sensitive. Put differently, the coindexing of the Q-domain variable with a F-variable is entirely optional; in principle, the Q-domain variable can get its value independently of the F-variable from the context.

Let us call this a CONTEXTUAL THEORY OF FSEs. The apparent effect of association with focus, on such a contextual theory, comes about in an indirect way: the meaning of ‹also› (and analogously ‹only›, etc.) refers to one or more contextually salient properties (which, also, hold true). As before, we assume independently that (contrastive) focus targets contextually salient meanings. If both focus and FSE (which, of course, on the contextual theory would be merely *pseudo*-FSEs) happened to use the same contextually salient meaning, we might wrongly get the impression that the FSE uses the F-alternatives themselves as a semantic argument.[7] For illustration, consider (26).

(26) a. (Kim danced with Sam.) Then she asked JO for a dance.
      b. (Kim danced with Sam.) She also asked JO for a dance.

---

[7] Such an approach to FSEs has been proposed at least as early as Taglicht (1984); later, more formal elaborations include (for various elements) Büring (1994), von Fintel (1994), Martí (2002), Roberts (1996), Schwarzschild (1997b) a.o.

To explain the focussing in (26a), we would assume that there is a contextually salient proposition of the form 'Kim asked x for a dance.' By assumption, the previous utterance makes such a proposition salient, because dancing with Sam contextually implies that Kim asked Sam for a dance.

Given this much, it seems safe to assume that the property 'ask Sam for a dance,' too, is contextually salient after the utterance of ‹Kim danced with Sam›. Context-sensitive ‹also› in (26b) then picks up that property and expresses that Kim asked Jo for a dance (literal meaning of VP) and that Kim asked Sam for a dance (contextually salient property). Thus the contextual theory of FSEs.

To complete such a theory, something has to be said about examples without context, such as (27).

(27)   Kim only asked JO for a favor.

Presented with (27) in isolation, we have no problem deducing that it implies that Kim didn't ask anyone other than Jo for a favor, that is, that the relevant properties to exclude are of the form 'ask x for a favor.' But since there is no context here, isn't that a strong argument *against* a contextual theory of FSEs?

Before concluding that, it is worthwhile noting that (27) with the accent pattern indicated is hardly an out-of-the-blue sentence. While no context is *given*, it still seems plausible to claim that some rather specific context needs to be *accommodated* in order to make sense of the accent pattern (this would hold regardless of whether ‹only› is present). Guided by something like the Contrastive Focus Rule (or the F-condition that comes with $\sim$), a hearer can conclude from the accenting alone that properties like 'ask x for a favor' must be (assumed to be) contextually salient, and accommodate a context in which they are. Since intonation is the only clue (27) gives about the context, and since ‹only›, like the accenting, requires some contextually salient properties (to exclude), one then proceeds to identify ‹only›'s exclusion domain with the contextual alternatives indicated by the focus. Put differently, since marked accent patterns give a rather detailed characterization of what must be assumed to be salient in the context, accent patterns provide a welcome cue for accommodating a context when forced to interpret ‹only› without one. Based on this reasoning, the contextual theory predicts that the apparent focus sensitivity of ‹only› should indeed be particularly striking *without* an explicit context. The more explicit a context is given, the greater the chances that ‹only› can be interpreted without considering focussing.

10.3.3 Focus sensitivity vs context sensitivity

A major argument for the contextual theory of FSEs would show that a focus in the scope of an FSE is not strictly speaking necessary. I sketch here an argument from Beaver and Clark (2003) showing that this is indeed the case for the adverbial ‹always›.[8] To appreciate the argument, note first the semantic similarity between ‹only› and ‹always›:[9]

---

[8] Such quantificational adverbs were analyzed as F-sensitive in Rooth (1985) and Krifka (1992); the first work to argue for a contextual approach to these seems to be von Fintel (1994).

[9] Beaver and Clark's (2003) example (1).

(28)   a. Sandy always feeds [FIDO]$_F$ Nutrapup.
       b. Sandy only feeds [FIDO]$_F$ Nutrapup.

As expected, (28b) means that Sandy has no properties of the form 'feed x Nutrapup' than that of feeding Fido Nutrapup. Sentence (28a) appears to mean more or less the same. Shifting the accent pattern brings about the expected shift in meaning, again for both ‹*always*› and ‹*only*›.

(29)   a. Sandy always feeds Fido [NUTRAPUP]$_F$.
       b. Sandy only feeds Fido [NUTRAPUP]$_F$.

It is not claimed that ‹*always*› and ‹*only*› are synonymous, only that they appear to show the same kind of focus sensitivity. Roughly, ‹*always*›'s meaning could be characterized as in (30).

(30^{DEF})   ‹*always VP*› denotes the property that is true of an individual x if, whenever any one of the properties in Π holds of x, that property is the ordinary denotation of VP.

According to an association with focus theory, the set Π in (30) is the set of VP's F-alternatives. According to a contextual theory, it would be a contextually given set of properties.

Exemplifying with (29a), that sentence would be true if whenever Sandy has any property like 'feed Fido x', she has the property 'feed Fido Nutrapup' (see e.g. Rooth, 1985, for an analysis along these lines). The question now is whether the set of properties 'feed Fido x' gets into the meaning of example (29a) by virtue of being the alternative set to VP, or by being (reconstructed to be) contextually salient.

Beaver and Clark (2003) proceed to show that indeed the variable Π in (30), that is, the semantic restriction of ‹*always*›, can be set regardless of focus under the right circumstances, such as those in (31).[10]

(31)   a. Mary always remembers to go to CHURCH.
       b. This is the cake I always order.

The natural interpretation for example (31a) says that whenever it is time for Mary to go to church, she remembers to do so. Setting the Q-domain of ‹*always*› (Π in definition (30) above) according to the accent pattern (which indicates a focus on ‹*church*› or some larger constituent containing it) yields wrong truth conditions like 'whenever Mary remembers something/to go somewhere, it is to go to church'.[11]

---

[10] Example (31a) is Beaver and Clark's (2003: (33)), example (31b) is loosely based on their examples (49) and (50).

[11] Beaver and Clark (2003) relate the actual reading to what they call the "factive use of the verb ‹*remember*›," presumably that ‹*remember to Q*› presupposes that Q needs to be done. So in example (31a) we get the presupposition that Mary is supposed to go to church, which serves to restrict ‹*always*›: whenever she is supposed to go to church, she remembers to do so.

Similarly, example (31b) is understood to mean that whenever I order something (in this cafe), it is this cake; this seems to be the case regardless of which element bears the NPA. For this reading to obtain, the alternative properties restricting ⟨*always*⟩ would have to be 'I order *x*' or 'I order an *x* cake.' But there is no focus on the object in the scope of ⟨*always*⟩; indeed, the object is not even in the syntactic sister of ⟨*always*⟩, so we cannot say that ⟨*always*⟩ in example (31b) above associates with the F-alternatives of its complement (see Section 10.4.2 for more on this reasoning).

It seems, then, that ⟨*always*⟩ presents a nice picture of what a *context* sensitive adverbial looks like: the apparent effect of focussing on the interpretation of ⟨*always*⟩ can be overridden by other elements that give cues to the context, such as presuppositional verbs or marked constructions like ⟨*this is . . .*⟩ in example (31b) above.

Strikingly, this picture is not at all shared by ⟨*only*⟩.

(32)   a. Mary only remembers to go to CHURCH.
       b. This is the cake I only order.

What is clear immediately is that examples (32a) and (32b) do not mean at all what examples (31a) and (31b) mean. Indeed, example (32a) means exactly what slavish association with focus would predict: That the only thing Mary remembers (to go to) is (going to) church. The effect is even more striking in example (32b): There is only one element in the syntactic scope of ⟨*only*⟩, the verb ⟨*order*⟩. And invariably one has to associate *that* with ⟨*only*⟩, yielding the rather implausible meaning that the speaker does not do anything else with that cake (e.g. eat it). Note that pragmatic consideration hardly favors this reading of example (32b), so if another construal were available in principle (as it was with ⟨*always*⟩ in example (31b)), it would probably be perceived. That only the rather weird reading is available strongly suggests that ⟨*order*⟩ in example (32b) is interpreted as the focus associated with ⟨*only*⟩—despite pragmatic pressure, and despite the fact that nothing in the written form of example (32b) marks it as accented—because it is a *grammatical* fact that ⟨*only*⟩ needs to associate with a focus within its syntactic sister.

Beaver and Clark (2003, 2008), using a battery of diagnostics, conclude that ⟨*only*⟩'s behavior is shared by ⟨*also*⟩, ⟨*even*⟩, and many of their synonyms, whereas frequency adverbs like ⟨*often*⟩, ⟨*usually*⟩, ⟨*mostly*⟩, and ⟨*never*⟩ pattern with ⟨*always*⟩. They call the former, but not the latter, "focus functional." Here, we continue to use the term "focus sensitive" for elements like ⟨*only*⟩, ⟨*also*⟩, and ⟨*even*⟩, which we take to be grammatically focus sensitive, and not amenable to the otherwise more parsimonious (and hence more attractive) strong, contextual theory. We may refer to ⟨*always*⟩ and similar adverbs as "pseudo-FSE," but these will not concern us in the remainder of this book.

10.3.4 Other instances of (apparent) focus sensitivity

Apart from particles like ⟨*only*⟩ and adverbs like ⟨*always*⟩, many other lexical items or constructions have been analyzed, at one point or another, as focus sensitive.

These include counterfactual conditionals (famously in Dretske, 1972, taken up in Rooth, 1985, 1996a among others), superlatives (Heim, 1985, 2000; Szabolcsi, 1986), adnominal quantifiers like ‹most› (Eckardt, 1999; Geilfuß, 1993; de Hoop, 1995; de Hoop and Solà, 1995; Herburger, 2000), the adverb ‹preferably› (Krifka, 1991/2: 43), ‹but› (Toosarvandani, 2010; Umbach, 2001), and ‹let alone› (Toosarvandani, 2010), among various others.

Several of these cases have received alternative analyses in terms of context-sensitivity, along the lines of the previous section, for example the adnominal quantifiers (Büring, 1996). An illustrative example is Eckardt's (2006) analysis of the German particle ‹noch›, 'yet,' which starts out hypothesizing lexical F-sensitivity of ‹noch›, but proceeds to show how that can be reduced to a sensitivity of ‹noch› to the current question under discussion.

A relatively clear case of an *apparent* FSE which turns out not to be one is sentential negation in English, which I will summarize now as an example of how to proceed on this kind of question (see also Partee, 1993). Jackendoff (1972: secs. 6.6 and 8.6) surmises that sentential negation (optionally) associates with focus, a position sometimes maintained in the subsequent literature. To illustrate the intuition, the examples in (33) would differ in meaning in that the noun ‹name› is negated in (33a), the possessive is negated in (33b), and the verb in (33c).

(33)   a. Trane didn't mention your NAME in court.
       b. Trane didn't mention YOUR name in court.
       c. Trane didn't MENtion your name in court.

Accordingly, (33a) implies that something else of the addressee's was mentioned in court, (33b) that someone else's name was, and (33c) that, while the addressee's name was not directly *mentioned* in court, it was brought up there in some other way.

It is crucial to emphasize, though, that the effect of focussing in the scope of negation, intuitively real though it may be, is not truth conditional, as can be seen in example (34).

(34)   Trane didn't $\left\{ \begin{array}{l} \text{mention your NAME} \\ \text{mention YOUR name} \\ \text{MENtion your name} \end{array} \right\}$ in court.

  Why should he $\left\{ \begin{array}{l} \text{involve you} \\ \text{mention anyone} \\ \text{bring it up} \end{array} \right\}$ at all?

Example (34) invokes no judgment of contradiction, so it is clear that the first clause cannot *entail* that, for example in (33b), Trane mentioned someone else's name. At most, we could claim that these sentences imply that the choice among the focus alternatives is under discussion, relevant, or salient. But as Rooth (1996a) aptly concludes, "this is so weak that there is no reason to adopt a logical form where

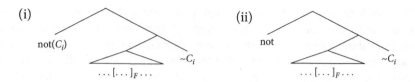

(i)   not(C_i)   ~C_i ...[...]$_F$...

(ii)   not   ~C_i ...[...]$_F$...

FIGURE 10.1   Negation (i) with, and (ii) without F-sensitivity (the latter opted for in Rooth, 1996a (and here)).

the negation has access to [the F-alternatives of its complement] as an argument. Instead, we can assume an LF with the geometry of [(ii) in Figure 10.1], where focus . . . does not interact with the negation."

What Rooth alludes to here is that an implication to the effect that the F-alternatives are salient will arise from a free focus alone (as in (ii) in Figure 10.1), with no need to associate that focus with the negation. Furthermore, on such a line of analysis, the fact that association of focus with sentential negation is, in Jackendoff's terms, optional—because the negation might itself be part of the "presupposition"—follows without further stipulation.[12] Thus in (35b), unlike (35a), the negation is itself part of the background, as in structure (35c), and no association-with-focus effect arises.

(35)   a. ([to the impatient loan shark] You can take any of these, while I'm getting the money together . . .!—) We won't take the STEreo.
        b. ([to the marshall seizing your assets:] Will you leave me something to keep in touch with the world?!—) We won't take the STEreo.
        c.

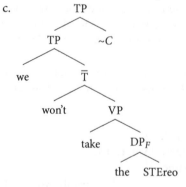

TP

TP   ~C

we   T̄

won't   VP

take   DP$_F$

the   STEreo

But why then the strong preference for "understanding" negation as F-related? Perhaps because a construal as in (35b) requires a combination of properties that is not easily obtained: An F-domain including the negation, and at the same time a rather narrow focus. Put differently, "negative" properties of the kind 'we won't take x' must be contextually salient in order to successfully value C in structure (35c), which in this case is accomplished via the question under discussion: what (which media device) will you leave me/not take? The normal strategy to accommodate

[12] See the discussion in Jackendoff (1972: 255ff).

a narrow focus under negation might likely be to take the F-domain to exclude the negation, as in (35a) (the salient question for which is 'What will you take?', which is arguably easier to accommodate as salient than the question 'What will you not take?').

The case of negation has been discussed here because it is instructive: Quite arguably, negation is *not* F-sensitive; it just, as a default in examples without context but with a narrow focus, triggers particular implicatures, namely that the corresponding *positive* question was under discussion (triggering, in turn, the quest for another, *correct* answer). The moral of this story, it seems to me, is that we should, as a rule, always explore the pragmatic route first: Couldn't the purported effect of F-sensitivity be derived from the pragmatics of focus, plus the semantics of the construction, alone? More precisely, the check list might run something like this: First, is the effect in question truly and always truth-conditional, non-cancelable? If no, could it not, as just said, be a conspiracy of lexical meanings, focus pragmatics, and world knowledge? Second, if the effect is truth conditional, could it be due to context-sensitivity—as argued for example by von Fintel (1994, 2004) and Beaver and Clark (2008) for the case of quantificational adverbs (see Section 10.3.3 above)—rather than F-sensitivity? Can the effect be canceled by cleverly disconnecting pragmatic contrast from quantificational domains, etc.? Or does it, on the other hand, show solid grammatical restrictions, as Beaver and Clark (2008) argue for ‹only› and its kin? Only, as a last resort, postulate F-sensitivity.

10.4 Odds and ends about FSEs

10.4.1 Presupposition and assertion

All FSEs imply the truth of their PREJACENT, that is, of the sentence they occur in minus their own semantic contribution. Arguably, the prejacent is *presupposed* in the case of exclusive particles like ‹only›, as suggested by examples like (36).

(36)   Did Kim only/merely/just/exclusively invite SAM to the party?

What (36) questions is the exclusivity; a 'no' answer implies that other people were invited to the party. Whether answered in the positive or in the negative (or not at all), the question itself already implies that Kim invited Sam to the party; the prejacent is thus a presupposition. The same conclusion suggests itself based on sentential negation.

(37)   Kim didn't only invite SAM to the party.

Example (37), like (36), implies that Sam was invited to the party, and negates that no one else was.

This is, remarkably, different for additive particles.

(38)   a. Did Kim also/even invite SAM to the party?
       b. Did Kim invite SAM to the party, too?

The questions in (38) imply that someone else was invited to the party, and ask whether Sam was. Likewise, the negation in (39) negates the prejacent while leaving the additive meaning untouched.

(39)   Kim didn't also invite SAM to the party.

It thus appears that with additive particles, the prejacent is asserted, while the additive meaning is presupposed, that is, the mirror image of the exclusive particles.

While this partitioning of the meaning components into assertion and presupposition then appears to be a lexical matter, it is striking that the division seems to neatly follow the line between additive and exclusive particles. An informal survey suggest that the same is true in many other languages as well. To the best of my knowledge, no explanation for this regularity has been offered in the literature.

10.4.2 Scope and domain of FSEs

At the very beginning of this chapter, I mentioned that the scope of FSEs quite regularly coincides with their syntactic c-command domain. In particular, it was shown in the discussion of DP-initial ‹only› (example (14) above) that the associated focus in this case has to be within the DP.

Relating back to the discussion of F-domains in Sections 2.3 and 7.1, we can confirm this diagnosis prosodically, using examples like (40).

(40)   Only the YOUNG dogs got SPECIAL food.

The focus associating with ‹only› in (40) is ‹young›. There is a second focus, on ‹special›, in the sentence, which is a free focus here. This can be confirmed semantically: If old dogs get ordinary food, (40) can still be true. That is, ‹only› does not exclude alternatives like 'the x dogs got y food', but only alternatives like 'the x dogs got special food.' Concomitant with that, the focus associated with ‹only› bears the last pitch accent within the subject DP—its domain—but not within the entire sentence. This accords with our generalization that focus bears the last pitch accent (or the highest stress) *within its domain*. We conclude that the focus domain of a focus associated with DP initial FSEs is the DP, that is, the sister (c-command domain) of the particle they associate with.

In fact, it holds quite generally that the domain of an associated focus is the sister of the FSE it associates with. The only clear exception to this rule in English is found with VP-initial ‹even›, as observed in Jackendoff (1972: 248ff): Unlike ‹only› and ‹just›, VP initial ‹even› can associate "backwards," with a focussed subject (Jackendoff, 1972: ex. (6.89)).

(41)   JOHN$_F$ even gave his daughter a new bicycle.

What, then, is the domain of ‹even› in this position? Note that (42), with an additional accent on ‹bicycle›, can be interpreted as synonymous with (42a) (‹even› associates with ‹bicycle›), or as synonymous with (42b), (‹even› associates either with both ‹John› and ‹bicycle›, or with the entire sentence).

(42) JOHN even gave his daughter a new BICYCLE
    a. John gave his daughter even a new bicycle.
    b. It is even the case that John gave his daughter a new bicycle.

Crucially, (42) cannot be interpreted as synonymous with (41); ‹even› cannot "ignore" the focus on ‹bicycle›. This suggests that indeed the entire sentence—not just ‹John› (as in the parallel sentence with ‹even John›)—is the domain of the focus associated with VP-initial ‹even› in (41). Any other focus within that domain—like that on ‹bicycle› in (42)—accordingly, must be interpreted as associating with ‹even› as well.

    None of this holds of other FSEs, say, ‹only›: A subject focus cannot associate with VP-initial ‹only› neither as the sole focus, (43a) (which cannot mean that only John gave his daughter a new bicycle), nor as one of several, (43b) (which cannot express that no one else gave their daughter anything).

(43) a. JOHN only gave his daughter a new bicycle.
     b. JOHN only gave his daughter a new BIcycle.

We thus conclude that with the, rather mysterious, exception of VP-initial ‹even›, the domain of an associated focus is the sister of the FSE it associates with.

    Recall from the discussion in Section 10.3 that one of Beaver and Clark's (2008) arguments for true F-sensitivity was the generalization that a focus must be within the syntactic domain of a (truly) FSE it is associated with. One example to illustrate that generalization was (32b), repeated below as (44a), along with more examples from English and German to show that it is not sufficient for ‹only/nur› to c-command the thematic position ("trace position") of the phrase it wants to associate with.

(44) a. This is the cake I only order.
       cannot mean: 'this is the cake such that I order only *it*'
    b. Dies ist die Torte, die ich nur gegessen habe.   (German)
       this is the cake that I only eaten have
       'This is the cake I only ate.' NOT 'This is the only cake I ate.'

(45) a. Which person did you only kiss?
       cannot mean: 'which is the person such that you kissed them and no one else?'
    b. Wen hast du nur geküsst?   (German)
       who have you only kissed
       'Who did you only kiss?' NOT 'Who is the only one you kissed?'

A notable exception to this generalization is found in German verb second clauses, in which a finite verb can be the associate of an FSE following it.

(46) a. Ich GUcke nur.   (German)
       I look only
       'I am just looking around (I am not about to buy anything).'

b. Ich SCHLAfe auch in diesem Zimmer.
   I   sleep   also in this   room
   'I also sleep in his room (I don't just work here).'

It appears that the position of the FSEs ⟨nur⟩ and ⟨auch⟩, 'only/also,' in such sentences systematically corresponds to the position these words would occupy in a parallel verb final clause.

(47) a. ... weil ich nur   GUCKe.   (German)
         since I only look

      b. ... obwohl ich auch in diesem Zimmer SCHLAfe.
             although I   also in this   room   sleep

Examples (46b) and (47b) are particularly instructive since in these contexts the position of ⟨auch⟩ may, for reasons of no concern to us here, be linearly separated from its focus, the verb, by a PP in the verb-end variant. In the verb second clause, (46b), the particle shows the same ordering relative to the PP (that is, the particle's position is not always sentence-final in these examples).

   Another instance of "backwards association with focus" is found with German ⟨auch⟩ (but not with the particles, corresponding to ⟨only⟩ and ⟨even⟩), which may associate with a preceding focus, as in (48a).

(48) a. MÜller schießt AUCH Tore.   (German)
         M.   shoots also goals
         'Müller, too, scores goals.'

      b. *?MÜller schießt Tore AUCH
          M.   shoots goals also
          'Goals also are shot by Müller.'

⟨Auch⟩, 'also,' in (48a) clearly associates with the subject in clause-initial position, where the sole pitch accents are on the subject and ⟨auch⟩ itself (and crucially, ⟨Tore⟩ cannot possibly be a focus). Example (48b) is there to show that, again, the thematic position of the focus appears to be relevant: a parallel construal is impossible if ⟨auch⟩ occurs in a position that is unambiguously lower than the subject's thematic position.[13]

   However, backwards AwF in example (48a) may not be contingent on fronting the focus to the initial position. Arguably, the source of (48a) is (49a)—in which ⟨auch⟩, 'also,' directly follows the subject—rather than (49b).

(49) a. Bekanntlich schießt MÜller AUCH Tore.   (German)
         as known   shoots M.   also goals
         'As is well known, Müller, too, scores goals.'

---

[13] Unlike other object DPs, bare plurals in German cannot scramble across subjects, except, marginally, if interpreted generically. Since a generic interpretation is out for pragmatic reasons in example (48b), the post-object position of ⟨auch⟩ clearly indicates that it occupies a very low position in the structure.

    b. Bekanntlich schießt auch MÜller Tore.
        as known   shoots also M.   goals
        'As is well known, Müller, too, scores goals.'

While both sentences in (49) are grammatical and appear synonymous, ‹Müller› is marked by a different kind of accent in examples (48a) and (49a) than in (49b), and, vaguely speaking, only (48a) and (49a) are pragmatically equivalent. So whatever enables backwards AwF in (49a) probably accounts (as a derivational source) for (48a) as well.[14]

    Examples like (46) may hint at a generalization along the lines of: head movement—unlike phrasal movement—does not "bleed" AwF. The case of (48a) and (49a) appears more idiosyncratic, as it applies to only one particle, ‹auch›, and probably hinges on a particular intonational marking. A larger investigation of the possibility of backwards AwF, including with English ‹even›, has, I believe, not been carried out yet.

10.4.3 Binding into focus (alternatives)

Krifka (1993, 1995) discusses cases in which the set of F-alternatives restricting a single FSE must co-vary with another expression. Our example (50) illustrates this kind of case.[15]

(50)   (Here are this year's grades, and here are the aggregate grades.)
        Most people think the aggregate grade only considers their grade from the
        PREvious year.
        (But in fact, it takes into consideration all four years.)

On its prominent reading (50) talks about people who think that their own grades from this year and the last, but not from two and more years back, go into the aggregate.[16] Figure 10.2 sketches a structure for this reading.

---

[14] A DP modified by ‹only› in English can take non-surface scope, as in (i).

(i)   They required only TWO languages to be SPOKEN.

Example (i) can mean that there are two specific languages (e.g. Spanish and Portuguese) of which active command is required. That is, ‹only› and ‹two languages› take logical scope above the intensional verb ‹required›. Still, the domain in which foci associate with ‹only›, and in which these foci must bear the final PA, is the DP, as witnessed by the following NPA on ‹spoken›, in keeping with the generalization given in the main text.

[15] Krifka's own example, (i) (ex. (25) in Krifka, 1995: 251, see also Krifka, 1993: 292ff), introduces an orthogonal complication in that the binding element, ‹every lady›, is within the scope of ‹only›.

(i)   John only introduced every lady to her partner at LEFT.

The sentence purportedly has a reading, however, on which it is falsified by John introducing even a single lady to the partner at her right, which means that ‹every lady› has to scope above ‹only› in a logical form (otherwise the sentence should only be falsified if John introduced every lady to her partners left *and* right), in which case the same configuration as in example (50) below arises.

[16] Note that the use of ‹most› virtually forces a singular dependent reading of ‹their›, as opposed to one where it refers to (some sub-group of) the people.

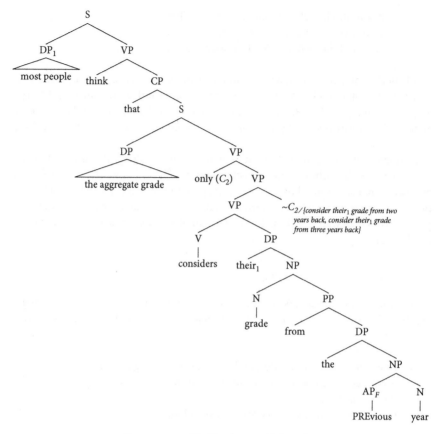

FIGURE 10.2   Binding into an F-domain.

Note that the F-alternatives of the lower VP covary with the matrix subject: $[\![\text{VP}]\!]_{\mathcal{F}} = \{\lambda x.x \text{ considers } g(1)\text{'s grade from } n \text{ years ago}| \; n \in \{1, 2, 3, 4 \ldots\}\}$, where $g(1)$ covaries with ‹*most people*›. But then for C_2 to denote a subset of these F-alternatives in each case (as required by $\sim$), the value of C_2 must itself be covarying with $g(1)$.[17] In other words, C_2 cannot just be a set of properties (regular VP meanings), which would yield the same Q-domain for ‹*only*› for each person ‹*most*› quantifies over.

To give a somewhat transparent rendering of what is needed, let us assume that the elements in C are in fact relations, not properties—something like ‘$\lambda x.\lambda y.y$ considers x's grade from n years ago.’ Furthermore, we need a class of operators that can turn a set of relations into a set of properties, call them BIA (“binding into alternatives”). The kind of representation we would get is indicated in Figure 10.3. BIA in Figure 10.3 must be defined as in (51).

---

[17] And notice that we do want a restricted set of alternatives to restrict ‹*only*› here, since we do not want ‘considering one's grades from this year’ in C_2.

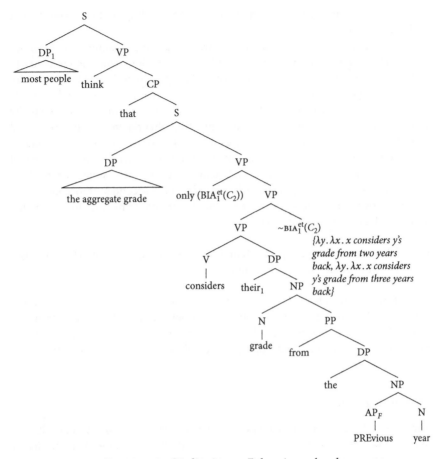

FIGURE 10.3   Binding into an F-domain, analyzed.

(51^{DEF})   for any index i, s.t. $g(i) \in D_{\tau_1}$, any type τ_2,

$$[\![\text{BIA}_i^{\tau_2}]\!]_O^g = \lambda \mathcal{C} \in D_{\{\langle \tau_1, \tau_2 \rangle\}}.\{c(g(i)) \mid c \in \mathcal{C}\}$$

Effectively, ‹BIA$_i$› is like a pronoun indexed i which combines with a F-alternative set and then combines $g(i)$, its value, with every F-alternative in that set to yield a new F-alternative set. So if $[\![C_2]\!]_O^g = \{\lambda y.\lambda x.x$ considers y's grade from two years back, $\lambda y.\lambda x.x$ considers y's grade from three years back$\}$, and $g(1) =$ Kim, then $[\![\text{BIA}_1^{\text{et}}(C_2)]\!]_O^g$ is $\{\lambda x.x$ considers Kim's grade from two years back, $\lambda x.x$ considers Kim's grade from three years back$\}$.

What is a bit awkward about this treatment is that BIA has to be applied to both occurrences of the F-variable C_2 in a structure including an FSE, as in Figure 10.3. This derives from the assumption that the C_2 that provides the Q-domain for ‹only› and the C_2 that imports the focus semantic value merely corefer, rather than one semantically binding the other. Plus we have to "custom tailor" the occurrence of

BIA to the demands of the F-domain at hand (depending on how many bound variables it contains).[18]

An alternative is to generalize to the worst case and assume that meanings in general, and F-alternatives in particular, are functions from assignments to ordinary denotations ($[\![\ ]\!]_{\mathcal{O}}$ and $[\![\ ]\!]_{\mathcal{F}}$, without a g parameter). This would require some internal re-wiring of these functions, but leave all representations the same.[19]

It may strike the reader as odd that C should at the same time be a contextually provided variable and be "bound into." But this phenomenon is not restricted to F-domain variables. Pseudo-FSEs, which we saw in Section 10.3 are arguably restricted by a contextually given (but not F-related) variable, show a parallel behavior. Thus ‹*always*› in example (52) quantifies over a set of situations in which someone paid for Hemingway's drink. ‹*Usually*› in the second sentence intuitively quantifies over the same set, only this time this set contains situations in which Toulouse-Lautrec is bought a drink.

(52)   When someone else paid, Hemingway always ordered scotch. Toulouse-Lautrec usually ordered [ABsinth]$_F$.

The set of situations here should thus be something like '*s* is a situation in which someone buys *him* a drink,' where *him* gets "re-bound" in each sentence; formally, again, the variable that provides the Q-domain for the frequency adverbs should be a function from individuals (or assignment functions) to sets of situations.

10.5 Indexed foci

The system of focus semantics used so far is UNSELECTIVE. A squiggle, or a FSE, will associate with any free focus in its c-command domain. This means in particular that no FSE or squiggle can associate with a focus across another FSE or squiggle. In Section 10.5.1 we will review some arguments that this is not empirically correct. This will lead us to a version of Alternative Semantics in which foci and FSEs are

---

[18] Notice that $[\![\ [_{VP}\text{considers their}\ldots]\ ]\!]^g_{\mathcal{F}}$ in Figure 10.3 is still a set of properties (though a different one for different gs, depending on the value of $g(i)$), not of relations; $\sim$ then "compares," for any g, the set of properties $[\![\ \text{VP}\ ]\!]^g_{\mathcal{F}}$ to the set of properties $[\![\ \text{BIA}^{et}_i\ ]\!]^g_{\mathcal{O}}$

[19] To give an idea, (i) gives a recursive definition of F-alternatives for such a system.

(i^{DEF})   ALTERNATIVE F-ALTERNATIVE CALCULATION
   a. If A is an F-marked terminal or non-terminal node of semantic type τ, then $[\![\ A\ ]\!]_{\mathcal{F}} = D_\tau{}^G, G$ the set of assignment functions
   b. otherwise (if A is not F-marked)
      1) If A is a terminal node, $[\![\ A\ ]\!]_{\mathcal{F}} = \{\lambda g'.[\![\ A\ ]\!]^{g'}_{\mathcal{O}}\}$
      2) If A is a non-branching node that dominates B, $[\![\ A\ ]\!]_{\mathcal{F}} = [\![\ B\ ]\!]_{\mathcal{F}}$
      3) for any branching node $[_A\ B\ C]$, $[\![\ A\ ]\!]_{\mathcal{F}} = \{\lambda g.b(g) \oplus c(g) \mid b \in [\![\ B\ ]\!]_{\mathcal{F}} \wedge c \in [\![\ C\ ]\!]_{\mathcal{F}}\}$, where $\oplus$ is the combination operation used in the ordinary semantic rules i.e. $[\![\ A\ ]\!]_{\mathcal{O}} = [\![\ B\ ]\!]_{\mathcal{O}}(g) \oplus [\![\ C\ ]\!]_{\mathcal{O}}(g)$.

Furthermore, we would need to redefine $[\![\ ]\!]_{\mathcal{O}}$ along parallel lines, as well as the definitions of ∃Clo and ∃F-Clo.

indexed, and selective association with focus is possible (Section 10.5.2). Additional arguments for such a semantics are presented in Section 10.5.3.

10.5.1 Nested foci

Krifka (1991/2) provides a systematic discussion of multiple foci and multiple FSEs. Of particular interest are configurations like in (53).[20]

(53)   a. John only introduced SUE to Fred.
         b. John also only introduced SUE to BILL

The meaning of (53b) can be paraphrased as in (54).

(54)   Bill, too, had Sue and no one other than Sue introduced to him (by John).

This means that ⟨*Bill*⟩ associates with ⟨*also*⟩, and ⟨*Sue*⟩ with ⟨*only*⟩. This pattern can be represented as in (55).[21]

(55)   John also, only$_2$ introduced SUE$_{F_2}$ to BILL$_{F_1}$.

Without the indexing, the focus semantic value of the VP would be 'introduce x to y'; ⟨*only*⟩ would unselectively associate with both yielding the meaning that John made no other introductions. Evidently, this is not the result we want.

   We could try to analyze (53b) as in (56).

(56)   John also$_{(1)}$ [$_{VP}$only$_{F(2)}$ introduced SUE$_{F(2)}$ to BILL]$_{F(1)}$

Note that the indices here are only for clarification. The intended association pattern would come about simply if each FSE associates with that focus that it minimally c-commands.

   Example (56) says that another thing John did was to introduce Bill to Sue and no one else. Due to the additive nature of ⟨*also*⟩, (56) should be true whenever (54) (=structure (55)) is, so we cannot construe an example that unambiguously shows that the focus of ⟨*also*⟩ is smaller, hence properly included in the domain of ⟨*only*⟩.

   But note that it would be unclear under the representation in (56) why the NPA falls on ⟨*Bill*⟩. Focus Realization predicts the nuclear accent on ⟨*Sue*⟩ in that case (since ⟨*Sue*⟩ is the sole focus of ⟨*only*⟩'s F-domain VP, and VP is the focus of the ⟨*also*⟩'s F-domain, the higher VP; if ⟨*Bill*⟩ were to bear the NPA, the greatest stress in ⟨*only*⟩'s F-domain would be on a non-focus).

   Moreover, we can construct examples with two instances of ⟨*only*⟩, which show the same configuration unambiguously.

---

[20] (Wold, 1995b: 280).

[21] Krifka (1991/2) uses indexing for illustration purposes only; his official proposal, cast in terms of structured meanings, does not need indices; see that paper for discussion.

(57) (You said that Mary only LOOKED$_F$ at the CDs you gave her.—)
No, I only said that Mary only LOOKED$_F$ at the BEATLES$_F$ CDs I gave her.
(I explicitly said that for all I know, she listened to all the Traffic albums.)

The meaning of (57) is (58a), corresponding to representation (58a-i), rather than (58b), which would be the meaning of (58b-i);

(58) a. the only things I said Mary looked at, but did not listen to, are the Beatles CDs.
(i) I only$_1$ said that Mary only$_2$ looked$_{F_2}$ at [the Beatles CDs]$_{F_1}$
b. I said that Mary looked at, but did not listen to, the Beatles CDs, and I didn't say anything else
(i) I only$_1$ said [that Mary only$_2$ looked$_{F_2}$ at the Beatles CDs]$_{F_1}$

Note that the meaning in (58b) would render the third clause in (57) contradictory since, due to the exclusive nature of ‹only›, the narrow focus version does not entail the wide scope version.

We thus take it that nested focus configurations are real, and that selective association with foci across other FSEs must be possible in principle (more configurations of nested foci appeared in our discussion of second occurrence focus in Section 7.3).

10.5.2 Formal intermezzo: a semantics for indexed foci

In this section we define a system in which foci and their operators, including ~ are indexed. This system could replace the unselective focus semantics used so far in this book; it builds on those in Kratzer (1991) and Wold (1995a, 1995b, 1996), but is more general than these.

Readers with no background in formal semantics might choose to skip this section and trust it that the indexing works in the way one intuitively expects. Furthermore, the system outlined in this section is implemented in such a way that it is "backwards compatible" with the index-less system, so that all LFs assumed so far are in fact interpretable using the new machinery.

To get indexed foci and selective association, we treat foci much like logical variables. Accordingly, the interpretation function ⟦ ⟧ now has two assignment functions: g, which assigns denotations to pronouns and traces in the usual way, and h, which assigns (alternative) denotations to focussed elements; accordingly, the focus marker F itself is indexed now.

Since foci can be of any semantic type, the focus assignment function h needs to "know" both the index on an F-marker and the semantic type of the constituent bearing it. Since the same is true for pronouns and traces, the general definition of an assignment function is as in (59).

(59^{DEF}) ASSIGNMENT FUNCTION
h is an assignment function iff it is a partial function on the set of type–number pairs s.t. for any semantic type τ, any natural number i, if $\langle i, \tau \rangle \in dom(h), h(\langle i, \tau \rangle) \in D_\tau$

The crucial definition is given in (60), which allows alternative denotations to be assigned to an F-marked element by manipulating h.

(60^{DEF})   for any expression α of type τ, any natural number n, $[\![\, \alpha_{F_n}\,]\!]^{g,h} =$
     a. $[\![\, \alpha\,]\!]^{g,h}$ if $\langle n, \tau \rangle$ is not in the domain of h,
     b. $h(\langle n, \tau \rangle)$ otherwise

By (60a), a focus can be "switched off" by removing it from the domain of the focus assignment h. Hence:

(61^{DEF})   ORDINARY MEANING
     For any expression α and assignment function g, $[\![\, \alpha\,]\!]^g_O =_{\text{def}} [\![\, \alpha\,]\!]^{g,()}$

By feeding $[\![\ ]\!]^{g,h}$ partial focus assignment functions h, we can now selectively "bind" foci. Example (62) illustrates.

(62)   John introduced Mary$_{F_1}$ to Bill$_{F_2}$.
     a. $[\![\, (62)\,]\!]^{g,()} = [\![\, (62)\,]\!]^g_O =$ John introduced Mary to Bill
     b. $[\![\, (62)\,]\!]^{g,[\langle 1, e \rangle\, \to\, \text{Sue}]} =$ John introduced Sue to Bill
     c. $[\![\, (62)\,]\!]^{g,[\langle 2, e \rangle\, \to\, \text{Mike}]} =$ John introduced Mary to Mike
     d. $[\![\, (62)\,]\!]^{g,\left[\begin{smallmatrix} \langle 1, e \rangle\, \to\, \text{Sue} \\ \langle 2, e \rangle\, \to\, \text{Mike} \end{smallmatrix} \right]} =$ John introduced Sue to Mike
     e. $\{[\![\, (62)\,]\!]^{g,\left[\begin{smallmatrix} \langle 1, e \rangle\, \to\, x \\ \langle 2, e \rangle\, \to\, y \end{smallmatrix} \right]} \mid x, y$ are individuals$\} = \{$John introduced x to $y \mid x, y$ are individuals$\} = [\![\, (62)\,]\!]^{g,h}_{\mathcal{F}}$ (see example (68))

To get the focus alternatives to a single focus or a set of foci, we define:

(63^{DEF})   I-ALTERNATIVE F-ASSIGNMENT FUNCTIONS
     for any set I of pairs $\langle n, \tau \rangle \in \mathbb{N} \times types$, and any assignment function h, let H^h_I be the set of assignment functions h' s.t. h' differs from h at most in the values it assigns to the $i \in I$.

(64^{DEF})   I-ALTERNATIVES
     for any set I of pairs $\langle n, \tau \rangle \in \mathbb{N} \times types$, any syntactic constituent α, the set of α's I-alternatives, relative to assignments g and h, written as $[\![\, \alpha\,]\!]^{g,h}_{\mathcal{F}_I}$ is $\{[\![\, \alpha\,]\!]^{g,h'} \mid h' \in H^h_I\}$

It thus holds that:

(65) $\{[\![\, (62)\,]\!]^{g,\left[\begin{smallmatrix} \langle 1, e \rangle\, \to\, x \\ \langle 2, e \rangle\, \to\, y \end{smallmatrix} \right]} \mid x, y$ are individuals$\} = \{$John introduced x to $y \mid x, y$ are individuals$\} = [\![\, (62)\,]\!]^{g,h}_{\mathcal{F}_{\{\langle 1, e \rangle, \langle 2, e \rangle\}}}$

$[\![\, A\,]\!]^{g,h}_{\mathcal{F}_{1,2}}$ abbreviates $[\![\, A\,]\!]^{g,h}_{\mathcal{F}_{\{\langle 1, e \rangle, \langle 2, e \rangle\}}}$; that is, we may omit the types, assuming they are picked according to the elements in A that bear focus features, and we omit set brackets. Generally, lists of integers may be written where officially we would have sets of type–number pairs, e.g. ⟨$only_1$⟩ instead of ⟨$only_{\{\langle 1,e\rangle\}}$⟩ or of ⟨$only_{\{\langle 1,\langle e,t\rangle\rangle\}}$⟩, etc. For illustration, here are two standard focus sensitive operators:

(66^{DEF})   a. $[\![\alpha[\sim_i C]]\!]_O^{g,h}$ is defined only if the existential closure of $g(C)$ entails the grand union of the existential closures of the elements in $[\![\alpha]\!]_{\mathcal{F}_i}^{g,h}$

   b. $[\![only_i\ VP]\!]_O^{g,h} = \lambda x.\forall p \in [\![VP]\!]_{\mathcal{F}_i}^{g,h}[p(x) \to [[\![VP]\!]_O^g(x) \to p]]$

And for illustration, here are some standard configurations:

(67)   a. operator binding focus F_1
   $OP_1 [...\alpha_{F_1}...]$

   b. operator binding focus F_1, but not F_2
   $OP_1 [...\alpha_{F_1}...\beta_{F_2}...]$

   c. operator binding foci F_1 and F_2
   $OP_{1,2} [...\alpha_{F_1}...\beta_{F_2}...]$ b.

   d. operator 1 binding focus F_1, operator 2 binding focus F_2
   $OP_2 [OP_1 [...\alpha_{F_1}...\beta_{F_2}...]]$
   $OP_1 [OP_2 [...\alpha_{F_1}...\beta_{F_2}...]]$

   e. one focus bound by two operators $OP_1 [OP_2 [...\alpha_{F_1,F_2}...]]$

10.5.3 Tanglewood

Kratzer (1991: 830) presents the exchange in (68) to argue for the need for an indexed focus semantics, which, for ease of later reference, we will assume to take place between Jones and Smith.

(68)   Jones: (What a copy cat you are! You went to Block Island because I did, you went to Elk Lake Lodge because I did. And you went to Tanglewood because I did.—)
   Smith: I only went to TANGlewood because you did.

In this context, the reply ⟨*I only went to Tanglewood because you did*⟩ is to be interpreted as (69).

(69)   the only place x such that Smith went to x because Jones went to x is Tanglewood

Example (68) involves VP ellipsis, and the crucial observation is that the missing VP is, on this reading, interpreted as covarying in focus with the pronounced VP. Let us assume with Kratzer that VP ellipsis is deletion at phonological form, then we have two possible underlying forms for (68), assuming unselective association with focus.

(70) a. I only went to [Tanglewood]$_F$ because you did ~~go to Tanglewood~~
'the only place x such that Smith went to x because Jones went to Tanglewood is Tanglewood'

      b. I only went to [Tanglewood]$_F$ because you did ~~go to [Tanglewood]$_F$~~
'the only x and y such that Smith went to x because Jones went to y are
Tanglewood and Tanglewood'

The readings resulting from these representations are given underneath each one.
Example (70a) is weaker than the intended reading: it does not exclude that
Smith went to Elk Lake because Jones went to Elk Lake, it only excludes that Smith
went to Elk Lake because Jones went to Tanglewood. Even a die-hard copy cat
could truthfully utter (71a). Example (71b), on the other hand is stronger than
the intended reading: It excludes Smith going *anywhere* because of Jones going
anywhere. It is, for example, false as soon as Smith went to New York (to visit the
Smiths) because Jones went to Boston (to visit the Joneses).

    The reading we are after could only be expressed, Kratzer argues, by an LF
like (71).

(71) I only₁ went to [Tanglewood]$_{F_1}$ because you did ~~go to [Tanglewood]$_{F_1}$~~

In (71), the two foci covary, as desired.

    There is of course something strange about the idea of a deleted focus. Usually,
the absence of any focus is seen as a precondition for deletion, hence the slogan:
"deletion is the most radical form of deaccenting." It is also noticeable that neither
(72a) nor (72b) has the interpretation (68) has.

(72) a. I only went to TANGlewood because you went to Tanglewood.
      b. I only went to TANGlewood because you went to TANGlewood.

That is to say, neither a deaccented nor a focussed rendering of ‹Tanglewood› in
a pronounced version of the second VP gives us the covarying reading. Rather,
(73a) means (71a), while (73b) means, if anything, something like 'I went no
other place than Tanglewood, because you went to Tanglewood.'[22] To exclude in
particular the covarying reading for (72b), Kratzer assumes that coindexing (and
hence covariation) for two foci is possible only under ellipsis/copying. Otherwise,
any two foci must be counter-indexed.

    An adequate paraphrase of (68) without ellipsis seems to be that in (73).

(73) I only went to TANGlewood because you went there.

Given that (73) has the reading we are after, we might as well assume that the full
structure of (68) is (74), rather than (71).

---

[22] There is a more plausible and more easily available reading of (72b), namely: 'the sole reason I went
to Tanglewood (of all places) is because you went to Tanglewood (of all places)'; but on that reading,
‹only› associates with the ‹because› clause, not the first ‹Tanglewood›.

(74)   I only went to TANGlewood because you did ~~go there~~

Does this possibility argue against focus coindexing? If ‹there› in (73) were co-bound by ‹only›, we would have to modify the restrictions on focus coindexing so as to allow it, in some cases, even outside of ellipsis (presumably exactly if the second apparently bound focus is a pronoun). Moreover, we have to explain how ‹there› in (73) can be interpreted as a focus without any prosodic prominence. In the alternative, we could assume that (73) and (74) are possible precisely *because* ‹there› is a pronoun, and as such can be bound by (and hence co-vary with) ‹Tanglewood› in the main clause. Structure (75) spells out this second possibility using syntactic scoping of ‹Tanglewood›.[23]

(75)   I only [TANGlewood$_F$], [[went to t_1] [because you did ~~go there~~$_1$]]]

Kratzer argues against such a structure using example (76), which has a similar co-varying reading.

(76)   I only contacted the person who chairs [the ZONING board]$_F$ before you did.

Here, the argument goes, ‹the zoning board› cannot possibly raise out of VP, since it is embedded within a complex NP and a relative clause, out of which movement should be impossible.

   We note, however, that here, too, a paraphrase with a pronoun is possible, albeit one in which the entire object DP, rather than the focus within it, is pronominalized.

(77)   I only contacted the person who chairs the ZONING board before you contacted them.

Kratzer seems to assume that ‹the zoning board› needs to bind into the second VP, but this is in fact not necessary. Even more in general, the mere fact that (77) and (73) have the readings they do clearly shows that bound readings with pronouns, but without ellipsis, are possible in these configurations.

   In sum, it is not entirely clear that Kratzer's Tanglewood example and its kin really require indexed foci. If they do, however, the system defined in Section 10.5.2 is able to capture them, provided we allow coindexing of foci in those cases in which Kratzer (1991) does.

---

[23] Structure (75) shows structural similarities to certain types of weak cross-over configurations: ‹Tanglewood› does not c-command ‹there› from an argument position, but rather seems to bind it and its own trace from a non-argument position (see Koopman and Sportiche, 1983; Büring, 2004; a.o.). However, as is well known, binding into an adjunct by an object is, whatever the reason, possible, as in Orson Welles' famous Paul Masson Commercial ‹We will sell no wine before its time› (see Barker, 2012 and the references there).

10.5.4 Are foci ever "absorbed"?

One aspect of Rooth's theory of focus we have not addressed yet is what happens to foci once they have been "retrieved" by a FSE. Rooth's (1992b) definition of the squiggle includes the clause in (78).

(78) $[\![\, [\delta \sim C]\,]\!]_\mathcal{F} = \{[\![\, \delta\,]\!]_\mathcal{O}\}$

What (78) expresses is that the focus semantic value of a focus domain δ gets "reset" or "defused" to the singleton containing δ's meaning. Any subsequent operators do not have access to foci c-commanded by $\sim C$.

The indexed focus system introduced in Section 10.5.2 does not include any such provision. The same focus can be accessed as many times as there are c-commanding FSEs. One way to motivate this are examples in which the same focus is associated with multiple FSEs.

(79)   a. John once only drank WINE$_F$.
       b. John also once only drank WATER$_F$

On an indexing approach, this can easily be represented:

(80)   John also$_1$ once only$_2$ drank WATER$_{F1,F2}$.

But such examples are beyond the expressive power of unselective Alternative Semantics if the lower FSE defuses the focus it associates with.

The question whether associated foci are at the same time free, contrastive foci is also a main theme of an unpublished paper by Roger Schwarzschild (Schwarzschild, 1993). Clearly, if FSEs were to defuse foci they associate with, no sentence level (or discourse level) rule or operator could subsequently associate with them. Associated foci should be "discourse inert." Schwarzschild argues that this is an incorrect prediction. He argues, for example, that it would be "unnatural" to analyze the focus on ‹Paul› as contrastive (with ‹the twins›) in (81a), but not (81b) (1993: 1).

(81)   a. (John saw the twins and) MAX saw PAUL.
       b. (John saw the twins but) MAX only saw PAUL.

In fact, given our current setting, if only ‹Max› were a free focus, we would require a focus antecedent like 'x only saw Paul', which is not present in (81b). To match ‹John saw the twins›, both ‹Max› and ‹Paul› must be sentence-level foci.

This shows that associated foci *may* at the same time be contrastive foci (i.e. be retrieved twice). It is more difficult to establish that associated foci *must* be free foci. Schwarzschild (1993) provides the examples in (82), to which I add (83).[24]

---

[24] Schwarzschild (1993: 20f).

(82)   Who did John see at the conference?
    A1:   He saw MARC at the conference (and that was the first and only time he ever saw Marc).
    A2:   He only saw MARC at the conference.
    A3: #He only saw Marc at the CONFERENCE.

(83)   A4: #He only saw MARC at the CONference.

While ‹Marc› in A2 can be both an answer focus and an associated focus (similar to example (81b)), A3 is impossible, even though the associated interpretation of the focus on ‹conference› should make A3 equivalent to A1. But since there is no antecedent for the free focus interpretation of ‹conference› in A3 (i.e. something like 'John (only) saw Marc at x'), Schwarzschild argues, it is infelicitous. Hence, even associated foci must be licensed, also, as free foci. Parallel reasoning applies to A4.

However, the infelicity of A3 and A4 could also be due to the *lack* of (nuclear) accent on the answer focus, ‹Marc›.[25] So all we can safely conclude from these examples is that an associated focus cannot "overwrite" a free focus.

Summarizing, we have seen arguments in this section that a single focus can be associated multiple times, either to multiple FSE, or as a bound and free focus at the same time. This means that "resetting" or "defusing" F-alternatives when they are retrieved by an FSE (or the squiggle) cannot be a general rule. In fact, I have not found any clear cases of an associated focus that is *not* also a free focus discussed in the literature, so it is possible, though not certain, that all foci are, at least *also*, contrastive. This also means that the fact that indexed focus semantics does not predict a "defuse after use" for associated foci is not a problem, but a virtue.

---

[25] And, in the alternative, if ‹Marc› in A4 *were* to bear the final pitch accent, the focus of ‹only› would no longer be the maximal stress in *its* domain; see the discussion in Section 7.3.2.

Bibliography

Allerton, D. J. and A. Cruttenden (1979). "Three reasons for accenting a definite subject." *Journal of Linguistics* 15: 49–53.

Ariel, Mira (1999). "Referring and accessibility." *Journal of Linguistics* 24: 65–87.

Ariel, Mira (2001). "Accessibility theory: An overview." In T. Sandeler, J. Schlipero- ord, and W. Spooren, eds., *Text Representation*, 29–87. Amsterdam: Benjamins.

Artstein, Ron (2004). "Focus below the word level." *Natural Language Semantics* 12(1): 1–22.

Barker, Chris (2012). "Quantificational binding does not require C-command." *Linguistic Inquiry* 43(4): 614–33.

Bartels, Christine (1999). *The Intonation of English Statements and Questions*. New York: Garland.

Bartels, Christine (2004). "Acoustic correlates of 'second occurrence' focus: Towards an experimental investigation." In Kamp and Partee (2004), 354–61.

Bäuerle, Rainer (1979). *Temporale Deixis—Temporale Frage*. Tübingen: Narr.

Baumann, Stefan and Martine Grice (2006). "The intonation of accessibility." *Journal of Pragmatics* 38(10): 1636–57. Special Issue: Prosody and Pragmatics.

Baumann, Stefan and Arndt Riester (2010). "Annotating information status in spontaneous speech." In *Proceedings of the Fifth International Conference on Speech Prosody*. Chicago.

Baumann, Stefan, Doris Mücke, and Johannes Becker (2010). "Expression of Second Occurrence Focus in German." *Linguistische Berichte* (221): 61–78.

Beaver, David and Brady Clark (2003). "*Always* and *Only*: Why not all focus sensitive operators are alike." *Natural Language Semantics* 11(4): 323–62.

Beaver, David and Brady Clark (2008). *Sense and Sensitivity: How Focus Determines Meaning*. Cambridge: Wiley-Blackwell.

Beaver, David, Brady Clark, Edward Flemming, Florian Jaeger, and Maria Wolters (2007). "When semantics meets phonetics: Acoustical studies of second occurrence focus." *Language 83* 83(2): 251–82.

Benincà, Paola and Nicola Munaro (2010). *Mapping the Left Periphery: The Cartography of Syntactic Structures, Volume 5*. Oxford & New York: Oxford University Press.

Bierwisch, Manfred (1966). "Regeln für die Intonation deutscher Sätze." In Deutsche Akademie der Wissenschaften zu Berlin. Arbeitsstelle Strukturelle Grammatik (1966), 99–201.

Bierwisch, Manfred (1968). "Two critical problems in accent rules." *Journal of Linguistics* 4: 173–8.

Blühdorn, Hardarik and Horst Lohnstein, eds. (2012). *Wahrheits—Fokus— Negation*. No. 18 in Linguistische Berichte Sonderheft. Hamburg: Buske.

Bocci, Giuliano (2013). *The Syntax–Prosody Interface. A Cartographic Perspective with Evidence from Italian*. Amsterdam: John Benjamins.

Bolinger, Dwight L. (1961). "Contrastive accent and contrastive stress." *Language* 37(1): 83–96. Reprinted in Bolinger (1965), ch. 7, 101–17.

Bolinger, Dwight L. (1965). *Forms of English: Accent Morpheme, Order*. Cambridge, MA: Harvard University Press.

Bolinger, Dwight (1972). "Accent is predictable if you're a mind reader." *Language* 48: 633–44.

Bolinger, Dwight (1982). "Intonation and its parts." *Language* 58: 505–33.

Bonomi, Andrea and Paolo Casalegno (1993). "*Only*: Association with focus in event semantics." *Natural Language Semantics* 2(1): 1–45.

Bosch, Peter and Rob van der Sandt, eds. (1994). *Focus and Natural Language Processing. 3 Volumes*. Stuttgart: IBM Deutschland GmbH.

Bosch, Peter and Rob van der Sandt, eds. (1999). *Focus—Linguistic, Cognitive, and Computational Perspectives*. Cambridge: Cambridge University Press.

Braun, Bettina (2005). *Production and Perception of Thematic Contrast in German*. Oxford: Peter Lang.

Braun, Bettina (2006). "Phonetics and phonology of thematic contrast in German." *Language & Speech* 49(4): 451–93.

Brentano, Franz (1874). *Psychologie vom empirischen Standpunkte*. Leipzig: Duncker & Humblot.

Bresnan, Joan (1971). "Sentence stress and syntactic transformations." *Language* 47: 257–81.

Brody, Michael (1990). "Some remarks on the focus field in Hungarian." In *UCL Working Papers in Linguistics 2*, 201–25.

Brown, Gillian (1983). "Prosodic structure and the given/new distinction." In Anne Cutler and D. Robert Ladd, eds., *Prosody: Models and Measurements*, vol. 14 of *Springer Series in Language and Communication*, 67–77. Heidelberg: Springer.

Brunetti, Lisa (2004a). "Are there two distinct foci in Italian?" *Southwest Journal of Linguistics* 23(2). https://www.quetia.com/library/journal/1G1-132534921/are-there-two-distinct-foci-in-italian

Brunetti, Lisa (2004b). *A Unification of Focus*. Padova: Unipress.

Brunetti, Lisa (2006). "Italian background: Links, tails, and contrast effects." In B. Gyuris, C. Pinōn L. Kálmán, and K. Varasdi, eds., *Proceedings of the Ninth Symposium on Logic and Language*. Budapest: Eőtvős Loránd University.

Brunetti, Lisa (2009). "On Links and tails in Italian." *Lingua* 119(5): 756–81.

Büring, Daniel (1994). "The interaction of focus, phrase structure, and quantification." No. 23 in MIT Working Papers in Linguistics, 75–94. Boston, MA: MIT Press.

Büring, Daniel (1996). "A weak theory of strong readings." In Galloway and Spence (1996), 17–34.

Büring, Daniel (1997a). "The great scope inversion conspiracy." *Linguistics & Philosophy* 20: 175–94.

Büring, Daniel (1997b). *The Meaning of Topic and Focus—The 59th Street Bridge Accent*. London: Routledge.

Büring, Daniel (2001a). "Let's phrase it!—focus, word order, and prosodic phrasing in German double object constructions." No. 49 in Studies in Generative Grammar, 101–37. Berlin & New York: De Gruyter.

Büring, Daniel (2001b). "What do definites do that indefinites definitely don't?" In Caroline Féry and Wolfgang Sternefeld, eds., *Audiatur Vox Sapientiae: A Festschrift for Arnim von Stechow*, no. 52 in Studia Grammatica, 70–100. Berlin: Akademie Verlag.

Büring, Daniel (2003). "On D-trees, beans, and B-accents." *Linguistics & Philosophy* 26(5): 511–45.

Büring, Daniel (2004). "Crossover situations." *Natural Language Semantics* 12(1): 23–62.

Büring, Daniel (2006). "Focus projection and default prominence." In Molnár and Winkler (2006), 321–46.

Büring, Daniel (2009). "Towards a typology of focus realization." In Zimmermann and Féry (2009), 177–205.

Büring, Daniel (2012a). "Predicate integration—phrase structure or argument structure?" In Kučerová and Neeleman (2012), 27–47.

Büring, Daniel (2012b). "What's new (and what's given) in the theory of focus?" In Sarah Berson, Alex Bratkievich, Daniel Bruhn, Ramon Escamilla, Amy Campbell, Allegra Giovine, Lindsey Newbold, Marta Piqueras-Brunet, Marilola Perez, and Russell Rhomieux, eds., *Proceedings of the Thirty-Fourth Annual Meeting of the Berkeley Linguistics Society, February 8-10, 2008*, 403–24. Berkeley, CA: Berkeley Linguistics Society.

Büring, Daniel (2013/15). "A theory of Second Occurrence Focus." *Language as a Cognitive Process/Language, Cognition and Neuroscience* 30(1–2): 73–87.

Büring, Daniel (2016). "(Contrastive) Topic." In Caroline Féry and Shinichiro Ishihara, eds., *The Handbook of Information Structure*. Oxford: Oxford University Press.

Büring, Daniel and Rodrigo Gutiérrez-Bravo (2001). "Focus-related word order variation without the NSR: A prosody-based crosslinguistic analysis." In Séamas Mac Bhloscaidh, ed., *Syntax at Santa Cruz 3*, 41–58.

Chafe, Wallace L. (1976). "Givenness, contrastiveness, definiteness, subjects, topics, and point of view." In Charles Li, ed., *Subject and Topic*, 25–56. New York: Academic Press.

Chomsky, Noam and Morris Halle (1968). *The Sound Pattern of English*. Cambridge, MA: MIT Press.

Cinque, Guglielmo (1993). "A null theory of phrase and compound stress." *Linguistic Inquiry* 24: 239–67.

Clark, Herbert (1977). "Bridging." In P. Johnson-Laird and P. Wason, eds., *Thinking*, 411–20. Cambridge: Cambridge University Press.

Clark, Herbert H. and Susan E. Haviland (1977). "Comprehension and the given-new contract." In Roy O. Freedle, ed., *Discourse Production and Comprehension*, 1–40. Norwood: NJ: Ablex.

Cohen, Philip R., Jerry Morgan, and Martha E. Pollack, eds. (1990). *Intentions in Communication*. Cambridge, MA: MIT Press.

Comrie, Bernard (1984). "Some formal properties of focus in Modern Eastern Armenian." *Annual Armenian Linguistics* 5: 1–21.

Constant, Noah (2006). *English Rise–Fall–Rise: A Study in the Semantics and Pragmatics of Intonation*. Master's thesis, University of California at Santa Cruz.

Constant, Noah (2012). "English rise–fall–rise: A study in the semantics and pragmatics of intonation." *Linguistics & Philosophy* 35(5): 407–42.

Cooper, William J., Stephen J. Eady, and Pamela R. Mueller (1985). "Acoustical aspects of contrastive stress in question–answer contexts." *Journal of the Acoustical Society of America* 77: 2142–55.

Cruschina, Silvio (2012). *Discourse-Related Features and Functional Projections.* Oxford Comparative Studies in Syntax. Oxford & New York: Oxford University Press.

Cruschina, Silvio and Eva-Maria Remberger (to appear). "Focus fronting." In Andreas Durfter and Elisabeth Stark, eds., *Manual of Romance Morphosyntax and Syntax.* Berlin: Mouton De Gruyter.

Cruttenden, Alan (1993). "The de-accenting and re-accenting of repeated lexical items." In *Proceedings of the ESCA Workshop on Prosody*, 16–19. Lund.

Cruttenden, Alan (2006). "The de-accenting of given information: A cognitive universal?" In Giuliano Bernini and Marcia L. Schwartz, eds., *Pragmatic Organization of Discourse in the Languages of Europe*, 311–56. The Hague: Mouton De Gruyter.

Crystal, David (1969). *Prosodic Systems and Intonation in English.* Cambridge: Cambridge University Press.

Currie, Karen L. (1980). "An initial 'Search for Tonics.'" *Language and Speech* 23: 329–50.

Currie, Karen L. (1981). "Further experiments in the 'Search for Tonics.'" *Language and Speech* 24: 1–28.

van Deemter, Kees (1999). "Contrastive stress, contrariety, and focus." In Bosch and van der Sandt (1999), 3–17.

Dekker, Paul and Herman Hendriks (1996). "Links without locations—information packaging and non-monotone anaphora." In Paul Dekker and Martin Stokhof, eds., *Proceedings of the Tenth Amsterdam Colloquium*, 339–58.

Delin, Judy and Ron Zacharski (1994). "A conversational model of information structure and intonation." In Bosch and van der Sandt (1994), 61–70.

Deutsche Akademie der Wissenschaften zu Berlin. Arbeitsstelle Strukturelle Grammatik (1966). *Studia Grammatica VII. Untersuchungen über Akzent und Intonation im Deutschen.* Akademie Verlag.

Diesing, Molly (1992). *Indefinites.* No. 20 in Linguistic Inquiry Monograph. Cambridge, MA: MIT Press.

Dretske, Fred (1972). "Contrastive statements." *Philosophical Review* 81: 411–37.

Drubig, H. Bernhard (2003). "Toward a typology of focus and focus constructions." *Linguistics* 41(1): 1–50.

Eady, Stephen J. and William J. Cooper (1986). "Speech intonation and focus location in matched statements and questions." *Journal of the Acoustical Society of America* 80: 402–15.

Eady, Stephen J., William Cooper, Gayle V. Klouda, Pamela R. Mueller, and Dan W. Lotts (1986). "Acoustical characteristics of sentential focus: Narrow vs. broad focus and single vs. dual focus environments." *Language and Speech* 29: 233–51.

Eckardt, Regine (1999). "Focus with nominal quantifiers." In Bosch and van der Sandt (1999), 166–86.

Eckardt, Regine (2006). "Was noch? Navigating in question–answer discourse." In Andreas Späth, ed., *Interface and Interface Conditions*. Berlin: Mouton De Gruyter.

É. Kiss, Katalin (1987). *Configurationality in Hungarian*. Dordrecht: Foris.

É. Kiss, Katalin (1998). "Identificational focus and information focus." *Language* 74: 245–73.

Erteschik-Shir, Nomi (1997). *The Dynamics of Focus Structure*. No. 84 in Cambridge Studies in Linguistics. Cambridge: Cambridge University Press.

Everaert, Martin and Henk van Riemsdijk (2006). *The Blackwell Companion to Syntax*. Malden/Oxford/Victoria: Blackwell.

Faber, David (1987). "The accentuation of intransitive sentences in English." *Journal of Linguistics* 23: 341–58.

Féry, Caroline (1993). *German Intonational Patterns*. Tübingen: Niemeyer.

Féry, Caroline (2011). "German sentence accent and embedded prosodic phrases." *Lingua* 121: 1906–22.

Féry, Caroline and Katharina Hartmann (2005). "The focus and prosodic structure of German Right Node Raising and Gapping." *The Linguistic Review* 22: 69–116.

Féry, Caroline and Shinichiro Ishihara (2009). "The phonology of Second Occurrence Focus." *Journal of Linguistics* 45: 285–313.

Féry, Caroline and Vieri Samek-Lodovici (2006). "Focus projection and prosodic prominence in nested foci." *Language* 82(1): 131–50.

von Fintel, Kai (1994). *Restrictions on Quantifier Domains*. Ph.D. thesis, University of Massachusetts, Amherst.

von Fintel, Kai (2004). "A minimal theory of adverbial quantification." In Kamp and Partee (2004), 137–75.

Fox, Danny (2007). "Free choice disjunction and the theory of scalar implicatures." In Uli Sauerland and Penka Stateva, eds., *Presupposition and Implicature in Compositional Semantics*, 71–120. Basingstoke: Palgrave-Macmillan.

Frascarelli, Mara (2000). *The Syntax–Phonology Interface in Focus and Topic Constructions in Italian*. No. 50 in Studies in Natural Language and Linguistic Theory. Dordrecht/ Boston/ London: Kluwer.

Frascarelli, Mara and Roland Hinterhölzl (2007). "Types of topics in German and Italian." In Kerstin Schwabe and Susanne Winkler, eds., *On Information Structure, Meaning and Form*, 87–116. Amsterdam: John Benjamins.

Fry, D. B. (1955). "Duration and intensity as physical correlates of linguistic stress." *Journal of the American Acoustic Association* 27: 765–9.

Fry, D. B. (1958). "Experiments in the perception of stress." *Language and Speech* 1: 205–13.

Fuchs, Anna (1976). "Normaler und kontrastiver Akzent." *Lingua* 38: 293–312.

Fuchs, Anna (1980). "Accented subjects in 'all-new' utterances." In Gunter Brettschneider and Christian Lehmann, eds., *Wege zur Universalienforschung: Sprachwissenschaftliche Beiträge zum 60. Geburtstag von Hansjakob Seiler*, 449–61. Tübingen: Narr.

Fuchs, Anna (1984). "'Deaccenting' and 'default' accent." In Dafydd Gibbon and Helmut Richter, eds., *Intonation, Accent and Rhythm: Studies in Discourse Phonology*, 134–64. Berlin, New York: De Gruyter.

Galloway, Teresa and Justin Spence, eds. (1996). *Proceedings of Semantics and Linguistic Theory (SALT) 6*, Ithaca, NY: CLC Publications.

Geilfuß, Jochen (1993). "Nominal quantifiers and association with focus." In Peter Ackema and Maaike Schoorlemmer, eds., *Proceedings of the Workshop on the Syntactic and Semantic Analysis of Focus*, 33–42. Utrecht: OTS (=OTS Working Papers TL-93-012).

Geurts, Bart and Rob van der Sandt (2004). "Interpreting focus." *Theoretical Linguistics* 30(1): 1–44.

Giegerich, Heinz J. (1992). *English Phonology*. Cambridge: Cambridge University Press.

Grabe, Esther (1998). *Comparative Intonational Phonology: English and German*. Ph.D. thesis, Katholieke Universiteit Nijmegen.

Grice, Martine, Stefan Baumann, and Rolf Benzmüller (2005). "German intonation in autosegmental-metrical phonology." In Sun-Ah Jun, ed., *Prosodic Typology: The Phonology of Intonation and Phrasing*, 55–83. Oxford: Oxford University Press.

Grimshaw, Jane (1997). "Projection, heads, and optimality." *Linguistic Inquiry* 28(3): 373–422.

Gryllia, Stella (2009). "Greek marks topics instead of foci." *The Linguistic Review, Special Issue on Topics Cross-Linguistically* 26: 177–205.

Guéron, Jacqueline (1980). "On the syntax and semantics of PP extraposition." *Linguistic Inquiry* 11(4): 637–78.

Guerzoni, Elena (2003). *Why* even *ask?*. Ph.D. thesis, MIT.

Gumperz, John (1982). *Discourse Strategies*. Cambridge: Cambridge University Press.

Gundel, Jeanette (1996). "Relevance theory meets the givenness hierarchy. an account of inferrables." In Thorstein Fretheim and Jeanette Gundel, eds., *Reference and Referent Accessibility*, 141–53. Amsterdam: Benjamins.

Gundel, Jeanette K. (1999). "On different kinds of focus." In Bosch and van der Sandt (1999), 293–305.

Gundel, Jeanette K. and Thorstein Fretheim (2004). "Topic and focus." In Laurence R. Horn and Gregory Ward, eds., *The Handbook of Pragmatics*, 175–96. Oxford: Blackwell.

Gundel, Jeanette, Nancy Hedberg, and Ron Zacharski (1993). "Cognitive status and the form of referring expressions in discourse." *Language* 69(2): 274–307.

Gunlogson, Christine (1999). "Rising declaratives." In *Proceedings of WECOL 99*.

Gunlogson, Christine (2001). *True to Form*. Ph.D. thesis, University of California, Santa Cruz.

Gussenhoven, Carlos (1983a). "Focus, mode, and the nucleus." *Journal of Linguistics* 19: 377–417. Reprinted as chapter 1 in Gussenhoven (1984).

Gussenhoven, Carlos (1983b). "A semantic analysis of the nuclear tones of English." Also published as ch. 6 of Gussenhoven (1984).

Gussenhoven, Carlos (1984). *On the Grammar and Semantics of Sentence Accents.* Dordrecht: Foris.

Gussenhoven, Carlos (2004). *The Phonology of Tone and Intonation.* Research Surveys in Linguistics. Cambridge: Cambridge University Press.

Gutzmann, Daniel (2008). *On the Interaction between Modal Particles and Sentence Mood in German.* Master's thesis, Universität Mainz.

Gutzmann, Daniel and Elena Castroviejo Miró (2011). "The dimensions of verum." In Olivier Bonami and Patricia Cabredo Hofherr, eds., *Empirical Issues in Syntax and Semantics 8 (Proceedings of CSSP 2009)*, 143–65. Paris: CNRS.

Gyuris, Beáta (2002). *The Semantics of Contrastive Topics in Hungarian.* Ph.D. thesis, Eőtvős Loránd University, Budapest.

Hajičová, Eva, Barbara Partee, and Petr Sgall (1998). *Topic–Focus Articulation, Tripartite Structures, and Semantic Content.* Dordrecht: Kluwer.

Halle, Morris and Jean-Roger Vergnaud (1987). *An Essay on Stress.* Cambridge: Cambridge University Press.

Halliday, M. A. K. (1967a). *Intonation and Grammar in British English.* The Hague: Mouton.

Halliday, M. A. K. (1967b). "Notes on transitivity and theme in English, Part II." *Journal of Linguistics* 3(2): 199–244.

Hamblin, C. L. (1973). "Questions in Montague Grammar." *Foundations of Language* 10: 41–53.

Hara, Yurie (2008). "Scope inversion in Japanese: Contrastive topics require implicatures." In *Japanese/Korean Linguistics 13.* CSLI Publication.

Hara, Yurie and Robert van Rooij (2007). "Contrastive topics revisited: A simpler set of topic-alternatives." In *Handout from the 38th Meeting of the North East Linguistic Society.* October 26–28, 2007, University of Ottawa.

Harris, Alice C. (1982). "Towards the universals of Q-word formation." In *Papers from the Parasession on Nondeclaratives*, 67–75. Chicago: Chicago Linguistic Society.

Hartmann, Katharina (2006). "Focus constructions in Hausa." In Molnár and Winkler (2006).

Hayes, Bruce (1982). "Extrametricality and English stress." *Linguistic Inquiry* 13(2): 227–76.

Hayes, Bruce (1995). *Metrical Stress Theory.* Chicago: The University of Chicago Press.

Hayes, Bruce and Aditi Lahiri (1991). "Bengali intonational phonology." *Natural Language & Linguistic Theory* 9: 47–96.

Hedberg, Nancy and Juan M. Sosa (2007). "The prosody of topic and focus in spontaneous English dialogue." In Lee et al. (2007), 101–20.

Heim, Irene (1982). *The Semantics of Definite and Indefinite Noun Phrases.* Ph.D. thesis, University of Massachusetts, Amherst.

Heim, Irene (1985). "Notes on comparatives and related matters." Unpublished ms., University of Texas, Austin.

Heim, Irene (2000). "Degree operators and scope." In *Proceedings of SALT X.* Ithaca, NY: CLC Publications.

Hendriks, Herman (2002). "Information Packaging: From cards to boxes." In Kees Van Deemter and Rodger Kibble, eds., *Information Sharing: Reference and Presupposition in Language Generation and Interpretation*. Stanford, CA: CSLI.

Herburger, Elena (2000). *What Counts: Focus and Quantification*. No. 36 in Linguistic Inquiry Monographs. Cambridge, MA: MIT Press.

Hirsch, Aron and Michael Wagner (2011a). "Context and prominence in English intransitive sentences." *Poster presented at ETAP 2, McGill University, September 23–25*.

Hirsch, Aron and Michael Wagner (2011b). "Patterns of prosodic prominence in English intransitive sentences." *Talk presented at GLOW 34, University of Vienna, April 28–30*.

Hirschberg, Julia and Gregory Ward (1991). "Accent and bound anaphora." *Cognitive Linguistics* 2(2): 101–21.

Hirschberg, Julia and Gregory Ward (1995). "The interpretation of the high-rise question contour in English." *Journal of Pragmatics* 24: 407–12.

Hirst, Daniel and Albert Di Cristo, eds. (1998). *Intonation Systems. A Survey of Twenty Languages*. Cambridge: Cambridge University Press.

Hobbs, Jerry R. (1990). "The Pierrehumbert–Hirschberg Theory of intonational meaning made simple: Comments on Pierrehumbert and Hirschberg." In Cohen et al. (1990), 313–23.

Höhle, Tilman M. (1982). "Explikation für 'normale Betonung' und 'normale Wortstellung'." In Werner Abraham, ed., *Satzglieder im Deutschen*, 75–153. Tübingen: Narr.

Höhle, Tilman (1992). "Über Verum-Fokus im Deutschen." In Jacobs (1991/2b), 112–41. (= *Linguistische Berichte* Sonderheft 4).

de Hoop, Helen (1992). *Case Configuration and Noun Phrase Interpretation*. Ph.D. thesis, Groningen. Published 1996 by Garland.

de Hoop, Helen (1995). "Only a matter of context?" Ms. Groningen.

de Hoop, Helen (1996). *Case Configuration and Noun Phrase Interpretation*. New York: Garland.

de Hoop, Helen and Jaume Solà (1995). "Determiners, context sets, and focus." In *WCCFL 14*.

Horvath, Julia (2000). "Interfaces vs. the computational system in the syntax of focus." In Martin Everaert Hans Bennis and Eric Reuland, eds., *Interface Strategies*, 183–206. Amsterdam: Holland Academic Graphics.

Horvath, Julia (2010). " 'Discourse features', syntactic displacement and the status of contrast." *Lingua* 120(6): 1346–69.

Hoskins, Steve (1996). "A phonetic study of focus in intransitive sentences." In *Proceedings of the Fourth International Conference on Spoken Language Processing*, 1632–5.

Howell, Jonathan (2011). *Meaning and Prosody: On the Web, in the Lab and from the Theorist's Armchair*. Ph.D. thesis, Cornell University.

Huddleston, Rodney (1994). "The contrast between interrogatives and questions." *Journal of Linguistics* 30: 411–39.

Huss, Volker (1978). "English word stress in the post-nuclear position." *Phonetica* 35(2): 86–105.

Inkelas, Sharon and Draga Zec, eds. (1990). *The Phonology–Syntax Connection.* Chicago and London: The University of Chicago Press.

Ippolito, Michela (2007). "On the meaning of some focus-sensitive particles." *Natural Language Semantics* 15(1): 1–34.

Ippolito, Michela (2008). "On the meaning of *only.*" *Journal of Semantics* 25(1): 45–91.

Irwin, Patricia (2011). "Intransitive sentences, argument structure, and the syntax-prosody interface." In Mary Byram Washburn, Katherine McKinney-Bock, Erika Varis, Ann Sawyer, and Barbara Tomaszewicz, eds., *Proceedings of the 28th West Coast Conference on Formal Linguistics,* 275–84. Somerville, MA: Cascadilla Press.

Jackendoff, Ray (1972). *Semantics in Generative Grammar.* Cambridge, MA: MIT Press.

Jacobs, Joachim (1983). *Fokus und Skalen.* Tübingen: Niemeyer.

Jacobs, Joachim (1984). "Funktionale Satzperspektive und Illokutionssemantik." *Linguistische Berichte* (91): 25–58.

Jacobs, Joachim (1988). "Fokus-Hintergrund-Gliederung und Grammatik." In Hans Altmann, ed., *Intonationsforschungen,* 89–134. Tübingen: Niemeyer.

Jacobs, Joachim (1991). "Implikaturen und 'alte Information' in W-Fragen." Tübingen: Niemeyer.

Jacobs, Joachim (1991/2a). "Einleitung." In Jacobs (1991/2b), 7–16. (= *Linguistische Berichte* Sonderheft 4).

Jacobs, Joachim, ed. (1991/2b). *Informationsstruktur und Grammatik.* Opladen: Westdeutscher Verlag. (= *Linguistische Berichte* Sonderheft 4).

Jacobs, Joachim (1991/2c). "Neutral stress and the position of heads." In Jacobs (1991/2b), 220–44. (= *Linguistische Berichte* Sonderheft 4).

Jacobs, Joachim (1992). *Integration.* Tech. Rep. 14, SFB 282, Düsseldorf, Köln & Wuppertal.

Jacobs, Joachim (1997). "I-Topikalisierung." *Linguistische Berichte* 168: 91–133.

Jacobs, Joachim (1999). "Informational autonomy." In Bosch and van der Sandt (1999), 56–81.

Jaeger, T. Florian (2004). "Only always associates audibly. Even if only is repeated The prosodic properties of second occurrence focus in English." Ms. Stanford University.

Jäger, Gerhard (2001). "Topic–comment structure and the contrast between stage-level and individual-level predicates." *Journal of Semantics* 18: 83–126.

Jun, Sun-Ah and Cécile Fougeron (2002). "The realizations of the accentual phrase in French intonatoin." *Probus* 14: 147–72.

Kahnemuyipour, Arsalan (2003). "Syntactic categories and persian stress." *Natural Language & Linguistic Theory* 21: 333–79.

Kahnemuyipour, Arsalan (2009). *The Syntax of Sentential Stress.* Oxford Studies in Theoretical Linguistics 25. Oxford: Oxford University Press.

Kallulli, Dalina (2006). "Triggering factivity: Prosodic evidence for syntactic structure." In David Montero, Donald Baumer, and Michael Scanlon, eds., *Proceedings of the 25th West Coast Conference on Formal Linguistics (WCCFL).* Somerville, MA: Cascadilla Proceedings Project.

Kallulli, Dalina (2009). "On the relation between givenness and deaccentuation: A 'best case' model." In Kleanthes Grohmann, ed., *Explorations of Phase Theory: Interpretation at the Interfaces*, 115–32. Berlin: De Gruyter.

Kallulli, Dalina (2010). "Belief will create fact: On the relation between givenness and presupposition, and other remarks." *Theoretical Linguistics* 36(2/3): 199–208.

Kamp, Hans and Barbara Partee, eds. (2004). *Context-Dependence in the Analysis of Linguistic Meaning*. Amsterdam: Elsevier.

Katz, Jonah and Elisabeth Selkirk (2011). "Contrastive focus vs. discourse-new: Evidence from prosodic prominence in English." *Language* 87(4): 771–816.

Katzir, Roni (2013). "A note on contrast." *Natural Language Semantics* 23: 1–11.

Kehler, Andrew (2005). "Coherence-driven constraints on the placement of accent." In Effi Georgala and Jonathan Howell, eds., *Proceedings from Semantics and Linguistic Theory XV*, 98–115. Ithaca, NY: Cornell University.

Kenesei, István (1998). "Adjuncts and arguments in VP-focus in Hungarian." *Acta Linguistica Hungarica* 45(1–2): 61–88.

Kenesei, István (2006). "Focus as identification." In Molnár and Winkler (2006), 137–68.

Kidwai, Ayesha (1999). "Word order and focus positions in Universal Grammar." In Rebuschi and Tuller (1999).

Kingdon, Roger (1958). *The Groundwork of Englich Intonation*. London: Longman.

Kiparsky, Paul (1966). "Über den deutschen Akzent." In Deutsche Akademie der Wissenschaften zu Berlin. Arbeitsstelle Strukturelle Grammatik (1966), 69–97.

Klinedinst, Nathan (2005). *Scales and Only*. Master's thesis, UCLA.

Koch, Karsten (2008). *Intonation and Focus in Nte?kepmxcin (Thompson River Salish)*. Ph.D. thesis, The University of British Columbia.

Kohler, Klaus J. (1991). "Terminal intonation patterns in single-accent utterances of German: Phonetics, phonology and semantics." *Arbeitsberichte des Instituts für Phonetik der Universität Kiel (AIPUK)* 25: 115–85.

Koopman, Hilda and Dominique Sportiche (1983). "Variables and the Bijection Principle." *The Linguistic Review* 2: 139–60.

Kraak, Remmert (1970). "Zinsaccent en syntaxis." *Studia Neerlandica* 4: 41–62.

Kratzer, Angelika (1991). "The Representation of Focus." vol. 6 of *Handbücher zur Sprach- und Kommunikationswissenschaft*, 825–34. Berlin: Walter De Gruyter.

Kratzer, Angelika (1995). "Stage Level and Individual Level Predicates." In Greg N. Carlson and Francis J. Pelletier, eds., *The Generic Book*, 125–75. Chicago: The University of Chicago Press.

Kratzer, Angelika and Elisabeth Selkirk (2007). "Phase theory and prosodic spell-out: The case of verbs." *The Linguistic Review* 93–135.

Krifka, Manfred (1984). "Fokus, Topik, syntaktische Struktur und semantische Interpretation." Ms., University of Munich.

Krifka, Manfred (1991/2). "A compositional Semantics for multiple focus constructions." In Jacobs (1991/2b), 17–53.

Krifka, Manfred (1992). "A Framework for Focus-Sensitive Quantification." In *SALT II: Proceedings of the Second Conference on Sematics and Linguistic Theory*. Working Papers in Linguistics 40, Ohio State University Columbus, 215–36.

Krifka, Manfred (1993). "Focus and presupposition in dynamic interpretation." *Journal of Semantics* 10: 269–300.

Krifka, Manfred (1995). "Focus and the interpretation of generic sentences." In Greg N. Carlson and Francis J. Pelletier, eds., *The Generic Book*, 238–64. Chicago: The University of Chicago Press.

Kuroda, Sige-Yuki (1972). "The categorical and the thetic judgement." *Foundations of Language* 9: 153–85.

Kučerová, Ivona (2007). *The Syntax of Givenness*. Ph.D. thesis, MIT.

Kučerová, Ivona and Ad Neeleman, eds. (2012). *Contrasts and Positions in Information Structure*. Cambridge: Cambridge University Press.

Ladd, D. Robert (1978). "Stylized intonation." *Language* 54: 517–40.

Ladd, D. Robert (1980). *The Structure of Intonational Meaning*. Bloomington: Indiana University Press.

Ladd, D. Robert (1988). "Declination 'Reset' and the hierarchical organization of utterances." *Journal of the American Acoustic Association* 84(5): 538–44.

Ladd, D. Robert (1996). *Intonational Phonology*. Cambridge: Cambridge University Press.

Ladd, D. Robert (2008). *Intonational Phonology, 2nd Edition*. Cambridge: Cambridge University Press.

Ladusaw, William (1994). "Thetic and categorical, weak and strong, individual and stage." In *SALT 4*.

Lakoff, George (1968). "Pronouns and reference." Mimeograph, Indiana University Linguistics Club, University of Indiana, Bloomington (published as Lakoff (1976)).

Lakoff, George (1976). "Pronouns and reference." In James D. McCawley, ed., *Notes from the Linguistic Underground, Syntax and Semantics, Volume 7*, 275–335. New York: Academic Press.

Leben, William (1973). *Suprasegmental Phonology*. Ph.D. thesis, MIT. Distributed by Indiana University Linguistics Club.

Lee, Chungmin (1999). "Contrastive topic: A locus of interface—Evidence from Korean and English." In Ken Turner, ed., *The Semantics/Pragmatics Interface from Different Points of View*, 317–42. Oxford: Elsevier.

Lee, Chungmin, Matthew Gordon, and Daniel Büring, eds. (2007). *Topic and Focus: Cross-linguistic Perspectives on Meaning and Intonation*. No. 82 in Studies in Linguistics and Philosophy. Dordrecht: Springer.

Lee, Chungmin, Ferenc Kiefer, and Manfred Krifka, eds. (2017). *Contrastiveness in Information Structure, Alternatives and Scalar Implicatures*. Dordrecht, Heidelberg, London, New York: Springer.

Legate, Julie Anne (2003). "Some interface properties of the phase." *Linguistic Inquiry* 34: 506–16.

Liberman, Mark and Janet Pierrehumbert (1984). "Intonational invariance under changes in pitch range and length." In M. Aronoff and R. T. Oehrle, eds., *Language Sound Structure*, 157–233. Cambridge, MA: MIT Press.

Liberman, Mark and Alan Prince (1977). "On stress and linguistic rhythm." *Linguistic Inquiry* 8: 249–336.

López, Luis (2009). *A Derivational Syntax for Information Structure*. No. 23 in Oxford Studies in Theoretical Linguistics. Oxford: Oxford University Press.

Ludwig, Rainer A. (2008). "Contrast for two." In Atle Grønn, ed., *Proceedings of Sinn und Bedeutung 12*, 384–98. Oslo: Ilos.

Maiden, Martin and Cecilia Robustelli (2000). *A Reference Grammar of Italian*. Chicago: NTC Publishing.

Martí, Luisa (2002). "Context reconstruction and informativity in the analysis of association with focus." Ms. University of Connecticut.

Mehlhorn, Grit (2001). "Produktion und Perzeption von Hutkonturen im Deutschen." In *Linguistische Arbeitsberichte*, no. 77, 31–57. Universität Leipzig: Institut für Linguistik.

Mehlhorn, Grit (2002). *Kontrastierte Konstituenten im Russischen. Experimentelle Untersuchungen zur Informationsstruktur*. Ph.D. thesis, Leipzig (= Europäische Hochschulschriften. Reihe 16: Slavische Sprachen und Literaturen).

Merchant, Jason (2008). "Variable island repair under ellipsis." In Kyle Johnson, ed., *Topics in Ellipsis*, 132–53. Cambridge: Cambridge University Press.

Miller, Judi (2006). "Focus." In Keith Brown, ed., *The Encyclopedia of Languages and Linguistics*, vol. 4, 511–18. Oxford: Elsevier.

Molnár, Valéria (1993). "Zu Pragmatik und Grammatik des TOPIK-Begriffes." In Marga Reis, ed., *Wortstellung und Informationsstruktur*, no. 306 in Linguistische Arbeiten, 155–02. Tübingen: Niemeyer.

Molnár, Valéria (1998). "Topic in focus. on the syntax, phonology, semantics and pragmatics of the so-called 'contrastive topic' in Hungarian and German." *Acta Linguistica Hungarica* 45(1–2): 89–166.

Molnár, Valéria and Susanne Winkler, eds. (2006). *The Architecture of Focus*. Studies in Generative Grammar 82. Berlin, New York: Mouton De Gruyter.

Neeleman, Ad and Kriszta Szendrői (2004). "Superman sentences." *Linguistic Inquiry* 35(1): 140–59.

Nespor, Marina and Irene B. Vogel (1986). *Prosodic Phonology*. Dordrecht: Foris.

Norcliffe, Elisabeth and T. Florian Jaeger (2005). "Accent-free prosodic phrases? Accents and phrasing in the post-nuclear domain." In *Interspeech 2005*.

O'Connor, J. D. and G. F. Arnold (1973). *Intonation of Colloquial English*. 2nd edn. London: Longmans.

Odden, David (1986). "On the role of the OBligatory COntour PRinciple in phonological theory." *Language* 62: 353–83.

Oshima, David Y. (2008). "Morphological vs. phonological contrastive topic marking." In Rodney L. Edwards, Patrick J. Midtlying, Colin L. Sprague, and Kjerti G. Stensrud, eds., *Proceedings of Chicago Linguistic Society (CLS)*, vol. 41–1, 371–84. Chicago: Chicago Linguistic Society.

Partee, Barbara H. (1993). "On the 'scope of negation' and polarity sensitivity." In Eva Hajičová, ed., *Functional Description of Language*, 179–96. Prague: Faculty of Mathematics and Physics, Charles University.

Pater, Joe (2000). "Non-uniformity in English secondary stress: The role of ranked and lexically specific constraints." *Phonology* 17: 237–74.

Pierrehumbert, Janet Breckenridge (1980). *The Phonology and Phonetics of English Intonation*. Ph.D. thesis, MIT.

Pierrehumbert, Janet and Julia Hirschberg (1990). "The meaning of intonational contours in the interpretation of discourse." In Cohen et al. (1990), 271–311.

Pierrehumbert, Janet B. and Shirley A. Steele (1987). "How many rise-fall-rise contours?" In *Proceedings of the 11th International Congress of Phonetic Sciences*. Tallinn.

Prince, Alan (1983). "Relating to the grid." *Linguistic Inquiry* 14: 19–100.

Prince, Alan and Paul Smolensky (1993). *Optimality Theory: Constraint Interaction in Generative Grammar*. Tech. rep., Rutgers University.

Prince, Ellen F. (1981). "Toward a taxonomy of given–new information." In Peter Cole, ed., *Radical Pragmatics* 223–55. New York: Academic Press.

Puskás, Genoveva (2000). *Word Order In Hungarian*, vol. 33 of *Linguistik Aktuell/Linguistics Today*. Amsterdam/Philadelphia: John Benjamins Publishing Company.

Rebuschi, Georges and Laurice Tuller, eds. (1999). *The Grammar of Focus*. No. 24 in Linguistik Aktuell/Linguistics Today. Amsterdam/Philadelphia: John Benjamins.

Reinhart, Tanya (1995). *Interface Strategies*. OTS Working Papers.

Reinhart, Tanya (2006). *Interface Strategies: Optimal and Costly Computations*. Cambridge, MA: MIT Press.

Riester, Arndt (2008). *The Components of Focus and their Use in Annotating Information Structure*. Ph.D. thesis, Universität Stuttgart. Arbeitspapiere des Instituts für Maschinelle Sprachverarbeitung (AIMS) Vol. 14(2).

Rizzi, Luigi (1997). "The fine structure of the left periphery." In Liliane Haegeman, ed., *Elements of Grammar: Handbook of Generative Syntax*, 281–337. Dordrecht: Kluwer.

Roberts, Craige (1996). "Information structure in discourse: Towards an integrated formal theory of pragmatics." In J. H. Yoon and Andreas Kathol, eds., *OSU Working Papers in Linguistics 49: Papers in Semantics*, 91–136.

Rochemont, Michael (1986). *Focus in Generative Grammar*. Amsterdam/Philadelphia: John Benjamins.

Röhr, Christine and Stefan Baumann (2010). "Prosodic marking of information status in German." In *Proceedings Speech Prosody 2010*, 100019: 1–4.

Röhr, Christine Tanja and Stefan Baumann (2011). "Decoding information status by type and position of accent in German." In *Proceedings 17th ICPhS*, 1706–09. Hongkong.

van Rooij, Robert (2010). "Topic, focus, and exhaustive interpretation." Paper presented at the 18th International Congress of Linguists. Available at http://staff.science.uva.nl/r.a.m.ovanrooij/Korea2008.pdf. To appear in Lee et al. (2017).

Rooth, Mats (1985). *Association with Focus*. Ph.D. thesis, UMass Amherst.

Rooth, Mats (1992a). "Reduction redundancy and ellipsis redundancy." In Steven Berman and Arild Hestvik, eds., *Proceedings of the Stuttgart Workshop on Ellipsis*, no. 29 in Arbeitspapiere des SFB 340, 1–26. University of Stuttgart.

Rooth, Mats (1992b). "A theory of focus interpretation." *Natural Language Semantics* 1: 75–116.

Rooth, Mats (1996a). "Focus." In Shalom Lappin, ed., *The Handbook of Contemporary Semantic Theory*, 271–97. London: Blackwell.

Rooth, Mats (1996b). "On the interface principles for intonational focus." In Galloway and Spence (1996), 202–26.

Rooth, Mats (1999). "Association with focus or association with presupposition." In Bosch and van der Sandt (1999), 232–44.

Rooth, Mats (2009). "Second occurrence focus and relativized stress F." In Zimmermann and Féry (2009), 15–35.

Saltarelli, Mario (1988). *Basque*. London: Croom Helm.

Samek-Lodovici, Vieri (2005). "Prosody–syntax interaction in the expression of focus." *Natural Language and Linguistic Theory* 23: 687–755.

Samek-Lodovici, Vieri (2006). "When right dislocation meets the left–periphery: A unified analysis of italian non-final focus." *Lingua* 116(6): 836–73.

Samek-Lodovici, Vieri (2009). "Topic, focus, and background in Italian clauses." In Andreas Dufter and Daniel Jacob, eds., *Focus and Background in Romance Languages*, vol. 112 of *Studies in Language Companion Series*, 333–57. Amsterdam/ Philadelphia: John Benjamins Publishing Company.

Sasse, Hans-Jürgen (1987). "The thetic/categorical distinction revisited." *Linguistics* 25: 511–80.

Sauerland, Uli (2005). "Don't interpret focus: Why a presuppositional account of focus fails, and how a presuppositional account of givenness works." In *Proceedings of Sinn und Bedeutung* 9, 370–84. Nijmegen.

Schmerling, Susan F. (1976). *Aspects of English Sentence Stress*. Ph.D. thesis, Austin.

Schubiger, Maria (1958). *English Intonation: Its Form and Function*. Tübingen: Niemeyer.

Schwarzschild, Roger (1993). "The contrastiveness of associated foci." Unpublished manuscript, Hebrew University of Jerusalem.

Schwarzschild, Roger (1997a). "Interpreting accent." Unpublished MS., Rutgers University.

Schwarzschild, Roger (1997b). "Why some foci must associate." Unpublished MS., Rutgers University.

Schwarzschild, Roger (1999). "GIVENness, AvoidF and Other Constraints on the Placement of Accent." *Natural Language Semantics* 7(2): 141–77.

Schwarzschild, Roger (2006). "Focus interpretations: Comments on Geurts and van der Sandt." *Theoretical Linguistics* 30(1): 137–47.

Selkirk, Elisabeth O. (1980). "The role of prosodic categories in English word stress." *Linguistic Inquiry* 11(3): 563–605.

Selkirk, Elisabeth O. (1984). *Phonology and Syntax: The Relation between Sound and Structure*. Cambridge, MA: MIT Press.

Selkirk, Elisabeth (1986). "On derived domains in sentence phonology." *Phonology Yearbook* 3: 371–405.

Selkirk, Elisabeth (1995a). "The prosodic structure of function words." In Laura Walsh Dickey, Jill Beckman, and Suzanne Urbanczyk, eds., *Papers in Optimality Theory*, no. 18 in University of Massachusetts Occasional Papers, 439–69. Amherst, MA: GLSA.

Selkirk, Elisabeth (1995b). "Sentence prosody: Intonation, stress, and phrasing." In John A. Goldsmith, ed., *The Handbook of Phonological Theory*, 550–69. London: Blackwell.

Selkirk, Elisabeth (2007). "Contrastive focus, givenness, and phrase stress." Ms. University of Massachusetts.

Selkirk, Elisabeth (2011). "The syntax–phonology interface." In John Goldsmith, Jason Riggle, and Alan C. L. Yu, eds., *The Handbook of Phonological Theory*, 2nd edn, 435–84. Oxford: Wiley-Blackwell.

Shue, Yen-Liang, Markus Iseli, Nanette Veilleux, and Abeer Alwan (2007). "Pitch accent versus lexical stress: Quantifying acoustic measures related to the voice source." In *Proceedings of Interspeech 2007*, 2625–8.

Stalnaker, Robert C. (1978). "Assertion." In Peter Cole, ed., *Pragmatics*, vol. 9 of *Syntax & Semantics*, 315–32. New York: Academic Press.

von Stechow, Arnim (1981). "Topic, focus, and local relevance." In Wolfgang Klein and Willem Levelt, eds., *Crossing the Boundaries in Linguistics*, 95–130. Dordrecht: Reidel.

von Stechow, Arnim and Susanne Uhmann (1986). *Some Remarks on Focus Projection*. Amsterdam: John Benjamins.

Steedman, Mark (1991). "Structure and intonation." *Language* 67: 260–96.

Steedman, Mark (1994). "Remarks on intonation and 'focus.'" In Bosch and van der Sandt (1994), 185–204.

Steedman, Mark (2000a). "Information structure and the syntax–phonology Interface." *Linguistic Inquiry* 31: 649–89.

Steedman, Mark (2000b). *The Syntactic Process*. Cambridge, MA: MIT Press.

Steedman, Mark (2007). "Information-structural semantics for English intonation." In Lee et al. (2007), 245–64.

Steedman, Mark (2014). "The surface-compositional semantics of English intonation." *Language* 90(1): 2–57.

Stommel, Hildegard (2011). *Verum-Fokus im Deutschen*. Marburg: Tectum.

Swerts, Marc, Emiel Krahmer, and Cynthia Avesani (2002). "Prosodic marking of information status in Dutch and Italian: A comparative analysis." *Journal of Phonetics* 4(30): 629–54.

Szabolcsi, Anna (1981). "Compositionality in focus." *Folia Linguistica* XV(1–2): 141–61.

Szabolcsi, Anna (1986). "Comparative superlatives." In Naoki Fukui, Tova Rapoport, and Elizabeth Sagey, eds., *Papers in Theoretical Linguistics*, no. 8 in MIT Working Papers in Linguistics, 245–65. Cambridge, MA: MIT Press.

Szendrői, Kriszta (2000). "A stress driven approach to the syntax of focus." Ms., University College London.

Szendrői, Kriszta (2001). *Focus and the Syntax–Phonology Interface*. Ph.D. thesis, University College London.

Szendrői, Kriszta (2003). "A stress-based approach to the syntax of Hungarian focus." *The Linguistic Review* 20: 37–78.

Szendrői, Kriszta (2004). "Focus and the interaction between syntax and pragmatics." *Lingua* 114(3): 229–54.

Szendrői, Kriszta (2006). "Focus movement (with special reference to Hungarian)." In Everaert and Riemsdijk (2006), 270–335.

Taglicht, Josef (1984). *Message and Emphasis: On Focus and Scope in English*. London. Langman.

Taglicht, Josef (1998). "Constraints on intonational phrasing in English." *Linguistics* 34: 181–211.

Takahashi, Shoichi and Danny Fox (2005). "Max elide and the re-binding problem." In *Proceedings of SALT XV*.

Terken, Jaques M. B. and Dik J. Hermes (2000). "The perception of prosodic prominence." In M. Horne, ed., *Prosody: Theory and Experiment—Studies Presented to Gösta Bruce*, 89–127. Dordrecht: Kluwer Academic Publishers.

Tomioka, Satoshi (2009). "Contrastive topics operate on speech acts." In Zimmermann and Féry (2009), 115–38.

Tomioka, Satoshi (2010). "A scope theory of contrastive topics." *Iberia* 2(1): 113–30.

Toosarvandani, Maziar Doustdar (2010). *Association with Foci*. Ph.D. thesis, University of California, Berkeley.

Torregrossa, Jacopo (2010). "Towards a taxonomy of focus types: The case of information foci and contrastive foci in Italian." *UCLA Working Papers in Linguistics* 15: 1–22.

Truckenbrodt, Hubert (1995). *Phonological Phrases: Their Relation to Syntax, Focus, and Prominence*. Ph.D. thesis, MIT. Published 1999 by MITWPL.

Truckenbrodt, Hubert (1999). "On the relation between syntactic phrases and phonological phrases." *Linguistic Inquiry* 30(2): 219–55.

Truckenbrodt, Hubert (2002). "Upstep and embedded register levels." *Phonology* 19: 77–120.

Truckenbrodt, Hubert (2004). "Final lowering in non-final position." *Journal of Phonetics* 32: 313–48.

Truckenbrodt, Hubert (2006). "Phrasal stress." In Keith Brown, ed., *The Encyclopedia of Languages and Linguistics*, vol. 9, 572–9. Oxford: Elsevier.

Truckenbrodt, Hubert (2007a). "The syntax–phonology interface." In Paul De Lacy, ed., *The Cambridge Handbook of Phonology*, 435–56. Cambridge: Cambridge University Press.

Truckenbrodt, Hubert (2007b). "Upstep of edge tones and of nuclear accents." In Carlos Gussenhoven and Tomas Riad, eds., *Tones and Tunes. Volume 2: Experimental Studies in Word and Sentence Prosody*, 349–86. Berlin: Mouton.

Truckenbrodt, Hubert (2012). "Semantics of intonation." In Claudia Maienborn, Klaus von Heusinger, and Paul Portner, eds., *Semantics: An International Handbook of Natural Language Meaning, Vol. 3*, no. 33 in Handbücher zur Sprach- und Kommunikationswissenschaft/Handbooks of Linguistics and Communication Science, 2039–969. Berlin: De Gruyter Mouton.

Truckenbrodt, Hubert and Daniel Büring (in preparation). "Correspondence at the Syntax–Phonology Interface."

Truckenbrodt, Hubert and Caroline Féry (2005). "Sisterhood and tonal scaling." In Merle Horne and Marc Van Oostendorp, eds., *In Boundaries in Intonational Phonology (Studia Linguistica 59.2/3)*, 223–43.

Truckenbrodt, Hubert, Filomena Sandalo, and Bernadett Abaurre (2009). "Elements of Brazilian Portuguese intonation." *Journal of Portuguese Linguistics* 8: 75–114.

Uechi, Akihiko (1998). *An Interface Approach to Topic/Focus Structure*. Ph.D. thesis, The University of British Columbia, Vancouver.

Uhmann, Susanne (1991). *Fokusphonologie*. Tübingen: Niemeyer.

Umbach, Carla (2001). "Contrast and contrastive topic." In Ivana Kruijff-Korbayová and Mark Steedman, eds., *Proceedings of the ESSLLI 2001 Workshop on Information Structure, Discourse Structure and Discourse Semantics*, 175–88. Helsinki. (available at http://www.coli.uni-saarland.de/~korbay/esslli01-wsh/).

Vallduví, Enric (1990). *The Informational Component*. Ph.D. thesis, University of Pennsylvania. (published 1992: Garland).

Vallduví, Enric and Elisabeth Engdahl (1996). "The linguistic realization of information packaging." *Linguistics* 34: 459–519.

Vallduví, Enric and Maria Vilkuna (1998). "On rheme and contrast." In Peter W. Culicover and Louise McNally, eds., *The Limits of Syntax*, vol. 29 of *Syntax and Semantics*, 79–180. New York: Academic Press.

Vallduví, Enric and Ron Zacharski (1993). "Accenting phenomena, association with focus, and the recursiveness of focus–ground." In Paul Dekker and Martin Stokhof, eds., *Proceedings of the Ninth Amsterdam Colloquium*.

Vanderslice, Ralph and Laura S. Pierson (1967). "Prosodic features of Hawaiian English." *Quarterly Journal of Speech* (53): 156–66.

Veilleux, Nanette, Stefanie Shattuck-Hufnagel, and Alejna Brugos (2006). "Lecture Notes from '6.911: Transcribing Prosodic Structure of Spoken Utterances with ToBI.'" Accessed April 27, 2015. License: Creative Commons BY-NC-SA.

Velupillai, Viveka (2012). *An Introduction to Linguistic Typology*. Amsterdam: John Benjamins.

Verhoeven, Elisabeth and Frank Kügler (2015). "Accentual preferences and predictability: An acceptability study on split intransitivity in German." *Lingua*, 165 B: 298–315.

Vilkuna, Maria (1989). *Free Word Order in Finnish. Its Syntax and Discourse Functions*. Ph.D. thesis, Helsinki.

Wagner, Michael (2005). *Prosody and Recursion*. Ph.D. thesis, MIT.

Wagner, Michael (2006). "Givenness and locality." In Jonathan Howell and Masayuki Gibson, eds., *Proceedings of the 16th Semantics and Linguistic Theory Conference*, 295–312. Ithaca: CLC Publications.

Wagner, Michael (2010). "Prosody and recursion in coordinate structures and beyond." *Natural Language and Linguistic Theory* 28: 183–237.

Wagner, Michael (2012a). "Contrastive topics decomposed." *Semantics and Pragmatics* 5(8): 1–54.

Wagner, Michael (2012b). "Focus and givenness: A unified approach." In Kučerová and Neeleman (2012), 102–47.

Ward, Gregory and Julia Hirschberg (1985). "Implicating uncertainty: The pragmatics of fall–rise intonation." *Language* 747–76.

Wilkinson, Karina (1996). "The scope of *even*." *Natural Language Semantics* 4: 193–215.

Williams, Edwin (1997). "Blocking and anaphora." *Linguistics Inquiry* 28: 577–628.

Winkler, Susanne (1997). *Focus and Secondary Predication*. Berlin/New York: Mouton De Gruyter.

Winkler, Susanne and Edward Göbbel (2002). "Focus, P-Movement and the NSR: A View from Germanic and Romance: Zubizarreta, M. L. (1998) Prosody, Focus, and Word Order." *Linguistics* 40(6): 1185–242.

Wold, Dag E. (1995a). "Binding Foci In Situ." MS., MIT.

Wold, Dag E. (1995b). "How to interpret multiple foci without moving a focused constituent." In Elena Benedicto, Maribel Romero, and Satoshi Tomioka, eds., *Proceedings of Workshop on Focus*, no. 21 in University of Massachusetts Occasional Papers in Linguistics, 277–89. UMass, Amherst: GLSA.

Wold, Dag (1996). "Long distance selective binding: The case of focus." In Galloway and Spence (1996), 311–28.

Worth, Dean S. (1964). "Suprasyntactics." In Horace G. Lunt, ed., *Proceedings of the Ninth International Congress of Linguistics*, 698–704. Den Haag/Paris: Mouton.

Wunderlich, Dieter (1991). "Intonation and contrast." *Journal of Semantics* 8(3): 239–51.

Xu, Yi and Ching X. Xu (2005). "Phonetic realization of focus in English declarative intonation." *Journal of Phonetics* 33: 159–97.

Zimmermann, Malte and Caroline Féry, eds. (2009). *Information Structure*. Oxford: Oxford University Press.

Zubizarreta, Maria Luisa (1998). *Prosody, Focus and Word Order*. Cambridge, MA: MIT Press.

Zubizarreta, María Luisa and Jean-Roger Vergnaud (2006). "Phrasal stress and syntax." In Everaert and Riemsdijk (2006), 522–68.

Zybatow, Gerhild and Grit Mehlhorn (2000). "Experimental evidence for focus structure in Russian." In Tracy H. King and Irina A. Sekerina, eds., *Formal Approaches to Slavic Linguistics. The Philadelphia Meeting 1999*. Ann Arbor: Michigan Slavic Publications.

Index